Life and Liberty in American

Sketches of a Tour in the
United States and Canada
in 1857-8

LIFE AND LIBERTY IN AMERICA

SKETCHES OF A TOUR IN THE
UNITED STATES AND CANADA
IN 1857-8

COSIMO CLASSICS
NEW YORK

Life and Liberty in America
Sketches of a Tour in the United States and Canada in 1857-8
© 2005 Cosimo, Inc.
All rights reserved. No part of this book may be used or reproduced in any manner whatsoever without prior written permission except in the case of brief quotations embodied in critical articles or reviews.
For information, address:

Cosimo, P.O. Box 416
Old Chelsea Station
New York, NY 10113-0416

or visit our website at:
www.cosimobooks.com

Life and Liberty in America, Sketches of a Tour in the United States and Canada in 1857-8 originally published by Harper & Brothers in 1860.

Library of Congress Cataloging-in-Publication Data
A catalog record for this book is available from the Library of Congress

Cover design by www.wiselephant.com

ISBN: 1-59605-431-X

PREFACE.

In pursuance of a long-cherished desire, the author of the following pages left London in October, 1857, for a tour in the United States and Canada. He traversed the Union from Boston to New Orleans, by St. Louis and the Mississippi, and returned to New York by land through the Slave States. He afterward visited Canada, and published from time to time in the *Illustrated London News* a few of the results of his observations, under the title of "TRANSATLANTIC SKETCHES." These sketches, after having received careful revision, have been included in the present work, and form about one third of its bulk. The remaining portions are now published for the first time, and include not only the chapters on the great social and political questions which, more than any mere records of travel, are of interest to the lovers of human liberty and progress, but nearly the whole of the Canadian tour. It is not to be expected that in a residence of less than a twelvemonth in America the author can have acquired a thorough acquaintance with the institutions of the country, or with the operations of social causes which the Americans themselves do not always comprehend. He makes no pretense at being oracular, but has contented himself with describing "LIFE" as he saw it, and "LIBERTY" as he studied it, to the extent of his opportunities, both in the North and in the South. He went to America neither to carp, to sneer, nor to caricature, but with an honest love of liberty, and a sincere desire to judge for himself, and to tell the truth, as to the results of the great experiment in self-government which the Anglo-Saxon and Anglo-Celtic races are making in America, under the most favorable circumstances, and with nothing, not springing from themselves, to impede or fetter their progress. He returned from America with a greater respect for the people than when he first set foot upon the soil. And if, with his European notions that a man's color makes no difference in his natural rights, he has come to the same conclusion as previous travelers, that "Liberty" in the New World is not yet exactly what the founders of the Union intended it to be, he trusts that he has expressed his opinions without bitterness, and that, while he can admire the political virtues of the republic, he is not obliged to shut his eyes to its defects or its vices. It is on American soil that the highest destinies of civilization will be wrought out to their conclusions, and the record of what is there doing, however often the story may be told, will be always interesting and novel. Progress crawls in Europe, but gallops in America. The record of European travel may be fresh ten or twenty years after it is written, but that of America becomes obsolete in four or five. It took our England nearly a thousand years, from the days of the Heptarchy to those of William III., to become of as much account in the world as the United States have become in the lifetime of old men who still linger among us. Those who bear this fact in mind will not concur in the opinion that books of American travel are likely to lose their interest, even amid the turmoil of European wars, and the complications created by the selfish ambition of rulers whose pretensions and titles are alike anachronisms in the nineteenth century.

London, May, 1859.

CONTENTS.

CHAP.		PAGE
I.	THE VOYAGE OUT	9
II.	NEW YORK	15
III.	BROADWAY BY NIGHT	22
IV.	HOTEL LIFE	29
V.	AMERICAN FIREMEN	34
VI.	FROM NEW YORK TO BOSTON	39
VII.	TO THE FALLS OF NIAGARA	47
VIII.	NIAGARA	52
IX.	NEWPORT AND RHODE ISLAND	64
X.	PHILADELPHIA	71
XI.	WASHINGTON	77
XII.	INTERVIEW OF INDIANS WITH THEIR "GREAT FATHER"	87
XIII.	AMERICANISMS AND AMERICAN SLANG	100
XIV.	THE IRISH IN AMERICA	112
XV.	FROM WASHINGTON TO CINCINNATI	117
XVI.	THE QUEEN CITY OF THE WEST	125
XVII.	ST. LOUIS, MISSOURI	138
XVIII.	THE MORMONS	147
XIX.	FROM ST. LOUIS TO NEW ORLEANS	151
XX.	"THE CRESCENT CITY"	162
XXI.	FROM LOUISIANA TO ALABAMA	178
XXII.	SOUTH CAROLINA	187
XXIII.	SOUTH CAROLINA—*continued*	192
XXIV.	A RICE PLANTATION	199
XXV.	SAVANNAH AND THE SEA ISLANDS	208
XXVI.	FROM SOUTH CAROLINA TO VIRGINIA	215
XXVII.	FROM RICHMOND TO WASHINGTON	224
XXVIII.	THE SOCIAL AND POLITICAL ASPECTS OF SLAVERY	231
XXIX.	PRO-SLAVERY PHILOSOPHY	247
XXX.	DECLINE OF THE SPANISH RACE IN AMERICA	258
XXXI.	BALTIMORE AND MARYLAND	270
XXXII.	FROM BALTIMORE TO NEW YORK	279
XXXIII.	AMERICAN LITERATURE, ART, AND SCIENCE	287
XXXIV.	PARTIES AND PARTY TYRANNY	300
XXXV.	ALBANY	309
XXXVI.	THE FUTURE OF THE UNITED STATES	314

CANADA.

CHAP.		PAGE
XXXVII.	FROM ALBANY TO MONTREAL	326
XXXVIII.	TO THE TOP OF BEL ŒIL	337
XXXIX.	THE ST. LAWRENCE	345
XL.	QUEBEC	355
XLI.	TORONTO	370
XLII.	HAMILTON, LONDON, AND OTTAWA	379
XLIII.	SHOOTING THE RAPIDS	387
XLIV.	EMIGRATION	396
XLV.	HOME AGAIN	407

LIFE AND LIBERTY

IN

AMERICA.

CHAPTER I.

THE VOYAGE OUT.

AT ten o'clock on the morning of Saturday, the 3d of October, 1857, the fine steam-ship *Asia*, Captain Lott, bearing the mails and about 150 passengers, left Liverpool for New York. The weather was the reverse of cheering. The rain fell, the wind blew, the Mersey showed its white teeth, and every thing betokened a rough voyage, and a vigorous demand for the steward's basin. The passengers were mostly Americans. Planters, cotton-brokers, and bankers from the South; merchants and manufacturers from the New England States; Americans from Virginia, South Carolina, and Alabama, who used the word "Yankee" as a term, if not of contempt, of depreciation, as we sometimes use it in England; and Americans from Connecticut, Massachusetts, and Vermont, who gloried in the appellation as the highest compliment that could be bestowed upon them; courtly gentlemen who would have graced any society in the world, and rough tykes and horse-dealers from the Far West, with about forty ladies and children, and five Englishmen, three of whom crossed the Atlantic for the first time, formed our company. It was not until the second day, when we were steaming along the southern shores of Ireland, that we began to grow social, to learn each other's names, to form ourselves into little cliques, coteries, and gossiping parties, and to receive and communicate information upon the pleasures and the perils of the Atlantic, upon the state of Europe and of America, upon the probable effects of the great Indian mutiny on the cotton trade of Charleston, Mobile, and New Orleans, upon the great commercial crash and panic at New York, upon the feelings of Englishmen toward Americans and of Americans toward Englishmen, or, in one phrase, "upon things in general."

The weather suddenly became mild and genial, and on Sunday morning, as we skirted the coast of Waterford and Cork, there was scarcely more motion in the sea or in our ship than if we had been steaming from London to Greenwich, or thridding our way amid the beautiful lochs of the Caledonian Canal. The breakfast, luncheon, dinner, tea, and supper tables were regularly crowded; there was not a single absentee from the five too frequent and too copious meals provided for us by our bountiful and urbane chief steward. The monotony of a long sea voyage is such that people eat for pastime. The sound of the bell for luncheon is an event; and dinner is a consummation of good things, as well as a consumption of them, to which all who are not smitten by sea-sickness look forward as the very crown and climax of the day, which the *gourmand* and the *gourmet* alike contemplate with pleasurable anticipations, and which nothing can impair but a stiff breeze. And such a breeze sprung up on the second day. Experienced travelers who had crossed the Atlantic scores of times—who spoke jauntily of our noble ship as a ferry-boat, and of the mighty Atlantic as "the Ferry," no larger, in their magniloquence, than that from Liverpool to Birkenhead — bade us "look out for squalls," and for the swell and roll of the ocean, as soon as we should pass Cape Clear and the Fassnett Lighthouse. They proved themselves true prophets. We had not left the rugged shores of the county of Kerry half an hour behind us before we made a most unpleasant acquaintanceship with the heaving billows of the Atlantic, and felt the *Asia* pitching in a heavy sea, with her bowsprit one moment running atilt at the clouds, and the next sinking as if it would poke a hole through the bottom of the ocean. In a few minutes our decks were cleared of all the fairer portion of the passengers; the crinolines disappeared; and for seven long and weary days the ruder and stronger half of creation were left in undisturbed but melancholy possession of the decks and the dining-tables. Nor did the greater number of the gentlemen fare, for a day or two, much better than the ladies. On the wings of the gale there rode a fiend—the fiercest, most unrelenting demon ever imagined, invented, or depicted—the archfiend Sea-sickness, in whose unwelcome presence life, nature, and humanity lose their charm, " the sun's eye hath a sickly glare," and death itself seems among the most trivial of the afflictions that can befall us. One of our English friends from Manchester, who was very sick and utterly miserable, created some amusement among those less miserable than himself. There was but one place on deck which afforded shelter from the beating rain, and the spray that washed over us in plenteous cataracts. This place was the general resort not only of the smokers, but of all those sufficiently convalescent to loathe and abhor the confined air of their state-rooms. The name originally given to this resort was the *Gridiron;* but the more significant application of the *Spit* was applied to it by a "Britisher" whom modesty forbids me to name, who detested tobacco and the streams of saliva which, whether "chawed" or smoked, it incited some portion of the Yankee passengers, and more especially a long, lean, leathery, unhealthy boy from Philadelphia, to discharge upon the floor. Seated in the "Spit" was our Manchester friend, as comfortless and as hopeless as man could look. We had been five days out, and it was impossible to walk the deck for the heavy seas and blinding spray that at every pitch or roll of the vessel came spouting over us. To eat was perilous, to drink was to invite sickness, to read was impossible, to talk was but vanity and vexation of spirit; and the sole resource was to woo the slumber which would not come, or to form deep though unspoken vows never again to cross the ocean in the expectation of deriving either pleasure or comfort from the trip. The vessel rolled heavily; and a "sea," bursting over the bulwarks, deluged the "Spit" and all within it till we stood six inches deep in water. "I'll be hanged," said the man of Manchester, "if I'll stand this any longer! Steward, call a cab!" We all smiled, and doubtless our smiles were ghastly enough, at the earnest jocosity of our friend's misery. It had, however, a good effect—homœopathically; it made us forget our sea-sickness for the better part of five minutes.

On the eighth night it blew a gale of wind, an indubitable storm, about which there could be no mistake. Our average rate of speed against the strong head wind since leaving Liverpool had been upward of eight knots an hour; but on that fearful night we did not exceed two and a half. The vessel groaned and creaked through all her timbers. The dull, heavy "thuds" or thumps of the roaring, raging seas staggered the *Asia* through the whole of her sturdy framework. It seemed at times as if, endowed with reason, she had made up her mind to resist the cruel aggression of the billows, and had stopped in mid career to deliberate in what manner she should, with the most power and dignity, show her sense of the insult; and then, as if learning wisdom in adversity, she resolved to hold on her course and show herself superior to the buffetings of fortune. To me, as to others, every minute of that night appeared to be as long as a day, and every hour was an age of suffering. To sleep in such a conflict of the elements was impossible. Even to remain in the berth, without being pitched head foremost out of it on to the cabin floor, and running the risk of broken limbs, was a matter of the utmost difficulty, and only to be accomplished by main strength and fruitful ingenuity of invention, and of adaptation to the unusual circumstances. Feet and hands were alike in requisition; and a hard grip of the sides of the berth was scarcely sufficient for security, unless aided by the knees and the elbows, and by a constant agony of watchfulness, lest a sudden sea should take the vessel unawares, and spill the hapless traveler like a potato out of a sack. And amid the riot of the winds and waves there was ever and anon a sound more fearful and distressing to hear—the moan of a sick lady, and the loud and querulous cry of a young child that refused to be comforted. For twelve unhappy and most doleful hours we plowed our way through the storm, praying for the daylight and the calm. At the first blink of morning every one capable of the exertion was dressed and upon deck, exchanging condolences with his fellow-travelers on the miseries of the night, or inquiring of the officers on watch what hopes there were of the moderating of the gale.

For six-and-twenty hours the storm raged, and for twelve hours after its cessation the ocean, with its long uneasy swell, bore traces on its white-crested waves of the perturbation that had been caused in it. On the tenth and eleventh days the sea was calm enough to admit of sports upon the lower deck, and several matches were made at shuffle-board, the marine substitute for the game of skittles. It was played with the greatest spirit, sometimes Ohio being matched against Kentucky, sometimes Charleston against New York, and frequently England against America. And, while this was the amusement on deck, cards, backgammon, and chess afforded relaxation to those who took no pleasure in robuster sport. Among other pastimes, a kind of masquerade was got up by the sailors, two of whom made a very respectable elephant between them, and one a very superior shaggy bear. On the back of the elephant rode the boatswain. The first part of the fun was that the elephant should continually throw him; and the second part was that he should continually remount—*per fas aut nefas;* all of which was effected according to the programme, and to the great amusement of the passengers, and especially of one little boy, eight years old, who laughed so immoderately as to suggest a fear that his mirth would end in convulsions. The bear also contributed his due share to the frolic; and the broad farce created as much hilarity among our hundred and fifty travelers as ever was excited on the London boards by Buckstone or Harley in the present day, or by Liston and John Reeve in the days of old. At the conclusion of the performances two of the passengers volunteered to go round with the hat, and nearly five pounds were the result of their solicitations. But the chief amusements of the younger and "faster" voyagers—smoking always excepted—were bets and lotteries. How many knots we should run in the next twenty-four hours; what latitude and longitude we should be in when our excellent captain made his noon-day observation; with what letter of the alphabet would commence the name of the pilot whom he should take on board on approaching New York; and how many miles, or scores of miles, we should be from shore when the pilot-boat first made its appearance, were but a few of the subjects of speculation on which ingenuity was displayed to kill time and to have something to think of. Ten to one was offered that on a certain day we should run 258 miles or upward. We ran 257 by the captain's calculation; and an amount of money changed hands on this question which was variously estimated in the ship at from £150 to £200.

It soon became evident that the adverse winds and rough weather would make our passage a longer one than the average, and that we should not reach New York under fourteen days. We passed over 1500 miles of ocean without having seen a sail but our own, affording no opportunity for the old maritime joke always palmed off upon landsmen, "sometimes we ship a sea, and sometimes we see a ship." After the twelfth day sailing-vessels and steam-ships were frequently met with, and we had abundant proofs that we were on the great highway of the nations, and in the most crowded part of the "Ferry."

On Friday, the 16th, at eight o'clock in the morning, a pilot, who had been on the look-out for us for four days, came on board, and informed us that we were 180 miles from land. He brought, at the same time, the news, distressing to very many of our company, that the commercial panic in New York had increased in intensity; that nearly, if not all the banks had suspended payment; and that there never had been a financial crisis of such severity in the whole history of the United States. At ten o'clock that night we were off Sandy Hook. The navigation being intricate, our entrance into the harbor was deferred until daylight; and at seven in the morning of Saturday, the 17th, having nearly completed our fourteenth day, we steamed for eighteen miles into the beautiful bay at the end of which stands New York, the Queen of the Western World, with New Jersey on the one side and Brooklyn on the other. The three form but one city in fact, though differing in name, like London and Westminster, and occupy a situation worthy in every respect of a metropolis that has no commercial rival or superior in the world—except London.

CHAPTER II.

NEW YORK.

New York, Nov. 25th, 1857.

IN one of his famous letters to the Pennsylvanians the late Rev. Sydney Smith accused the whole American people of pride, conceit, and presumption. Smarting under a sense of injuries inflicted upon him, not by the State or city of New York, which had not the remotest connection with his grievances, real or supposed, he hurled this sweeping denunciation against all the states—declaring, among other odd things, in his own odd way, "that this new and vain people could never forgive England because Broadway was inferior to Bond Street." It is fourteen years since the Rev. Sydney Smith thus disburdened his mind, prompted to do so by the fact, disagreeable to him, that his pockets had been previously disburdened by his own desire of making more than five per cent. by the transatlantic investment of his money. The lapse of years has made a great difference in the aspect of Broadway, as well as in that of New York generally. But, whatever may have been the appearance of this great artery of New York in that remote period of its history—a period when, as travelers told us, pigs prowled about the principal thoroughfares, and lay down at night on the marble door-steps of marble palaces in snug and affectionate familiarity with Irish immigrants—Sydney Smith's assertion of the inferiority of Broadway to Bond Street is ludicrously untrue at the present time. Bond Street! quotha? Bond Street is no more to be compared to Broadway for beauty, extent, life, bustle, and wealth, than a dingy old farthing of the reign of George III. to a bright new sovereign of the days of Queen Victoria. There is no street in London that can be declared superior, or even equal, all things considered, to Broadway. It is a street *sui generis*, combining in itself the characteristics of the

Boulevard des Italiens at Paris, and of Cheapside or Fleet Street in London, with here and there a dash of Whitechapel or the Minories, and here and there a dash of Liverpool and Dublin. It is longer, more crowded, and fuller of fine buildings than the Boulevard des Italiens; it is as bustling as Cheapside; and, more than all, it has a sky above it as bright as the sky of Venice. Its aspect is thoroughly Parisian. Were it not for the old familiar names of Smith, Jones, and Brown over the doors of the stores and warehouses, and the English placards and advertisements that every where meet the eye, the stranger might fancy himself under the maximized government and iron grip of Napoleon III., instead of being under that of the minimized and mild government of an American republic—a government so infinitesimally light in its weight, and carried on by persons so little known, that strangers in this, the "Empire State," as it is called, and even the citizens themselves, are scarcely more cognizant of the name of the governor than a Londoner is of the name of the high sheriff of Flintshire or of the lord lieutenant of Merioneth.

England has given names to the people in Broadway, but France and Continental Europe seem to have given them their manners. Flagstaffs on the roof of every third or fourth house, banners flaunting from the windows, a constant rat-tat-too of drums as detachments of the militia regiments (and very fine regiments they are, and very splendidly accoutred) pass to and fro, all add to the illusion; and it is only the well-known vernacular of the city of St. Paul's, spiced occasionally with the still more piquant vernacular of the city of St. Patrick's, that bring the cheated fancy back to the reality, and prove to the Englishman that he is among his own people.

Were there any thing like uniformity in the design of its long lines of buildings, Broadway would be one of the three or four most magnificent streets in the world. Even without any general design—for each man builds exactly as he pleases—the street, in its details, surpasses any single street that England or the British Isles can show. From the Battery facing the sea, where Broadway has a very ignoble commencement, to Trinity Church, there is nothing remarkable about it; but from Trinity Church, of brown stone, with its elegant spire, to Grace Church, built entirely of white marble, a distance in a straight line of nearly three miles, and thence on to Union Square, and the statue of Washington, Broadway offers one grand succession of commercial palaces. Formerly —and perhaps when Sydney Smith wrote—the houses were for the most part of brick gayly colored, with here and there a house of brown stone or granite. But the brick is in gradual process of extirpation; and white marble—pure, glittering, brilliant, without speck or flaw—is rapidly taking its place. The St. Nicholas Hotel, one of the most sumptuous buildings in New York, is a palace of white marble, with upward of one hundred windows fronting Broadway. To the right, and to the left, and in front, are other palaces of the same material, pure as Parian—larger than the largest warehouse in St. Paul's Church-yard, and devoted to the same or similar purposes; some for the wholesale, but the great majority for the retail trade. "Dry-goods" or linen-drapers' stores compete with each other in the use of this costly stone; and such has been, and is, the rage for it, that in a few years hence a house of any other material than marble, granite, or iron will be the exception to the rule in Broadway, and in the main thoroughfares leading from it to the east and the west. Most of these buildings, taken separately, are fine specimens of architecture, but the general effect is not striking, from the total absence of plan and method, already alluded to, and which seems to be inevitable in a country where every man is a portion of the government and of the sovereignty, and considers himself bound to consult nobody's taste but his own. But this peculiarity is not confined to America, or St. Paul's Church-yard would not be what it is, and the noble proportions of the Cathedral would not be marred as they are by the too close proximity of the hideous warehouses that have been gradually piled up around it—monuments alike of commercial pride and bad taste. Brown stone edifices rank next in size and number to the marble palaces; and a few of cast iron, with elegant Corinthian pillars, add to the variety of architecture in the Broadway. Conspicuous among the edifices that give its most imposing character to this busy and beautiful street are Stewart's dry-goods store, the iron palace of Messrs. Haughwout and Co., such hotels as the St. Nicholas, the Metropolitan, the Lafarge House, the St. Denis, the Clarendon, the New York, and the Astor House. The last-mentioned was some years ago the boast and pride of New York, and the wonder of strangers; but the city has outgrown its southern limits, and stretched itself far away into the north and northwest, and new hotels like the St. Nicholas and the Metropolitan have dwarfed the Astor House in size and eclipsed it in splendor. The St. Nicholas makes up from 500 to 700 beds, and the Metropolitan nearly as many. Both of these, as well as the others mentioned, represent the magnificent scale on which the New Yorkers do business, as well as the more than Parisian publicity with which families eat and drink and pass the day.

Enough for the present on the street architecture of Broadway. A few words on its physical and moral aspects are necessary to complete the picture. On each side of the street are rows of American elm, with here and there a willow or a mountain ash. At this date all the trees are leafless, except the willows, which still droop in green beauty, though somewhat shriveled in their leaves by the frosts of the last three nights. The roadway is excellently paved with granite, and the foot pavements are equally good. But let not the traveler be deceived into the idea that the part is a specimen of the whole. Broadway monopolizes nearly all the good pavement as well as cleanness of New York; and the streets that branch off from it on each side are uneven, dirty, and full of deep holes and ruts, through which carriage-driving is far from being agreeable. If there be any exception, it is in the Fifth Avenue—the Tyburnia or Belgravia of New York—where the richest people live in marble and stone palaces, not quite so large as the business palaces of Broadway, but sufficiently luxurious and imposing. The street swarms with omnibuses, somewhat smaller and more inconvenient than the omnibuses of London. Nearly the whole of them are painted white.

No one rides outside, for the satisfactory reason that there are no seats. They have no conductors. The passenger, on entering, is expected to pay his fare to the driver through a hole in the roof; and, if he neglect to do so, the driver begins to drum with his fist on the top, to attract attention, and forthwith pokes his hand through the aforesaid hole for the money, with an objuration against the passenger more emphatic than polite, and often in the choicest brogue of the county of Cork. When the passenger wants to descend he pulls a cord, the vehicle stops, and he opens the door for himself, and goes about his business. The New Yorkers consider themselves, and are considered by others, to be a fast people ; but they have no Hansom, and, indeed, no cabs of any description. They have not yet advanced beyond the lumbering old hackney-coach with two horses, which disappeared from the streets of London more than five-and-twenty years ago. A few cabs, it appears, were recently introduced, but Cabbie, being in a free country, where municipalities make good laws, but are not strong enough to enforce them, insisted upon fixing the fares himself, at something like a dollar a mile. As might have been predicted, the scheme did not work, and Cabbie, instead of lowering his price, disappeared altogether, and betook himself to other schemes and projects for making an easy living, or emigrated to the Far West. The hackney-coaches with two horses are conducted upon such a system of extortion that one job per diem may be considered tolerably good pay. Let not the stranger who comes to New York for the first time imagine that there is any law for him if he have a dispute with the hack-driver. The New York Jehu, who is generally an Irishman, charges what he pleases, and I, and doubtless many others, before and since, had to pay two dollars (eight shillings and fourpence) for a drive of less than two miles, and there was no redress for the grievance, nor any thing but submission. Had a bargain been made beforehand, one dollar would doubtless have been accepted; but a hackney-coach is, at the best of times, and in all circumstances, such an expensive and litigious luxury in New York that few people, unless newly-arrived strangers, think of using one.

The great avenues that run parallel with Broadway are provided with lines of rail, on which numbers of very excellent cars, each capable of accommodating, with perfect ease and comfort, from twenty to thirty passengers, are drawn by horses —an arrangement which might be introduced into some of the main thoroughfares of London with much advantage.

Broadway is the fashionable promenade—the Regent Street and Hyde Park, as well as the Cheapside and Fleet Street of New York. Let us take a look at the people. A few carriages—several of them with coronets upon the panels, though on what principle no one can tell—mingle among the white omnibuses; and here the negro coachmen come into competition with the Irish. The ladies of New York who go shopping in Broadway are evidently fond of dress. Let them not be blamed; for what lady is not? Some of the journals have been ungallant enough to attribute the late commercial panic almost exclusively to the extravagance in personal adornment of the fair sex; but, without joining in this silly assertion, or saying one word in disparagement of that charming and better portion of human kind, truth compels me to state that, as regards the mere volume and circumference of hoop or crinoline, the ladies of London and Paris are, to those of New York, but as butterflies compared with canary birds. The caricatures of the crinoline mania which the world owes to its excellent friend *Punch*, if exaggerations of English fashions, are no exaggerations of those of New York; and to get along Broadway, where there is no tacitly understood and acknowledged law of the pavement as in England, and where every one takes the wall as it pleases him or her, is no easy matter. Even without these abominable hoops, it would be difficult for an Englishman, accustomed to have the wall at his right hand, to make any progress, unless by a series of provoking zigzags; but, hustled by crinolines, the best thing for the gallant man who is in a hurry is to step off the pavement into the road. Nor have the fair ladies all the hoops to themselves. The dark ladies share with them the passion, or the sentiment of the monstrosity, and inflate their garments to the most ridiculous proportions. Little negro girls of fourteen or fifteen years of age, with bright-colored parasols, bright cotton and silk dresses of a width surpassing any credence but that of the eyes of the beholder, flounder awkwardly to and fro; and aged negresses, equally splendid and equally rotund, waddle like hippopotami among their Anglo-Saxon and Celtic fellow-creatures, as if they had been rigged out maliciously by some hater of crinoline, and launched into the street to convert their fairer sisters to the use of a more elegant form of dress, upon the same principle as the ancients inculcated sobriety by the spectacle of their drunken slaves. There is not only a craze for crinoline here, but crinoline itself is crazy— huge, unwieldy, preposterous, and in every way offensive.

Another feature of Broadway is the number of Irish and Germans who swarm in it, on it, and round about it. The Irish seem to have the news trade to themselves; and the newsboys and newsgirls, selling the cheap daily newspapers, are to be met with at every corner, and blockade the entrances to all the principal hotels. Ragged, barefooted, and pertinacious, they are to be found in the streets from dawn till past the dark, crying out "The glorious news of the fall of Delhi!" The last " terrible explosion on the Ohio—one hundred lives lost!" or the last "Attempted assassination in a lager beer cellar!" They recall the memories of the old country by their garb, appearance, and accent, if not by their profession; while their staid elders, male and female, who monopolize the apple-stalls, look far sleeker and more comfortable than their compeers do at home, and show by their cozy appearance that they have prospered in the new land. The Germans are more quiet, and pursue more responsible callings.

CHAPTER III.

BROADWAY BY NIGHT.

New York, Dec. 1, 1857.

"I ENVY you your trip to America," said mine urbane and friendly host of the Waterloo Hotel, at Liverpool, as, two months ago, he took leave of me at his door, and wished me a safe and speedy passage across the Atlantic. There seemed to be nothing very enviable in the matter, for the wind had been howling all the night, the mercury in the glass was falling, the rain was beating against the windows, and the prospects of the voyage, all things considered, seemed the reverse of agreeable.

"And why?" said I, with a faint and, doubtless, unsuccessful attempt to look comfortable and happy.

"Because," replied he, his joyous features beaming out into a still greater refulgence of smiles than they had previously worn, "you will get such delicious oysters! New York beats all creation for oysters."

Mine host spoke the truth. There is no place in the world where there are such fine oysters as in New York, and the sea-board cities of America; fine in flavor, and of a size unparalleled in the oyster beds of Whitstable, Ostend, or the once celebrated Rocher de Cancale. Nor has the gift of oysters been bestowed upon an ungrateful people. If one may judge from appearances, the delicacy is highly relished and esteemed by all classes, from the millionaire in the Fifth Avenue to the "Boy" in the Bowery, and the German and Irish emigrants in their own peculiar quarters of the city, which (*soit dit en passant*) seem to monopolize all the filth to be found in Manhattan. In walking up Broadway by day or by night— but more especially by night—the stranger can not but remark the great number of "Oyster Saloons," "Oyster and Coffee Saloons," and "Oyster and Lager Beer Saloons," which solicit him at every turn to stop and taste. These saloons—

many of them very handsomely fitted up—are, like the drinking saloons in Germany, situated in vaults or cellars, with steps from the street; but, unlike their German models, they occupy the underground stories of the most stately commercial palaces of that city. In these, as in the hotels, oysters as large as a lady's hand are to be had at all hours, either from the shell, as they are commonly eaten in England, or cooked in twenty, or, perhaps, in forty or a hundred different ways. Oysters pickled, stewed, baked, roasted, fried, and scolloped; oysters made into soups, patties, and puddings; oysters with condiments and without condiments; oysters for breakfast, dinner, and supper; oysters without stint or limit—fresh as the fresh air, and almost as abundant—are daily offered to the palates of the Manhattanese, and appreciated with all the gratitude which such a bounty of nature ought to inspire. The shore of Long Island, fronting the Long Island Sound, for one hundred and fifteen miles, is one long succession of oyster-beds. Southward, along the coast of New Jersey, and down to Delaware, Pennsylvania and Virginia, and northward and eastward to Rhode Island and Massachusetts, the same delicacies abound, and foster a large and very lucrative commerce. In City Island, the whole population, consisting of 400 persons, is employed in the cultivation of oysters. The City Islanders are represented as a very honest, peculiar, and primitive community, who intermarry entirely among themselves, and drive a very flourishing business. The oyster which they rear is a particular favorite. Other esteemed varieties come from Shrewsbury, Cow Bay, Oyster Bay, Rock Bay, Saddle Rock, Virginia Bay, and Spuyten Duyvel. It is related of an amiable English earl, who a few years ago paid a visit to the United States, that his great delight was to wander up and down Broadway at night, and visit the principal oyster saloons in succession, regaling himself upon fried oysters at one place, upon stewed oysters at another, upon roasted oysters at a third, and winding up the evening by a dish of oysters *à l'Anglaise*. On leaving New York to return to England, he miscalculated the time of sailing of the steamer, and found that he had an hour and a half upon his hands.

"What shall we do?" said the American friend, who had come to see him off.

"Return to Broadway," said his lordship, "and have some more oysters."

As nearly all the theatres are in Broadway, the Broadway oyster saloons command at night a traffic even larger than by day. "*Fruges consumere nati*" may designate humanity elsewhere, but here the quotation may be out of place, for man seems born to consume "oysters."

Seated in one of these saloons, and amused at the satisfaction with which a company of Germans were consuming pickled oysters, and inhaling the *Lager bier*, which the United States owe to the German immigration, I heard a sudden rush and rumble in Broadway.

"What is the matter?" said I.

"Only a fire," replied an American friend; "but don't move. Nobody thinks any thing about fires here. Fires are familiar incidents. They are an institution of the country; we are proud of them. Besides, we do not believe all the alarms of fire that are raised, for the 'boys' like to have a run. If your own walls are heated by a conflagration next door, you may bestir yourself, but not till then."

"But I have heard much of the firemen, and should like to see some of them."

"They also are an 'institution' in America, and if you have not seen them we will go round to their bunk-rooms."

"Bunk-rooms?" I inquired, suggestively, for the word was new.

"Yes, bunk-rooms; where they bunk together."

"Bunk together?"

"Yes; bunk, sleep, chum, live together."

We emerged into Broadway. But there was no fire. It was only a procession of firemen, with their engines (or en-*gines*, as the word is generally pronounced in America), their ladders, and their hooks. Thousands of people lined both sides of Broadway. It was a lovely night, clear, crisp, and cold, and the rays of the moon fell upon the marble edifices with a brilliancy as if they had fallen upon icebergs or the snowy summits of hills. Every object was sharp and distinct; and the white spire of Grace Church, more than a mile distant, stood out in bold relief against the blue sky, as well defined in all its elegant tracery as if it had not been more than a hundred yards off. It was a grand "turn out" of the firemen. Each company had its favorite engine, of which it is as fond as a captain is of his ship, gayly ornamented with ribbons, flags, streamers, and flowers, and preceded by a band of music. Each engine was dragged along the streets by the firemen in their peculiar costume — dark pantaloons, with leathern belt around the waist, large boots, a thick red shirt, with no coat or vest, and the ordinary fireman's helmet. Each man held the rope of the engine in one hand, and a blazing torch in the other. The sight was peculiarly impressive and picturesque. I counted no less than twenty different companies, twenty engines, and twenty bands of music—the whole procession taking upward of an hour to pass the point at which I stood. The occasion of the gathering was to receive a fire company on its return from a complimentary visit to another fire company in the adjoining Commonwealth of Rhode Island, a hundred miles off. Such interchanges of civility and courtesy are common among the "boys," who incur very considerable expense in making them, the various companies presenting each other with testimonials of regard and esteem in the shape of silver claret-jugs, candelabra, tea services, etc. But the peculiarities of the firemen, the constitution of their companies, the life they lead, and their influence in the local politics and government of the great cities of the Union, are quite a feature in American civic life, totally different from any thing we have in England, and so curious in every way as to deserve the more elaborate consideration which I propose to give them hereafter.

My present purpose is with the night aspects of Broadway —a street that quite as much as any street in London or Paris affords materials for the study of life and character. In one respect it is superior to the streets of London. Being the main artery of a great and populous capital, it may be supposed that vice reigns rampant within it as soon as night has

B

darkened. But, whatever may be the amount of licentiousness in the city, it does not expose itself to public view in the open, glaring, unblushing, brazen, and disgusting manner in which Londoners behold it in the Haymarket, Piccadilly, Regent Street, and the Strand. I do not speak of hidden immorality; but, as regards the public exhibition of vice, New York is infinitely more modest than London, and almost as modest as Paris. We know, however, that the outside appearance of Paris is but hypocrisy, and a cloak to vice more shameless—or shameful—than any thing of which London has ever been guilty; and perhaps the same may be said of New York. However, upon this point I forbear to dwell. I simply record the fact that, to all outward appearance, New York is much more decent and decorous than London.

A few nights after the torchlight procession of the firemen, when making my way from the Astor House to the St. Nicholas, in the midst of a thick drizzling rain, I was somewhat surprised to see a shower of rockets and blue-lights blazing from the middle of the street, and to hear a confused war of shouting voices, the blast of trumpets, and the beat of drums. But the majestic roar of the multitude—the grandest sound in nature—predominated above all other noises. Broadway was impassable. All the omnibuses had turned out of their usual track, and were making their way by the back streets and parallel avenues to their several points of arrival and departure. Had such a gathering been permitted in the streets of London by night, there might have been fears for the safety of the Bank of England and the Mint; and had it occurred in the streets of Paris, the empire of the third Napoleon would have stood a chance of once more giving way to a republic or some other form of government; but in New York—where there is scarcely a policeman to be seen—it seemed to excite no alarm, but considerable curiosity. As I pushed, or insinuated myself as well as I could through the dense mass, the rockets kept pouring up to the sky in more rapid succession; the uproar of the people's voices swelled louder and louder; and when I came within one hundred yards of the St. Nicholas, I found that that building was the very point of attraction, and that an excited orator was addressing a still more excited auditory from the balcony. Thickly scattered among the multitude were grimy fellows in their shirt-sleeves, who held aloft blazing torches, and, at each rounded period of the orator's address, waved them in the air, and signaled the crowd to cheer, shout, and huzza. I could not obtain admission into my own abode for the pressure of the multitude, but, after a quarter of an hour, succeeded in getting ingress by the back door. Making my way to the balcony, I discovered that the speaker was the Mayor of New York, elected by universal suffrage, who was addressing his constituents at that late hour —nearly eleven o'clock—and soliciting at their hands the honor of re-election to the mayoralty. That upturned sea of human faces, heedless of the rain that beat down upon them, eagerly intent upon the hard words that the mayor was launching against his political opponents—the moving, excited, surging, roaring mass, irradiated, as it swayed to and fro, by the gleam and glare of hundreds of torches wildly waved in the air, formed a most picturesque spectacle.

The mayor, brother of the theatrical speculator, to whom the world owes the nuisance and the slang of the so-called "negro" minstrelsy, had been accused by his opponents in the press, and at public meetings, of every crime, public and private, which it was possible for a man to commit short of murder, and in terms so gross and open that the horsehair wig of any judge in England might have stood on end with surprise at the audacity of the libels, if brought under his cognizance for trial. But the mayor, unabashed and undismayed, seemed to consider the charges against his character to be quite consistent with the ordinary tactics of party strife, and contented himself with simple retaliation, and the use of the broadest, most vernacular *tu quoque* which it was possible to apply. It was difficult to avoid feeling some alarm that, if the police were not requisite in such a meeting, the firemen speedily would be, either from the effects of the rockets and Roman candles, or from those of the torches. But no harm came of the demonstration; and a dozen or twenty similar meetings by torchlight have since been held by the mayor and his rivals in other parts of the city. Surely a population among whom such nightly saturnalia are possible without a general assault upon all the shops and stores in the city has an innate respect for the laws of *meum* and *tuum*? But politics are the life of this people. Every man is a voter; and every officer, general or local, president, governor, mayor, alderman, city or state treasurer, the officers of the militia, even the firemen, are elected by universal suffrage and the ballot-box.

But, with all this respect for property—if these midnight and torchlight meetings of an excited multitude in one of the richest streets in the world prove, as they seem to do, the inherent peaceableness and respect for law of citizens—New York is not a city where either life or property is very secure. The daily journals teem with accounts of murder, robbery, and outrage; and this morning one of the most influential papers asserts in its most prominent leading article that during the past three years New York has been sinking in the scale of public respectability; that citizens resort to the expedients of border life, and assume the habits of a semi-barbarous society for the preservation of their property and the safety of their persons; that ladies are stopped and robbed in the broad light of day; that murderous affrays take place with practical impunity to the perpetrators within reach of the public offices and under the very eye of the chief magistrate of the city; and that decent people go about their daily business armed as if an enemy lurked in every lane and gateway of the streets.

This, it is to be hoped, is an exaggeration in the interest of the rival candidate for the office of mayor; but there can, unfortunately, be no doubt that the police of New York is not equal to its duties, and that robberies, accompanied with violence and murder, are of more frequent occurrence here than in any other city in the world of the same size and population. Whether the citizens of New York relish the prospect or not, they will have, ere many years, to increase their taxes and their police force, and regulate it more stringently, and by some more efficacious mode than by universal suffrage, and by the votes of the very "rowdies" and blackguards they wish to repress, if they will not resort, in the last extremity of desperation, to the Californian substitution of a Vigilance Committee.

CHAPTER IV.

HOTEL LIFE.

New York, Dec. 9, 1857.

PRAISE the cities of America, admire the greatness and wealth of the country, extol the enterprise and "go-ahead-ativeness" of the people, or expatiate on the glorious future before the republic, and there is a class of persons in this city who reply to your enthusiasm with a sneer, and assert that they have "heard all that sort of thing before," and " can stand a great deal of it" without evil consequences to their health or digestion. But if, on the other hand, the stranger, in the exercise of his independent judgment, presume to disapprove or condemn any thing in the manners of the people, or hint a doubt as to the perfect wisdom of any one of their social or political institutions, the porcupines of the press raise their quills, and grow exceedingly angry. To them optimism or pessimism, or the medium between the two, is equally distasteful. No matter how honest may be the praise or how gentle the expression of disapproval, they do not like it. They seem to suspect all praise to be a sham or a mockery, and to feel all dispraise to be an insult and an outrage. In these respects they differ from Englishmen, all of whom can bear with the most patient equanimity the rubs that would almost drive such sensitive Americans out of their wits. It must be confessed, however, that the more reflective among the Americans, who have seen the world, and are more assured of the strength and position of their mighty republic, take things more easily; accept praise as their due in the same generous spirit in which it is offered; and endeavor to learn wisdom from the criticism of people who cross the Atlantic to see, hear, and judge for themselves. Even if they do not agree with the adverse criticism, they have philosophy and common sense enough to be undisturbed by it, even when it seems to be hostile. It is a pity, however, that such gentlemen and philosophers are not more common both in the press and in society.

In describing the aspects of hotel life in New York and in the other great cities of America as they have impressed me, it is possible that I may incur the displeasure of those who hold that the " things of America" should, like the "*cosas de España*," be kept sacred from all foreigners as things which they can not understand, and which they must not touch upon except under the penalty of ridicule or misinterpretation of motives. Nevertheless, if my judgment be imperfect, it shall, at all events, be honest; and, as regards this particular question of hotel life, there are many thousands of estimable and reflecting men and women in America who, I feel confident, will agree in the estimate I form of it.

The hotels in the great cities of America—in New York, Philadelphia, Baltimore, Washington, New Orleans, Chicago, Boston, etc.—are conducted on a peculiar system, and in a style of much magnificence. The British Isles possess no such caravansaries. Even the monster Hôtel du Louvre in Paris is scarcely to be compared with such establishments as the St. Nicholas, the Metropolitan, the Astor House, and many others in New York. Some of them make up from five hundred to a thousand beds, and others from two to five hundred. The country is so immense, the distances from point to point are so great—such as from New Orleans to Boston, or from New York to Chicago, Detroit, and the Far West; the activity of commerce is so incessant, and its ramifications so extensive, that a much larger class of people than with us is compelled by business, public and private, to be continually upon the move. In England, hotels are conducted in a style suitable to the days of solitary horsemen, gigs, and the mail-coach, and moulded upon such limited necessities as then existed; but in America the hotels and the railways grew together, and have been made to fit into each other. Large hotels are of positive necessity; and, were they solely confined to travelers, would deserve the praise of being, what they really are, the finest, most convenient, and best administered establishments in the world. It is not their fault that they have, in the course of time, and by the force of circumstances, been devoted to other uses, and that they have become the permanent homes of families, instead of remaining the temporary residences of strangers.

For a fixed charge of two dollars and a half a day (about ten and sixpence English) the traveler has a comfortable bedroom, the use of a drawing-room, dining-room, reading-room, and smoking-room, and the full enjoyment of a liberal tariff, or bill of fare, for breakfast, luncheon, dinner, tea, and supper. The two dollars and a half include all charges for servants, and every charge whatever that can be fairly included under the head of board and lodging, except wine, beer, and spirits. There is no charge for wax-lights—that flaring pretext for extortion in England. The cookery is in general excellent. The breakfast is bounteous, and at the leading hotels is spread from eight o'clock till twelve, between which hours fish, flesh, and fowl, fresh meat and salt meat, eggs, omelets, wheaten bread, rye bread, corn bread, corn cakes, rice cakes, and buckwheat cakes (the last-mentioned a greater delicacy than England can show), are liberally distributed. From twelve o'clock till two the luncheon is spread with equal profusion; and from two to six there is a succession of dinners, the getting up of which, at the St. Nicholas, the Metropolitan, or the New York, would do credit to the Reform Club and its excellent *chef de cuisine*. As soon as dinner is over, tea commences, and as soon as tea is cleared away the cloths are laid for supper, so that from eight in the morning till midnight there is one continual succession of feasts, at which governors of states, members of Congress, judges, generals, ex-presidents of the republic, the magnates of commerce and the law, and all the miscellaneous and less distinguished public, male and female, sit down. Whether the traveler do or do not partake, it is the same to the landlord. He may eat once, twice, thrice, or all day long, if he pleases. The price is two dollars and a half, even should he be a popular celebrity—have many friends—and take all his meals abroad. If ladies and families prefer to have apartments of their own, the price for lodging varies from three to five or ten dollars a day, according to the extent or elegance of accommodation required. In like manner, the board of each individual, supplied in a private apartment, is raised from two and a half to four dollars per diem. The consequence is that very few people board in their private rooms, and that nearly all breakfast, dine, and sup in public, except the very young children, for whose convenience there is a separate *table d'hôte*.

It will thus be seen that for the traveling community these hotels are very comfortable, very luxurious, very cheap, and very lively. In consequence of the great difficulty which private families experience in procuring cooks and housemaids in a country where menial service is considered beneath the dignity of a native-born American, where service is called "help," to avoid wounding the susceptibility of free citizens, and left almost exclusively to negroes and the newly-imported Irish, who too commonly, more especially the female portion of them, know nothing whatever of any household duties, and whose skill in cookery scarcely extends to the boiling of a potato, the mistresses of families keeping house on their own account lead but an uncomfortable life. In England the newly-married couple take a house, furnish it, and live quietly at home. In the cities of America—for the rule does not apply to the rural districts—they too commonly take apartments at the hotel, and live in public, glad to take advantage of the ready means which it affords of escape from the nuisances attendant upon inefficient, incomplete, and insolent service. The young wife finds herself relieved from the miseries and responsibilities of housekeeping, and has nothing to think of but dress, visiting, reading, and amusement. Brides who begin married life in hotels often continue in them from youth to maturity, without possessing the inestimable advantage and privilege of any more secluded home. To those who know nothing of domestic affairs, and to those who are willing to attend to them, but can not procure proper "help" in their household, the hotel system is equally well adapted. It saves trouble, annoyance, and expense; but at what a cost of the domestic amenities! Perhaps not above one half of the people who daily sit down to dinner in these superb establishments are travelers. The remainder are permanent residents —husbands, wives, and children. To eat in public now and then may be desirable; but for ladies to take all their meals every day, and all the year round, in the full glare of publicity; to be always full dressed; to associate daily—almost hourly —with strangers from every part of America and of the world; to be, if young and handsome, the cynosure of all idle and vagrant eyes, either at the *table d'hôte* or in the public drawing-room—these are certainly not the conditions which to an Englishman's mind are conducive to the true happiness and charm of wedded life. And it is not only the influence of this state of things upon the husband and wife to which an Englishman objects, but its influence upon the young children, who play about the corridors and halls of such mansions, and become prematurely old for want of fresh air and exercise, and overknowing from the experiences they acquire and the acquaintances they contract. Perhaps "fast" people may consider such objections to savor of "old fogyism." But reasonable people will not. The system is peculiar to America, and, therefore, strikes the attention more forcibly than if it were common to the civilized world.

It is, doubtless, more the misfortune than the fault of American families that they live so much in this style; for, without good servants who know their duty, and are not too supercilious and saucy to perform it, it is impossible for a lady, without shortening her life and making herself worse than a slave, to have a comfortable and happy home, or to govern it with pleasure or advantage either to herself or her family. Recently the New York and Philadelphia newspapers have been filled with the details of two scandalous cases —one ending in a tragedy—of which a New York and a Philadelphia hotel were the scenes, and in both of which the fair fame of ladies was sacrificed. To these painful exposures it is not necessary to make farther allusion; but they are so fresh in the public recollection that they can not be passed over, even in this cursory glance at some of the evils attendant upon the undue publicity of female life in such monster hotels as I have endeavored to describe.

To all the hotels is attached an establishment known as the "bar," where spirituous liquors are retailed under a nomenclature that puzzles the stranger, and takes a long acquaintanceship with American life and manners to become familiar with. Gin-sling, brandy-smash, whisky-skin, streak of lightning, cock-tail, and rum-salad, are but a few of the names of the drinks which are consumed at the bar, morning, noon, and night, by persons who in a similar rank of life in England would no more think of going into a gin-shop than of robbing the bank. Fancy a gin-palace under the roof of, and attached to, the Reform or the Carlton Club, and free not only to the members, but to the world without, and both classes largely availing themselves of it to drink and smoke, both by day and by night, and you will be able to form some conception of the "bar" of an American hotel, and of the class of people who frequent it. But can such a system conduce to any virtuous development of young men in this republic? The question admits of many replies; and without presuming, on so short an acquaintance with the country, to speak with authority, I leave it for the consideration of those who desire that America should be as wise and happy in the private relations of her citizens as she is free and independent in her relations to the great comity of the world.

CHAPTER V.

AMERICAN FIREMEN.

New York, Dec. 21, 1857.

WHATEVER the Americans are proud of—whatever they consider to be peculiarly good, useful, brilliant, or characteristic of themselves or their climate, they designate, half in jest, though scarcely half in earnest, as an "institution." Thus the memory of General Washington—or "Saint" Washington, as he might be called, considering the homage paid to him—is an institution; the Falls of Niagara are an institution; the

Plymouth Rock, on which the Pilgrim Fathers first set foot, is an institution, as much so as the Blarney Stone in Ireland, to which an eloquent Irish orator, at a public dinner, compared it, amid great applause, by affirming that the Plymouth Rock was the "Blarney Stone of New England." "Sweet potatoes" are an institution, and pumpkin (or punkin) pie is an institution; canvas-back ducks are an institution; squash is an institution; Bunker's Hill is an institution; and the firemen of New York a great institution.

The fire system, in nearly all the principal cities of the Union is a peculiarity of American life. Nothing like it exists in any European community. As yet the city of Boston appears to be the only one that has had the sense and the courage to organize the fire-brigades on a healthier plan, and bring them under the direct guidance and control of the municipality. Every where else the firemen are a power in the state, wielding considerable political influence, and uncontrolled by any authority but such as they elect by their own free votes. They are formidable by their numbers, dangerous by their organization, and in many cities are principally composed of young men at the most reckless and excitable age of life, who glory in a fire as soldiers do in a battle, and who are quite as ready to fight with their fellow-creatures as with the fire which it is more particularly their province to subdue. In New York, Philadelphia, Baltimore, and other large cities, the fire service is entirely voluntary, and is rendered for "the love of the thing," or for "the fun of the thing," whichever it may be. The motto of one fire company at New York, inscribed on their banner, is,

"Firemen with pleasure,
Soldiers at leisure;"

a couplet which characterizes the whole spirit of their organization. The firemen are mostly youths engaged during the day in various handicrafts and mechanical trades, with a sprinkling of clerks and shopmen. In New York each candidate for admission into the force must be balloted for, like a member of the London clubs. If elected, he has to serve for five years, during which he is exempt from jury and militia duty. The firemen elect their own superintendents and other officers, by ballot, as they were themselves elected, and are divided into engine companies, hook and ladder companies, and hose companies. The engine and accessories are provided by the municipality; but the firemen are seldom contented with them in the useful but unadorned state in which they receive them, but lavish upon them an amount of ornament, in the shape of painted panels, silver plating, and other finery, more than sufficient to prove their liberality, and the pride they take in their business. The service is entirely voluntary and gratuitous, having no advantages to recommend it but those of exemption from the jury and the militia, and leads those who devote themselves to it not only into great hardship and imminent danger, but into an amount of expenditure which is not the least surprising part of the "institution." The men—or "boys," as they are more commonly called—not only buy their own costume and accoutrements, and spend large sums in the ornamentation of their favorite engines, or hydrants, as already mentioned, but in the furnishing of their bunk-rooms and parlors at the fire-stations. The bunk or sleeping rooms, in which the unmarried, and sometimes the married, members pass the night, to be ready for duty on the first alarm of fire, are plainly and comfortably furnished, but the parlors are fitted up with a degree of luxury equal to that of the public rooms of the most celebrated hotels. At one of the central stations, which I visited in company with an editor of a New York journal, the walls were hung with portraits of Washington, Franklin, Jefferson, Mason, and other founders of the republic; the floor was covered with velvet-pile carpeting, a noble chandelier hung from the centre, the crimson curtains were rich and heavy, while the sideboard was spread with silver claret-jugs and pieces of plate, presented by citizens whose houses and property had been preserved from fire by the exertions of the brigade; or by the fire-companies of other cities, in testimony of their admiration for some particular act of gallantry or heroism which the newspapers had recorded.

If the firemen be an "institution," fire itself is an institution in most American cities. Whether it be carelessness, or the habitual overheating of all houses, public and private, by the system of flues, furnaces, and stoves which are in ordinary use, or the combustibility of the materials of which houses are built, or a combination of all these causes, and perhaps many others, it is certain that fires are much more common in America than they are in Europe. Into whatever city the traveler goes, he sees the traces of recent conflagration; sometimes whole blocks, or often whole streets or parishes leveled to the ground, or presenting nothing but bare and blackened walls. So constant appears to be the danger, that the streets of New York, Boston, and other cities are traversed in all directions by telegraphic wires, which centre invariably at the City Hall, and convey instantaneously to head-quarters, day or night, the slightest alarm of fire. By an ingenious system, due to the scientific sagacity of Mr. Moses G. Farmer and Dr. W. F. Channing, of Boston, and brought to its present perfection in 1852, the alarm is rapidly transmitted from any part of the circumference to the centre, and from the centre back again, through an almost countless number of radii, to the whole circumference of the city. In a lecture delivered before the Smithsonian Institution at Washington, Dr. Channing explained the fire organization of a city by stating that "from the central station at the City Hall go out wires over the house-tops, visiting every part of the city and returning again. These are the signal circuits by which the existence of a fire is signalized from any part of the city to the centre. Strung on these circuits, or connected with them, are numerous *signal boxes* or signalizing points, of which there may be one at the corner of every square. These are cast-iron, cottage-shaped boxes, attached to the sides of the houses, communicating, by means of wires inclosed in a wrought-iron gas-pipe, with the signal circuit overhead. On the door of each signal box the number of the fire district, and also the number of the box or station itself in its district, are marked, and the place in the neighborhood where the key-holder may be found is also prominently notified. On opening the door of the signal box a crank is seen. When this is turned it communicates to the centre the number of the fire district and of the box, and nothing else. Repeated turns give a repetition of the same signal. By this means any child or ignorant person who can turn a coffee mill can signalize an alarm from his own neighborhood with unerring certainty. Connected with the signal circuits at the central office, where they all converge, are a little alarm-bell and a register, which notifies and records the alarm received from the signal box. The galvanic battery which supplies all the signal circuits is also placed at the central station. If a fire occurs near signal box or station 5, in district 3, and the crank of that box is turned, the watchman or operator at the central station will immediately be notified by the little bell, and will read at once on his register the telegraphic characters which signify district 3, station 5. Having traced the alarm of a fire from a signal box into the central station, the next question is, how shall the alarm be given from that centre to the public? From the central station proceed also several circuits of wires, called alarm circuits, which go to the various fire-bells throughout the city, and which are connected with striking machines similar in character to the striking machinery of a clock, but liberated by telegraph. The operator at the central station is enabled, by the mere touch of his finger upon a key, to throw all the striking machines into simultaneous action, and thus give instantaneous public alarm."

It is certainly a triumph of science to be enabled by means of one instrument to ring simultaneously all the alarm-bells in every steeple and tower of a great and populous city, and call out the fire companies with their engines, ladders, ropes, hooks, and hose, and designate to each of them at the same moment the particular spot in the city which is threatened with devastation, although the very completeness of the arrangement, and the necessities which called it into existence, are sufficient to prove that there is something wrong either in the house-building or the house-heating of America, or in the absence of the careful attention which in other parts of the world renders fire less frequent.

The assertion is frequently made by Americans, whenever

the subject of fires is mentioned, that many fires are purposely caused by the "boys" for the sake of a frolic, or a run, or in a spirit of rivalry between two or more companies, who desire to compete with each other in the performance of deeds of daring, or who long, as they sometimes do, for a street fight to wipe out some ancient grudge which had its origin at a fire. The statement is repeated on American authority, and must go for what it is worth—as something which may be false, but which is believed by many estimable citizens of the republic to be true. In Philadelphia and Baltimore alarms of fire are regularly expected on Saturday nights, when the "boys" have received their week's wages, and are ripe for mischief. In Boston, where the firemen are paid by the city, and where they are entirely under the control of the municipality, fires are less frequent than elsewhere, and fights among the firemen are entirely unknown. New York and the other great American cities must ultimately resort to the same system, or continue to pay the penalty not only of constant loss of life and property, but of the preponderance of a very unruly and dangerous class in the lower strata of their population.

The firemen throughout the Union have a newspaper of their own, devoted exclusively to their interests, and to the promulgation of facts and opinions relating to the fraternity.

CHAPTER VI.

FROM NEW YORK TO BOSTON.

October, 1857.

IN fine weather—or perhaps in any weather—the pleasantest mode of traveling between New York and Boston is by steam-boat through the Long Island Sound to Fall River, a distance of upward of 200 miles, and from Fall River by railway to Boston, 54 miles. Railway traveling in the United States is not agreeable. Such easy luxury as that of a first-class carriage in England or in France is not to be obtained for love or money. In a land of social equality, every one except the negro travels in the first class. The servant and the mistress, the navvie, the peddler, the farmer, the merchant, the general, the lawyer, the senator, the judge, and the governor of the state, with their wives, their sons, and their daughters, and even the Irish bogtrotter, who, before he left Ireland, would as soon have thought of taking the chair from the viceroy, or the pulpit from the Roman Catholic Archbishop of Dublin, as of traveling in a first-class carriage, but who, in this country, handles more money in a day than he saw in the old country in a month, and who waxes saucy in proportion to his cash, all mingle together in one long car, by no means so comfortable as a second-class carriage on any of the principal lines in Great Britain.

These cars accommodate each from sixty to eighty travelers, and in the winter are warmed by stoves burning anthracite coal, which stoves and which coal are among the greatest afflictions and miseries of the country. Every place to which an unfortunate stranger can resort is overheated by these abominable contrivances. They burn out all the elasticity and moisture of the atmosphere; they quicken the pulse, inflame the skin, and parch the tongue. Hotels, private houses, railway cars, all are alike rendered intolerable by their heat, until, oppressed by the sulphury and palpitating hotness, depressed in spirit, weakened in body, and well-nigh suffocated, the stranger accustomed to the wholesome fresh air rushes out to get a gulp of it, and takes cold by the suddenness of the transition. Perhaps the universal use of these stoves may account for the sallowness of so many of the American people, which contrasts so remarkably with the ruddy freshness of the English. An equal freshness is seldom to be seen here except in young children and among new-comers. He who would avoid this nuisance, as well as such other discomforts of the rail as the want of all support for the back or the head in long journeys, rendering sleep an almost unattainable blessing, should travel by the steam-boats whenever he has a chance. Against the steam-boats the only objection is that they sometimes blow up or take fire. But these are rare occurrences; and no man of ordinary nerve and courage who is compelled to travel need alarm himself unduly by the anticipation of such catastrophes. As every man believes all men to be mortal except himself, so most travelers believe that every boat may explode, or burn, or be wrecked except the particular boat by which they happen to take their passage. Were it not so, who would travel, unless from the direst necessity? The steamers that ply in the Long Island Sound are, as regards all their interior arrangements, as handsome and luxurious as the railway cars are the reverse. For a slight extra charge, only amounting to one dollar in the distance between New York and Boston, a private state-room or cabin can be obtained, fitted up with every comfort and convenience. Why similar privacy and comfort are not obtainable on the railways it is difficult to say. Though huge, unwieldly, and ungraceful when seen from the outside, with their machinery working on the top, the river and 'long-shore steamboats, when examined from within, are worthy of the name of floating palaces. The saloons, three deep, one above the other, and affording a promenade the whole length of the vessel, are large and airy, richly carpeted, and decorated with velvet and gold, with easy-chairs, fauteuils, and sofas, and all appliances either for waking or for sleeping. Some of them make up from 600 to 800 berths, in addition to the private state-rooms. The tables are bountifully spread for meals, and the negro stewards and waiters, who are the best servants procurable in the United States, and far superior to the Irish, their only competitors in this line of business, are attentive and obliging.

Expecting to dine on board, I took no dinner in New York, but found at six o'clock that tea only was provided. The tea, however, had all the bounteousness of a dinner—fish, flesh, fowl, pastry, and dessert; every thing except beer or wine. Seeing this, I asked the jet-black negro who waited on me to bring me some lager beer.

"Can't do it, sar," said he, with a grin; "it's against the rules, sar."

"What rules?"

"The rules of the ship. Ours is a temperance boat, sar."

"Then why don't you advertise it as a temperance boat, that people may take their choice?"

"All the same, sar," said the negro; "'zackly the same. Can't let you have beer or wine at the table; but you go on, sar, to the barber's shop, and thar you'll get every thing you want, sar—whisky, rum, brandy, wine—all sorts thar, sar."

It was even so. In each steamer is a barber's shop, handsomely fitted up, and where the traveler can have his hair cut, or cleaned, or washed, or where he may be shaved by a black barber, and where, whether the boat be a temperance boat, or a boat for the moderate enjoyment and use of the liquid blessings of life, he can obtain gin-slings, and cock-tails, and whisky-skins, and all the multifarious spirituous drinks of America. The only interference with his personal liberty in the matter is that he must take his drink in the barber's sanctum, and can not have it served to him in any other part of the ship. I mention this fact for the edification of Exeter Hall, and of those who would introduce the Maine Liquor Law, or something like it, into England, as one out of many proofs which might be adduced to show how great a "sham" is the operation of that prohibitive and tyrannical measure in the country which gave it birth.

Boston, the capital of the small but ancient, wealthy, and intelligent commonwealth of Massachusetts, the model and most conservative state of the Union, is one of the most picturesque as well as important cities of America. The original Indian name of the small peninsula on which it is built was "Shawmut," or the "Living Fountains." From the three hills on which it stands, which have been now partly leveled, it obtained from the early settlers the name of Tremont, or Trimountain—a name still given to it by poets and orators when they strive to be particularly eloquent. In compliment to the Rev. John Cotton, the Vicar of Boston, in Lincolnshire, who emigrated here for conscience' sake, with the other hardy and honest Englishmen, who have obtained the honorable name of the "Pilgrim Fathers," it received from the early settlers the name of Boston. Since that day it has grown to be a city of 180,000 inhabitants, and the nucleus of quite a congeries of other cities almost as important as itself. These stretch around it on every side, but are divided from it either by the arms of the sea or by the pleasant waters of the Charles River. Charlestown, Cambridge, Roxbury, Brighton, Brookline, and Chelsea are so closely united to Boston as virtually to form part of it on the map, although most of them are independent cities, governed by their own magistrates and municipalities. The total population of Boston and the outlying cities, towns, and villages is upward of 400,000. Boston city is divided into South Boston, East Boston, and Boston Proper. The old city, or Boston Proper, stands on a peninsula, surrounded by salt water on three sides, and on the fourth by the brackish water of the Charles River, which, at its confluence with the sea, spreads out like a small lake. It is connected by a narrow strip of land, not more than two feet above high water, and called the Neck, with the suburb or city of Roxbury. Bunker's or Bunker Hill—so named, according to some, from Bunker's Hill in Lincolnshire, and according to others from Bunker's Hill in the town of Nottingham, is not in Boston, but in the adjoining city of Charlestown, with which it has communication by four bridges—two for ordinary traffic, and two for the railways.

The 750 acres of ground on which old Boston is built was occupied, in the year 1635, by the Rev. John Blackstone, the only inhabitant, as well as the sole owner of the soil. Mr. Blackstone sold the land for £30 English money. There are now many sites in the city worth as much per square yard. Boston is very picturesque, very clean, and very English. It has not the French and foreign aspect of New York, but is altogether quieter and more sedate, and justifies, by its outward appearance, the character it has acquired of being the Athens of the New World, the mart of literature, and the most intellectual city in America. Not that this high character is willingly conceded to it by people who live beyond the limits of Charleston, Roxbury, and Cambridge; for the New Yorkers, the Philadelphians, and many others, so far from taking the Bostonians at the Bostonian estimate of themselves, hold their high pretensions in scorn, and speak contemptuously of them as utter "Yankees." There can, however, be no doubt, all jealousy and rivalries apart, that the society of Boston is highly cultivated and refined, and that, if it do not excel, it is not excelled by that of any city in the Union.

The great charm of the scenery of Boston is its Common or Park—a piece of ground covering about forty acres, and open on one side to the Charles River, over the estuary of which, and the heights beyond, it commands from every part a series of extensive and beautiful views. The other sides of the Common are occupied by the residences of the principal inhabitants—noble stone buildings most of them—and representing a rental ranging from £300 to £800 or £1000 per annum. House-rent is exceedingly high in all the great American cities, and is at least double that of houses of the corresponding style in London. In all distant views the State House dominates the city as the highest and most conspicuous object, around which every thing else is concentrated. The view from the top of this edifice well repays the labor of the ascent, and affords an unrivaled panorama of the busy, populous, and thriving home which the descendants of the ancient English Puritans have made for themselves in the New World. In the Common, surrounded by a railing to protect it from injury, stands a venerable elm, with an inscription stating that it is believed to have been planted before the first settlement of Boston as a colony, and that it began to exhibit signs of old age a quarter of a century ago. Its boughs are inhabited by a colony of tame gray squirrels. To throw nuts to these graceful little creatures, and watch their gambols, is one of the principal amusements of the nursemaids and children of Boston, as well as of many older and wiser persons. There are similar colonies in the other elms in some of the principal streets. The squirrels are general favorites, and have no enemies except among the cats, which occasionally make an inroad upon them and diminish their numbers, to the great disgust and indignation of the well-minded population. It may be mentioned as an interesting fact in natural history that the elms in Boston planted by the English settlers from slips or seeds brought from England retain their leaves much later than the native American elms. At this advanced period of the year may be noticed, amid the leafless or the brown and yellow trees that grace the Common, seven elms of most luxuriant green foliage, which seem not to have lost a leaf, or to possess a leaf in the slightest degree discolored. These are the English elms, sturdy Britons, flourishing in a vigorous old age, while their Yankee brethren, seedy, sapless, and wobegone, look as sallow as if they too, like their human compatriots, smoked immoderately, chewed tobacco, spat, lived in heated rooms, and, in their over-eagerness to get rich, did injustice to their physical nature.

The principal street of Boston is Washington Street, a long and not very even thoroughfare, but picturesque and English in its character, and containing some very handsome shops. The most interesting, if not the most prominent of them, is the "book-store" of Messrs. Ticknor and Fields—two associates who have published more poetry, and, if report speak truly, made more money by it than any other publishers in America. Their store is the lounge and resort of all the literary celebrities of Boston and Harvard University. Here Longfellow, poet, scholar, and gentleman, looks in to have a chat. Here Professor Agassiz, who has rendered himself doubly dear to Boston by refusing to leave it on the invitation of Napoleon III., and the offer of a large salary in Paris, shows his genial and benevolent face, more contented to live humbly in a land of liberty, than ostentatiously and luxuriously in a land of thraldom. Here Oliver W. Holmes, the "Autocrat of the Breakfast Table," who ought to be well known in England, comes to give or receive the news of the day. Here the amiable Prescott, the historian, and one of the most estimable of men—to have shaken whose hand is a privilege—sometimes looks in at the door with a face like a ray of sunshine. Here poets, poetesses, lecturers, preachers, professors, and newspaper editors have combined, without premeditation, to establish a sort of Literary Exchange, where they may learn what new books are forthcoming, and talk together upon literature and criticism.

Boston is the great metropolis of lecturers, Unitarian preachers, and poets. Perhaps for poets it would be better to say rhymers or versifiers, and I make the correction accordingly. The finest churches in the city—with the tallest and handsomest spires, and the most imposing fronts and porticoes, belong to the Unitarians. Lecturers have been so richly endowed by the Lowel bequest, that the Bostonians, over-belectured, often experience a feeling of nausea at the very suggestion of a lecture, or worse still, of a series of them; and as for poets and poetesses, or, as I should say, rhymers and versifiers, both male and female, their name is "legion upon legion." In walking along Washington Street, and meeting a gentlemanly-looking person with a decent coat and a clean shirt, the traveler may safely put him down as either a lecturer, a Unitarian minister, or a poet; possibly the man may be, Cerberus-like, all three at once. In Boston the onus lies upon every respectable person to prove that he has not written a sonnet, preached a sermon, or delivered a lecture; and few there are above the station of the lowest kind of handicraftsmen who could lay their hands upon their hearts and plead not guilty to one or the other of these charges.

Within an easy ride by rail from Boston, and almost near enough to form a suburb, is the city of Cambridge, celebrated as the seat of the Harvard University, the most serviceable educational institution in America. Harvard has no pretensions to rival its British namesake either in wealth or architectural beauty, and is but a modest assemblage of unconnected and unattractive looking buildings. But it has turned out some of the best men in America, and to be its president is one of the greatest honors to which a citizen of Massachusetts can aspire.

It is not any portion of the plan of this book to record private conversations or private hospitalities. If it were, much might be said of Cambridge and Harvard, and of the choice spirits whom it was my privilege to meet on my short but most pleasant visit to its classic purlieus. Let it suffice to say that in my remembrance it is sacred to the name and to the companionship of such men as Longfellow, Agassiz, Lowell, and the excellent and venerable Josiah Quincy, long the president of the University. The last-named gentleman is one of the few survivors of the British era. He was born a British subject before the Declaration of Independence, and still survives in a green and illustrious old age to shed honor upon American liberty.

CHAPTER VII.

TO THE FALLS OF NIAGARA.

Nov. 3d, 1857.

IT was a beautiful morning when I took the train from Boston for the Falls of Niagara. The foliage was not in the full bloom and flush of that autumnal glory which makes the month of October so lovely in America, but the trees were far from bare. The "pride of India," the alanthus, and the elm, were shorn of their splendors, and were all but leafless; but the oaks, and, more especially, the maples, glittered in green, brown, and crimson magnificence. Nothing can surpass the beauty of the American maples at this season, when their leaves, turned to a blood-red color by the first touch of the winter frosts, gleam, fairest of the fair, amid the yellowing foliage of oaks and beeches, the bright green of the fir-trees, and the more sombre verdure of the omnipresent pine. The sky was cloudless, and the atmosphere so transparent that remote objects were brought out sharply and distinctly, as if close to the eye. To the mind of one accustomed to the English and Scottish landscape, there was one defect in the character of the scenery, and that was the absence of the green grass, earth's most beautiful adornment in the British Isles, but which is nowhere to be seen on the American continent after the early summer. The heat of July parches and withers it, and in autumn and winter there may be said to be no grass at all—nothing but shriveled herbage, dry as stubble, and of the same color. But otherwise the landscape was as fair as poet or painter could desire, and the delicious blue of the sky, and the hazy, dreamy stillness of the Indian summer, made amends even for the absence of grass. If nature had not spread a carpet, she had certainly hung curtains and drapery of regal magnificence.

Though I ardently desired, I yet dreaded to see Niagara. Wordsworth at Yarrow "had a vision of his own," and was afraid lest he should undo it by making too close an acquaintanceship with the reality. Such were my feelings on drawing near to the falls. Unlike a celebrated traveler from England, who had, very shortly before my visit, been at Buffalo— within two hours' journey by railway, yet had never had the curiosity, or found the time, to look at Niagara face to face, I was positively pervaded, permeated, steeped, and bathed in a longing desire to behold it; and my fears but arose from the excess of my love. The season was not the most favorable that could have been chosen; but, as one who might never have another opportunity, I determined, whatever welcome the weather might give me—whether amid rain, hail, or snow— to gaze upon this wonder of creation while yet it was in my power, and to hear that great voice preaching in the wilderness, and singing forever and ever the old and eternal anthem, " God is great !"

Our first resting-place of importance was at Albany, the political capital of the State of New York; our next at Utica, ninety-five miles from Albany, where it was originally my intention to remain for two or three days, to visit the Trenton Falls, as beautiful, though not so grand, as Niagara, and by many travelers preferred to the more stupendous marvel of the two. But, on learning that the hotel, the only house in the place, had long been closed for the season, I held on my way. A sudden fall of snow, just as I was debating the question, was the last feather that broke the back of the camel of Doubt, and made me press on to my journey's end. From Utica—a place of considerable trade, and with a population of upward of 20,000—our train started to Rome, and from Rome to Syracuse. After leaving the last-mentioned place we lost sight for a while of this classical nomenclature, and traversed a region where Asiatic names were in greater favor—through Canton to Pekin—leaving Delhi on the left. Thence we emerged into a district where the towns of ancient and modern Europe and Africa seemed to have had a stiff battle to perpetuate their names in the New World, and where Attica, Athens, Geneva, Palmyra, Hamburg, Carthage, Algiers, and Glasgow were scattered about in the most perplexing confusion. On either side of the way the stumps of trees that had been cut down by the pitiless axe of the settlers, and the black, charred, ghost-like stems of monarchs of the forest, which, to save labor, they had attempted to destroy by fire, stood in the utterness of their desolation. The swamps of dark moss-colored water, amid which they rotted, reflected their melancholy grandeur, undisturbed by any ripple larger than had been occasioned by a falling leaf. The villages and towns, most of them aspiring to be called cities, presented invariably the same rude, unfinished appearance. Mingled amid the log huts, the cabbage-gardens, and the squash-fields, were churches, chapels, hotels, stores, banks, mills, and printing-offices, most of them incomplete at that time, but doubtless, ere this, in full activity of life and business. Irish and Germans seemed to form the bulk of the community. "Gasthaus," in German characters, was a word that continually met the eye; while the ubiquitous pig, and such names over the doors as O'Driscoll, Murphy, O'Brien, and O'Callaghan, unequivocally affirmed the fact that the Germans had not entirely monopolized the farms, the fields, the shanties, and the stores of the country. At Rome an old man got into our car, who did us the favor of remaining with us for upward of fifty miles of our journey. He plied during the whole of the time a vigorous trade in some quack medicine of his own concoction, which he declared to be "good for fevers, agues, dyspepsias, rheumatisms, and colics." The price was a dollar a bottle; and among the sixty persons in our car he succeeded in getting no less than nine customers by dint of the most impudent and vexatious pertinacity I ever beheld. But trade of every kind is so congenial with the spirit of the American people, that no display of it at any time, and under any circumstances, seems to be offensive, but, on the contrary, to be admired as something "smart" and praiseworthy. Having exhausted our car and my patience, the peddler disappeared into the car adjoining, where he no doubt carried on the same series of performances. We were no sooner relieved of his presence than a book-hawker made his appearance, and left a prospectus with every traveler, to study or to cast upon the floor, and after a sufficient interval returned for orders. But the book-trade did not appear to be very prosperous, and he gathered up his prospectuses to do service on a future occasion. Then, changing his literary business for that of a dealer in maple-candy, peppermint-drops, cakes, and apples, he allowed us no cessation from importunity until we arrived at the city of Rochester, where a new set of plagues of the same class took possession of us, and accompanied us the whole way to Niagara.

At Rochester—a city of nearly 50,000 inhabitants, seated upon the Genesee River, whose magnificent falls give it an amount of water-power which any city in the world might envy—the New York Central Railroad crosses the stream upon a bridge much more substantial than such structures usually are in the United States. But the bridge being within a hundred yards above the fall, the passengers by rail can not obtain even a glimpse of the cataract as they pass. On a subsequent occasion I stopped a night at Rochester to view the fall. When this part of the world was a wilderness the Genesee must have been eminently grand and beautiful. Even now, when there is not a tree upon the banks, and when a succession of flour, paper, and other mills has monopolized all the available space on both banks, and filched from the great fall itself a hundred little streams, that discharge their power over the wheels of as many mills and factories, the rush of the mighty river is a noble sight. Man has disfigured the banks, but the stream itself is not only too unmanageable to be brought into subjection to his uses, but too vast in its loveliness and grandeur to be sensibly impaired, or made other than beautiful, whatever he may do to it.

It had been dark for two hours before we reached Niagara City, sometimes called "The City of the Falls;" and when the train stopped I distinctly heard the dull, heavy roar of earth's most stupendous cataract. All the great hotels were closed for the season. The Cataract House, and the International, on the American side, and the Clifton House, on the Canadian shore, were alike deserted and sealed against the visitor. No place remained available for a nightly lodging but a third, or, I might say, a fifth-rate hotel, considering the style of the accommodation and the cookery, and thither I betook myself and engaged a bed. I had no sooner made all my arrangements for the night than I sallied out to take a glimpse of the moonlight glory of Niagara. I had some difficulty in finding my way. The guides had all departed weeks previously, and there was not even a stray inhabitant in the wide, muddy, unfinished streets of Niagara City. A few pigs still prowled about in the miry ways, a few German *Gasthäuse* were still open, but there were no other sounds or sights of life in all the melancholy place. The International Hotel, a huge block, about three times as large as the Reform Club— had all its shutters up; and the shops and stores of the Indian dealers in furs, moccasins, and stuffed birds were closed. At last, in my perplexity, I was constrained to enter a German beer-house to ask my way to the falls. The honest German to whom I put the question stared at me with genuine astonishment. He seemed to think that I had either lost my senses, or that I had never possessed any.

"Do you want to cross to the other side?" he asked, in tolerably good English; "because, if you do, it is late for the ferry, and I advise you to go to the Suspension Bridge."

"How far is it?" said I.

"Two miles," he replied.

"But I only want to take a look at the falls," I rejoined.

"To-night?"

"Yes, to-night; why not?"

"To-night! But why not wait till daylight? But I beg your pardon; you must surely be an Englishman? Nobody else would be absurd enough to want to see the falls at such a time, and risk his neck in the attempt. The ferryman lives on the Canadian side, and is not likely to come across for you, even if you can make him hear, which is doubtful."

I thought so too, considering the noise which Niagara made,

and which I could hear as the bass to the shrill treble of the German's speech; but he kindly directed me to the ferry-house with a shrug of pity, and the parting consolation that, if I failed to get across that night, I could see the falls in the morning, which, in his opinion, would be quite soon enough for any rational being.

The ferry-house was as deserted as the hotels. Its door was open, but the interior was almost pitch dark; and after groping about for some minutes, reluctant to return without a sight of the falls, I discovered that the ferry-house was on the top of the high bank (about two hundred feet from the level of the stream), and that passengers were let down by ropes in a car upon a sloping rail. Dreading to tumble down the incline, and meeting with no living creature to appeal to for aid or information, I made my way back to the "Clarendon"—the cheapest and most uncomfortable of all American hotels; got more than ankle-deep in mire; met several pigs and one passenger; and, for that evening, left the falls unvisited. But I fell asleep with their mighty music ringing in my ears, and next morning was more than repaid for my disappointments by the sight of Niagara in all its glory.

CHAPTER VIII.

NIAGARA.

No description that I had read of Niagara—whether written by poet, romance-writer, geologist, or mere tourist and traveler—conveyed to my mind any adequate idea of the reality. I had formed a Niagara in my mind, but it was another and a very different Niagara from that which my senses disclosed to me—immensely higher, more noisy and more confused, and lacking the majestic regularity, order, and calm though stupendous power of the actual torrent which my eyes beheld. I was prepared to be astonished at its grandeur and magnificence; but my feelings in gazing upon it, day after day and evening after evening, were not so much those of astonishment as of an overpowering sense of law, mingled with a delicious pleasure, that filled my whole being, and made my brain dizzy with delight. That I may not be accused of an attempt at fine writing in my description of this wondrous waterfall, I shall exhaust all my adjectives at once. Having poured out my praises in one gush, I shall relapse into the soberest description I can command of what I saw, and endeavor to present an unimpassioned narrative of its effects upon my mind. Any enthusiastic traveler, deeply impressed with the grace, the loveliness, and the sublimity of such a scene, will speedily reach the limit of his vocabulary. To himself, or, better still, to some congenial companion of either sex, he can but repeat the old and well-worn epithets, grand, beautiful, stupendous, awful, majestic, and magnificent. This done, he must, if he still feel, resort to silence, as more demonstrative than speech. There are no more adjectives which he can use; but he feels that there is an infinitude of uninvented words in the depths of his consciousness which, if he could but drag them into being, would serve to explain to others how keenly the spiritual beauty of Nature had wrought itself into the spiritual nature of man, and into every sense of his physical and material existence. But, as these words can not be uttered, silence is the best relief and the only alternative. An English lady emphatically declared Niagara to be "sweetly pretty!" and an American lady declared it to be "handsome!" Possibly the fair speakers exhausted in these epithets the whole wealth of their admiration; and yet, faulty as their language was, they might have as thoroughly enjoyed the beauty of the cataract, and been as deeply impressed with its majesty, as travelers who made use of a more appropriate phraseology. There are minds which feel so acutely the overpowering loveliness of nature, and the imbecility of any language to express their sympathies and emotions, even the richest that ever grew and germinated into logic or poetry, that their enforced dumbness becomes ultimately so painful as to disturb the fine balances of Reason, and put the harp of Imagination out of tune. The well-known lines of Byron express this instinctive emotion, when, speaking of another fall, less glorious than Niagara, he says,

"One can't gaze a minute
Without an awful wish to plunge within it."

Niagara has this fascination about it in a very high degree. The beautiful boa constrictor, glaring with its bright and deadly eyes at a rabbit or a bird, has a similar power; and the poor little quadruped or biped, fascinated, bewildered, undone, and wrought into a phrensy by the overwhelming glamour of the snake, rushes deliriously into perdition. Thus Niagara bewilders the senses of the too passionate admirers of its beauty. Many are the tragical stories which are recounted of the fair girls, the young brides, and the poetic souls who have thrown themselves into the torrent for the speechless love they bore it, and floated into death on its terrific but beautiful bosom.

Before shifting my quarters from the desolate hostelry of the Clarendon at the City of the Falls, and repairing to the excellent accommodation of the Monteagle House, two miles distant, near the Suspension Bridge, I sallied out at dawn of day to the ferry, and was rowed across the Niagara River, about half a mile below the falls. From this point, amid the comparative quiet of the waters, the first glimpse of Niagara conveyed a feeling that partook of disappointment. I had expected the falls to be much higher; and if the water had poured from a precipice a thousand feet above me, I should not, perhaps, have considered that the guide-book makers and the tourists had led me to expect too much. The eye was unfamiliar with the distance and with the grandeur of the surrounding objects; and, as the result of my experience, I advise the traveler not to take his first view of Niagara in this manner. The majesty is too far off to be appreciated. There is no measurement within reach by which the size can be tested; and the noblest waterfall in the world suggests a weir —no doubt above the average size of weirs, but a weir nevertheless. The eye too often makes fools of our other senses, until it is taught to know its own littleness and imperfection, and to be humble accordingly. In the summer season a little steam-boat, appropriately named the *Maid of the Mist*, runs up into the very spray of the cataract. From its deck a magnificent spectacle is doubtless to be obtained; but at the time of my visit this vessel had long ceased its excursions, and was safely moored for the winter at "Biddle Stairs." There were no tourists, and even the guides had taken their departure. No lingering remnant of that troublesome confraternity lay in wait for a stray traveler like myself, to tire his patience, disencumber him of his loose cash, and mar the whole effect of the scenery by his parrot-like repetition of the old story, from which all soul, freshness, and meaning had departed. Thus I had Niagara all to myself. It was my own dominion; and I ruled over it unadvised, untroubled, and undirected. I discovered its beauties gradually as best I could, and made my way from place to place with as much of the true spirit of discovery and adventure latent and stirred within me as moved the first white man who ever gazed upon its marvels; and, instead of narrating how and in what way I saw them, let me, for the benefit of any future travelers who may read these lines, explain in what sequences of grandeur and beauty they should explore the stupendous scenery of the river, the islands, and the falls, so as to reach the climax where the climax should be naturally expected, and to go on, from good to better, and from better to best, in one grand and harmonious crescendo, and thus extract from it a music of the mind sufficient to make even the sublimest harmonies of Beethoven appear tame and commonplace.

Proceeding first to the narrow and apparently frail bridge which connects the main land of the village, or "City," formerly called Manchester, with Bath Island, and thence with Goat Island—lovely enough to deserve a more beautiful name —the mind of the traveler will be impressed with a spectacle which to me, unprepared for it, seemed as grand as Niagara itself. Here is to be obtained the first glimpse of the rapids ere the whole overflow of the great lakes—Superior, Michigan, Huron, and Erie, covering a superficies of no less than 150,000 square miles—a space large enough to contain England, Scotland, and Ireland, with room to spare—discharge themselves over the precipice into the lower level of Lake Ontario. In a distance of three quarters of a mile the Niagara

River gallops down an incline of fifty-one feet. Such a bubbling, boiling, frothing, foaming, raging, and roaring as occur in that magnificent panorama it was never before my good fortune to see or hear. Were there nothing but the sight of these rapids to repay the traveler for his pains, it would be worth all the time and cost of the voyage across the Atlantic. It was like looking up a mountain of furious water to stand upon the bridge and gaze toward the torrent. I will not call it angry, though that is the epithet which first suggests itself. Anger is something sharp and short, but this eternal thunder is the voice of a willing obedience to unalterable law. There is no caprice or rage about it; nothing but the triumphant song of gravitation, that law of laws, which maintains the earth in perpetual harmony with heaven. On the side of the "City" were several mills for flour, corn, and paper, which had borrowed an exterior thread from the mighty web of waters to help in performing the operations of human industry. But these scarcely marred the effect of the scene, and were to some extent useful in affording a contrast of the littleness of man with the ineffable greatness of Nature. The builders of the bridge, taking advantage of the havoc made by the waters in days gone by—perhaps five hundred thousand years ago—supported it partially on a great rock lifting its head a few feet above the foam; standing at this point, I counted the islets scattered on either side, and stretching downward to the very brink of the fall. Besides Goat Island, about a mile in circumference, which separates the American from the Canadian fall, I made out nineteen isles and islets; some no larger than a dining-table, others twenty or a hundred times as large, and several of them supporting but a single tree, and others two or three trees, blooming and flourishing amid the war of waters, and suggesting to the unpracticed eye a fear that every moment would be the last both of them and their vegetation.

There is a toll of twenty-five cents for passing over this bridge to Goat Island; but the toll once paid frees the traveler for a year. It is calculated that forty thousand persons pass annually, yielding a handsome revenue to Mr. Porter, the proprietor of the island. The father or grandfather of this gentleman, a surveyor, is said to have procured Goat Island from the State of New York in part payment of his bill for surveying the rapids and their neighborhood. The Indian Emporium, purporting to be kept by the descendants of the famous "Black Hawk," was still open on the occasion of my visit; and the fans, the moccasins, the purses, and all the little knick-knacks which the Indians manufacture of moose skins, beads, and birch bark, were spread out for sale. Having paid tribute here, I passed on to the wilderness. Though Goat Island is laid out into carriage-drives and by-paths, it exists otherwise in a state of nature. The trees are unpruned forest-trees, though marked occasionally by the busy knives of the ubiquitous Joneses and Smiths, who, though transplanted to new soil, are as deeply imbued with the traditional failing of their British ancestors for carving or scrawling their inillustrious names on trees and public monuments as their kindred in the "old country." In this lovely spot the undergrowth of fern and brushwood is wild and luxuriant in the extreme. The beauty and variety of the island surpass, I should think, that of any island in the world; although, when contemplating the turbulence around, and the *débris* of past convulsions which strew the run of the river above and below, it is difficult to avoid a feeling that ere long Goat Island will be entirely swept away, or scattered into fragments at the foot of the falls.

To the left, down a little by-path, there is a small cataract, perhaps about ten feet in width, separated by huge boulder stones from the main current, which, if it existed in Great Britain or in any other part of Europe, would attract admiring crowds from all quarters to behold it, but which here dwindles into comparative insignificance amid the mightier marvels that surround it. Lodore among the English lakes, and Foyers in Inverness-shire, beautiful and even sublime as they may be, are but as ribbons to this. And this itself is but as a ribbon compared with Niagara.

The next point is the American Fall, roaring down into the abyss, one hundred and sixty feet below, in one immense sheet of slaty-green water. Beautiful exceedingly! *Vedi Napoli e poi mori!* say the Italians; but to see this fall is to reach a higher climax: and—if Death be agreeable—to have a greater motive for confessing that Life has nothing grander to show. The traveler can approach to the very brink of the fall, and, if he pleases, dabble his feet in it without danger; but let him wade two or three feet only, and he is gone—down! down! like a speck, into Death and Eternity! Looking over the avalanche of waters, where they roll smoothly and irresistibly as Fate, I beheld a couple of hawks or other birds of prey hovering half way down, fishing for the dead or stupefied fish that are hurled through the boiling spray. Farther down the Niagara stream—white as cream at the foot of the precipice, but half a mile below as tranquil apparently as if nothing had happened—is seen, at a distance of two miles, the noble Suspension Bridge. Over its airy and seemingly perilous fabric passes the railway that connects the New York Central Railway, by the Great Western Railway of Canada, with Michigan, Wisconsin, Minnesota, and the "Far West."

And now for the culminating point—at Prospect Tower, forty-five feet high, and built on the very edge of Goat Island between the two falls. From the top of this edifice, amid the "hell of waters," is to be obtained the most magnificent view of the whole scenery of Niagara, above and below, and down the arrowy deeps of the ever-boiling caldron.

The Great Canadian or Horseshoe Fall is in reality Niagara itself. The American Fall, stupendous as it is, must be considered no more than an offshoot from the main cataract. "Oh, that Great Britain and the United States would go to war!" said an enthusiastic American; "and that the United States might gain the day! We would stipulate for the annexation of the Great Horseshoe Fall as a *sine qua non* of peace, and after that we would be friends forever!" And no wonder that the Americans so love it, for the Horseshoe Fall is alike the greatest marvel and the principal beauty of the New World. Here, at all events, man and his works are impotent to mar or diminish the magnificence of nature. No wheels of mills or factories can be set in motion by a cataract like this. It would dash into instant ruin the proudest pyramid, palace, temple, or manufactory that imperial man ever erected since the world began. He who would utilize such a flood must be as cautious as a homœopathist. To use more than an infinitesimal portion of its exuberant strength would be to court and to meet annihilation. The mass of water pours over the rocks in one lucent and unbroken depth of upward of twenty feet; for although no magician and no plummet has ever sounded the dread profundity, even within a mile of the final leap, a condemned lake steamer, the *Detroit*, drawing eighteen feet of water, was carried over the falls as lightly as a cork. She never touched the rocks with her keel until she was precipitated, still shapely and beautiful, a hundred and fifty feet below, and then down, down, no one knows, or ever will know, how many fathoms, into a lower deep scooped out by the incessant action of the falls in the very bowels of the earth, to reappear, a few minutes afterward, a chaotic and unconnected mass of beams, spars, and floating timber.

It is a long time before the finite senses of any human being can grasp the full glory of this spectacle. I can not say that I ever reached a satisfactory comprehension of it. I only know that I gazed sorrowfully, and yet glad, and that I understood thoroughly what was meant by the ancient phrase of "spell-bound;" that I knew what fascination, witchcraft, and glamour were; and that I made full allowances for the madness of any poor, weak, excited human creature who, in a moment of impulse or phrensy, had thrown him or herself headlong into that too beautiful and too entrancing abyss.

When the first sensations of mingled awe and delight have been somewhat dulled by familiarity with the monotonous majesty, so suggestive of infinite power, and so like an emblem of eternity—though impossible for man's art to picture it under such a symbol—the eye takes pleasure in looking into the minutiæ of the flood. The deep slaty-green color of the river, curdled by the impetus of the fall into masses of exquisite whiteness, is the first peculiarity that excites attention. Then the shapes assumed by the rushing waters—

shapes continually varying as each separate pulsation of the rapids above produces a new embodiment in the descending stream—charm the eye with fresh wonder. Sometimes an avalanche of water, striking on a partially hidden shelf or rock half way down the precipice, makes a globular and mound-like surge of spray; and, immediately afterward, a similar downflow, beating on the very same point, is thrown upward, almost to the level of the Upper Niagara, in one long, white, and perpendicular column. Gently, yet majestically, it reaches the lower level by its own independent impetus, without being beholden to the gravity of the sympathetic stream from which it has been so rudely dissevered. And then the rainbows! No pen can do justice to their number and their loveliness. No simile but the exquisite one of Byron at the Italian waterfall, which, compared with Niagara, is but a blade of grass to some oaken monarch of the woods, can adequately render the idea of any spectator who has a soul for natural beauty as he gazes on the unparalleled spectacle of such an Iris as it was my good fortune to behold:

"Love watching Madness with unalterable mien!"

But the sensations of one man are not the sensations of another. To one, Niagara breathes turbulence and unrest; to another it whispers peace and hope. To one it speaks of Eternity; to another merely of Time. To the geologist it opens up the vista of millions of years; while to him who knows nothing of, or cares nothing for, the marvels of that science, it but sings in the wilderness a new song by a juvenile orator only six thousand years old. But to me, if I can epitomize my feelings in four words, Niagara spoke joy, peace, order, and eternity. To other minds—dull, prosaic, and money-grubbing—Niagara is but a great water-power gone to waste, and not to be compared, in grandeur of conception or execution, to the Suspension Bridge that crosses the river two miles below. "Niagara is a handsome thing," said a guest at the Monteagle House to his neighbor; "but what is it to the bridge? The bridge! why, I hold *that* to be the finest thing in all God's universe!" It was no engineer who spake thus, but a man from a dry-goods store in Chicago, and doubtless a very worthy man too; though, if I could have had my will of him, he never should have had a vote for Congress, for the election of President, or even for the nomination of mayor or sheriff of Chicago. I would have inflicted summary justice upon him, and in the very scene and moment of his offense deprive him forever of all the rights of citizenship.

It was in traversing the ferry from time to time, and entering into conversation with the ferryman and the chance passengers in his boat, that I learned the minute and, to me, interesting particulars of what may be called the private history and romance of the falls. Many were the sad stories told of wobegone and desperate creatures who had chosen the terrific platform of the Horseshoe Fall, or of the Tower at Goat Island, as the scenes of their violent exit from a world which they fancied had used them ungratefully; of young brides who had come thither to rush out of an existence where they had staked all on the chance of domestic happiness and gained nothing but broken hearts; of young men and of old men (but never of old women), sick of the world, and of all its pleasures and sorrows, who had here taken the fearful leap from Time into Eternity. And how is it, O learned doctors of lunacy and mania, that old men commit suicide so frequently, and old women so seldom? Many, too, were the stories told of Indians and others who, sailing peaceably and incautiously in their canoes or boats from Erie to Chippewa, had been sucked into the irresistible current and precipitated in the sight of agonized spectators into the abyss below. The ferryman did not personally remember the catastrophe of the *Caroline* steamer cut adrift by the gallant Colonel (now Sir Allan) M'Nab in the Canadian rebellion, and sent blazing over the falls; but the incident will long be told in Canadian story and the annals of border warfare. The ferryman stated, as the result of his experience and that of all his predecessors, that the dead bodies washed ashore in the vicinity of the ferry-house were always found in a state of nudity, and that he never heard of an instance in which a corpse had been recovered with the slightest shred or vestige of a garment adhering to it. One tragedy was fresh in his recollection—that of a young man who, about five months before the period of my visit, had called for and drunk off at a draught a bottle of Champagne at the Clifton Hotel, then engaged and paid for a carriage to drive him to the Table Rock, and, in sight of the driver and of other people who never suspected his intent, had proceeded from the carriage to the edge of the Great Fall, coolly walked into deep water, and been washed over the precipice before even a voice could be raised to express the horror of the by-standers. His body was not found until several days afterward, perfectly nude—Niagara having, according to its wont, stripped him of all his valuables as well as of his life, and cast him upon mother earth as naked as he was at the moment he came into it. Many also, according to the ferryman, were the waifs and strays that fell to his share in his lonely vocation—large fish drawn into the current and precipitated over the falls, quite dead; aquatic fowl, skimming too near the surface of the rapids in search of prey, and caught by the descending waters; and logs of timber, and fragments of canoes and other small craft, which he collected on the shore to make his Christmas fire, and help to keep a merry blaze in the long and severe winters of the climate. Niagara, according to the testimony of all who dwell near it, is never more beautiful than in the cold midwinter, when no tourists visit it, and when the sides of the chasm are corrugated and adorned with pillars and stalactites of silvery frost, and when huge blocks of ice from Lake Erie, weighing hundreds of tons, are hurled down the rapids and over the falls as if they were of no greater specific gravity than feathers or human bodies, to reappear half a mile lower down the river, shivered into millions of fragments. It is a tradition of Niagara that, in 1822 or 1823, such a thick wall of ice was formed above Goat Island that no water flowed past for several hours, and that in the interval the precipice at the Horseshoe Fall was perfectly bare and dry. A picture of the scene, painted at the time, is still in existence. What a pity that no geologist or poet was present and that we have not his report upon the appearance of the rocks over which tumbles the eternal cataract, that never, perhaps, at any previous period unveiled its flinty bosom to the gaze of the petty pigmies who wander on its shores, and call themselves the lords of the creation.

But a small portion of the once widely-projecting Table Rock is now in existence, the remainder having suddenly given way four or five years ago. It seems to have been loosened in some of its internal crevices by the action of the frost. A horse and gig had been standing on the projection less than a minute before the rock gave way, and the action of their removal was perhaps the immediate cause of the catastrophe. But sufficient of the rock still remains to afford a footing whence a fine view of the whole panorama of the falls is attainable.

In consequence of the absence of guides, and, indeed, of every person from whom I could obtain information, I did not penetrate, as I might have done, behind the Horseshoe Fall. The mighty cascade, in pouring over the precipice its ninety millions of gallons of water per hour, curves outward, and leaves behind it a chamber which daring travelers, determined to see every thing, make it a point to visit. The feat is both painful and dangerous, and was not to be thought of by a solitary wayfarer like myself. "It may be supposed," says a well-known American writer who achieved it, "that every person who has been dragged through the column of water which obstructs the entrance to the cavern behind the cataract has a pretty correct idea of the pains of drowning. It is difficult enough to breathe, but with a little self-control and management the nostrils may be guarded from the watery particles in the atmosphere, and then an impression is made upon the mind by the extraordinary pavilion above and around which never loses its vividness. The natural bend of the cataract and the backward shelve of the precipice form an immense area like the interior of a tent, but so pervaded by discharges of mist and spray that it is impossible to see far inward. Outward the light struggles brokenly through the crystal wall of the cataract, and, when the sun shines directly on its face, it is a scene of unimaginable glory. The footing is rather unsteadfast—a small shelf, composed of loose and slippery stones, and the abyss boiling below, like—it is difficult to find a comparison. On the whole, the undertaking is rather pleasanter to remember than to achieve."

For many days I lingered in the purlieus of Niagara. I often walked from the Suspension Bridge along the Canadian shore, getting at every turn a new glimpse of loveliness; and on other occasions have sat for hours on Prospect Tower, with no companions but a favorite book and the eternal music of the falls. In storm, in shine, in moonlight, and in mist—in all weathers and at all hours—I have feasted on the beauty and tranquillity of the scene; for, as soon as the ear becomes accustomed to the roar of the waters, they descend with a lulling and soothing sound. And when I was compelled to take my farewell look and travel to new regions, I repeated to myself, neither for the first nor the last time, "I have lived, and loved, and seen Niagara."

CHAPTER IX.

NEWPORT AND RHODE ISLAND.

November 22, 1857.

THE governors of the several states of the Union have some, but not much patronage. That their salaries are far from considerable may be inferred from the fact that one estimable gentleman of my acquaintance, who rules over a territory as large, and much more fertile than England, enjoys the not very munificent allowance of $1500, or about £300 per annum, to support his dignity; but they have the power of life and death, or, rather, the privilege to commute the punishment of death into imprisonment for life or for a term of years; and they have the quasi imperial or royal right to open the session of the Legislature by speech or address, and in some states, but not in all, to bring the session to a premature close. In the early times of the republic, the governors of the states thought it necessary to surround themselves with more splendor and ceremonial. John Hancock, the first governor of Massachusetts after the Revolution, rode about Boston in a gilt coach with four horses. A Loyalist paper, published in New York a year prior to the recognition of American independence, stated of Hancock that he appeared in public "with all the pageantry of an Oriental prince; and thus he rode in an elegant carriage, attended by four servants, dressed in superb liveries, mounted on fine horses richly caparisoned, and escorted by fifty horsemen with drawn sabres, the one half of whom preceded and the other half followed his carriage." But things have greatly changed since that day. The present Governor of Massachusetts, a very eloquent and able man, formerly a working blacksmith, who was lately Speaker of the House of Representatives, and is now an aspirant for the presidency, walks to the State House when he has to deliver a message to the Legislature, and boards at the public hotel, having no house of his own in the capital of the commonwealth of which he is the chief magistrate. The same simplicity prevails elsewhere. Among the few privileges not already mentioned which the governors still enjoy in New England and New York, and perhaps farther south, is that of appointing, by their sole authority, a day of general thanksgiving or of humiliation. Thanksgiving-day is generally fixed in November, and corresponds in its festive character to the celebration of Christmas in England. The people shut up their stores and places of business; go to church, chapel, or conventicle in the forenoon or afternoon, or both, and devote the remainder of the day to such social pleasure and jollity as the custom of the place may sanction. The dinner, at which the *pièce de rigueur* is roast turkey, is the great event of the day. As roast beef and plum pudding are upon Christmas-day in Old England, so is turkey upon Thanksgiving-day among the descendants of the Puritans in New England. Yesterday was Thanksgiving-day at Newport, in the little but prosperous Commonwealth of Rhode Island—the smallest state in the Union, but not the least proud or wealthy. To borrow a description from the old popular ballad, "American Taxation," written by a New England patriot in 1765:

"It is a wealthy people
   Who sojourn in this land;
Their churches all with steeples
   Most delicately stand;
Their houses like the gilly
   Are painted white and gay:
They flourish like the lily
   In North Americay.

"On turkeys, fowls, and fishes
   Most frequently they dine;
With well-replenished dishes
   Their tables always shine.
They crown their feasts with butter,
   They eat, and rise to pray;
In silks their ladies flutter,
   In North Americay."

Business, and not pleasure, brought me to Rhode Island, and to the fashionable, but at this season deserted watering-place of Newport. This elegant little town, or "city," is of easy access from New York or Boston, and during the summer months is crowded with visitors from all parts of the Union; and where—strange anomaly in a country said to be so strict and prudish—the ladies and gentlemen bathe together, "the ladies," according to the unimpeachable authority of Belle Brittan, "swimming about in white trowsers and red frocks—a costume gayer than the chorus of an Italian opera," and the gentlemen, according to another authority, in a costume almost as decent, though by no means so picturesque. But the pleasure hotels were all shut up, and no place open but the excellent Aquidneck House, sufficiently large to accommodate all, and fifty times more than all, the travelers who at that season were likely to come to Newport on business. Newport consists principally of one long street on the shore of Narragansett Bay, and has an air of greater antiquity than is common among the towns of New England. It is a clean, white, quaint, and agreeable place; but during the bathing season all its life and bustle are transferred to the other side of the narrow island on which the town is built, and to the western shores of the bay, known as the first, second, and third beaches.

Newport is a place of historical note, having been held by the British forces during the Revolution, and almost destroyed by them before the independence of the United States was officially recognized. They are said to have burned 480 houses, to have battered down the light-house, broken up the wharves, used the churches for riding-schools, and cut down all the fruit and ornamental trees before taking their departure; and by these, and the other more legitimate consequences of the warlike occupation of the place, to have reduced the population from 12,000 to 4000. But, if these barbarities were really committed, there seem to remain no traces of animosity on the part of the present generation, and to be an Englishman is a passport to the kind offices of the principal inhabitants. An attempt to release Newport from British occupation was made in 1778, under the combined forces of Count L'Estaing, the French admiral, and General Sullivan, the United States commander, in which expedition Governor Hancock, of Massachusetts, and General Lafayette commanded divisions. The attempt was unsuccessful; and was commemorated in a Loyalist ballad of the day, to the air of "Yankee Doodle:"

> "'Begar!' said Monsieur, 'one grand coup
>   You bientôt shall behold, sir:'
> This was believed as gospel true,
>   And Jonathan felt bold, sir.
>
> "So Yankee Doodle did forget
>   The sound of British drum, sir—
> How oft it made him quake and sweat,
>   In spite of Yankee rum, sir.
>
> "He took his wallet on his back,
>   His rifle on his shoulder,
> And vowed Rhode Island to attack
>   Before he was much older."

There is an old building at Newport, which stands in the public square in the upper town, of which the origin and the objects have excited considerable controversy. By some it is alleged to have been erected by the Norsemen in their pre-Columbite discovery of America, and by others it is alleged to be merely an old stone mill. But, as architectural antiquities in any part of the American continent north of Mexico are utterly unknown or non-existing, it may be supposed that strenuous battle is done on behalf of the theory that this building is the remnant of a Norse tower, and that the supporters of the mill theory and of its modern erection receive but small toleration at the hands of the people of Newport. Professor Rafn, under date of 1839, affirms that the building was erected at a period decidedly not later than the 12th century, as there is no mistaking the style, which is that of the round-arch style; the same which in England is denominated Saxon, and sometimes Norman architecture. It is upon a legend brought into connection with this ruin that Longfellow has founded his poem of the "Skeleton in Armor."

Among the pleasanter memories that attach to Newport is one which affirms that in a cottage near the second beach, beyond a place called Purgatory, Bishop Berkeley wrote several of the works which have handed his name down to posterity.

Though I had no opportunity to visit Providence, the capital, or any of the other cities of Rhode Island, that small republic has so interesting a history, both past and present, as to demand not only a record from the pen, but the sympathetic appreciation of every passing stranger who has any thing to say about the "*cosas Americanas.*" It is distinguished, in the first place, as the smallest of the thirty-two states of the Union, being only about forty-seven miles long by thirty-seven broad. Though for the most part continental, it derives its name from the little island in Narragansett Bay on which Newport is built, and contains a population of less than 150,000 souls. Its second and more admirable claim to distinction arises from the fact that, while its people govern themselves at somewhat less than one dollar per head per annum, they pay nearly twice as much for public education as for all the other expenses of the state. The governor's salary is $1000 (£200) per annum; the civil, military, and miscellaneous expenses are $50,000 (£10,000); while the direct grant from the state for educational purposes is $35,000 (£7000), and the local expenses for the same object are $50,000 (£10,000) more—or, in all, $85,000. Where is the other state, great or small, upon the globe, that can glorify itself by such a fact as this? And, in the last place, Rhode Island may lay greater claim to being the cradle of religious liberty than any republic, kingdom, or empire in the world.

The early Puritans and Pilgrim Fathers, who shook the dust of England from the soles of their feet, and sailed across the Atlantic to find a spot where they might worship God in their own way, without molestation from the strong arm of secular authority, did not always mete out to others the measure which they insisted upon for themselves. The Puritan settlers in Massachusetts became as intolerant of others, when settled in their new homes, as the religious oppressors in England from whose oppression they had escaped, and decreed the penalties of fine, imprisonment, and even death against all who would not conform to the observances and the doctrine of that sectarianism which they arrogantly considered as containing the whole and only truth of God. Among other stanch and uncompromising men to whom this Puritan intolerance was intolerable was Roger Williams, who boldly proclaimed in Massachusetts, to the scandal and alarm of the magistracy, that conscience was free, and that in a Christian and a free state no man ought to be troubled or called to account for his religious opinions, whatever they might be. This was too bold for Massachusetts, and too wicked, in the opinion of the ruling classes, to be endured. Williams was warned of the danger of persisting in preaching such doctrines, but he would not flinch from his principles; and, ultimately, after a series of sufferings in the wilderness, the history of which has lately been given to the world, he fled from the inhospitable soil in a canoe, with five companions, to seek amid the kinder savages a few acres of land to cultivate, and a corner of the earth where he might pray to God in his own fashion. Sailing and rowing on this forlorn expedition, he arrived after many days at a little arm of the sea stretching inward from the Bay of Narragansett. Here he saw an Indian standing upon a rock, who made friendly gestures, and called to him in English, "What cheer?" The words seemed of good omen; Roger Williams landed; was kindly received by the chiefs; fixed his abode on the adjoining land; received a large grant of territory, and gave it the name of Providence. Close to the spot where he landed is the site of the city of the same name, and capital of Rhode Island. In the course of time, other men and women flying from persecution, and being invited by Williams to join him in what he called his "place of shelter for persons distressed for conscience," gathered about him in considerable numbers. To the most able and enterprising of these Williams freely gave portions of the land which he had received from the Indians, and the colony increased and prospered. The words, "What cheer?" were adopted as the motto of the state thus singularly formed; and in 1644 Williams proceeded to England, and procured a charter from King Charles I., constituting his settlements into a colony under the style and title of the "Plantations of Providence and Rhode Island." This charter requiring amendment and extension, Williams, then a venerable old man, paid a second visit to England in 1663, and obtained a new charter from Charles II. By this charter the citizens were empowered to elect their own governor—a greater degree of liberty than was accorded in those days to Massachusetts and other states, whose governors were appointed by the crown. Thanks to such men as Roger Williams, and to such also as William Penn in Pennsylvania, and Lord Baltimore in Maryland—though the last two did not suffer in the cause as Williams did—absolute religious toleration has become the law of the whole American Union; and Puritanism, while retaining its other features, has ceased to persecute. It is said that no stone or memorial marks the spot where this patriot of liberty is buried. Memorials and monuments of Washington are to be found every where; but surely Rhode Island, and the friends of religious freedom in America, owe it to themselves to do honor to the dust of one quite as worthy of honor, in his own way, as Washington himself.

CHAPTER X.

PHILADELPHIA.

Philadelphia, Dec. 19, 1857.

RETURNING from the beautiful Niagara to Boston, and from Boston to New York, I thence proceeded to Philadelphia, the capital of Pennsylvania, the "Keystone State." Pennsylvania derives this title as being the "keystone" of American liberty, and the scene of the ever-memorable Declaration of Independence. The point of departure from New York is at Jersey City, over the Hudson or North River Ferry, and the point of arrival is at Camden, on the River Delaware, exactly opposite to the city of the Quakers, to which the passengers are conveyed by one of the monster steam ferry-boats common in all the rivers of the Union. The road passes the whole way through the flat alluvial districts of New Jersey—a state which the New Yorkers declare to stand in the same anomalous relation to the Union as that occupied by the town of Berwick-upon-Tweed to the kingdoms of Great Britain and Ireland. But New Jersey can afford to despise the joke, if joke it be; for, though one of the smallest, it is one of the most prosperous states of the Republic.

Philadelphia, eighty-seven miles by rail from New York, is the second city of the Union, with a population of about 500,000 souls. It stands upon a level with the waters of the Delaware, and does not possess within its whole boundaries a natural eminence one third of the height of Ludgate Hill. It contains a large number of churches and chapels, but none of them is distinguished for architectural beauty of dome, tower, or spire. The whole place is formal, precise, and unattractive, leaving no impression upon the mind of the traveler but that of a weary sameness and provoking rectangularity. Except in Chestnut Street (the centre of business) and Walnut Street (the fashionable quarter), all the streets of the city are built on the same model. The same third-rate houses—of the kind which the Englishman sees in Birmingham and Manchester—seem to rise on every side, all of one color and of one shape; all with green Venetian blinds on the upper, and with white blinds on the lower stories; all equally prim, dull, and respectable. The foot-pavements are of the same color as the houses, neither drab nor red, but a mixture of both, suggestive of the story of the English Quaker of the old school, to whom, as he sat behind his desk at his warehouse in Manchester, was delivered a packet, with a bill requesting payment. The old Quaker opened the packet, and found a red hunting-coat.

"What is this?" he said to the messenger. "There is a mistake here, friend."

"No," said the messenger; "'tis a coat for Mr. Thomas."

"Thomas," said the father to the young Quaker, who had become smitten with an unquakerly passion for hunting, "is this for thee?"

"Yea, father," replied the son.

"And what is it?" rejoined the sire.

"A coat," replied the son.

"Yea, Thomas; but what color is it?"

"Why," said Thomas, somewhat bewildered, and scratching his head to expedite the delivery of the tardy answer, "it's a kind of fiery drab."

Such is the color of Philadelphia—the Quaker city, the city of Brotherly Love, or, according to the disparaging assertion of New Yorkers, the city of "brotherly love and riots." It is fiery drab wherever you turn—fiery drab houses, fiery drab pavements, fiery drab chapels, and fiery drab churches. One peculiarity of Philadelphia, in addition to the unvarying rectangularity of its streets, is, that the carriage-ways are always dirty and the foot-ways always clean. Nobody purifies, or cares to purify, the carriage-road, but every body seems to be bent upon cleaning the fiery drab pavements. Morning, noon, and night the work of ablution goes on. Negro men and women, with a fair admixture of Irish female "helps," are continually squirting water over the pavements from gutta-percha tubes, and twirling the moisture from their ever-busy mops over the lower garments of the wayfarers, till the streets run with water. The passing vehicles continually churn up the mud, and the road is never allowed to dry, unless under the irresistible compulsion of the thermometer below zero.

The population of Philadelphia is not so largely imbued with the Quaker element as might be supposed from its history and origin. Though William Penn was its founder, and is, to some extent, its patron saint, the co-religionists of William Penn, so far from being in the majority, do not number above 30,000 out of 500,000 inhabitants. Scotchmen and descendants of Scotchmen are numerous; Irish and descendants of Irish are also numerous; and Germans and descendants of Germans more numerous still. To the Germans, Philadelphia owes the establishment within the last five years of several extensive breweries, and the introduction to every part of the Union of a taste for "*lager bier*," an excellent beverage well suited to the climate, and resembling the Bavarian beer of Europe, though by no means so strong or so aromatic as the *lager bier* of Vienna, from which it derives its name. Prior to the introduction of this novelty, beer was very little in America. English porter, stout, and ale, besides being exorbitantly dear, were not well suited to the climate, but *lager bier* supplied the very article required. It was exactly to the taste of the Germans, and from them a love of it has gradually extended to all sections and races of the American people. The rich consume oysters and Champagne; the poorer classes consume oysters and *lager bier*, and that is one of the principal social differences between the two sections of the community. If Messrs. Bass or Allsopp ever had a chance of extending their trade into America, the *lager bier* breweries of Philadelphia have seriously diminished it. What American will give thirty-seven cents (eighteen pence English) for a pint of English pale ale or porter, when he can procure a pint of home-brewed lager for five cents?

There are some fine stores, banks, and warehouses in Chestnut Street, and some showy buildings of granite and white marble in course of construction. There are also some superior private houses of marble and granite in Walnut Street. It is one of the peculiarities of Philadelphia that the door-steps of every house that has any pretensions to style are of white marble. At this season, however, the white marble of the door-steps is covered up with wood, and workmen are busily employed in the principal thoroughfares in incasing the steps in planks of deal in preparation for the frost; they would otherwise be so slippery as to be dangerous to life and limb; so that the luxuriousness of a Philadelphian door-step is somewhat like that of a "dress poker" in England—something for show rather than for use.

There are but two public buildings in the city which will repay the visit of any traveler who is pressed for time, and these are the State House, or Independence Hall, in Chestnut Street—the most venerable and the most venerated building in America—and the Girard College, at the outskirts of the town. No stranger should omit visiting them both. The State House is illustrious as the place where the first American Congress held its sittings, and where, on the ever-memorable 4th of July, 1776, the Declaration of Independence was adopted, and read to the assembled people, and publicly proclaimed from the steps fronting the street. The building has been jealously preserved as it stood in that day, and the room in which the solemn conclave was held—now called the Hall of Independence—is adorned with the same internal fittings and decorations as on the day that made America a free and great nation. Cold is the heart, and stagnant the fancy and imagination of any man, whatever his nation or habits of thought, who can stand unmoved in this simple chamber, or be unimpressed by the noble thoughts and generous aspirations which its history excites. On every side are relics of the great departed—portraits of the high-souled and fearless men who affixed their signatures to the document which severed their connection with the country of their birth and their ancestors. These men loved the old country as a true son loves the unjust and hard-hearted father in spite of his injustice and obstinacy, and with the yearning hope, strong as nature itself, that the father will relent, or, if he do not relent, acknowledge that age has its faults as well as youth, and that the duty of age is to be tolerant and forgiving. They entered upon a career which, when they began it, was rebellion, but which afterward became revolution, with many forebodings, and with a deep, earnest, religious sense of the responsibility they had undertaken. Among other relics of the time and the men are the walking-stick of Washington and the writing-table of Benjamin Franklin. The table has a ticket upon it announcing it for sale, upon the condition that the purchaser do not remove the relic from Philadelphia, and that he allow the public to have access to it at stated times. The price is only 120 dollars, about £24 sterling; but the city of Philadelphia, according to the janitor of the hall, is too poor to purchase it, being deeply involved in debt, without a cent which it can fairly call its own. Another relic, still more interesting than either of these, is the great bell, which, on the 4th of July, 1776, rang to the people the joyous tidings of the Declaration of Independence, and which now bears, and bore long before its sonorous voice was called into requisition on that august occasion, the prophetic inscription, "*Proclaim liberty throughout the lands, and to all the peoples thereof.*" This bell, a sacred one to all Americans, is now past service; and having been accidentally cracked some years ago—like Big Ben of Westminster—was removed from the belfry to the hall, where it now stands surmounted by a stuffed eagle. Either the eagle is too small for the bell, or the bell is too large for the eagle—a disparity which strikes all visitors. On mentioning my impression to the janitor, he admitted the fact, and stated that last year an American gentleman, who entertained the same idea, sent him a splendid eagle, nearly three times as large as the actual occupant of the place of honor. Unfortunately, however, the big eagle had but one wing; and, as a disabled eagle upon a cracked bell would have afforded but too many opportunities to the gibers of gibes and the jokers of jokes, the gift was respectfully declined, and the little eagle, strong, compact, and without a flaw, holds his seat upon the relic, until some more ponderous and unexceptional bird shall be permitted to dethrone him.

The Girard College is a noble building of white marble—beyond all comparison the finest public monument on the North American continent. It is built on the model of a Grecian temple of the Corinthian order; is 218 feet long, 160 broad, and 97 high, and closely resembles the beautiful Townhall of Birmingham, the great difference between the two being the dazzling whiteness and more costly material of the Philadelphian edifice. The grounds of the main building and its four contiguous halls cover forty-five acres. Stephen Girard, the founder, originally a poor French emigrant, came to Philadelphia at ten years of age, without a penny or a friend, and, as a merchant and banker in the city of his adoption, accumulated a fortune of upward of six millions of dollars, the greater portion of which he bequeathed to the college which bears his name. The college and grounds cost two millions of dollars, or £400,000 sterling, and their endowment about as much more. The institution is for the support and education of orphan boys, such as Girard himself was when he first came to Philadelphia. The peculiarity of the institution is that no religious doctrine whatever is permitted to be taught within its walls. The Bible, without comment, is read night and morning to the boys; but such a dislike had the founder to priests and clergymen of all denominations, that no minister of religion is permitted even to enter within the walls of the college. The question is put to all visitors whether they are clergymen; and, if the reply be in the affirmative, they are refused admittance. Upon these, as well as upon the personal grounds of their own disinheritance, the will was contested by the numerous relations of Girard. The poor boy had no relations and no friends when he came to Philadelphia, but France produced a whole colony of relatives before and after his death. But in all countries rich men have more cousins than they are aware of. After a long course of litigation, the sanity of the testator, as well as the morality of the will, was established by the courts, and upward of three hundred boys are now receiving within the walls of the college a plain education to fit them for the duties of life. In the entrance-hall is a fine marble statue of Stephen Girard, surmounting a sarcophagus containing his remains—for it was another command in his will that he should not be buried in consecrated ground. In an upper chamber of the building are preserved his household furniture, his day-books and ledgers, his china, his pictures, and his wearing apparel. Among the latter is a pair of blue velvet knee-breeches which he wore at the time of his death—very threadbare and shabby—and adorned with several patches far more substantial than the garment whose deficiencies they attempted to hide.

CHAPTER XI.

WASHINGTON.

Washington, Jan. 11, 1858.

WASHINGTON, the official and political capital of the United States, is beautifully situated on the Potomac, a wide but not deep river, at a distance of upward of 250 miles from the ocean. It is 226 miles from New York, 136 from Philadelphia, and 40 from Baltimore, and contains a population of upward of 60,000 souls, of whom 8000 are free blacks, and 2000 slaves. The city is laid out into wide streets and avenues— wider than Portland Place in London, or Sackville Street in Dublin. The avenues, as the principal thoroughfares are called, radiate from the Capitol, or Palace of the Legislature, as their centre, and are named after the thirteen original States of the Federation. Pennsylvania Avenue, leading direct from the Capitol to the White House, or mansion of the President, is about a mile in length, and of a noble width, but contains few buildings of a magnitude commensurate with its own proportions. The houses on each side are for the most part of third-rate size and construction, and, in consequence of the spaciousness of the roadway, look even meaner and smaller than they are.

Washington, with a somewhat unsavory addition, which it would offend polite ears to repeat, was called by a late celebrated senator the "city of magnificent distances," and well justifies the title. On every side the distances stretch out in apparently interminable lines, suggesting to the stranger who walks through the city at night, when the gas lamps show their fairy radiance at long intervals, a population of at least a million of souls. But at daylight the illusion vanishes. The marks of good intention and noble design are every where apparent, but those of fulfillment are nowhere to be found. All is inchoate, straggling, confused, heterogeneous, and incomplete. In the same street are to be found a splendid marble edifice of a magnitude such as would make it the ornament of any capital in the world, while opposite and on each side of it are low brick houses, crazy wooden sheds, and filthy pig-sties, suggestive of the Milesian element in the population. Such a street is F Street, in which the Patent-office is situated, and such streets are H and I Streets, where many of the diplomatic corps and the fashion of Washington have taken up their residence. And here it may be mentioned that the founders of the city seem to have exhausted their inventive ingenuity when they named the principal streets after the States of the Union. Having taxed their imagination to this extent, or having no imagination at all, they resorted to the letters of the alphabet as a mode of nomenclature. When they had exhausted these—an easy matter in a growing city—they brought arithmetic to the rescue of their poverty, as was done in New York, Philadelphia, and other cities. Thus, in receiving cards and returning visits, the stranger may not unfrequently find that he has been called upon by Mr. Jones, of No. 99 Ninety-ninth Street, or must visit Mr. Brown, at No. 3 Third Street, or Mr. Smith at No. 22 Twenty-second Street. The system has its advantages, no doubt, but is somewhat stiff and mathematical, and ignores a very cheap but very effective mode of rendering honor to the great men of the country, living or dead—the giving of their names to the public thoroughfares. If Washington gave his name to the city, why should not the names of other great Americans be given to its streets?

Besides its noble Capitol, with its towering dome, Washington possesses many elegant public buildings, such as the White
 ......e mansion, the Treasury buildings, the

THE CAPITOL AT WASHINGTON.

Patent-office, and the Post-office. Were these edifices, which are mostly of white marble, concentrated, as they might and ought to have been, in the great artery of Pennsylvania Avenue, instead of being scattered over various portions of the city, Washington might have possessed at least one street to rival or surpass the Rue de Rivoli in Paris. But the opportunity has been lost, and can never again recur. Still, it is impossible not to believe that Washington will yet become one of the most splendid cities on this continent. It has all the elements of beauty as well as of greatness, both in itself and its immediate environs; and when it becomes as populous as New York, which it is likely to be in less than fifty years, unless the seat of government be transferred in the interval to some such place as St. Louis, nearer to the centre of the republic, the inferior buildings that line its spacious streets will disappear, and its "magnificent distances" will be adorned with an architecture worthy of the capital of fifty, perhaps of a hundred, young and vigorous republics.

The site of Washington was chosen by George Washington himself, who laid the corner-stone of the Capitol on the 18th of September, 1793. At that time, and for some years afterward, the sittings of the Legislature were held in Independence Hall, Philadelphia. The city stands in the District of Columbia, in territory ceded for the purpose by the Commonwealth of Virginia and Maryland, and covers an area of sixty square miles. Originally its measure was one hundred square miles; but in 1846, forty square miles were restored to the Commonwealth. The design as well as the location of the city is due to the genius of Washington, under whose directions the plans were executed by Major L'Enfant. The limits extend from northwest to southeast about four miles and a half, and from east to southwest about two miles and a half. The circumference of the city is fourteen miles, and the aggregate length of the streets is computed at 199 miles, and of the avenues sixty-five miles. The average width of the principal thoroughfares is from seventy to one hundred and ten feet.

The original Capitol was so much damaged by the British invading force in the unfortunate war of 1814, that in the following year it was found necessary to reconstruct it. In 1828 it was entirely repaired; and in 1851, being found insufficient for the increasing business of the nation, it was determined to add two wings to it, which are at the present time in process of construction, together with a new and lofty dome of iron, from the plans and under the superintendence of Captain Meigs, the architect. The Capitol contains the halls or chambers of the Senate and the House of Representatives. The former numbers 64, and the latter about 250 members. It also contains the hall of the Supreme Court, where nine judges, robed, but not bewigged—and the only functionaries, except those of the army and navy, who wear an official costume—sit to administer justice, and to control and regulate the whole action of the government, in a manner quite unknown to the Constitution of Great Britain. The Capitol is built of white marble, and gleams in the sunshine of this beautiful climate in a manner trying to the eyes of an Englishman accustomed to the murky sombreness of the public monuments of London.

The White House, or President's mansion, is of freestone, painted white in imitation of marble. It is a plain but elegant building, befitting the unpretending dignity of the popular chief magistrate of a country where government is minimized, and where the trappings and paraphernalia of state and office are unknown or uncongenial. Here the President—a man who possesses, during his term of office, a far greater amount of power and patronage than the sovereign of any state in Europe, except the Emperors of France, Russia, and Austria—transacts, without any unnecessary forms, and with no formality or ceremony at all, the business of his great and growing dominion. Here he receives, at stated days and periods, ladies or gentlemen who choose to call upon him, either for business or pleasure, or from mere curiosity. Here he shakes hands with the courtly and urbane embassadors of European powers, or with the veriest "rowdies" from New York, or "plug-uglies" from Baltimore, who either have, or fancy they have, business with him, and that, too, without the necessity of a personal introduction. There is no man in the United

States who has such a quantity of hand-shaking to get through as the President. Throughout the whole country, every body shakes hands with every body else, though the ladies are far more chary of the privilege than the ruder sex. If the gentlemen would but shake hands less, and the ladies would shake hands a little more, America would be perfectly delightful to the man of many friends and acquaintances. Perhaps the President, if not a happier, would be a better satisfied chief magistrate.

Washington has no trade or commerce of its own, and is deserted for nearly half the year. It therefore presents a greater number of the characteristics of a fashionable watering-place that of a capital city. But, as the country increases in wealth and population, Washington will increase with it, and will gradually lose the provincial appearance which it now presents, and assume the completeness to which its position as the seat of the Legislature and of all the departments of government entitle it. Never was there a place in which office-hunters and place-seekers more assiduously congregate. The ante-chambers of the President are daily thronged with solicitants—with men who think they helped to make the President, and who are consequently of opinion that the President should help to make them. I thought, when presented to Mr. Buchanan, that he seemed relieved to find that I was an Englishman, and had nothing to ask him for—no little place for self, or cousin, or friend, or son, for which to beg his all-powerful patronage. "Gentlemen," he said, when the crowd was ushered pell-mell into his presence, without the intervention of any stick (gold or silver) in waiting, "I must take you by the miller's rule—first come first served. Have the goodness to state your business as shortly as possible, as I have much to do and little time to do it in." And so the crowd passed up, each man shaking hands with the chief magistrate, and receiving a polite, and, in many instances, a cordial reception. Whether they received any thing else at that or at any future time, or whether they still linger on, feeding upon hopes deferred, which make the heart sick, is best known to themselves; but I saw enough to convince me that it is not an easy thing to be a popular President.

I passed New Year's day at Washington, and such a day I never passed before, or wish to pass again. With two generals and a colonel—one of the generals a member of Congress for the city of New York, and the other an ex-member, and the whole three excellent, amiable, and accomplished gentlemen, and having nothing military about them but their titles—I was engaged from daylight till ten o'clock at night in a constant whirl and chase of visiting and card-leaving. Engaging a hack carriage for the day for some exorbitant sum—five, if not ten times the usual charge—we sallied forth, each armed with at least a couple of hundred cards, and drove to leave them at the places where etiquette and custom demanded. Let me attempt to give the list. First, there was the President—upon whom and his fair niece every body in Washington made it his or her business to call, from the embassadors of foreign powers down to the book-keepers and clerks at the hotels, and the very rowdies of the streets. Next there were the foreign ministers, whose ladies remained at home for the especial purpose; then came the married members of the government, and the members of Congress, all of whom expected to receive the homage and the good wishes of their friends on New Year's day; and, lastly, every married lady in Washington with whom one had ever exchanged a word or made an obeisance to. At nearly all of these places—with the sole exception of the President's house—the visitor was expected to partake of refreshments, or to pretend to do so. But my companions, being old stagers at the business, reserved themselves for the best places, and only on three occasions on that memorable day did our eating or drinking amount to more than the veriest and most barefaced sham. Washington was one scene of hurry-scurry from morning to night, and the penance done by the fair ladies in receiving such miscellaneous crowds must have been sorely trying to their physical if not to their mental comfort. But they bore it with good-humor; and, if I had not had other reasons to carry away a vivid recollection of the beauty, grace, elegance,

AMERICAN INDIANS WAITING FOR THE PRESIDENT.

and unaffected amiability of the ladies of America, the experience of that day of toil would have been more than sufficient to justify such a remembrance in the case of the ladies of Washington.

CHAPTER XII.

INTERVIEW OF INDIANS WITH THEIR "GREAT FATHER."

Washington, Jan. 14, 1858.

I WAS present a few days ago at a great ceremonial interview between the President of the United States and delegations from three tribes of Indians—the Poncas, the Pawnees, and the Pottawatomies. Each delegation was totally unconnected with the other, and the Pawnees and Poncas were ancient and hereditary foes; but, being in the presence of their "Great Father," as they termed the President, they looked upon each other with as much polite unconcern as the same number of civilized "swells," not formally introduced, might have displayed at a fashionable assembly in London or Paris. They did not appear to think of each other, but of their "Great Father," the splendor of his mansion, and the business which had brought some of them two thousand miles from their wilderness to the head-quarters of American civilization. The interview was highly picturesque; and, although in some respects it might seem to the careless observer to partake of the ludicrous, its predominant character was that of pathos, if not of solemnity. On one side was Civilization, represented by the venerable and urbane President, "with his head as white as snow," and surrounded by his secretaries and chiefs of departments, by the beauty and fashion of Washington, by senators and members of the House of Representatives, and by the ministers of foreign powers. On the other side was Barbarism, represented by the hostile tribes in their wild and striking costume—their red and blue blankets wrapped closely around them; their long, straight black locks stuck full of eagle plumes, bound together by uncouth head-gear of all shapes, and colors, and modes of manufacture; their ears laden and overladen with ponderous rings; their necks adorned with necklaces of bears' claws, artistically wrought together; their breasts and shoulders with the scalps which they had taken from their enemies; their hands grasping the spear, the tomahawk, and the war-club; and their faces, and sometimes their hair, daubed over with masses of red, blue, green, and yellow paint, disposed in fantastic forms and patterns in accordance with the rules of the only heraldry—for such it is—to which they are accustomed, and as much subject to law and ordinance of hereditary descent as the heraldry of the griffins, boars' heads, lions rampant and couchant, bloody hands, and other insignia of the heralds' colleges of Europe.

The interview took place by appointment in the great or east room of the presidential mansion. By eleven o'clock a considerable number of spectators had assembled, and at half past eleven the Indians made their appearance, each delegation being accompanied by its interpreter. The Pawnees, sixteen in number, were first in the order of entrance—a fine body of men, some of them naked to the waist, and some wearing buffalo robes or blankets, and all of them adorned with the full paraphernalia of paint and feathers which the red men like to display on great and solemn occasions. They were preceded by a little white lady of twelve or thirteen years of age, the daughter of an American gentleman who had charge of the delegation on behalf of the government. The Indians had adopted this little girl as the daughter of their tribe. A sort of *fille du régiment*, she seemed quite proud of her position as the pet of the savages, and accompanied them as part of the show in all their public appearances. Many remarks were made by the white spectators on the theatrical nature or bad taste of this display, not on the part of the Indians, but on that of the living parents of this child. Had she been a foundling of the forest, the case would have had its noble and touching aspects; but at her age, with a living father able to take care of her, the propriety of this companionship was held to be more than questionable. Next to the Pawnees followed the Poncas, six in number, similarly accoutred and bedizened —fine, stalwart, but melancholy men, with a dignity impressed on their features and gleaming from their eyes which even the grotesque eccentricities of red and blue paint were unable to impair. These, also, were accompanied by an interpreter—a border trader of European blood, who had picked up their language in a long career of commercial intercourse, perhaps in the exchange of fire-water for the spoils of the chase, or in other bargains as little to the advantage of the simple red men. Last of all came the Pottawatomies, nine in number, dressed in shabby European costume. This tribe claims to be wholly or half civilized; but they seem to have received nothing from civilization but its vices and defects, and to have lost the manly bearing, the stoical dignity, and the serene self-possession, as well as the costume and habits of other Indian tribes. They afforded a very marked contrast to the Pawnees and Poncas. They had an air of cunning, servility, and meanness in every lineament of their countenances and motion of their bodies, as well defined and unmistakable as the seedy shabbiness and awkwardness of their costume. A little red and blue paint would have added a positive grace to their sallow, baboon-like faces, would have made them look real instead of unreal, and shown them to be the savages which they actually were. These poor Pottawatomies were somewhat out of favor. They had a special grievance and wrong to detail to the President; but, having chosen to come to Washington without the permission of the official agent charged with the administration of Indian affairs, they were there at their own cost and risk. Not so the Pawnees and Poncas, who had been specially invited by the proper authorities, and whose expenses were paid by the government from the day they had left their own hunting-grounds, and would be paid back to their own homes in the same way, after they had seen all the sights and partaken of all the gayeties of the capital.

At twelve o'clock precisely the President entered the east room and took his position in the centre of a square, of which the Indians formed three sides and the spectators the fourth. The Indians, who till this time had been silent and wondering spectators of the rich carpet, the curtained windows, and gilded cornices of the reception-room—no doubt the most magnificent specimens of the white man's wealth, power, and ingenuity which their eyes had till that moment beheld—turned their looks to the President, but made no motion or gesture, and uttered no sound expressive either of their curiosity or the respect which they evidently felt. The President's head leans slightly on his shoulder, and this little defect, added to his kindliness of expression and his venerable white hair, gives him the appearance of still greater benignity, and as if he were bending his head purposely to listen to the complaints, the requests, or the felicitations of those who have occasion to address him. The four chiefs of the Pawnees and the twelve men of the tribe were severally introduced. The President cordially shook hands with them, looking all the time as if he really felt that paternal interest in their character which his position commanded, but which he was not able to express to them in their own language. There was one Indian of this tribe—a short but well-formed man, about fifty years of age, and deeply pitted with the small-pox, who wore human scalps after the fashion of epaulets, besides a whole breast-plate of such ghastly adornments, and held in his hand a war-club thickly studded with brass nails, who was introduced by the interpreter as the bravest of his people—the "plus brave des braves," the Marshal Ney of his race—who had taken more scalps than any living Indian. Upon this individual the President seemed to look with more than common interest. Indeed, the eyes of all present were directed toward this redoubtable chief; but there was nothing forbidding or ferocious in his appearance. His face and bearing expressed stoical endurance and resolute self-reliance, but neither cruelty nor cunning. The Poncas and their chief went through the same ceremony, and met the same reception; and even the unbidden Pottawatomies were welcomed by their "Great Father" as kindly as if they had been regularly invited to his presence, Mr. Buchanan all the while wearing that good-humored smile which seems natural to him. It was obvious that he was quite as much interested in his red children as they were in their white father, a feeling that none could help sharing who was a witness of the scene.

The presentations over, the President made a short speech, welcoming the Indians to Washington, expressing his readiness to hear whatever they might have to say, and redress any real grievances of which they might have to complain, if they came within the scope of the government to redress, and were not solely due to their own faults and mismanagement. This being three times translated by the three several interpreters—for no one of the tribes understood the language of the other—each tribe signified its approval: the Poncas by an emphatic guttural sound not unlike the peculiar "Oich! oich!" of the Highlanders of Scotland, the Pawnees by the exclamation of "Lowar!" and the Pottawatomies by a short "Ugh! ugh!"

And now began the speech-making in reply to the President's invitation. The four chiefs of the Pawnees, one chief of the Poncas, and one of the Pottawatomies, expressed in succession the object of their journey to Washington. The Pawnees had come to ratify a treaty already made with the government, to see their "Great Father," to learn from him how to grow rich like white men, and no longer to be "poor." The Poncas had come to make a treaty for the sale of their lands in Nebraska, to look with their own eyes upon their "Great Father," whom they judged by the splendor around him to be rich, and to be visibly favored by the "Great Spirit." The Pottawatomies had come unbidden to request that an allowance, paid to them semi-annually by treaty, should be paid annually, to save trouble. All the spokesmen dwelt upon their poverty and wretchedness. Some of them held up their arms and exposed their bosoms to show that they were naked. They wanted to be taught how to be rich; to earn, like the white man, the favor of the Great Spirit, and no longer to be poor. Poverty—extreme poverty—was the key-note of their lamentations, the mournful burden of their whole song. "We are," said one of them, looking right into the eye of the President, and approaching so near that his breath must have felt warm on Mr. Buchanan's cheek as he spoke, "the children of the Great Spirit as much as you are. We have traveled a long distance to see you. At first we traveled slowly. At every place we stopped we expected to find you. We inquired of the people, and they told us you were a long way off. We have found you at last, and we are glad. We see by these things" (pointing to the gilded walls, to the carpets, and the curtains) " that you are rich. We were rich in the days that are past. We were once the favorites of the Great Spirit. The very ground on which we now stand" (and the orator, for such he was, stamped significantly with his feet upon the carpet as he spoke) " once belonged to our fathers. Now we are poor—we are very poor. We have nothing to shelter us from the cold. We are driven from our possessions; and we are hungry. We have come to you to help us. The Great Spirit, through the mouth of the 'Great Father,' will speak to us, and tell us what we are to do. Let us be rich, like the white man, and be poor no longer."

Such was their melancholy and invariable supplication. At every repetition of the word " poor"—when translated in the hardest, coldest, boldest manner by the interpreters—there was a laugh among a portion of the white spectators, who should have known better—a laugh that seemed to me grievously out of place, and which somewhat perplexed the poor Indians, as was evident by the surprise expressed upon their faces. To them their poverty was no laughing matter. They had come to Washington purposely to speak of it. In their simplicity of heart, they believed that the President had it in his power to remove it, and they had lost faith in their own customs, manners, and modes of life, to keep them on a level with the white men; and why should they be laughed at? The President gave them excellent advice. He told them that they always would be poor as long as they subsisted by the chase; that the way to be wealthy was to imitate the industry of the white men—to plow the land, to learn the arts of the blacksmith, the carpenter, the builder, and the miller; and, above all things, to cease their constant wars upon each other. " I learn," he added, " that the Pawnees and Poncas now present are deadly enemies. It is my wish, and that of the Great Spirit who implanted it in my breast, that they should be enemies no more; that, in my presence, they should shake hands in token of peace and friendship." This was explained to

INTERVIEW OF INDIANS, ETC.

them by the interpreters. The enemies made no sign of assent or dissent beyond the usual guttural expression of their satisfaction. "I wish," said the President, "to join your hands together, and that the peace between you should be perpetual." The chiefs of the hostile tribes advanced, and shook hands, first with the President, and then with each other. One man only gave the left hand to his former enemy; but this was explained by the interpreter, who stated that the right hand was withheld by the Pawnee because it had slain the brother of the Ponca, but that the new friendship between the two would be equally as sacred as if the right hand had affirmed it.

"Will they keep the peace?" inquired a gentleman of the President.

"I firmly believe they will," replied Mr. Buchanan. "A peace ratified in the presence of the 'Great Father' is more than usually sacred." And in this opinion he was corroborated by each of the three interpreters.

And so ended the ceremony. I have seen much of the Indians during my stay in Washington—seen them at the theatre, looking intently and inquiringly at the pirouettes of Signora Teresa Rolla, a celebrated *danseuse* now here—seen them in the streets and thoroughfares looking vacantly around them, and seen them at the Arsenal, receiving from the hands of General Floyd, the Secretary at War, the rifles and the muskets which are given to them as presents by the government before they return to the wilderness. On each occasion I have been much impressed with the native dignity and intelligence of these poor people. But their doom is fixed. Between them and the whites there is no possible fraternization. The white men who act as the pioneers of civilization, and push their way into the far wilderness, are ruder, rougher, and more ferocious than the Indians. Between them there is constant animosity; and the red men, being the weaker of the two, stand no chance with their white assailants, who shoot them ruthlessly down for small offenses, punish slight robbery with death, and bring whisky and rum to the service of destruction when readier means are found to be unattainable.

The red men are fast disappearing: only 314,622 of them, little more than half the number of the population of Philadelphia, remain in the territories of the United States; and these are rapidly diminishing from small-pox, internecine war, and the rifles and the whisky-bottles of the whites:

"Slowly and sadly they climb the western mountains,
And read their doom in the departing sun."

In Mexico and in South America they still thrive, or increase, and amalgamate and intermarry with the European races; but in the United States and Canada, where the Anglo-Saxon race predominates, they will in a few years disappear altogether from the land which was once their own, and leave no trace behind them but the names of a few rivers and mountains, and here and there of a state that takes an Indian appellation in default of an Anglo-Saxon one—such as Minnesota, Iowa, Kansas, Wisconsin, and Michigan. Their fate is inevitable, but is none the less sad. The ancient Britons survive in their progeny, but the aborigines of North America are dying out, and their blood will form no portion of that great republic which is so rapidly rising to overshadow the world.

During the stay of the Indians at Washington, public notification was made by bills and placards, and privately to the keepers of the hotels and spirit-shops, that no intoxicating liquors should be served to them, and that gentlemen would refrain from treating them. The notification was doubtless very necessary. In company with Mr. Charles Lanman, of Georgetown, I paid the Poncas and the Pawnees a visit at their hotels. I was received on both occasions with much courtesy, the chiefs presenting their hands in American fashion, and shaking mine very heartily. They seemed to pass their time in smoking, playing cards, or mending their leggins and moccasins. *Wa-ga-suppe*, or the *Whip*, the Ponca chief, gave us some particulars of his life, which were translated to us by the interpreter.

He said he was born on Middle River, in the Territory of Nebraska, and was about fifty-six years of age. "The first creature he killed, when a mere child, was a ground squirrel, and he had killed, since that time, at least ten thousand buffaloes. He always aimed at the heart; frequently one arrow caused death, but he had often sent ten arrows into a buffalo without killing him. He had sometimes sent an arrow right through a buffalo's neck. He once killed a perfectly white buffalo, and never saw but this one. He always hunted these animals on horseback. Once he and another man went after the same animal, because it was large and fat. He was ahead, but his companion shot and wounded the animal; he was angry, and in his desperation took out his knife, and while on the run seized the animal's horns and cut its throat. On another occasion he had a horse killed under him by an angry bull, the body of the horse having been ripped open by one horn, while the other went through his own leg. At another time, when pursuing a buffalo toward a deep river, where the bank was twenty feet high and abrupt, the buffalo made a sudden turn, and at the very instant that he shot an arrow—which killed it—the horse which he rode, alarmed by the buffalo's roar, leaped into the river and was drowned. He himself was not injured."

But his exploits as a hunter were surpassed by his deeds as a horse-thief. The people whom he chiefly robbed of their horses were Pawnees and Comanches. "He had traveled a thousand miles upon one of these expeditions—been gone a hundred and twenty days, and captured or stolen six hundred horses. He never sold a horse, but always made it a point to give them to the poor, the old, and the feeble of his tribe. It was his cunning in stealing horses, and his liberality in giving them away, that caused him to be elected chief. He and his party once traveled five hundred miles simply for the purpose of stealing a spotted horse of which he had heard, and he got the prize. He had had five wives: one died, he abandoned three for their infidelity, and one he still cherished. He had been the father of eleven children. The prairie was his home. The summer lodges of his tribe are made of buffalo skins; those which they inhabit in the winter are made of turf. He had never been sick a day. He had never been afraid to risk his life, but always disliked to kill human beings. He had never killed but one man, and the circumstances were these: he had been four days without food on a horse-stealing expedition when he came to a deserted Pawnee village. He was disgusted, and hunger filled him with hate and revenge. At that moment he discovered a solitary Pawnee approaching the village. He shot him down, and, after scalping him and breaking his neck, out of pure wickedness, he left him thus exposed, by way of letting the Pawnees know, on their return, that he had been there."

On questioning him about his ideas of a future state, he said that he expected to go, after death, to the white man's heaven. "There was but one heaven for all men."

The Pawnee chief, whom we visited at another part of the city, said his name was *Ne-sharo-lad-a-hoo*, or the Big Chief. "He did not know where he was born, but it was somewhere in the Territory of Kansas. He was about sixty years old. He had never been much of a hunter: his people called him too lazy and fat for a huntsman. He claimed to be very brave, however, and had devoted his whole life to horse-stealing; had been twelve days without food, and the illness which followed that abstinence was very severe; he was delirious with hunger, and that was the only time he had known what it was to be sick. He had been the husband of four women, and the best of them all was one he had stolen. He had taken four scalps during his life. He once entered a Mexican encampment at night when all were asleep, and, 'just for the fun of it,' walked entirely through, and carried off thirty horses." When asked what he would have done if he had been discovered, he said, "he would have put an arrow into every eye that opened." One of the scalps he had taken belonged to a Ponca, and the only brother of the man he had killed was one of those who stepped up and shook hands with him in the presence of the President. In speaking of his people, this man said that they had once been notorious for their cruelty. In illustration of this, he said, "When we took a handsome girl as prisoner, we kept her for a few weeks, and treated her well; but after a certain time we tied her to a stake, had a great feast and much dancing, and then burned her to death. Some of us cut off pieces of her flesh, and the boys of the tribe shot into her body little arrows made of prairie grass. But this was long ago, and it was very bad. Our people thought it would please the Great Spirit; but we are wiser now."

The truth was, they were frightened out of this horrible practice by being told that the *small-pox* by which they had once been scourged was sent by the Great Spirit as a punishment for such wickedness. These people hardly know the use of a canoe, but journey exclusively on horseback. This man told us he had known several persons who had been scalped and yet survived. Such men, however, were always considered disgraced, and they had a tradition that all such men congregated in some distant country and lived in caves. Like the Comanches and Blackfeet Indians, the Pawnees have but few friends among the prairie tribes.

The following official statement—the latest published by the United States government—gives the names of all the Indian tribes left within the limits of the Union, their place of location, and their numbers, as estimated by the Indian agents and other officials:

Name of Tribe.	No. of Souls.	Place of Residence.
Apaches	7,000	New Mexico Territory.
Apaches	—	Texas.
Apaches	320	Arkansas River.
Assinaboines	3,360	Upper Missouri River.
Arickarees	800	do.
Arrapahoes	3,000	Arkansas and Platte Rivers.
Anadahkoes, Caddoes, and Ionies	500	Texas.
Blackfeet	7,500	Upper Missouri River.
Cherokees	17,530	West of Arkansas.
Cherokees	2,200	North Carolina, Tennessee, Georgia, and Alabama.
Choctaws	16,000	West of Arkansas.
Choctaws	1,000	Mississippi.
Chickasaws	4,787	West of Arkansas.
Creeks	25,000	do.
Creeks	100	Alabama.
Chippewas of Lake Superior		Michigan.
Chippewas of Lake Superior	4,940	Wisconsin.
Chippewas of Lake Superior		Minnesota Territory.
Chippewas of the Mississippi	2,206	do.

98 LIFE AND LIBERTY IN AMERICA.

Name of Tribe.	No. of Souls.	Place of Residence.
Chippewas and Ottawas	5,152	Michigan.
Chippewas of Saginaw	1,340	do.
Chippewas of Swan Creek, etc.	138	do.
Chippewas of Swan Creek, etc.	33	Kansas Territory.
Cayugas	143	New York.
Catawbas	200	North and South Carolina
Christians or Munsees	44	Kansas Territory.
Crows	3,360	Upper Missouri River.
Crees	800	do.
Caddoes	—	Texas.
Comanches and Kioways	20,000	do.
Comanches	—	New Mexico Territory.
Comanches	3,600	Arkansas River.
Cheyennes	2,800	Arkansas and Platte Rivers.
California Tribes	33,539	California.
Delawares	902	Kansas Territory.
Gros Ventres	750	Upper Missouri River.
Ionies	—	Texas.
Iowas	433	Kansas Territory.
Kickapoos	344	do.
Kickapoos	—	Texas border.
Kioways	—	Texas.
Kioways	2,805	Arkansas River.
Kansas	1,370	Kansas Territory.
Keechies, Wacoes, and Towacarros	300	Texas.
Kaskaskias	—	Kansas Territory.
Lipans	560	Texas.
Miamis	207	Kansas Territory.
Miamis	353	Indiana.
Mandans	250	Upper Missouri River.
Minatares	2,500	do.
Menomonees	1,930	Wisconsin.
Missourias	—	Nebraska Territory.
Munsees	—	Kansas Territory.
Kuscaleros or Apaches	400	Texas.
Navajoes	7,500	New Mexico Territory.
Oneidas	249	New York.
Oneidas	978	Wisconsin.
Onondagas	470	New York.
Ottawas	—	Michigan.
Ottawas	249	Kansas Territory.
Omahas	800	Nebraska Territory.
Ottoes and Missourias	600	do.
Osages	4,098	West of Arkansas.
Oregon Territory Tribes	13,000	Oregon Territory.
Poncas	700	Nebraska Territory.
Pottawatomies	236	Michigan.
Pottawatomies of Huron	45	do.
Pottawatomies	3,440	Kansas Territory.
Pawnees	4,000	Nebraska Territory.

INTERVIEW OF INDIANS, ETC.

Name of Tribe.	No. of Souls.	Place of Residence.
Piankeshaws, Weas, Peorias, and Kaskaskias	220	Kansas Territory.
Pueblo Indians	10,000	New Mexico Territory.
Quapaws	314	West of Arkansas.
Stockbridges	13	Kansas Territory.
Stockbridges	240	Wisconsin.
Sioux of the Mississippi	6,383	Minnesota Territory.
Sioux of the Missouri	15,440	Upper Missouri River.
Sioux of the Plains	5,600	Platte and Arkansas Rivers.
St. Regis Indians	450	New York.
Senecas	2,557	do.
Senecas (Sandusky)	180	West of Arkansas.
Senecas and Shawnees (Lewistown)	271	do.
Shawnees	851	Kansas Territory.
Sacs and Foxes of Mississippi	1,626	do.
Sacs and Foxes of Missouri	180	do.
Seminoles	2,500	West of Arkansas.
Seminoles	500	Florida.
Tuscaroras	280	New York.
Towaccaros	—	Texas.
Tonkawas	400	do.
Utah Territory Tribes	12,000	Utah Territory.
Utahs	2,500	New Mexico Territory.
Wacoes	—	Texas.
Wichitas	950	do.
Weas	—	Kansas Territory.
Winnebagoes	2,546	Minnesota Territory.
Winnebagoes	208	Kansas Territory.
Wyandots	554	do.
Washington Territory Tribes	14,000	Washington Territory.
Wandering Indians of Comanches, Cheyenne, and other tribes	17,000	New Mexico Territory.
Total number	314,622	

CHAPTER XIII.

AMERICANISMS AND AMERICAN SLANG.

EVERY country has its own slang or "argot," though it is not every language that has a word to express this particular form of the ultra-vulgar vernacular. American slang is more interesting to an educated Englishman than the slang of France, Germany or any other country. The slang of ancient Greece and Rome, with the exception of a very few words imperfectly understood, is lost to the moderns, or it might perhaps interest us as greatly as the classical speech which has come down to us, for the new light it might throw upon the manners, characteristics, and domestic life of the ancient peoples. But as this is no longer a possible subject of study for the learned or unlearned, and as slang at home is unhappily too familiar to be considered of any importance, the peculiar idioms, perversions, and revivals of words in common use among our American cousins, striking us by their novelty, acquire by that means a certain sort of dignity, and become valuable to the student both of history and literature. They show the up-springings and germinations of language. They prove how much points of difference in national character, and even climate and accidental circumstances of politics or trade, can influence and change the well-established words of the dictionary; how a noun, verb, or adjective, without being in the least degree changed in its pronunciation, can insensibly glide into a meaning totally different from that with which it was originally associated; and how new words are coined, and are always coinable by and under new circumstances. In these respects, the study even of "slang" is profitable, whether the student be a philosopher in the largest sense of the word, or merely a philologist. Etymology is a fiery and often unmanageable hobby-horse to ride, but those who ride it wisely may do good service. During my residence in America, I noted down from day to day not only the single words and forms of expression, but the phrases used both by educated and uneducated men with whom I held conversation, and also the idioms in books and newspapers which grated harshly or sounded strangely to my English ears. To these I added words which, if not ungraceful and vulgar in themselves, had a flavor of novelty and foreignness. A few of these words have been introduced from America into England, and have a positive value for expressing tersely the complicated ideas which, without their aid, could not have been forcibly rendered in any other way. Others, again, derived from Dutch, German, or Spanish roots, although they have no individual merit to recommend them to the estimation of the English scholar, stand as simple Americanisms, with such justification as geography can afford them. And how much geographical distances, even small, can influence and change a noble language, we may see by the study of the varieties of English spoken in such slightly divergent localities as London, Cornwall, Newcastle, Wales, Ireland, Edinburgh, and Aberdeen.

The "Great West" of the United States—the home of the hardiest and roughest population, and which contains the largest admixture of the foreign races of Europe—is the birthplace of the greatest number of new words. But even here the new words are more commonly revivals of local and provincial Anglo-Saxon and Anglo-Scandinavian words still in use in the rural districts of England, although they have dropped out of polite life and literature, than "annexations" from an entirely foreign source. When we see in our classical England itself—where, if any where, the best and purest English ought to be spoken—the growth and acceptance of such a word as "starvation," and of another that has not an equal antiquity to recommend it—the odious but fashionable word in Parliament and newspapers, "to 'ventilate' a subject," we can not be surprised that in the New World the old language should partake of the colors of the clime, and undergo transformations more or less decided. "Humbug" has become a good word by virtue of time and possession; and for the same reason, "to Barnumize" may finally become naturalized on both sides of the Atlantic, and express the action of him who would resort to the *ne plus ultra* of all possible humbug for the filling of his pockets at the expense of the public. Valuable is any one word which can be made to express an idea so complicated.

First of all, I cite a few words that have lost in America their original English meaning.

To exercise means to agitate, vex, or trouble. Thus it is said of a senator in Congress that he is *exercised* by the great question he is about to bring forward, or that Mr. —— was much *exercised* by an attack upon him in a newspaper.

Bright means "clever." A clever man, or a man of talent, would in America be called a "bright" man.

Clever means "amiable and courteous." A "clever" captain is one who is friendly, attentive, and polite to his passengers. Among the recommendations sometimes advertised in the Mississippi and Ohio steam-boats is that the captain and clerk are the "cleverest" on the line, and for this reason agreeable to the ladies.

Amiable means "stupid." A member of the House of Representatives, and a most worthy man, was highly offended at hearing his friend called "amiable" by an Englishman. He thought the phrase implied a reproach or a sneer, and declared that the word "amiable" was synonymous with what in English slang is called "spooney." "You may call a woman 'amiable,'" said he, "but not a man."

Skinflint, which in England signifies "over-sensitive," in America means "stingy and parsimonious."

Smart means "sharp." A smart man is one who would do a dishonest act in business if he could manage to keep on the safe side and avoid the law.

Among the pure Americanisms may be cited the following:

To honeyfugle, to gloze, flatter, bamboozle, or "take in."

High falutin or *high verlooten* signifies high-flown, exaggerated, and bombastic in speech or writing.

To loaf, to idle or dawdle.

A loafer, a dawdler or idler.

Splurge, a display, an outburst of expenditure, such as to create a sensation among the by-standers or witnesses.

To make a splurge may be rendered by the common English vulgarism, "to cut a dash."

To cave in, to give way, to collapse.

To stump, to address public meetings in the open air—a phrase derived from the fact that popular orators in most circumstances often stand on stumps of trees, as the most available platforms.

To stump a state, to go on a tour of political agitation through a state.

Platform, the recognized principles and creed of a political party. This phrase is of English origin, and is to be found in the political tracts and in the sermons of the days of Cromwell.

A plank of the platform, one principle out of the many agreed upon by a party.

Buncombe or *Bunkum*. A diffuse and angry orator having made a somewhat irrational and very unnecessary speech in the House of Representatives at Washington where nobody thought it worth while to contradict him, was afterward asked by a friend who met him in Pennsylvania Avenue why he had made such a display? "I was not speaking to the House," he replied; "I was speaking to Buncombe"—a county or district by the majority of whose votes he had been elected. Hence Buncombe or Bunkum has become a phrase in America, and, to some extent, in England also, to express that extra parliamentary oratory which appeals to the passions or prejudices of the outside people, or sections of the people, and not to the reason and sound sense of a deliberative assembly.

To vamose, to decamp or vanish.

Pile, a fortune.

To make a pile, to make a fortune.

Swanger, a dandy or "swell."

A muss, a slight quarrel or disturbance.

A cuss, a curse—applied to a person.

A mean cuss, a cursedly mean person.

Mung, sham, false, pretended.

Mung news, a fabrication.

Bender, a spree.

To go on a bender, to go on a spree.

To fix, to dress, to adorn, to trim. The phrase is applied either to the human figure, as when a lady says she will "fix herself;" or to an article of attire, as when she says her cap, her bonnet, or dress, has been "fixed" or ornamented; or to a dish for the table, as to "fix" a steak with onions—a chicken with mushrooms, etc.

Fixings, trimmings, adornments.

Caucus, a preliminary political meeting, and gathering together of the party, to decide upon ulterior movements.

To lobby, to use private influence for the passing of bills through the Legislature.

Grit, the real grit, the true grit. These words or phrases are used to signify a person of superior worth, solidity, and genuineness, as distinguished from another who is inferior, or merely "chaff." The miller is evidently the parent of this expression.

Declension "I have been writing," said a lady, "several declensions to dinners and balls." The word is equivalent to refusal, but it seems to mean refusal for reasons assigned—a declinature.

Bogus, false or sham; said to be derived from the name of a man notorious for issuing counterfeit notes. Hence "bogus" news, a "bogus" meeting, a "bogus" baby, a "bogus" senator, a "bogus" convention.

To foot a bill, to sign or accept bill.

Whole-souled, a very common phrase in America to express a hearty enthusiastic person. In "Lloyd's Railway Guide," the Bradshaw of America, it is stated of one of the hotels in a principal city that "Colonel ——, the proprietor, is a whole-souled landlord."

Fits. To "give a man fits" is an expression continually used, and seems to mean, to assault, or give a man a disagreeable surprise, either by words or by blows, or by a public exposure.

Jesse. To "give Jesse" or "particular Jesse" are phrases equivalent to the preceding.

Bim. Hit him *bim* in the eye—*i. e.*, right in the eye.

Realize—Realizing. It is a favorite pulpit phrase to say that a person has a "realizing sense of the goodness of God."

Dépôt, a railway station.

Fizzle, a slight quarrel or controversy.

A stampede, a rush, a multitudinous exit.

Socdologer, a knock-down blow. There is a species of fish-hook of this name.

To overslaugh, a word apparently derived from the German or old English, like onslaught, and signifying to strike over.

Rocks, money—a Californian phrase.

To squirm, to wriggle like a worm.

To tote, to carry.

To tote the plunder, a slang phrase for "carry the luggage."

To wilt, to wither.

Wilted, withered.

Ge-a-headative, progressive, "fast."

A dough face, a man easily moved to change his opinion; a person to be wrought upon and modeled to any particular shape, like a piece of dough.

Boss, a master; "a boss barber," "a boss butcher," are common expressions.

Shyster, a blackguard.

Cracker, a biscuit.

Nut anvil, a nut-cracker.

In all great American cities there are, as there are in the cities of Europe, rude youths, who vent the exuberance of their animal spirits in acts of daring that too often savor of what might not unjustly be called blackguardism. But in America such persons are of more importance in the social scale than they are with us, for they have votes if they have reached the age of twenty-one, and they have aggregate political influence in addition if they happen to be members of the fire-companies, or to be otherwise enrolled and enregimented. The ruffians of this sort have names that differ in different cities. In New York there are "Bowery boys," "Spiggots," "High-binders," and "Rowdies." The last word has already reached England, and threatens to become naturalized. In Washington they have

"Swipers;"* in Philadelphia "Dead Rabbits;" and in Baltimore, "Plug-uglies," "Rosebuds,"† and "Blood-tubs." In the New England States, where the municipal government is generally far more settled, and where a volunteer fire service is not the rule, but the exception, these Ishmaels are not to be found, and the order and regularity approach to, or equal that of the streets of London, where a "Plug-ugly," a "Dead Rabbit," or a "Blood-tub" would stand no chance against the police.

Among other Americanisms that strike the attention of a stranger, though doubtless they would not be noticed by a native-born American of the highest culture and refinement, simply from the fact of the familiarity, are such mispronunciations as "ben" for "been," "air" for "are," and "was" for "were;" "ant-*eye*-slavery" for "anti-slavery," "Eye-taly" for "Italy," "Eye-talian" for "Italian," "dye-plomatic" for "diplomatic," and invariably "*my*self" for the more subdued mode in which we in the "old country" pronounce these two egotistical syllables. "Engine" is generally "en-*gine*," though "machine" retains the English pronunciation.

Among the idiomatic and proverbial expressions that differ from those of the mother country are such as the following: "I reckon," which is the distinctive mark of the Southerners,

---

* "Last night, at about half past eleven o'clock, another of those murders which have been so frequent of late in Washington, by the hands of rowdies, was committed on the corner of Ninth Street and New York Avenue. Marcellus Stoops, a quiet young man, a messenger in the Treasury Department, while walking leisurely along in company with another young man, was shot with a pistol. He died a few minutes afterward, and before Dr. Duhamel, who was sent for, could reach the spot. Eight or ten men of the fighting club here, called "Swipers," have been arrested, and it is stated that one of the leaders, called Johnson, shot the unfortunate young man. Washington has become the most lawless place in the world."—*New York Herald, April* 4, 1858.

† "'Democrat of the old school' informs us that the 'Rosebuds,' charged with rowdyism at the last Baltimore election, and acquitted in the Circuit Court of Baltimore on the 4th inst., were good Buchanan Democrats, and were acquitted by a Know Nothing jury, because the evidence plainly showed the police to be in the wrong."—*New York Herald, February* 14, 1859.

as "I guess" is of the people of the New England States and of the North generally. "All aboard," or "All aboord," is the invariable cry of the conductors and officials of the railway stations or dépôts when they wish the passengers to take their seats. This is not the only nautical phrase in general use among the Americans. "Where do you hail from?" is often asked; and it is not uncommon to be told that Mr. or Mrs. So-and-so has been "hauled up" with a fever. To be "under the weather" is to suffer from cold. To "give a man hell" is to beat him, bully him, or, as our prize-fighters would say, "punish" him. To make a man "smell hell" is a phrase with a similar meaning. I remember hearing, in the Parliament of one of the Southern States, an angry orator declare, that if the gentleman from—say Buncombe (not the honorable member for Buncombe, as with us), dared to repeat out of the house what he had said in the house, he would make him "smell hell." A common expression in the Southern States to denote an ambuscade is that "there is a nigger in the fence." In the Northern States the same meaning is conveyed by the phrase, possibly English in its origin, "There's a cat in the meal-tub." A man of great importance in his own estimation or that of the world, is called a "big bug." Thus I Street in Washington, the residence of the foreign embassadors, bankers, and other important persons, is said to be inhabited by the "big bugs." A person of note and great wealth is said to be "some punkins" (or pumpkins). And instead of the common English phrase, that "it is well to wash the dirty family linen at home," the Western people have the more striking and significant phrase, that "every man should skin his own skunk." The skunk is fortunately unknown in England, but it is a little animal that smells ten thousand times worse than a polecat, and of which, if the least odor gets into the clothes or garments of man or woman, the only remedy is to burn them. "To play 'possum" is equivalent to the old London phrase of "shamming Abraham," the opossum having a trick of pretending to be dead when it finds that all other means of escape from its enemies are unavailing.

A bunch of sprouts. An Englishman who had steamed down the Mississippi with a captain who was not "clever" in the American sense of the word, seeing on his arrival at New Orleans a great assemblage of people at the levée, and hearing a disturbance, asked the captain what was the matter.

"Oh, nothing particular," said the captain. "It is only Jones, an editor, who has quarreled with Smith, another editor, and given him a whole bunch of sprouts."

"A bunch of sprouts!" inquired the Englishman.

"Yes, a bunch of sprouts," said the captain.

"And what *is* a 'bunch of sprouts?'" inquired John Bull, bewildered.

"Don't you know!" rejoined the captain.

"I don't," said John Bull.

"Then more fool you," was the reply, on giving which the captain turned upon his heel and walked away.

The Englishman, not altogether discouraged, applied to the clerk for information.

"Oh! editors are always quarreling here," he replied. "It is but one editor who has given another a bunch of sprouts."

"But what *is* a 'bunch of sprouts?'"

"Don't you know?"

"Not I."

"Why, what a fool you must be!"

The story is that the Englishman has asked the same question since that day, no one knows how many years ago, of thousands of people, but never obtained an answer; that the idea has taken entire possession of his mind; and that he is wandering over the United States asking every one he meets, "What is a 'bunch of sprouts?'" Receiving no satisfactory reply, he hurries on from place to place, and from person to person, worn to a skeleton, the mere shadow of a man—a kind of flying Dutchman—a spectral presence—a wandering Jew—asking the old, eternal question, never to be answered on this side of the grave, "What is a 'bunch of sprouts?'" Should this unhappy citizen of our fortunate isles ever read these pages, the spell that is upon him will be broken, and he will learn that a "bunch of sprouts" is a slang expression for the whole discharge of a revolver—barrel after barrel.

To attempt to make a vocabulary of the political slang words that every now and then arise in the United States, live their little day, and sink into oblivion, but which, while they last, sorely puzzle all who are not Americans, would be an endless and an unsatisfactory task. Such words and phrases as "Hard Shells," "Soft Shells," "Locofocos," "Know Nothings," and others, which float about on the stormy ocean of politics until they are ingulfed or rot away, are ephemeral by their very nature. Invented by newspapers or stump orators, they tickle the public fancy for a time. They enjoy considerable popularity while current, but they are so entirely local as scarcely to merit explanation beyond the limits of the country which produces them.

A rich and fruitful source of slang expressions is to be found in the names of drinks in such Southern and Western States as the agents of the Maine Liquor Law have hitherto assaulted in vain. "Gin-sling," "brandy-smash," "a streak of lightning," "whisky-skin," "mint-julep," "cocktail," "sherry-cobbler," and others, are more or less known, both by name and by nature, on this side of the Atlantic, and need not be farther particularized. In the South—and possibly the phrase extends northward to New York, and westward beyond Chicago—a dram, or small glass of spirits, is called a "smile."

Let no American reader of these pages misinterpret the motives which induce a traveler from the old country, that still presumes to be the home of the language as well as of the race, to note the differences which climate and circumstances may make in such a familiar matter as the daily speech of the semi-educated or the wholly vulgar. In England, the changes which the spoken language undergoes from generation to generation are very many, and such is the ever-increasing intercourse between the United States and the British Isles, that a word introduced in the one speedily becomes known in the other, and if it have any terseness or appositeness to recommend it, becomes naturalized in both countries. It takes a long time to secure even for a good and valuable word a place in the dignified niche of a dictionary, in which respect our dictionary makers err on the side of undue conservatism. Man is not made for language, but language is made for man; and the English spoken at the time when Columbus discovered America is not the English spoken either in England or America at the present time. Even the common talk of the fathers of the present generation differed in many respects from the common talk of the men of the year 1859, and the copiousness, if not the elegance, of the noblest tongue, all things considered, spoken in the present age of the world, is continually increased by inventions, revivals, and, it may be said, robberies, or, at the least, appropriations and assimilations from other languages, less fortunate and wealthy. It were to be wished, however, that those who have the ear of their countrymen, either as great orators or great writers, would, instead of being led away, as they sometimes are, by a foolish fashion for a word, as ladies are by a stupid fashion for red stockings or red petticoats, and other ebullitions of the scarlet fever, bethink themselves how many excellent words have dropped out of use since the days of Chaucer, or even more recently, since those of Shakspeare. Some of these words are of the highest value both to orators and poets, and it would be much better to revive them than to coin other words out of foreign or vulgar materials, which do not and never can harmonize so thoroughly with the genius of our tongue as the sturdy, pithy, able-bodied words of our Anglo-Saxon and Anglo-Scandinavian ancestors. The Scottish, and even the Northumbrian, Yorkshire, Lincolnshire, Suffolk, and Cornish dialects of the English language contain many excellent words that the greatest writers since the days of Pope and Addison have never thought of using, but by aid of which our literature would be all the richer if men of influence with the pen would judiciously and cautiously endeavor to reintroduce them. Why, for instance, should we have "rather," and not "rathe" and "rathest?" Why not naturalize the Scottish "gloaming," "glamour," "cannie," "douce," "bonnie," "cantie," "sonsie," "daft," "wud," "wowff," and many other honest words that have not their synonyms in English literature? The archæological dictionaries and glossaries of the British Isles contain mines of treasure, which, when we consider of what elements the population of the United States and Canada is mainly composed, lead us to hope that our language, like our race, may achieve new triumphs, and attain greater wealth and power in the new regions to which it has been transplanted than it ever attained in the original cradle of its birth and growth. If he who makes a blade of grass grow where grass never grew before, is to that extent a public benefactor, is not he who coins a new word to express a new meaning, or an old meaning that could not be otherwise expressed without a periphrasis or a whole sentence to itself, or, better still, who revives a good old word that ought never to have been allowed to die, a public benefactor also? I think so, and for that reason have dwelt at greater length upon the subject of Americanisms in speech than I should otherwise have considered myself justified in doing.

In addition to these, there are Americanisms in writing which strike the traveler by their novelty. To an Englishman it would seem odd if, instead of Birmingham on the address of a letter, there were simply " Bir.," or instead of London, " Lon.," or of Manchester, " Man." But such abbreviations are the rule and not the exception in America. Every state in the Union has its recognized abbreviation, which is always a monosyllable, wherever it is possible so to make it. New York, New Jersey, New Hampshire, Rhode Island, North Carolina, and South Carolina, are the sole exceptions to the monosyllabic arrangement, and are commonly written and printed N. Y., N. J., N. H., R. I., N. Ca., and S. Ca. The other states are,

Maine..................Me.	Alabama.............Ala.
Vermont..............Vt.	Mississippi...........Miss.
Massachusetts.......Mass.	Missouri ....Mo.
Connecticut.........Conn.	Louisiana............La.
Pennsylvania ....Pa.	Arkansas.............Ark.
Delaware ....Del.	Tennessee............Tenn.
Maryland............Ma. or Md.	Kentucky ....Ky.
Virginia..............Va.	Ohio....................O.
Georgia...............Ga.	Michigan.............Mich.

Indiana...............Ind.	Iowa..................Io.
Illinois................Ill.	Wisconsin...........Wis.
Florida...............Fla.	Minnesota...........Min.
Texas.................Tex.	California...........Cal.

In like manner, the name of the city of Baltimore is abbreviated into Balto. A busy, "go-ahead" nation has not time to write the names of its states and cities in full. If this be not the reason, it is difficult to find another.

CHAPTER XIV.

THE IRISH IN AMERICA.

Washington, January, 1858.

STANDING at the bar of Willard's Hotel, in Washington, in company with two distinguished senators and three members of Congress, and taking, all of us, a slight noonday refection of crackers (biscuits) and lager beer, our conversation turned upon the great rebellion in India, and upon the indomitable "pluck" and energy displayed by the British soldiers and commanders, and especially by the gallant Havelock, in confronting and subduing the mutineers. The execrations lavished upon the name of Nana Sahib, and the fervent praises showered upon that of Havelock by my American friends, could not have been surpassed for honest intensity in any circle in England. Every one of them seemed to feel proud that he was of the same blood and lineage as the conquerors of India, and, although the great struggle was far from concluded, each predicted that it could but have one result—the utter discomfiture of the foe, and the triumphant vindication of British supremacy in every portion of our Eastern empire.

"It is the blood, sir," said one of the senators—"the noblest and best blood in the world—a blood that never was conquered, and never will be."

At this moment, a person who had been hanging on, and listening to the conversation—an Irishman by his accent, and who, as it afterward appeared, had not been above five years in America—burst in upon us with a volley of oaths so awful and so disgusting that no gentleman or man of common decency would whisper them, much more print them, and imprecated such wrath of heaven upon England and upon Englishmen in India and at home, that I fairly lost breath in the excess of my surprise at hearing such abominable sentiments in the mouth of a human being. That every English man, woman, and child in India should be put to the sword, was but one of the hideous wishes which he formed, and his whole speech, gesture, and demeanor suggested the idea that he was a maniac rather than a sane man. It did not appear, however, that he was mad. He was a well-known "citizen," I was told, and much respected; and, though much more violent in his Anglophobia than the Irish generally, he but expressed a feeling only too common among men of his race who have left Ireland for Great Britain's good, and brought their passions and their prejudices into the great arena of American politics.

The incident suggested the propriety of making some inquiries into the condition of the Irish in the United States, and to the sources of their continually and openly avowed hatred toward England. It can not be denied that the Irish immigration has been of incalculable service to the development of the resources of the United States, and more especially of the North and West. As servants, or "helps," instead of the negroes—to the employment of whom many persons have an aversion—and as strong, sturdy laborers doing all the rough work of the country, especially building and the making of canals and railroads, they have supplied a great public want, and aided immensely in the material progress of the country. The native-born American, of Anglo-Saxon descent, looks upon all rough labor, except that of the farm, as somewhat derogatory from his dignity. It is for him to labor with his brains rather than with his thews and sinews; to barter, not to dig and delve; and to set others to hard work rather than do the hard work himself. And the able-bodied Irish supplied the very help he needed, and both parties to the bargain were satisfied—the Americans in getting the work done, and the Irishman in getting as much wages in one day as he could have got in Ireland or in England in a week. But here the satisfaction of the Americans came to an end. The new-comer, though not entitled to a vote until after a residence of a certain number of years in the country, either found means himself, or had them found for him by others, to claim the privilege before he had been a week on American soil. Instances have been known, during hot election contests in the state or the municipality of New York, when the whole male immigration landed in the morning from a Cork or Liverpool vessel has voted ere the afternoon for one "ticket" or the other. This abuse, and the general dictatorialness of the Irish party, when, after due naturalization and long residence, they had acquired the legal right to vote, and had been marshaled by their ecclesiastical and lay leaders into one unbroken phalanx, led to the establishment of what is sometimes called the " Know-nothing," and sometimes the " American" party. The main object of this organization, whatever be its proper designation, was to prevent all but native-born Americans from voting at elections; and there can be little doubt, if they could have succeeded in this object, that the anti-British feeling which is so often fomented in the States for purposes wholly domestic and internal, would speedily diminish, if it did not die out altogether. And it is well that the British people should understand how it is that, from time to time, so much jealousy and ill feeling are expressed toward England by speakers and writers in the United States. The most influential, if not the largest portion of the American people, are the descendants of Englishmen and Scotchmen— men who, when they speak from their hearts of England, her laws, her literature, and her example, might borrow the words of Oliver Wendell Holmes, and exclaim,

"Our little mother isle! God bless her!"

The descendants of the French, the Germans, and the Norwegians, who form another large class in America, have no ill feeling toward England. They are a patient, plodding, and industrious people, and if they do not love her, they certainly do not hate her. The party that hates England, and which it is sometimes expedient to propitiate even at the cost of reason, justice, and propriety, exists mainly in the Irish immigration. The Hiberno-Americans, as a body, entertain a religious as well as a political hatred toward Great Britain—a hatred which would doubtless expire were it not fostered for purposes of ecclesiastical domination and influence, or encouraged for the selfish objects of ambitious demagogues, who strive to raise themselves into notoriety and power by arts that in the Old Country have ceased to be profitable in ceasing to be dangerous. Parties in America are divided in reality into the pro-slavery and anti-slavery parties, and—with some minor shades of difference, that are as shifting as the glass beads and fragments in a kaleidoscope—into the Republican and Democratic parties. These are the two great and essential divisions, shift and change as they may; and, these being pretty nearly balanced, the Irish party, well drilled and organized, and keeping aloof until victory must be declared on some one of the many issues that are continually raised, is able but too often to turn the scale. Hence the Hiberno-Americans are hated and yet courted by both; and hence every now and then it is found that statesmen who have no sympathy for the Irish and the priests deem it necessary to angle for Irish votes by anti-English orations, which it would greatly grieve these statesmen to be taken in England at their American value.

Whenever the election for President draws near, and for at least eighteen months before the final decision of the struggle, it may be noticed that the American press, both of the North and the South, gets up a grievance against England. If it be not the right of search, or the enlistment question, or a disputed boundary in the far Northwest, or a fishing case in the Bay of Fundy, or the right of way across the Isthmus of Panama, or the Mosquitian Protectorate, it will be something else; perhaps something of no greater moment than a leading article in *The Times*, or some other London journal of note or influence. Hard words will be used; much "bunkum" will be spoken; and from the press the vituperation will spread to the floor of Congress, until Englishmen, partly alarmed and partly amused, are compelled to ask in genuine bewilderment what it all means? It means nothing, except that the two great American parties, opposing each other for some object, or to carry the election of some candidate for high office, and deeming every vote of importance in a contest too evenly balanced to be comfortable for either, desire to have the Irish on their side. And the straw with which the Irish are most easily tickled is abuse of England. Predict that the sun of England's greatness is set forever, and the Irishman will think you the pink of orators. Assert that Brother Jonathan will "lick" John Bull into immortal "smash," and all creation along with him, and Paddy O'Rourke will flourish his shillaly, and vent his ecstasy in prolonged ululations.

But the leading statesmen of America, though they are condemned at times to use such agencies for the accomplishment of purposes which have not the remotest connection with English politics, despise the tools with which they do this work, and look with unfeigned alarm upon the prospect of any serious misunderstanding with Great Britain. It is not race or blood, so much as religion, that creates the ill-feeling of Roman Catholic Irishmen toward Protestant England. And this animosity, which does not affect the German immigration, even when newly arrived, is found by experience to be greatly weakened in the second generation. The children born of Irish parents upon American soil, sent in ordinary course to the excellent schools so bountifully provided in all the states, are assimilated to the common American type, and in their youth and maturity cease to look upon England with the vindictiveness of their progenitors. They cling affectionately to the name and to the memory of the green isle, but do not find it absolutely essential to their love of Ireland that they should hate England. If a few of the fathers inveigh against the Sassenach with the bloodthirsty bitterness of the zealot whose exhibition of himself in the public room at Willard's has led to these observations, it is satisfactory to think that the virus is weakened in the children, and that a cause so beneficent for the change is to be found in the operation of the school system and the extension of education.

CHAPTER XV.

FROM WASHINGTON TO CINCINNATI.

Cincinnati, January 19, 1858.

PRIOR to leaving Washington, my friends—and among their names I might mention, if it were a portion of my design to detail private gossip, some of the most illustrious public men in America—gave me a parting dinner at Gautier's well-known restaurant in Pennsylvania Avenue. It is not necessary to say more of this dinner than that it was luxuriously served, the cooking as scientific, and the wines as rare, as if the symposium had been in Paris or London. Furthermore, it led to the production of the following lines, which the author recited in lieu of making a speech:

JOHN AND JONATHAN.

I.

"SAID Brother Jonathan to John,
 'You are the elder-born,
And I can bear another's hate,
 But not your lightest scorn.
You've lived a life of noble strife,
 You've made a world your own:
Why, when I follow in your steps,
 Receive me with a groan?

II.

"'I feel the promptings of my youth,
 That urge me evermore
To spread my fame, my race, my name
 From shore to farthest shore.
I feel the lightnings in my blood,
 The thunders in my hand,
And I must work my destiny,
 Whoever may withstand.

III.

"'And if you'd give me, Brother John,
 The sympathy I crave,
And stretch your warm fraternal hand
 Across the Atlantic wave,

I'd give it such a cordial grasp
  That earth should start to see,
And ancient crowns and sceptres shake,
  That fear both you and me.'

IV.

"Said Brother John to Jonathan,
  'You do my nature wrong;
I never hated, never scorn'd,
  But loved you well and long.
If, children of the self-same sire,
  We've quarrel'd now and then,
'Twas only in our early youth,
  And not since we were men.

V.

"'And if with cautious, cooler blood,
  Result of sufferings keen,
I sometimes think you move too fast,
  Mistake not what I mean.
I've felt the follies of my youth,
  The errors of my prime.
And dream'd for you—my father's son—
  A future more sublime.

VI.

"'And here's my hand—tis freely given—
  I stretch it o'er the brine,
And wish you from my heart of hearts
  A higher life than mine.
Together let us rule the world,
  Together work and thrive;
For if you're only twenty-one,
  I'm scarcely thirty-five.

VII.

"'And I have strength for nobler work
  Than e'er my hand has done,
And realms to rule and truths to plant
  Beyond the rising sun.
Take you the West and I the East;
  We'll spread ourselves abroad,
With trade and spade and wholesome laws,
  And faith in man and God.

VIII.

"'Take you the West and I the East;
  We speak the self-same tongue
That Milton wrote and Chatham spoke,
  And Burns and Shakspeare sung;

And from our tongue, our hand, our heart,
　　Shall countless blessings flow
To light two darkened hemispheres
　　That know not where they go.

IX.

"'Our Anglo-Saxon name and fame,
　　Our Anglo-Saxon speech,
Received their mission straight from heaven
　　To civilize and teach.
So here's my hand, I stretch it forth;
　　Ye meaner lands look on!
From this day hence there's friendship firm
　　'Twixt Jonathan and John!'

X.

"They shook their hands—this noble pair—
　　And o'er the 'electric chain'
Came daily messages of peace
　　And love betwixt them twain.
When other nations, sore oppress'd,
　　Lie dark in sorrow's night,
They look to Jonathan and John,
　　And hope for coming light."

Leaving unvisited until another opportunity the large and flourishing city of Baltimore, we started from Washington for Cincinnati, by the Baltimore and Ohio Railway, at the early hour of four on a cold morning of January. The rain fell in torrents—in drops larger than fall in England in the heaviest thunderstorms of July or August. The long, wide avenues of the capital were silent and deserted, and the few gas-lights threw a flickering radiance over the swollen gutters, that rolled along like mimic rivers to join the neighboring stream of the Potomac. I had made so many friends at Washington—met so many of the most able, most eloquent, and most influential members of the House of Representatives and of the Senate—been at so many balls, parties, and dinners, and seen so much of the beauty, fashion, elegance, and grace which centre at Washington during the full tide of legislative business, that I left the city with regret. For the first thirty miles of the journey, and until the morning light streamed through the windows of the car, I was but half awake. I had confused visions of presidents, embassadors, governors, generals, colonels, judges, members of Congress, secretaries of state, editors of newspapers, beautiful women, and painted savages, tomahawks in hand, and scalps around their shoulders, all mingling and mixing together in saturnalian dance, lingering at times to drink my health in bumpers of Catawba, and then all melting away into empty air. At last we stopped at the Relay House, and our engine letting off steam banished from my hazy memory these dim and blurred recollections of the past.

From Washington to the Relay House the road runs northeast through a portion of Maryland. At this point, at a distance of nine miles from Baltimore, the rails from Washington and Baltimore unite. The road then strikes due west to Harper's Ferry, where it enters the State of Virginia—so named after Queen Elizabeth. In this land of newness, where even such modern antiquity is something to be proud of, the Virginians designate their commonwealth by the pet name of "the Old Dominion," and love to trace their descent from Englishmen of the days of Shakspeare and the Stuarts. At Harper's Ferry the Shenandoah River unites with the Potomac, and the railway crosses the united stream by a fine bridge of nine hundred feet in length, and then runs through a picturesque mountain gorge for several miles, the Potomac foaming and flowing beneath, and steep, precipitous rocks rising grandly on either side. From this point to the little city of Cumberland—famous for its productive coal-mines, and situated high amid the ridges of the Alleghany Mountains—the scenery offers a constant succession of beauties and sublimities. The engineering difficulties that have been surmounted by the projectors and builders of this line are only equaled in Europe by the famous railway from Vienna to Trieste across the Simmering Alps. But with the Austrian line the Baltimore and Ohio Railway may well stand comparison. The passage of the Alleghanies is as noble an exhibition of skill and enterprise as the passage of the Styrian Alps; and the rapid descent of the mountain, within a few miles of Wheeling, 379 miles from Baltimore, is a much greater feat than any thing of the kind attempted on any other railway in the United States. I was unfortunate enough to travel over the most sublime portion of the road in the night, and thus to lose the opportunity of describing from personal experience the scenery of the Alleghanies. From six in the morning until dark in the evening we made only 178 miles; and when we reached busy and smoky Cumberland nestled amid the mountains, the sun was setting in such a blaze of glory as to prompt the desire to wait for his reappearance in the east ere we recommenced our journey. But this was not to be. It was dark night when we reached Altamont, forty-five miles farther, and learned from the guide-book, and the not very communicative or urbane conductor of our train, that we were at the culminating point of the line, and at a height of 2626 feet above tide-water at Baltimore. From Altamont to Wheeling, on the River Ohio, a distance of 156 miles, the descent is not much less than 2400 feet. The road crosses several rivers—among others, the rapid and rejoicing Youghiogheny; the falls of Snowy Creek; the Cheat River, 310 feet wide; the beautiful Monongahela (giving its name to some famous but very bad whisky), which is crossed by a viaduct 650 feet long; and the Fish Creek, a tortuous mountain stream which makes so many twists and windings ere it reaches the Ohio that the makers of the railway found it necessary to cross it no less than eight times on substantial bridges before they could leave it behind them. As for the tunnels on this road, their name is legion—one of them, the Kingwood Tunnel, being a cut of 4100 feet through the solid rock; and the Welling Tunnel, 1250 feet.

But the rapid descent of the line from the lower summit of the Alleghany Ridge to Benwood on the Ohio, four miles from Wheeling, is the most marvelous portion of the journey. The descent is effected by a series of zigzags, first down an inclined plane for several hundred yards, then back again down another inclined plane of equal or greater length, then forward once more on the same principle, then back again, and so on until the base of the mountain is reached—the locomotive and its train literally going down stairs. Should any one who reads these pages ever travel on this line, let him travel by daylight if he wishes to see this marvelous descent and some of the finest scenery in America.

F

We arrived at the little dingy, dull city of Wheeling, in Western Virginia, before daylight on Sunday morning, and found that we could get no farther until Monday. Here we were saluted by the first snow of the season, and severally hastened to our beds to snatch the sleep which it is next to impossible to win, or even to woo, in a hot, frowsy, uncomfortable railway car, containing from fifty to sixty people, and a demoniacal furnace burning anthracite coal. Without a proper place to stow away one's hat; with no convenience even to repose the head or back, except to the ordinary height of a chair; with a current of cold outer air continually streaming in, and rendered necessary by the sulphurous heat of the furnace; and with the constant slamming of the doors at either end of the car, as the conductor goes in and out, or some weary passenger steps on to the platform to have a smoke, the passenger must, indeed, be "dead beat" who can sleep or even doze in a railway car in America. For these reasons right glad were we to reach Wheeling, and for these reasons we postponed the pleasure of making any more intimate acquaintance with it than sheets and pillows would afford until the hour of noon.

At length, refreshed by sleep, by ablution, and by breakfast, we sallied forth to look at the town and at the Ohio. The town was covered with a dense smoke—for it burns soft coal, and has several large manufactories of nails, screws, and other useful articles of iron—and some of its tall chimneys continue to vomit forth soot even on the day of rest. It is not to be inferred from this that work is done in Wheeling on the Sunday, but only that the fires are not extinguished. Perhaps this is only to save the trouble of rekindling on the Monday, for coal is so plentiful and cheap as to be retailed at one cent and a half (three farthings) a bushel. This cheapness, however, did not prevent our host at the hotel from putting down in the bill one dollar (four shillings and twopence) for the consumption in our room of less than half a bushel of the commodity, which dollar I paid, after being assured, in answer to a suggestion to that effect which I threw out for our host's consideration, that it was not a mistake, but the regular charge.

FROM WASHINGTON TO CINCINNATI. 123

The Ohio River is a yellow and turbid stream, bearing down in its broad and rapid current countless particles of fine yellow sand and clay, which it washes daily, nightly, and hourly from its soft, rich banks. It is crossed at Wheeling by a fine suspension bridge, erected on the site of one still finer, which was blown down by a hurricane two years ago. The immediate banks of the river at this point are not steep. Ranges of hills, crowned with wood, rise on either side, within a short distance, to the height of several hundred feet, and suggest, with the sole exception that there are no ruined castles, the picturesque beauties of the Rhine. There is almost daily steam-boat communication between Wheeling and Cincinnati, but, as the distance by water between the two points, in consequence of the many windings of the river, is about 600 miles, and that by railway only 240, most travelers who are pressed for time choose the latter and more expeditious route. As this was our condition, we started at 11 o'clock on Monday morning by the rail, and reached the Burnet House, Cincinnati, at 10 at night. We found rooms prepared for our reception, fires lighted, supper ready, excellent Catawba, and a cordial welcome from Colonel Coleman, the landlord of one of the largest, most noted, and most luxurious hotels in America.

The suspension bridge at Wheeling divides Western Virginia from the State of Ohio or the Buckeye State. This name was given to it in derision, but was afterward adopted by the people of Ohio, and changed from a phrase of contempt into one of endearment. A citizen of Ohio is a Buckeye. Meeting an Englishman settled in Ohio, who presented to me his three daughters, I inquired if they were English. "No," he replied, "they are Buckeyes." And what, it may be asked, is the meaning of the word? Buckeye is a species of wild chestnut, which grows so plentifully in every part of the state as to be its one pervading and prevailing tree. Its fruit bears a fancied resemblance to the eye of the buck or fawn, and hence its name. Both the leaves and the fruit are poisonous to cattle; but in this respect, like the human creatures who love tobacco, and chew it, they persist in indulging themselves with what is not good for them to such an extent that the farmers of Ohio detest the tree as a public nuisance, and would be glad if it could be totally extirpated, to make room for some other of greater utility and with fewer demerits. And doubtless the farmers will have their way sooner or later.

The snow which had fallen during the night had all disappeared before we entered the State of Ohio. The day was mild and genial, and the sun shone brilliantly. The soil as far as Columbus, the capital, a distance of 120 miles, is one deep, rich, soft stratum of disintegrated limestone, so fertile that for forty years, without change of crop, or the use of the smallest particle of manure, it has continued to grow maize, or Indian corn, in such immense quantities, that the crops rot upon the earth for want of hands to gather in the harvest. In this month of January many thousands of acres of produce are still unharvested; and the cattle, looking like pigmies amid the lofty stalks of twelve or fourteen feet high, are turned in to feed at their leisure and their pleasure. The land rolls in beautiful swelling hills, fit for the cultivation of the vine, and already crowned with many noble vineyards. From Columbus to Cincinnati—another ride of 140 miles—the country is of the same rich, fertile, and beautiful character—so beautiful, so rich, so well calculated for the happy sustenance of twenty or thirty millions of the human race, instead of two millions only who now inhabit and endeavor to cultivate it, as to recall the saying of the governor of the neighboring State of Indiana, who declared, with a profanity which drew upon him a clerical rebuke, that "the Almighty must have been in a good humor when he created Indiana and Ohio." This commonwealth is nearly as large as England, and has natural resources enabling it to feed as great a population as that of the British Isles. It is the favorite resort of the German immigration, and is estimated to number about 500,000 of that people, of whom about one fourth are Jews.

CHAPTER XVI.

"THE QUEEN CITY OF THE WEST."

Cincinnati, January 27, 1858.

CINCINNATI is as yet the greatest city of the "Great West." How long it will remain so depends on the progress of population in Missouri, and in the city of St. Louis, on the Mississippi, which many persons who fancy they look "ahead" much farther than their neighbors declare to be the central city of the Confederation, and the future capital of the United States. But a few years ago, Cincinnati was the Ultima Thule of civilization. All beyond it was wilderness and prairie. Behind it stretched the unbroken forest, where the Red Man prowled, tomahawk in hand, or the illimitable plains, where roared and fed countless herds of scarcely more savage buffaloes. The man is yet living, in hale old age, who felled the first tree in Ohio, and helped to clear the ground on which now stands what its inhabitants call the "Queen City of the West." Cincinnati is estimated to have a population of nearly 250,000 souls; contains miles of well-built and handsome streets, many stores, banks, and warehouses, public institutions, worthy by their architectural beauty to adorn any metropolis in the world, and about one hundred churches, chapels, and synagogues. Of the churches but two have any pretensions to elegance or splendor. One is the Episcopal Church, as yet unfinished; and the other the Roman Catholic Cathedral of St. Peter's, built of white freestone, and deserving to rank among the finest ecclesiastical edifices in America.

The original name of Cincinnati is said by the original settlers, and such of their descendants as can carry their memories back to such remote antiquity, to have been Losantiville. It was the intention of the first immigrants and backwoodsmen to build a city at North Bend, eighteen miles higher up the river. But Fate and Love (for there is a love-story in the history) willed it otherwise. The United States' officer in command at North Bend having become enamored of the young wife of an old pioneer, the lady was removed by her husband to Fort Washington, where Cincinnati now stands. The gallant officer followed shortly afterward, and reported officially that Fort Washington, and not North Bend, was the proper site for a military station and city. His influence or his reasons prevailed. North Bend was abandoned, and Fort Washington became the site of the future city of Cincinnati, or, as the Americans generally pronounce it, *Sinsnahta.* The name was changed a short time after its foundation to that which it now bears, in honor of the society of " the Cincinnati." It is the sixth city of the Union for population, wealth, and commerce, ranking immediately after New York, Philadelphia, Baltimore, Boston, and New Orleans. It is crowned with a coronal of perpetual and very dense black smoke, so black and dense as almost to hide it from the view of the spectator passing over in the ferry-boat to the Kentucky shore, or looking down upon it from the adjacent height of Mount Adams and the hill of the Observatory. Next to Manchester and the great manufacturing towns of Yorkshire, Lancashire, and Staffordshire, it may be called the smokiest city in the world, and in this respect far murkier than London, and far murkier than any city ought to be allowed to remain in a civilized country, and in an age of scientific progress and sanatory improvement. But, disagreeable as the smoke of Cincinnati may be, it affords an unmistakable proof of its industrial and commercial activity. The city contains several large manufactories of railway cars and locomotives; a distillery, which produces whisky and alcohol at the rate of 2500 barrels per week, a large proportion of which lately found its way to France, to aid in the manufacture of "native" cogniac; two or three manufactories of household furniture for the supply of the "Far West;" and many minor establishments for the manufacture of agricultural implements and tools.

But the chief wealth of Cincinnati is derived from the hogs raised in the rich agricultural districts of Ohio, and slaughtered here to the number of about 600,000 annually. The slaughter-houses are the great curiosities of the place; but, having a respect for hog as an article of diet, and relishing, at fitting seasons, both the ham and the rasher of bacon, I would not impair that respect or diminish that relish by witnessing the wholesale slaughter of the animal, however scientifically the slaughtering might be effected. I therefore left the slaughter-houses unvisited, contented to believe, upon hearsay, the marvelous tales which are related of the dexterity of the slaughterers, who, armed with heavy hammers, which they hold in both hands, are sometimes known to stun as many as sixty hogs in a minute, leaving them in that state to an assistant butcher, who, with almost equal rapidity, follows in their wake, and cuts their throats before they have time to recover from the stunning blow and vent their alarm by a single shriek. The 600,000 hogs slaughtered in the city are converted into packed merchandise with less noise than often attends the killing of one porker in the farmsteads of England. From the moment when the hog received the first hammerstroke until it was singed, cleaned, cut up, placed in brine, and packed in a cask for exportation, not more than two hours were formerly suffered to elapse. But this celerity, being unnatural, led to mischief. The pork, drowned in brine before it had time to become cold, caused a fermentation in the pickle, and this fermentation, in its turn, caused a disease in the pork which was called measles, and which, whether deserving or not of this appellation, rendered it unwholesome. Much injury was thus done to the trade. The cause of the mischief was fully reported upon by the British consul at New Orleans; and the men of Cincinnati, made wise by experience, now stay their hands and allow the pork to cool before they pickle it.

All Cincinnati is redolent of swine. Swine prowl about the streets and act the part of scavengers until they are ready to become merchandise and visit Europe. Swine are driven into it daily and hourly by every avenue, but not one of them ever goes out again alive. Barrels of them line all the quays; cartloads of their carcasses traverse the city at all seasons; and palaces and villas are built, and vineyards and orchards cultivated, out of the proceeds of their flesh, their bones, their lard, their bristles, and their feet.

In the early days of the pork trade, the feet and entrails of the swine were cast as rubbish on to the quays and streets, or swept into the waters of the Ohio, to be thence transferred, via the Mississippi, into the Gulf of Mexico. But the Cincinnatians have learned more wisdom, and not the smallest portion of the animal is now allowed to be wasted. The entrails are boiled into lard; the feet are prepared as an article of food, or stewed into glue; and the blood, carefully collected, is used for various chemical purposes, besides being employed in the manufacture of black-puddings for home consumption. The average value of the hog before he is slaughtered is about ten dollars, or £2 sterling, so that from this source alone one million and a quarter sterling is annually brought into the purses of the farmers and people of Ohio and of its chief commercial city of Cincinnati. So plentiful are swine in Ohio, so much more plentiful and cheap in some parts than coals, that ere now pork has been burned instead of fuel to keep up the fires of steam-boats on the Ohio. Only three days ago I read a newspaper paragraph in reprobation of such cruel extravagance.

Another source of wealth has recently been developed in Ohio, chiefly by the skill, enterprise, and public spirit of one man, Mr. Nicholas Longworth, to whom America owes the introduction of the grape culture for the purpose of winemaking.

With its endless varieties of soil, and with climates of all degrees of heat and cold; in some parts sunny as Naples, Spain, and Barbary, and in others as temperate as France and Germany, it was to be expected that America possessed one or more indigenous grapes. Mr. Longworth, of whom and of whose exertions in the cause of temperance and of good wine I might say much more than space and time will allow, has calculated that the varieties of grapes in America amount to no less than the almost incredible number of five thousand. But no one knew how to turn the boundless treasure to proper account, for the production of it lay upon the surface, but might as well have been like the pearls that Gray sings of—perdu in the dark, unfathomed caves of ocean, until Mr. Longworth appeared. And then the hills gushed into fertility, and the world received the gift of Catawba.

The earliest mention of the vine in America dates as far back as 1564, when wines were made both in Florida and Louisiana. The Jesuits—men with keen eyes to spy out the fatness of the land, and who, in all countries, have proved themselves skillful cultivators of the soil, were among the first to appropriate good locations to themselves and to plant vineyards. Unluckily, the French government of that day, through a stupid feeling of jealousy, ordered all the vineyards of Louisiana to be destroyed, lest American wines should compete injuriously with those of France in the markets of the world. Were it not for this barbarous folly, the Southern States of the Union might long ago have produced wine as well as cotton, rice, and sugar. But, in consequence of the absolute nature of the prohibition, the vineyards were abandoned, and the wild grapes of the North American continent were left to their own vagrant fancies, to be eaten by the wolf and the fox, or the Red Indian, undisturbed by the care or the pruning-knife of the vintager.

John Bull loves his beer, and cares but little for wine. When he can afford the juice of the grape, he likes it strong. There was a time, if we are to rely upon tradition, and upon the evidence of old songs and ballads, when the favorite drink of the upper classes was claret; and next to claret, Burgundy. But the famous treaty concluded with Portugal in 1759, and known as the Methuen Treaty, introduced unsuspecting John to a new and more potent beverage called Port, and vitiated the national taste. Most people remember the epigram as regards the effect which Port wine had upon the Scotch:

> "Firm and erect the Caledonian stood,
> His meat was mutton, and his claret good.
> 'Let him drink Port!' the British statesman cried:
> He drank the poison, and his spirit died!"

John Bull is now, unluckily, so accustomed to the full-bodied, brandied wines of Portugal and Spain, that he does not appreciate the light, harmless wines of France and Germany. As for the wines of Cincinnati, scarcely one Englishman in ten thousand has ever heard of them. The late Duke of Wellington, who, if we are to believe some of his over-ardent admirers, knew every thing, and was as universal a genius as Shakspeare, was in this respect in advance of his countrymen. He had tasted Catawba wine; for, when a gentleman from Cincinnati was introduced to him two years before he died, he said, "Oh, I know Cincinnati. It is the residence of Miss Groesbeck, and is famous for Sparkling Catawba; Catawba's a good wine!"

It was not until the year 1799 that the grape culture excited much attention in America. Shortly before that time the wild "sand" grape, that grew on the banks of the Ohio in great profusion, was subjected to the wine-press by some French settlers in the Marietta District. This wine, even at that early period, was pronounced to be almost equal to Rhenish. The late Mr. John Dufour, one of the Swiss pioneers who emigrated to America in 1805, improved upon the efforts of his predecessor. But the progress of the new thing was slow, and it was not till some years after the death of this gentleman that the real Bacchus of the West appeared in the person of Mr. Nicholas Longworth, of Cincinnati — a man whom the Greeks would have apotheosized; and who, if he had lived two thousand years ago, and done as much for his country and the world as he has done in our day, would have been ranked among heroes and demi-gods, and loomed largely on our imaginations through the haze and mist of antiquity. Like Bacchus of old, he has taught the people how to cultivate and press the grape, and to use it for health, and strength, and length of days. Mr. Longworth, considering the variety of soil and climate in America, and the abundance of wild grapes that grow from Virginia southward and westward, arrived at the conclusion — which proved to be a sound one — that if wine could be produced in the Old World, it could also be produced in the New. Thirty or forty years ago he made some experiments with French and German grapes, but they were failures, as many great enterprises are at their commencement. In a letter to the Cincinnati Horticultural Society dated three years back, he says, "I have for thirty years experimented on the foreign grape, both for the table and for wine. In the acclimation of plants I do not believe, for the White Sweet Water does not succeed as well with me as it did thirty years since. I obtained a large variety of French grapes from Mr. Loubat many years since. They were from the vicinity of Paris and Bordeaux. From Madeira I obtained six thousand vines of their best wine grapes. Not one was found worthy of cultivation in this latitude, and all were rooted from the vineyards. As a last experiment, I imported seven thousand vines from the mountains of Sura, in the vicinity of Salins, in France. At that point the vine region suddenly ends, and many vines are there cultivated on the north side of the mountain, where the ground is covered with snow the whole winter long, from three to four feet deep. Nearly all lived, and embraced about twenty varieties of the most celebrated wine grapes of France. But, after a trial of five years, I was obliged to throw them all away. I also imported samples of wine made from all the grapes of Europe. One variety alone—the celebrated Arbois wine, which partakes slightly of Champagne character—would compete with our Catawba."

The results of Mr. Longworth's hopeful perseverance, indomitable energy, and long experience, not only in his own city and neighborhood of Cincinnati, but elsewhere on the American continent, were, that he abandoned the European grape, and selected out of the 5000 indigenous varieties eighty-three. From these eighty-three he again selected twelve as alone fit for the production of wine. These twelve were the Catawba, the Cape, the Isabella, the Bland's Madeira, the Ohio, the Lenoir, the Missouri, the Norton's Seedling, the Herbemont's Madeira, the Minor Seedling, the White Catawba, and the Mammoth Catawba.

Having resolved to concentrate his attention upon Catawba, with its rich muscadine flavor, first found growing on the banks of the Catawba River in Carolina, he succeeded, about ten years ago, in producing out of it the Sparkling Catawba wine, which competent judges, who have tasted all the wines of the world, declare to be equal to any sparkling wines which Europe can boast, whether they come from the Rhine or the Moselle, or from the Champagne districts of France. Perhaps these pages will be the first intimation that the English people will receive of the existence of this bounty of nature; but there is no risk of false prophecy in the prediction here hazarded, that not many years will elapse before both the dry and the sparkling Catawba will be recognized in Europe, as they are in America, as among the purest of all wines, except claret and Burgundy. No red wines of any great delicacy or value have been produced in Ohio, or any other state of the Union; but Mr. Longworth, Mr. Robert Buchanan, Mr. Werk, and other eminent growers near Cincinnati, are of opinion that wines equal both to red and white Burgundy will be successfully grown in Ohio, South Carolina, and California. As yet there are no symptoms in America that the clarets of France will ever be surpassed or equaled. But far different is it with French Champagne, who as the Queen of Wines must yield her sceptre and throne to one purer and brighter than she, who sits on the banks of the Ohio, and whom Mr. Longworth serves as chief adviser and prime minister.

Longfellow, worthy to celebrate the wines of Longworth, sings of Catawba:

"'This song of mine
Is a song of the vine,
To be sung by the glowing embers
Of wayside inns
When the rain begins
To darken the drear Novembers.

*   *   *

"For richest and best
Is the wine of the West,
That grows by the beautiful river,
Whose sweet perfume
Fills all the room
With a benison on the giver."

Mr. Longfellow maintains, with all the fervor of an American as well as of a poet, that European wines are drugged and poisoned; that Port burns, and is the mother of podagra; that sherry is a sham, and that Champagne is a vile concoction, born of turnips and of gooseberries, not of the vine:

> "Drugged is their juice
> For foreign use,
> When shipped o'er the reeling Atlantic,
> To rack our brains
> With the fever pains
> That have driven the Old World frantic.
>
> * * * *
>
> "To the sewers and sinks
> With all such drinks,
> And after them tumble the mixer!"

But not so with Catawba; for Catawba is pure. Hear, ye lovers of wholesome drink, another ditty from a native of the Old Country, who knows how to appreciate the dainty luxuries of the New:

CATAWBA WINE.

> "Ohio's green hill-tops
> Glow bright in the sun,
> And yield us more treasure
> Than Rhine or Garonne;
> They give us Catawba,
> The pure and the true,
> As radiant as sunlight,
> As soft as the dew,
> And fragrant as gardens
> When summer is new:
> Of all the glad vintage
> The purest and best,
> Catawba the nectar
> And balm of the West!
>
> "Champagne is too often
> A trickster malign,
> That flows from the apple,
> And not from the vine.
> But thou, my Catawba,
> Art mild as a rose,
> And sweet as the lips
> Of my love, when they close
> To give back the kisses
> My passion bestows.
> Thou'rt born of the vintage,
> And fed on its breast,
> Catawba the nectar
> And balm of the West!

"When pledging the lovely,
 This sparkler we'll kiss;
When drinking to true hearts,
 We'll toast them in this;
For Catawba is like them,
 Though tender, yet strong,
As pleasant as morning,
 And soft as a song,
Whose delicate beauty
 The echoes prolong.
Catawba! Heart-warmer!
 Soul-cheerer! Life-zest!
Catawba the nectar
 And balm of the West!"

Mr. Longworth's son-in-law kindly gave our party an invitation to accompany him on a visit to the vineyards. They are situated on a hill-top and slope overlooking the windings of the beautiful Ohio—beautiful at a distance, but somewhat thick and turbid on a close inspection. We there found an old soldier of Napoleon, from Saxe-Weimar, who fought at Waterloo, and afterward retired to his native fields to cultivate the vine. Mr. Longworth having sent to Europe for persons skilled in the manufacture of Rhenish and Moselle wines, had the fortune to discover this excellent old man, good soldier, and skillful vintager. Soon after his arrival he was placed in the responsible position of chief wine-maker and superintendent under Mr. Longworth. Under the guidance of this venerable gentleman—Mr. Christian Schnicke—we traversed the vineyards, learned the difficulties he had surmounted and yet hoped to surmount; the varieties of grape on which he had made experiments; the names of the wines he had succeeded in producing, and the number of acres that, year after year, he brought under cultivation. We ended by repairing to his domicil, on the crown of the hill, where he set before us bread and cheese, and a whole constellation of native wines. Among others were Dry Catawba and Sparkling Catawba, both excellent; a not very palatable wine produced from grapes imported from the Cape of Good Hope; and two other wines almost equal to Catawba itself—one from the grape called the Isabella, rosy-red as the morning, and

THE BANKS OF THE OHIO.—MR. LONGWORTH'S VINEYARDS.

sparkling as the laughter of a child; the other a dry wine, of a pale amber color, clear, odoriferous, and of most delicate flavor, and almost equal to Johannisberger. This wine, it appeared, had not arrived at the honors of a name; was not known to commerce; and was simply designated by Mr. Schnicke as the wine of the Minor Seedling grape. As so excellent a beverage could not remain forever without a name, it received one on this occasion in the manner recorded by Colonel Fuller in the following extract from a letter to the *New Orleans Picayune:* "On visiting Mr. Longworth's vineyard in the neighborhood of Cincinnati, vineyards which yield from six to seven hundred gallons to the acre, we found the 'boss' to be an old soldier of Napoleon the Great, and as devoted to the memory of the emperor as he is enthusiastic in the culture of the vine. Producing a very choice brand of the color of amber, and with a bouquet that filled the room, called the wine of the Minor Seedling, objection was taken to the name, but not to the article; so it was there and then christened 'Mackay' wine, in honor of the poet who was present. Mr. Longworth afterward confirmed the new name in a prose as well as a poetical epistle."

It is, to some extent, owing to the increase of the cultivation of the vine in Ohio that so many Germans have settled in Cincinnati and the neighborhood. There are about fifty thousand of these people in the city, of whom one fourth are Jews. The Germans inhabit a district of their own, over the Miami Canal, which runs through a district of Cincinnati. To this canal they have given the name of the Rhine, and on its banks they have erected concert-gardens such as they have in Germany. Here, embowered *unter den Lauben*, they congregate on Sunday evenings, the old stagers with wooden shoes on their feet and night-caps on their heads, and the young in a more cosmopolitan costume, to drink lager beer, smoke long pipes, and sing the songs of "Fatherland." They have also erected a German theatre, established German schools, and one or two, if not more, German newspapers.

It should not be omitted from this record of Catawba and the vintage of America that Mr. Longworth was the first friend of Mr. Hiram Powers, so well known as the sculptor of the "Greek Slave." Mr. Powers, as he takes pleasure in remembering, was greatly aided in the early struggles of his professional career by Mr. Longworth. Nor is Hiram Powers the only artist whom the Western Bacchus has befriended, for Mr. Longworth uses his great wealth to noble purposes, and never more willingly than in aiding the artist of genius up those few first steps of the ladder of fame which it is always difficult, and sometimes impossible, to climb.

CHAPTER XVII.

ST. LOUIS, MISSOURI.

St. Louis, Jan. 31st, 1858.

WESTWARD—ever westward! After no less than four accidents to our train on the Ohio and Mississippi Railway, happily involving no other evil consequences than the smashing of the company's engine and two or three cars, the sacrifice of many valuable hours, and the loss of an amount of patience difficult to estimate, though once possessed by all the passengers, myself included, we arrived at the miserable village, though called a city, of Jeffersonville, in Indiana, nearly opposite to Louisville, in Kentucky, on the River Ohio. The train was due at an early hour of the afternoon, but did not reach Jeffersonville until half past nine in the evening, long before which time the steam ferry-boat had ceased to ply, and the captain of which refused to relight the fires of his engines to carry the passengers across. We saw the lights of the large city gleaming temptingly across the stream, but there being no means of conveyance, we were all reluctantly compelled to betake ourselves to the best inn at Jeffersonville, and bad, very bad, was the best. We had had nothing to eat or to drink all day, in consequence of the accident to our train having befallen us in an out-of-the-way place, and in the very heart of the wilderness; and such of us as were not teetotalers looked forward to a comfortable supper and glass of wine, or toddy, after our fatigue and disappointments. But, on asking for supper and wine at the hotel, we were told by mine host that we were in a temperance state, and that nothing in the way of drink would be served except milk, tea, coffee, and lemonade. A thoughtful friend at Cincinnati had given us on starting a bottle of Bourbon whisky twenty years old; and we told mine host that, if he would provide us with glasses, hot water, sugar, and a corkscrew, we should enjoy his meat, find our own drink, and set Fate at defiance. Hot water he had, glasses he had, sugar he had, but no corkscrew. Under the circumstances, he advised us either to break off the neck of the bottle, or go round to the shop of the apothecary in the adjoining street. He thought that personage would be able to draw the cork for us, or "loan" or sell us a corkscrew. Colonel Fuller and myself held a council of war, and resolved, lest we should waste the liquor, to make friends with the apothecary. A corkscrew was procured from that respectable practitioner—not borrowed, but bought and paid for, and after a fair supper, and some excellent toddy, we turned into our miserable beds. Next morning at an early hour, glad to leave Jeffersonville and all that belonged to it, we crossed in the steamer to Louisville, and once more found ourselves in a land of plenty and comfort, in a flourishing city, in an excellent hotel—the "Galt House," one of the best conducted establishments in America; in a state where the Maine Liquor Law was only known by name, and where it was not necessary to go to the apothecary's shop to obtain, by a sneaking, hypocritical, false pretense, the glass of wine, beer, or spirits that custom, taste, health, or absolute free-will and pleasure demanded.

Louisville is the principal commercial city of the State of Kentucky, well situated on the Ohio, and having direct communication with the Mississippi, and with all the immense internal navigation of these great rivers. It contains a population of upward of 60,000, and next to Cincinnati, which it aspires to rival, is the greatest emporium of the pork trade on the North American continent. The annual number of hogs slaughtered here is nearly 300,000, and is yearly increasing.

On the second night after our arrival, I and my fellow-traveler were alarmed several hours after we had retired to rest by the loud cry of "Fire! fire!" several times repeated in the lobby adjoining our rooms. I rushed out of bed, opened the door, and saw a negro woman rushing frantically past. She called "Fire! fire!" and passed out of sight. Another door was opened, and a woman's voice exclaimed, "It is not in the Galt House; there's no danger!" In the mean time, as quick as thought, an uproar of bells and the rattle of engines were heard; and knowing how frequent fires were in America, and how much more frequent at hotels than in other places, we prepared ourselves to escape. But, by the blaze that suddenly illumined our bedrooms, we saw that the conflagration was at the opposite "block" or row of buildings, at a manufactory of naphtha and other distilled spirits. The fire raged till long after daylight, and all efforts to subdue it being utterly futile, the "boys" with the engines directed their energies to save the adjoining buildings, in which they happily succeeded. At breakfast in the morning we learned from the negro waiter who attended us that the fire had proved fatal to his good master. The landlord of the hotel had lain for three days previously at the point of death, and the noise and alarm created by the fire, and the dread lest it should extend to his premises, had acted so powerfully on his weakened frame that he had expired in a paroxysm caused by the excitement.

There is nothing to detain a traveler in Louisville unless it be private friendship and hospitality, of both of which we had our share. After three days we took our departure for St. Louis, but found it as difficult to quit Louisville as it had been to arrive at it. We crossed to Jeffersonville to take the train for the Mississippi, and were in the cars within ten minutes of the appointed time. We had not proceeded five hundred yards from the "dépôt," or station, when our locomotive, which happily had not put on all its steam, ran off the rails, and stuck hard and dry upon the embankment. Here we waited two hours in hope of assistance, but none being forthcoming, we made the best of the calamity, and returned to our old quarters at Louisville for another day. On the morrow we again started for the same place; but this time being more successful, we arrived, traveling at the rate of not more than fourteen miles an hour, at the bank of the great river Mississippi. For a week previously I had been looking forward with pleasant anticipation to the first glimpse of the "Father of Waters." But at this point the scenery is not picturesque. The shores are low, flat, and unvaried by the slightest elevation; but the stream itself—broad, rapid, and turbid, and swarming with steam-boats and river craft—has associations of wealth and power which go far to make amends for the absence of natural beauty. Cincinnati was at no remote period the Ultima Thule of civilization, and the farthest city of the West. But in America the "West" is very difficult to fix. Ask the people of Cincinnati, and they will tell you it is at St. Louis. At St. Louis it is in the new territory of Kansas. At Kansas it is at Utah, the paradise of the Mormons. At Utah the West is in Oregon; and at Oregon it is in California or Vancouver's Island, and the shores of the Pacific Ocean. Every one remembers Pope's line—

"Ask where's the North? At York, 'tis on the Tweed;"

and how he ends by giving up the inquiry in despair of an answer, looking for it only

"In Nova Zembla or the Lord knows where."

In America the true West is quite as difficult to "locate," and is pushed so far from one ocean toward the other, by the restless love of adventure, by the *auri sacra fames*, and by the "go-ahead-ativeness" characteristic of the Anglo-Saxon race on this continent, that West and East melt insensibly into each other, and the ultra-occidentalist finds himself looking at China and Japan in the Far East before he is aware that he has reached the limit of his researches.

St. Louis remains, next to Cincinnati, the greatest city of the West; but, as its growth has been more rapid than that of its sister on the Ohio, and as it contains within itself far greater elements of prosperity and increase, it is likely, within a few years, to surpass it in trade, population, and extent. It is already the largest and most flourishing place between Cincinnati and San Francisco, and will, in all probability, within a quarter of a century contain and employ half a million of people. It is situated on the Mississippi, about twenty miles below the point at which that river, pure and lucent in all its upper course, receives the dark and muddy waters of the Missouri. It was founded so early as the year 1746, by Laclede, a Frenchman, and named in honor of St. Louis of France, or, as some say, of Louis XV., who, though a Louis, was assuredly no saint. Until its transfer to the United States in 1804, it remained a village of a few log huts, inhabited by trappers, who traded with the red men for the spoils of the forest, exchanging bad rum and execrable brandy for peltry, and detestable muskets, warranted not to go off, for furs that sold exceedingly well in the markets of Europe. The first brick house in St. Louis was built in 1813; and the first steam-boat arrived at its *levée*, or quay, in 1817, having taken six weeks to ascend the Mississippi. This voyage is now performed in six days; but, before the introduction of steam, when flat-bottomed boats were rowed, or otherwise painfully propelled up the stream, it occupied from six to seven months. After all, America need not crow so very loudly over the " Old Country." It is steam that has been the making of them both, and given them their wonderful impulse. Were it not for steam, what would be England's place in the world? And were it not for steam, what would the United States of America be? England would be better off than the United States as regards wealth and population, and civilized America would be a mere strip on the seaboard, as it was in the days of Washington, when it took months to go up and down the Mississippi, and when a man might lose not only his time, but his scalp, in the perilous adventure. It was not until 1820, when the population of St. Louis was under 5000, that the place became of any importance. Twenty years afterward the population reached 17,000. In 1852 it exceeded 100,000, and in 1857 it was variously estimated at from 150,000 to 180,000. It is still rapidly increasing. English, Irish, German, and the surplus population of such old states and communities as Massachusetts, Connecticut, and others in New England, continually flock into it, and beyond it, to add to its wealth, and to develop the resources of the great and fertile regions lying between the Mississippi and the Rocky Mountains, and the remote sources of the Missouri. Men are still living in the city, owners of "town lots," for which they paid, forty years ago, the government price of one dollar and a quarter per acre. These lots, in consequence of the enormous rise in the value of real estate, are not to be obtained at the present day under six hundred or sometimes one thousand dollars per foot frontage, and are covered with noble buildings and lines of commercial palaces. These prosperous citizens and millionaires deserve their good fortune; and if there be any who envy them, they go out into the back woods, still farther west, in the hope that equal luck will attend their own speculations in land and their own conflicts with the border savages. Such men are the pioneers of civilization, and bear the brunt and heat of the battle. In early life they hold their lands on the sufferance of the Indians, and have to guard their possessions like beleaguered fortresses in an enemy's country, with the warwhoop ringing in their ears, and the murderous tomahawk suspended continually over their heads.

St. Louis, via Washington and Cincinnati, is about 1200 miles from New York, 20 miles below the mouth of the Missouri, and 174 miles above the junction of the Ohio with the Mississippi. Above, it commands the navigation of the Missouri for nearly 2000 miles, and of the Mississippi to the Falls of St. Anthony for 750. Below, it commands the Mississippi for 1295 miles to New Orleans, and from New Orleans to the Gulf of Mexico, 94 miles. Besides this extent of direct riverine traffic, it commands that of the various tributaries of the Mississippi; rivers, many of them larger than the Rhine or the Danube, such as the Ohio, navigable from its junction with the Mississippi at Cairo, to Pittsburgh, in Pennsylvania, a distance of 1000 miles; the Red River, navigable for 1100 miles; the White River, for 400 miles; the Tennessee, for 600 miles; the Cumberland, for 300 miles; the Wabash, for 300 miles; and many others inferior in length or importance to these, but navigable for a hundred or two hundred miles beyond the point of their confluence with the larger streams to which they run.

The levee of St. Louis extends along the right bank of the Mississippi for nearly six miles, about half of which length is densely built upon. No city in the world offers to the gaze of the spectators such a vast assemblage of river steam-boats. As many as one hundred and seventy, loading and unloading, have been counted along the levee at one time. These vessels, which, like all those that ply on the Mississippi and the Ohio, are of peculiar construction, painted white, and with two tall black funnels, are built for internal traffic, and would play but a sorry part in the salt water if the wind blew ever so little. But for riverine purposes they are admirable, and, were it not for the occasional mischance of a collision in the fog, or the still more frequent casualty of a blow-up from the bursting of a boiler, would afford the traveler the safest, as they do the pleasantest, mode of conveyance in America. The people of St. Louis are as proud of their steam-boats as of their city. One of them, in conversation with a newly-arrived emigrant from the "Old Country," who had discoursed too well and too wisely to please his listener on the wealth, power, and greatness of England, put a stop to all farther argument by exclaiming, like a man of large ideas, "Darn your little island! when I was there I found it so little I was afeerd I should tumble off. Look you, sirree! we've steam-boats enough at St. Louis to tow Great Britain out into the Atlantic and stick her fast — opposite New York harbor!" But, as just observed, these steamers are but frail affairs, and one hour of an Atlantic storm would be sufficient to make wrecks of all that ever plied or ever will ply upon the drumly bosom of the "Father of Waters." Had the "Britisher" thus rebuked possessed ideas commensurate with those of his Yankee friend, he might have rejoined that it would take the combined strength of all the steamers between St. Louis and New Orleans to tow the *Great Eastern* from Dover to Calais, and that the whole fleet would in all probability perish in the gigantic attempt.

For steam tonnage it is estimated that St. Louis is the third

ST. LOUIS, MISSOURI.

city in the Union. New York ranks first, with a tonnage in the year 1854 of 101,478; New Orleans second, with a tonnage of 57,147; and St. Louis third, with a tonnage little inferior to that of New Orleans itself, amounting to 48,557. The manufactures of St. Louis are numerous and important, and comprise twenty flour-mills, about the same number of saw-mills, twenty-five founderies, engine and boiler manufactories and machine-shops, eight or ten establishments engaged in the manufacture of railroad cars and locomotives, besides several chemical, soap, and candle works, and a celebrated type foundery, which supplies the whole of the Far West with the types that are absolutely necessary to the creation of all new cities in the wilderness. A church, a forge, a hotel, and a daily newspaper—with these four, aided by a doctor or two, and as many lawyers and bankers, a newly-named city will take its place on the map, and speculators who have bought land at a dollar and a quarter per acre will look to make their fortunes by simply holding on to their purchase until streets run over their grounds, and they become in America such men as the Duke of Bedford, Lord Portman, and the Marquis of Westminster are in London, and Lord Derby in his town of Preston.

St. Louis contains two theatres, and the two finest lecture-rooms in the United States. The upper and lower rooms of the Mercantile Library Association are unrivaled for this purpose; and neither New York nor Boston contains any lecture-rooms at all to be compared to them for elegance of construction and decoration, or adaptability to the end proposed.

The city contains at most times a large floating population of Englishmen—of a class that America is not very anxious to receive, and is at this moment somewhat puzzled what to do with—the Mormon emigration. These fanatics, who are mostly recruited from the manufacturing districts of Wales and the north and middle of England, with a few from Scotland, make St. Louis their resting-place, on their way from New York to the Salt Lake City, and recruit both their energies and their finances before starting on their long and perilous overland pilgrimage to Utah. They generally remain here for a year, and, being for the most part expert handicraftsmen or mechanics, they manage without much difficulty to procure employment. Those who have no trades set up small grocery stores, or betake themselves to the easy, and, in America, most profitable occupation, of hackney-coach drivers. Horses are cheap; horse-feed is cheap; but riding in carriages in every part of the Union is most exorbitantly dear. The Jehus, having no law to control them, and no fear of policeman or magistrate before their eyes, charge exactly what they please. To drive from a steam-boat to a hotel that may happen to be less than a hundred yards distant is seldom to be accomplished under a dollar; and a drive which in London would be overpaid at two shillings, costs two dollars in any American city except Boston, which in this respect is a city of law and order, and an example to the whole of the Union. Either at this profession or some other the Mormons make money, and generally depart from St. Louis well laden with the spoils of the Gentiles, leaving the next batch from England to imitate their example.

The mineral resources of St. Louis and the State of Missouri are abundant. About eighty miles to the westward of St. Louis, on a line of railway which is nearly completed, exist two hills or "mountains" of iron ore. One is called the Iron Mountain, and the other the Pilot Knob. The base of the Iron Mountain, in the country of St. Francis, covers an area of about five hundred acres. It rises to a height of about 270 feet, and is estimated to contain above the surface no less than 200 millions of tons of iron ore, yielding from sixty-eight to seventy per cent. of pure iron. The ore below the surface is probably quite as abundant. Over an area of 20,000 acres, in the plain from the midst of which this singular mountain rises, are scattered huge blocks of similar formation, some of them sharp-pointed and pyramidal, and deeply imbedded in the earth; others, unshapely and cumbrous, are lying loose upon the soil, and seeming as if they had dropped from the moon, or were the *disjecta membra* of some broken asteroid wandering in too close proximity to the sphere of the earth's attraction, and dashed to pieces in their fall against the superior planet, where they have at length found a resting-place. The Pilot Knob is eight miles farther to the west of St. Louis, and rises to the height of seven hundred feet. It contains quite as large an amount of iron ore as the Iron Mountain, though the percentage of pure iron differs by one or two degrees. There is a third hill in the vicinity, called the Shepherd Mountain, which is almost equally rich in iron; besides a plateau covered with loose iron ore, which is to be gathered in nuggets and blocks from the weight of one or two pounds to lumps of three and four hundred. As Missouri possesses coal as well as iron, these mountains will in due time make her richer than if she possessed all the gold of California or Australia. Several blast-furnaces have been at full work in this region for the last four years, and many more are in process of erection.

The country around St. Louis contains not only these immense quantities of iron, but large mines of copper and lead, and some excellent quarries of what has been called "Missouri marble." Many of the public buildings in St. Louis are composed of this stone, which is of a brownish-gray color, and susceptible of a high polish. Altogether St. Louis is one of the most flourishing places in America. It is full of life and activity, but too densely covered with a pall of smoke to be a very agreeable abode for more than a day or two to the traveler who journeys either for health or recreation.

CHAPTER XVIII.

THE MORMONS.

St. Louis, February, 1858.

THE collision between the government of the United States and the singular theocracy of the Mormons, which has established itself in the Great Salt Lake Valley, under the presidency of Brigham Young, and which took place in the "fall" of last year, was inevitable, sooner or later. The United States proclaim perfect liberty of religion — perfect liberty even of the grossest superstition and fanaticism — so that

Brigham Young and his apostles and elders may, if it so please them, and if they can afford the extravagance, indulge themselves with a hundred wives apiece, and exclaim, like their kindred Mohammedans, that " God is great, and Joe Smith is his prophet !" without forfeiting thereby the right of the Territory of Utah or Deseret to be admitted in due time, with its own laws, religion, and customs, among the sovereign republics of the United States. Brigham Young, the choice of the people, was for many years, *de jure* as well as *de facto*, the Governor of Utah, and as fully entitled to be so as the respective Governors of New York, Massachusetts, Virginia, Pennsylvania, or any other state, are to administer the laws of those commonwealths. It would have been well if the question had been left in that state for twenty or thirty years—if the Mormons had been allowed, in the wilderness where they have fixed their abode, to govern themselves in their own way, and to give their knavish and disgusting superstition rope enough to hang itself. It was highly desirable for a thousand reasons that no violence should be done, or seem to be done, to that great principle of religious freedom and equality which the founders of the Union established. Unfortunately, however, the question was hurried forward with undue and unwise haste. From small beginnings the Mormons have grown into a large community; and from equally small beginnings of interference the government of the United States was drawn on, step after step, to assume a position with respect to them from which there was no honorable escape on either side. To do the Mormons justice—and, much as the world must loathe their filthy doctrine, they are entitled to fair consideration—they did their utmost to avoid collision. When their pretended prophet was cruelly and treacherously murdered by a gang of bloodthirsty ruffians, and elevated into the dignity of martyrdom; when they were driven from one settlement to another, and finally expelled from Nauvoo, their new Zion—they withdrew beyond the Rocky Mountains, that they might be out of the way of all neighbors—that they might live with a belt of wilderness around them, and wive, thrive, work, and worship after their own fashion. But it was not decreed that they should remain in this state of isolation.

Deseret, or Utah, is in the high road from the Atlantic to the Pacific. The discovery of gold in California, which was partly due to Mormon agency, has made their territory a station, through which the civilization and the trade of the Atlantic sea-board must pour to the sea-board of the Pacific, and drawn them into that community of Anglo-Saxon nations with whom they have so little in common but their industry, their pluck, and their mother tongue. The inevitable collision was thus hastened. The Mormons refused obedience to the laws of the United States; drove from their territory the officers of the supreme government legally appointed; overruled the authority of the President and Congress of the United States —by the mere will of Brigham Young, a theocrat and a despot, as well as the choice of the people—and rendered it impossible for the government at Washington, without loss of dignity and sacrifice of principle, to do other than enforce obedience by the strong arm of physical force. If left alone, Mormonism, like other mischiefs and absurdities, might have died out, and given the world no farther trouble. But it is the fortune or the fatality of religions, new or old, and of forms of faith of every kind, that they thrive upon obstruction and hostility. Nothing in its previous history did so much for Mormonism as the murder of Joe Smith.

The next great aid and impetus which their cause received was the savage expulsion of the Mormons from Missouri, and their exodus, in the midst of a severe winter, with their goods and chattels, their plows, their oxen and their kine, their wives and their children, across the wilderness for upward of two thousand miles, and through the gorges of the Rocky Mountains to the Great Salt Lake, where they succeeded in establishing themselves, amid dangers and difficulties unparalleled in history. It only needed a hostile collision with the army of the United States to make Mormonism a still greater fact than it is, and to establish it, perhaps, too firmly to be shaken. The United States government sent, late last autumn, a small force of only 2500 men, of whom only one half were really available, to reduce the fanatics to obedience; and the Mormons, in a rude, wild country, defended by mountain passes, in which a hundred men might destroy an invading force of fifty times their number, resolved to do battle against their assailants. Upon the rule that all is fair in war, the Mormons engaged the Indian tribes in their defense. Seventy-five wagons, containing the stores and provisions of the United States' army, fell into their hands; they burnt up all the grass and every green thing for two hundred miles on the route which the soldiers had to take; and, animated with the fiercest spirit of resistance, they organized a force, independent of their Indian auxiliaries, three times as numerous as that of their invaders. Every man capable of bearing arms was enrolled; and they had a mounted troop of shepherds, huntsmen, and others, well skilled in the use of the rifle, every man of whom knew all the mountain passes and gorges, of which their adversaries were totally ignorant. But, after a great show of resistance and still greater bluster, the Mormons, finding the ultimate hopelessness of the struggle, unexpectedly made a *quasi* submission at the last moment; and the United States' government, glad of an opportunity to end this impolitic struggle, appointed another governor—not a Mormon—in the room of Brigham Young. Thus did President Buchanan and his cabinet retire from a false position.

To coerce the Mormons into submission, and to compel them to conform to the laws of that great Union of which their territory forms a part, may or may not have been a desirable object to attempt; but to have made the attempt and failed would have been a political and social crime of the highest magnitude. Its results would have fanned the flame of Mormon fanaticism and audacity, and brought into their ranks a whole army of scamps, filibusters, and soldiers of fortune ready to fight for any cause that promised pay, promotion, and power, and that added the additional inducement, potent with such scoundrels, of a harem with as many wives as Brigham Young or Heber Kimbal. The United States, having entered upon this war, were bound to conquer; but it can scarcely be asserted by the warmest friends of the administration that the victory was a brilliant one for the federal government. The struggle will be renewed at a future time.

There is no room for such fanatics in the United States territory, wide as it is, and they must "clear out" as civilization spreads westward. Whether their next home will be in Mexico or in British territory is impossible to predict. They are certainly not wanted on British ground; and Mexico would not be the worse of their company, but might probably be the better for the infusion of a little more vigorous blood, and of a new superstition not more degrading than its own.

CHAPTER XIX.

FROM ST. LOUIS TO NEW ORLEANS.

New Orleans, Feb. 20, 1858.

ON leaving St. Louis our sensations were not of the most agreeable kind. Two days previously the steamer *Colonel Crossman* had burst her boiler near a place called New Madrid, several hundred miles down the river, and the papers were filled with accounts of the calamity, and with long lists of the killed and wounded. As we drove down to the levee to secure our state-rooms on board of the *Philadelphia*, the Irish newsboys thrust into our hands the *St. Louis Republican* of that morning, bawling out, "Horrible accident! bursting of the *Colonel Crossman*—fifty people killed!" This was not pleasant; but all the passengers—there were sixty or seventy of us—consoled themselves with the hope that such a calamity would endow with extra caution, for at least a month to come, every captain, pilot, engineer, and stoker on the Mississippi. And so we took our voyage, satisfied that our captain was "clever" both in the English and the American sense of the word, and that the clerk, the next in authority, was equally so. The crew and stokers were all negro slaves; and this was a circumstance to be deplored perhaps, but not to be remedied; for the recklessness of the negroes—recklessness caused not by wickedness, but by want of thought, want of responsibility, and want of moral dignity, consequent upon the state of slavery—is doubtless one cause, among many, of the frequency of accidents in all the waters where they form the crews of the navigating vessels.

We had on board the *Philadelphia* at starting from the levee 1000 head of chickens, 400 turkeys, 1100 sheep, 180 hogs, 2000 barrels of flour, 1990 sacks of corn, 400 barrels of pork, besides two or three hundred bales of hemp and cotton, and a load of fuel. In traveling for such long distances in the United States, any one from England who has journeyed for even a thousand or five hundred miles on the Continent of Europe is impressed not alone with the comfort and freedom of being able to go so far without that curse of our old and, in some respects, semi-barbarous civilization — the passport, with its fees and its visés, its delays and its obstructions, and its often insolent and always greedy gendarmerie and officials, but with the unvarying sameness of aspect presented by the landscape, the cities, and the people. There is little that is picturesque on the great lines of travel, for the Ohio and Mississippi are but monstrous drains.

The Mississippi flows through a loose, soft soil, and a flat woody country, with here and there a bluff or headland of reddish sandstone. But even these breaks to the prevailing uniformity are unknown at the last twelve hundred miles of its monotonous course. The cities, too, appear to be all built upon the same model. The long rectangular streets, the monster quadrangular hotels, the neat new chapels and flaring stores, seem repeated every where, with little or no variations of aggregate or detail, and the people have the same look, the same swagger, the same costume, the same speech, so that the traveler, not being startled at every hundred or two hundred miles of his course, as in Europe, by the apparition of a new uniform, a new style of building, by being addressed in a new language by waiters or officials, or by seeing new and unfamiliar names over the shop doors and at the corners of the streets, forgets the enormousness of the distances that he is passing through, or only remembers them by their tediousness. But, though the scenery of the Mississippi has but little attraction after the first few hours, the incidents that occur by day and night are novel enough to interest and instruct

THE MISSISSIPPI STEAM-BOAT "PHILADELPHIA."

every traveler who has his eyes open and his wits about him. And foremost among these incidents are the lading or discharging of cargo, and the taking in of wood. The steamers invariably burn wood, for coal is too dear for this purpose. On either bank of the Mississippi, as the traveler is borne down its steady current, he may observe at every four or five miles' distance piles of wood. These are cut by the negroes for their masters, the owners of the forests and the plantations, and heaped near the shore for the convenience of the steamers. When a steamer requires wood, it touches at any one of these points, takes what it wants, and either leaves the money or a note of what has been taken, to be settled hereafter. Sometimes the planter will be glad to take corn or pork in exchange; and if it be inconvenient to him to leave a negro or any other person in charge to take the chance of a passing boat, he leaves a notification of his wants and wishes on the pile of wood, and the captain, if it be possible, complies with his wishes. If not, he leaves a memorandum stating the reason why, and a note for the money—perhaps the money itself. When the operation of taking in wood is performed at night, it is picturesque in the extreme. The steamer rests with her prow upon the bank; a plank is laid from the lower deck to the shore; an iron stove, hoisted up on an iron pole, is filled with fire, which burns merrily, and casts its red flickering glow upon the rapidly descending current, and a gang of negroes, singing at their work, pass on shore and return laden with logs of cottonwood and cypress, and pile it upon the deck ready for the all-devouring furnace. In five or six hours it will need a fresh supply, and the operation will be repeated at least thirty or forty times in the 1200 miles. The fuel bill for the voyage between St. Louis and New Orleans averages, down stream, about 1000 dollars, or £200, and for the upward voyage about 250 dollars more.

All travelers have heard much of the "snags" and the "sawyers" upon the Mississippi. A snag is an agglomeration of trunks and branches of trees, borne down by the ever-varying current of the river, that is continually encroaching either on the left bank or on the right, and sometimes on the one curve and sometimes on the other, and washing away the trees that grow too near to the margin. A sawyer is a single trunk that has been fixed diagonally by the action of the stream. If an ascending vessel happens in the dark to run against one of these formidable instruments of destruction, she may be ripped up in her whole length before there is time to stop the engine. We on our voyage experienced no difficulties from either of these sources of evil. Every year they are becoming of less frequent occurrence, the United States government having established a series of flat-bottomed steamers expressly to dredge for, collect, and carry away these *disjecta membra*. But the snags and sawyers, though no longer so formidable or so many as in the days of yore, are still numerous enough to tax all the vigilance of the pilots and captains of the Mississippi boats, especially when ascending the stream. Our course was downward, and for that reason the less dangerous.

Another peculiarity of the Mississippi is its numerous beds and curves, to which may be added the bayous, or streams, running out of instead of into the main current, thus reversing the process to which we are accustomed in the Old World, where the small streams feed the large ones. For many hundred miles the Mississippi flows upon a ridge above the adjoining country, and, breaking loose now and then, lets off a portion of its superabundant waters into the lower region, forming a stream called a bayou, that is largest near its source, and smallest at its termination. The bayous often end in stagnant pools, the haunt of the alligator, and the hot-beds of fever and malaria. The bends of the river may be understood in their pattern, but not in their magnitude and multitudinousness, by any one who has stood upon the battlements of Stirling Castle, and seen "the mazy Forth unraveled." At one place a canal of less than two miles has been constructed, which saves a navigation of upward of twenty miles; and occasionally, after heavy falls of rain, the stream itself, making a new channel across slight obstruction, forsakes its devious ways, and goes directly to its purpose miles adown. But the Mississippi is one of the most shifting of rivers, always eating away its own banks, flooding the country at one side, and leaving it dry on the other, and next day taking a fancy to return to its old bed, in obedience to some inscrutable law which in its results looks more like caprice than order.

When we left St. Louis, the Mississippi, or, as the people call it familiarly and affectionately, the "Mississip," was covered with floating ice. Two days before we arrived at New Orleans we steamed into another climate—warm, balmy, and delicious as England is in the first week of June.

The following rhymed version of our seven days' adventures on the bosom of the "Father of Waters" was written during the voyage. The verses have the merit of fidelity to the truth in all their incidents and descriptions of scenery. It may be said of them, even by their author, that they helped in their composition to beguile the monotony of a very long voyage of 1295 miles, and that, if they yield no amusement to the reader, they yielded some to the writer:

"DOWN THE 'MISSISSIP.'

I.

" 'Twas a wintry morning, as the clock struck ten,
That we left St. Louis, two dejected men;
Gazing on the river, thick with yellow mud,
And dreaming of disaster, fire, and fog, and flood;
Of boilers ever bursting, of snags that break the wheel,
And sawyers ripping steam-boats through all their length of keel:
Yet, on shipboard stepping, we dismissed our fears,
And beheld through sunlight, in the upper spheres,
Little cherubs, waving high their golden wings,
Guarding us from evil and its hidden springs;
So on Heaven reliant, thinking of our weans,
Thinking of our true-loves, we sailed for New Orleans:
Southward, ever southward, in our gallant ship,
Floating, steaming, panting, down the Mississip.

II.

"Oh, the hapless river! in its early run
Clear as molten crystal, sparkling in the sun;
Ere the fierce Missouri rolls its troublous tide
To pollute the beauty of his injured bride;
Like a bad companion poisoning a life,
With a vile example and incessant strife;
So the Mississippi, lucent to the brim,
Wedded to Missouri, takes her hue from him;
And is pure no longer, but with sullen haste
Journeys to the ocean a gladness gone to waste;

Thus our idle fancies shaped themselves that day,
Mid the bluffs and headlands, and the islets gray :
Southward, ever southward, in our creaking ship,
Steaming through the ice-drifts down the Mississip.

III.

"In our wake there followed, white as flakes of snow,
Seven adventurous seagulls, floating to and fro,
Diving for the bounty of the bread we threw,
Dipping, curving, swerving—fishing as they flew—
And in deep mid-current, throned upon a snag,
Far away—a rover from his native crag,
Sat a stately eagle, Jove's imperial bird,
Heedless of our presence, though he saw and heard ;
Looking so contemptuous, that human nature sighed
For a loaded rifle to slay him for his pride ;
But superb, defiant, slowly at his ease,
Spreading his wide pinions, he vanished on the breeze :
Southward, flying southward, far beyond our ship,
Floating, creaking, panting, down the Mississip.

IV.

"In a blaze of glory shone the sun that day ;
In a blaze of beauty, fresh as flowery May,
A maid from Alabama came tripping on the deck—
Bright as heaven above us—pure without a speck,
Singing songs till twilight freely as the lark
That for inner gladness sings, though none may hark :
Songs of young affection, mournful songs of home,
Songs of happy sadness, when the fancies roam
From th' oppressive Real to the fairy Far
Shining through the Future, silvery as a star :
And the sun departed in his crimson robe,
Leaving Sleep, his viceroy, to refresh the globe.
Thus we traveled southward in our gallant ship,
Floating, drifting, dreaming, down the Mississip.

V.

"Brightly rose the morning o'er the straggling town,
Where the broad Ohio pours its waters down
To the Mississippi, rolling as before,
Seeming none the wider for increase of store ;
And they said, 'These houses scattered on the strand
Take their name from *Cairo*, in the Eastern land,
And shall be a city at some future day,
Mightier than Cairo, dead and passed away.'
And we thought it might be, as we gazed a while ;
And we thought it might not, ere we passed a mile :
And our paddles paddled through the turbid stream
As we floated downward in a golden dream ;

Southward, ever southward, in our panting ship,
Idling, dawdling, loafing, down the Mississip.

VI.

"Sometimes in Missouri we delayed an hour,
Taking in a cargo—butter, corn, and flour;
Sometimes in Kentucky shipped a pile of logs,
Sometimes sheep or turkeys, once a drove of hogs.
Ruthlessly the negroes drove them down the bank,
Stubbornly the porkers eyed the narrow plank,
Till at length, rebellious, snuffing danger near,
They turned their long snouts landward, and grunted out their fear.
And the white-teethed 'niggers,' grinning with delight,
Rode them and bestrode them, and charged them in the fight!
And then came shrill lamenting, and agony and wail,
And pummeling, and hoisting, and tugging at the tail,
Until the swine were conquered; and southward passed our ship,
Panting, steaming, snorting, down the Mississip.

VII.

"Thus flew by the slow hours till the afternoon,
'Mid a wintry landscape and a sky like June;
And the mighty river, brown with clay and sand,
Swept, in curves majestic, through the forest land,
And stuck into its bosom, heaving fair and large,
Many a lowly cypress that grew upon the marge—
Stumps, and trunks, and branches, as maids might stick a pin,
To vex the daring fingers that seek to venture in.
O travelers! bold travelers! that roam in wild unrest,
Beware the pins and brooches that guard this river's breast!
For danger ever follows the captain and the ship,
Who scorn the snags and sawyers that gem the Mississip.

VIII.

"Three days on the river—nights and mornings three,
Ere we stopped at Memphis, the port of Tennessee,
And wondered why they gave it such name of old renown—
A dreary, dingy, muddy, melancholy town,
But rich in bales of cotton, o'er all the landing spread,
And bound for merry England, to earn the people's bread;
And here—oh! shame to Freedom, that boasts with tongue and pen!—
We took on board a "cargo" of miserable men;
A freight of human creatures, bartered, bought, and sold
Like hogs, or sheep, or poultry—the living blood for gold;
And then I groaned remorseful, and thought, in pity strong,
A curse might fall upon us for suffering the wrong—
A curse upon the cargo, a curse upon the ship,
*Panting, moaning, groaning, down the Mississip.**

---

* This poem has been extensively copied into the American papers;

IX.

"Here our songster fled us, the little gipsy queen,
  Leaving us a memory of gladness that had been,
  And through the dark night passing, dark without a ray,
  Save the light we carried, we held upon our way;
  Darkness on the waters—darkness on the sky—
  Rain-floods beating o'er us—wild winds howling high—
  But, safely led and guided by pilots who could tell
  The pulses of the river, its windings and its swell,
  Who knew its closest secrets by dark as well as light,
  Each bluff or fringing forest, each swamp or looming height—
  Its gambols and caprices, its current's steady law,
  And at the fourth day dawning we skirted Arkansaw;
  Southward, steering southward, in our trusty ship,
  Floating, steaming, panting, down the Mississip.

X.

"Weary were the forests, dark on either side;
  Weary were the marshes, stretching far and wide;
  Weary were the wood-piles, strewn upon the bank;
  Weary were the cane-groves, growing wild and dank;
  Weary were the tree-stumps, charred and black with fire;
  Weary was the wilderness, without a house or spire;
  Weary were the log huts, built upon the sand;
  Weary were the waters, weary was the land;
  Weary was the cabin with its gilded wall,
  Weary was the deck we trod—weary—weary all:
  Nothing seemed so pleasant to hope for or to keep,
  Nothing in the wide world so beautiful as sleep,
  As we journeyed southward in our lazy ship,
  Dawdling, idling, loafing, down the Mississip.

XI.

"Ever in the evening, as we hurried by,
  Shone the blaze of forests, red against the sky—
  Forests burned for clearings, to spare the woodman's stroke,
  Cottonwood and cypress, and ash and giant oak—
  And from sleep upspringing, when the morning came,
  Seemed the lengthening landscape evermore the same,
  Evermore the forest and the rolling flood,
  And the sparse plantations and the fertile mud;
  Thus we came to Princeton, threading countless isles;
  Thus we came to Vicksburg, thrice three hundred miles;
  Thus we came to Natchez, when the starlight shone,
  Glad to see it—glad to leave it—glad to hurry on—

---

but it may be mentioned as a sign of the sensitiveness of public opinion on the subject of negro slavery that the eight lines referring to the cargo of slaves were invariably omitted in all the journals except those of Massachusetts and the other New England States.

Southward, ever southward, in our laden ship,
Fuming, toiling, heaving, down the Mississip.

XII.
"Whence the sound of music? Whence the merry laugh?
Surely boon companions, who jest, and sing, and quaff?
No! the slaves rejoicing—happier than the free,
With guitar and banjo, and burst of revelry!
Hark the volleyed laughter! hark the joyous shout!
Hark the nigger chorus ringing sharply out!
Merry is the bondsman; gloomy is his lord;
For merciful is Justice, and kind is Fate's award.
And God, who ever tempers the winter to the shorn,
Dulls the edge of sorrow to these His lambs forlorn,
And gives them cheerful natures, and thoughts that never soar
Into that dark to-morrow which wiser men deplore.
So sing, ye careless negroes, in our joyous ship,
Floating, steaming, dancing, down the Mississip.

XIII.
"At the sixth day dawning all around us lay
Fog, and mist, and vapor, motionless and gray:
Dimly stood the cane-swamps, dimly rolled the stream,
Bayou-Sara's house-tops faded like a dream;
Nothing seemed substantial in the dreary fog—
Nothing but our vessel drifting like a log:
Not a breath of motion round our pathway blew—
Idle was our pilot, idle were our crew—
Idle were our paddles, idle free and slave—
Every thing was idle but the restless wave,
Bearing down the tribute of three thousand miles
To the Southern Ocean and its Indian isles;
Thus all morn we lingered in our lazy ship,
Dozing, dreaming, nodding, down the Mississip.

XIV.
"But ere noon, uprising, blew the southern breeze,
Rolling off the vapor from the cypress-trees,
Opening up the blue sky to the south and west,
Driving off the white clouds from the river's breast;
Breathing in our faces, balmy, from the land,
A roamer from the gardens, as all might understand;
Happy as the swallows or cuckoos on the wing,
We'd cheated Father Winter, and sailed into the Spring;
And beheld it round us, with all its sounds and sights,
Its odors and its balsams, its glories and delights—
The green grass, green as England; the apple-trees in bloom;
The waves alert with music, and freighted with perfume—
As we journeyed southward in our gallant ship,
Singing and rejoicing down the Mississip.

XV.

"On the seventh day morning we entered New Orleans,
The joyous 'Crescent City'—a Queen among the Queens—
And saw her pleasant harbor alive with tapering spars—
With 'union-jacks' from England, and flaunting 'stripes and stars,'
And all her swarming levee, for miles upon the shore,
Buzzing, humming, surging, with Trade's incessant roar;
With negroes hoisting hogsheads, and casks of pork and oil,
Or rolling bales of cotton, and singing at their toil;
And downward—widening downward—the broad majestic river,
Hasting not, nor lingering, but rolling on forever;
And here, from travel resting, in soft ambrosial hours,
We plucked the growing orange, and gathered summer flowers,
And thanked our trusty captain, our pilot, and our ship,
For bearing us in safety down the Mississip."

CHAPTER XX.

"THE CRESCENT CITY."

New Orleans, Feb. 25, 1858.

IN descending the great River Mississippi our anticipations of New Orleans were of the most agreeable kind. We had no misgivings of plague or yellow fever, and dreaded far more the explosion or burning of the steam-boat to which we had intrusted the safety of our limbs and lives than any calamity attendant on the proverbial sickliness of the great city of the south. Nor is New Orleans more subject to the great scourge, of which the recollection is so intimately associated with its name, than Mobile, Charleston, Savannah, and other places in the same latitudes. The yellow fever, when it appears in the fullness of its ghastly majesty, generally affects the whole sea-board, and showers its unwelcome favors upon the just and upon the unjust, upon green and breezy Savannah as freely as upon the closely-packed lanes and alleys of the "Crescent City." But in winter, spring, and early summer, New Orleans is as healthy as London. These pleasant anticipations were not doomed to disappointment. New Orleans was in the full tide of its most brilliant season, and every thing and every body seemed devoted to enjoyment; and, certainly, the contrast with the lands and the scenery which we had left a week before was as agreeable as it was remarkable. On bidding farewell to St. Louis we left the winter behind us; and on approaching Baton Rouge, the state capital of Louisiana, and within one hundred and twenty-five miles of New Orleans, it was a physical as well as a mental luxury to note the difference of climate with which a few days' voyage had made us acquainted. There were no more floating ice-fields on the Mississippi; no more cold winds or leafless trees; no more stunted brown and withered grass, such as that which had wearied our eyes for many hundreds of miles previously, but, by a transformation as complete and rapid as that in a fairy pantomime, the land was covered with all the beauty and glory of the early spring. The sky was of bright, unclouded blue; the grass beautifully green; the plum, peach, and apple trees were in full and luxuriant bloom of white and purple; and the breeze that blew in our faces came laden with the balm of roses and jessamines. The sugar plantations on either bank of the river, with the white houses of the proprietors, each in the midst of gardens, of which the orange-tree, the evergreen oak, the magnolia, and the cypress were the most conspicuous ornaments, gleamed so cheerily in the sunshine that we could not but rejoice that we had turned our backs on the bitter north, and helped ourselves to an extra allowance of vernal enjoyment. For a few days it seemed like a realization of the poetical wish of Logan, in his well-known apostrophe to the cuckoo:

> "Oh, could I fly, I'd fly with thee!
> We'd make with social wing
> Our annual visits o'er the globe,
> Companions of the spring."

Steam was the cuckoo of this occasion—a cuckoo whose monotonous notes have in this land made the remotest wildernesses to smile with beauty and fertility. The simile may not be a very good one, but let it pass. The effect of the change of climate upon the spirits of all the passengers was decided. The taciturn became talkative; the reserved became communicative. The man of monosyllables expanded into whole sentences; and the ladies, like the flowers by the river side, felt the bland influence of the skies, and bloomed into fresher loveliness. The wearisome and apparently interminable forests of cypress and cottonwood, through which our vessel had been steaming for five days previously, were left far in our wake; and the landscape around us was alive, not only with the bustle of commercial and agricultural business, but with all the exhilarating sights and sounds of that sweet season when nature leaps to the kisses of the sun. This was on the 13th of February, the day before St. Valentine's. In England, in the ancient epoch of our traditional poetry, ere Chaucer, the "morning star of song," had arisen upon our land, the anniversary of St. Valentine, when the birds begin to choose their mates, was considered to be the first day of spring. May not the fact suggest a change of the seasons in the old land within the last five or six hundred years? And may it not help to prove that the climate enjoyed by our forefathers in the twelfth century was similar to that which now blesses the people of the sunny South in the nineteenth? But, leaving this point to the curious and to the weatherwise, I must own that, while walking out on St. Valentine's-day in the beautiful green meadows near Algiers, on the side of the Mississippi opposite to New Orleans, I was ungrateful enough to complain (to myself) that something was wanting to complete my enjoyment. The homesickness was upon me, and I was dissatisfied with the green grass because there were no buttercups, daisies, cowslips, or primroses among it. And here let me state that none of these flowers are to be found on the North American continent except in conservatories, where they are not exactly the same as our beautiful wild English varieties. But if there be no daisies, it must be confessed that there are violets in the South, for I gathered bunches of them on the 14th of February; but, alas! they had no scent, and did not betray themselves by their fragrance before the eye was aware of their proximity, like the sweet violets of Europe. But then it may be said for Nature in these latitudes that she gives so much odor to the orange blossoms, the roses, the bay-spice, and the jessamines, as to have none to spare for such humble flowers as violets. Let me also confess, *en passant* (and still under a qualm of the homesickness), that I found another deficiency, I will say defect, in the landscape, to which all the surpassing loveliness of the atmosphere failed to reconcile me, which was, that the air was silent, and that no skylarks, " true to the kindred points of heaven and home," sang in the blue heavens. There are no larks in North America, nor, as far as I have been able to discover, any other bird with a song as joyously beautiful and bountiful. America has the bluebird and the mockingbird; but those who love to hear the lays of that speck of delicious music, that diamond-like gem of melody which twinkles in the " blue lift" and hails the early morn at heaven's gate, may expect the gratification in the Old World, but not in the New.

But this is a digression, and we have yet to reach New Orleans. For a distance of several hundred miles, where the river skirts the shores of the great cotton-growing states of Mississippi, Arkansas, and Tennessee, cotton plantations, with their negroes busy at work to feed the hungry mills of Lancashire, meet the eye on both sides of the stream. But on entering Louisiana the traveler sees that the cultivation of sugar replaces to a great extent that of cotton. I regret that I had not time or opportunity to visit either a sugar or cotton plantation on my way down the river, that I might have studied for a few days the relationship between the master and the slave, and have tested by my own experience the benevolent and patriarchal character, rightly or wrongfully, but universally given to it in the South. But on this subject I shall possibly, with more experience, have something to say hereafter. In the mean time I could but notice how little of this rich country was cultivated, and how thin a belt of land made profitable by the plow extended between the dark river and the darker forest which bounded the view on every side. But this belt is gradually widening. The axe and the torch are clearing the primeval forest; and the cotton-growing states of Mississippi and Alabama, and the sugar-growing state of Louisiana, are annually adding to the wealth of America and of Great Britain by increasing the area of profitable culture, and developing the resources of a soil that contains within its bosom fertility enough to clothe and feed the whole population of Europe and America. The sugar plantations have seldom a river breadth of more than five acres, but they extend all but indefinitely into the forest beyond. Some of them reach for one mile, others for three or even ten miles, into the wilderness of cypress-trees and dismal swamps that for hundreds of miles fringe the shores of the "Father of Waters."

New Orleans stands on the left bank of the Mississippi, about a hundred miles from its mouths, on a crescent-like bend of the river, whence its name of the "Crescent City." By means of the continual deposits of the vast quantities of mud and sand which it holds in solution, and brings down from the great wilderness of the Far West, the Mississippi has raised its bed to a considerable height above the level of the surrounding country, and is embanked for hundreds of miles by earthen mounds or dikes, of six or eight feet in height, called levees. This name was originally given by the French, and is still retained by the dwellers on the banks of the Mississippi and Ohio. A levee of this kind protects New Orleans. As many parts of the city are lower than the bed of the river, no portion of the drainage finds its way into what in other cities is the natural channel, but runs, from the direction of the stream, into the swamps of the lower country toward Lake Pontchartrain. As there is very little fall in this direction, New Orleans, as may be supposed, is ill drained. It is a matter of considerable difficulty and great expense to drain it, even as inefficiently as such untoward circumstances will allow. What drainage there is is upon the surface, and even at this early season of the year the smell affects painfully the olfactory nerves of all who prefer the odors of the rose to those of the cesspool. The population of the city is about 120,000, of whom one half or more are alleged to be of French extraction. The French call themselves, and are called, Creoles—a term that does not imply, as many people suppose, an admixture of black blood. Indeed, all persons of European descent born in this portion of America are strictly, according to the French meaning of the word, Creoles. New Orleans is less like an American city than any other in the United States, and reminds the European traveler of Havre or Boulogne-sur-Mer. From the admixture of people speaking the English language it is most like Boulogne, but the characteristics of the streets and of the architecture are more like those of Havre. The two languages divide the city between them. On one side of the great bisecting avenue of Canal Street the shop-signs are in French, and every one speaks that language; on the other side the shops and the language are English. On the French side are the Opera House, the restaurants, the cafés, and the shops of the modistes. On the English or American side are the great hotels, the banks, the Exchange, and the centre of business. There is one little peculiarity in New Orleans which deserves notice as characteristic of its French founders. In other American cities no effort of imagination is visible in the naming of streets. On the contrary, there is in this respect an almost total absence of invention. New York, Philadelphia, Washington, Cincinnati, and St. Louis seem to have exhausted at a very early period of their histories the imagination or the gratitude of their builders. Street nomenclature has been consigned to the alphabet at Washington, where they have A Street, B Street, C Street, D Street, etc. At New York the streets are named from First Street up to One Hundred and Eighty-eighth or even to Two Hundredth Street. At Philadelphia imagination in this particular matter seems to have reached its limit when it named some of the principal thoroughfares after the most noted and beautiful trees that flourished on the soil—

> "Walnut, Chestnut, Spruce, and Pine,
> Hickory, Sassafras, Oak, and Vine."

Having stretched so far, it could go no farther, and took refuge, as New York did, in simple arithmetic. At Cincinnati, where the same system prevails, the street-painters do not even take the trouble of adding the word street, but simply write Fourth or Fifth, as the case may be. In that pleasant and prosperous place you order an extortionate coach-driver to take you, not to Fourth Street, but to Fourth. Not so in New Orleans. The early French had greater fertility of fancy, and named their streets after the Muses and the Graces, the

Nereids and the Oreads, the Dryads and the Hamadryads, and all the gods and goddesses of Olympus. Having exhausted their classic reminiscences, they next, as a gallant people, bethought themselves of the names of their fair ladies—dames and demoiselles—and named some of the newer streets after the Adèles, Julies, Maries, Alines, and Antoinettes, whom they held in love or reverence. When these failed they betook themselves to the names of eminent men—in their own and in ancient times—to those of Lafayette or Washington, or to the founders of New Orleans, the Carondelets and the Poydras. It is, perhaps, too late for New York and other great American cities to alter the system they have established; but to name a street after a public benefactor, a statesman, a warrior, a philosopher, or a poet, or even after the Muses and the Graces, seems preferable to so tame and prosaic a method of nomenclature as that afforded by the alphabet or the multiplication table.

The most prominent public building in New Orleans is the St. Charles Hotel, an edifice somewhat in the style and appearance of the Palace of the King of the Belgians at Brussels. During the twelve days that our party remained under its hospitable roof it contained from seven hundred to seven hundred and fifty guests, and its grand entrance-hall, where the gentlemen congregate from nine in the morning till eleven or twelve at night, to read the newspapers, to smoke, to chew, and, let me add, to spit, presented a scene of bustle and animation which can be compared to nothing but the Bourse at Paris during the full tide of business, when the *agioteurs* and the *agens de change* roar, and scream, and gesticulate like maniacs. The Southern planters, and their wives and daughters, escaping from the monotony of their cotton and sugar plantations, come down to New Orleans in the early spring season, and, as private lodgings are not to be had, they throng to the St. Louis and the St. Charles Hotels, but principally to the St. Charles, where they lead a life of constant publicity and gayety, and endeavor to make themselves amends for the seclusion and weariness of winter. As many as a hundred ladies (to say nothing of the gentlemen) sit down together to

THE LEVEE AT NEW ORLEANS.

breakfast—the majority of them in full dress as for an evening party, and arrayed in the full splendor both of their charms and of their jewelry. Dinner is but a repetition of the same brilliancy, only that the ladies are still more gorgeously and elaborately dressed, and make a still greater display of pearls and diamonds. After dinner the drawing-rooms offer a scene to which no city in the world affords a parallel. It is the very court of Queen Mob, whose courtiers are some of the fairest, wealthiest, and most beautiful of the daughters of the South, mingling in true Republican equality with the chance wayfarers, gentle or simple, well dressed or ill dressed, clean or dirty, who can pay for a nightly lodging or a day's board at this mighty caravansary. To rule such a hotel as this in all its departments, from the kitchen and the wine-cellar to the treasury and the reception-rooms, with all its multifarious array of servants, black and white, bond and free, male and female—to maintain order and regularity, enforce obedience, extrude or circumvent plunderers, interlopers, and cheats, and, above all, to keep a strict watch and guard over that terrible enemy who is always to be dreaded in America—Fire—is a task demanding no ordinary powers of administration and government, but it is one that is well performed by the proprietors, Messrs. Hall and Hildreth. Their monster establishment is a model of its kind, and one of the "sights" of America.

So much for the in-door life of New Orleans. Its out-door life is seen to greatest advantage on the levee, where steamboats unloading their rich freights of cotton, sugar, and molasses from Mississippi, Arkansas, and Tennessee, and of pork, flour, corn, and whisky from the upper and inland regions of Missouri, Illinois, Ohio, and Kentucky, present a panorama that may be excelled in Europe for bustle and life, but not for picturesqueness. The river can scarcely be seen for the crowd of steam-boats and of shipping that stretch along the levee for miles; and the levee itself is covered with bales of cotton and other produce, which hundreds of negroes, singing at their work, with here and there an Irishman among them, are busily engaged in rolling from the steamers and depositing in the places set apart for each consignee. These places are distinguished one from the other by the little flags stuck upon them —flags of all colors, and mixtures of colors, and patterns; and here the goods remain in the open air, unprotected, until it pleases the consignees to remove them. New Orleans would seem, at the first glance, to overflow with wealth to such an extent as to have no room for storage. The street pavements actually do service for warehouses, and are cumbered with barrels of salt, corn, flour, pork, and molasses, and bales of cotton, to such an extent as to impede the traffic, and justify the belief that the police must be either very numerous and efficient, or the population very honestly disposed. The docks of Liverpool are busy enough, but there is no life or animation at Liverpool at all equal to those which may be seen at the levee in the "Crescent City." The fine open space, the clear atmosphere, the joyousness and alacrity of the negroes, the countless throngs of people, the forests of funnels and masts, the plethora of cotton and corn, the roar of arriving and departing steam-boats, and the deeper and more constant roar of the multitude, all combine to impress the imagination with visions of wealth, power, and dominion, and to make the levee as attractive to the philosopher as it must be to the merchant and man of business.

One day, weary of the sights and sounds of trade, and anxious for fresh air, I crossed to Algiers on the opposite side of the Mississippi. Here, while admiring the orange groves, but regretting that the oranges were bitter, and overhearing the strange names given to the negroes by one another, and by the Creole masters and mistresses—such names as Hercule, Lysandre, Diane, Agamemnon, and Hector—I was much amused by the fervent ejaculations of a man who had evidently been drinking. Talking loudly to himself, but slowly and deliberately, he said, "Damn every thing! damn every body! Yes, but there's time enough to damn every thing, and it's not my business to go out of the way to do it. Besides, I have no authority to damn any thing, and, for that matter, to damn any body but myself, which I do most heartily. Damn me!" and he passed on, reeling.

On the third day after our arrival, New Orleans was excited

beyond the limits of its ordinary propriety by the revelries of the "Mystick Krewe of Comus"—an association of citizens whose names are known only to the initiated, who annually celebrate the festival of Mardi Gras by a procession through the city. The procession on this occasion represented Comus leading the revels, followed by Momus, Janus, Pomona, Vertumnus, Flora, Ceres, Pan, Bacchus, Silenus, Diana, and, in fact, the whole Pantheon of the Greek mythology, male and female, all dressed in appropriate costume. The "Krewe" assembled at nine o'clock in Lafayette Square, and, having obtained permission of the mayor to perambulate the city with torch-lights, started in procession through the principal streets to the Gayety Theatre, where the performers in the masque, to the number of upward of one hundred, represented four classical tableaux before a crowded audience. They protracted the festival till midnight; but during that night and the preceding day no less than three assassinations by maskers were perpetrated in the open street. The circumstances, horrible to a stranger, appeared to excite no sensation among the natives. But New Orleans is in this respect on a par with Southern Italy. Human life is a cheap commodity, and the blow of anger but too commonly precedes or is simultaneous with a word; and among the counterbalancing disadvantages of a too warm and too luxurious climate, this predisposition to the stiletto or the bowie-knife is not the least disagreeable or the least remarkable.

The swamps of the great cotton-growing states of Louisiana, Mississippi, and Alabama are a striking feature of the southern landscape. The traveler, whether he proceed by the steam-boats on the great rivers, or along the dreary lines of railway that pierce, often in a straight line, for hundreds of miles through the jungle and the wilderness, speedily becomes familiar with their melancholy beauty, though he seldom has occasion to penetrate far into their dangerous solitudes. No part of the rich state of Louisiana, and but few portions of the states of Mississippi, Arkansas, and Tennessee, are more than two hundred feet above the level of the Gulf of Mexico. The majestic rivers which give names to these states, and many others which are tributary to these larger arteries, such as the Red River, the Tombigbee, and the Ohio, overflow their banks every year, and, breaking over the artificial levees that are raised to restrain them within their natural channels, lodge their waters in the low grounds and hollows of the forests. There being no fall by which they can return again to the parent or any other stream or outlet, the waters simmer in the hot sun, or fester in the thick, oppressive shadow of the trees, where nothing flourishes but the land-turtle, the alligator, the rattlesnake, and the moccasin—the latter a small but very venomous reptile. An area of no less than 9000 square miles between the Mississippi and Red River is periodically submerged; and the Alabama and Tombigbee Rivers, in many parts of their course, are as treacherous and unruly as the Mississippi itself, and commit as much havoc on the low-lying districts within twenty or thirty miles of their banks. Between the city of New Orleans and the Lake Pontchartrain, in a carriage-drive of six miles over the celebrated Shell Road (the best road in America, though not to be compared with Regent Street, Oxford Street, or the New Road), the traveler may see a miniature specimen of the prevalent scenery of the American swamps. He may admire the luxuriant forest-growth, festooned with the graceful ribbons of the wild vine, the funereal streamers of the tillandsia, or Spanish moss, drooping from the branches of pine, cottonwood, cypress, and ever-green oaks—weird-like all, as witches weeping in the moonlight; and underneath, amid the long, thick grass, the palm and palmetto spreading their fanlike leaves in beautiful profusion. At the roots of the trees, many of them charred and blackened by fire, sleeps the dull, calm water, sometimes in a smaller pool, dyed to a color like that of porter or coffee by the decayed vegetation of successive years, but in the larger pools, often four or five feet deep, lying clearer and more translucent than when it left the turbid receptacle of the parent Mississippi. But on the banks of the great river itself, between St. Louis and Natchez, may be seen in more perfection the apparently interminable forests of cottonwood and cypress, whose deep recesses, far beyond the present reach of cultivation, or the probable capabilities of existing negro labor, stretch the "dismal swamps"—worthy of the name—where men seldom venture, even in pursuit of sport, which elsewhere makes them brave so many dangers. The atmosphere in the summer months, when the vegetation is in its greatest beauty, is too deadly even for acclimated white men and for those in the South. None but negroes may brave the miasmata with impunity. Their lungs seem of a texture coarse enough to imbibe the foul air without damage, and their coarse skins repel the noxious vapors that are fatal to the white race.

It is to places like these, in the innermost recesses of the swamps, that the rebellious negro, determined upon freedom, flies in pursuit of the blessing, and where he hides and skulks, armed to the teeth, until opportunity serves him to travel by what the Americans call the "underground railway" to Canada, where, and where only, he can be safe from the marshals and constables of the United States.

And what, it may be asked, is the "underground railway?" When and by whom the name was first applied it is difficult, if not impossible, to state, but it simply means the system by which the friends of the negro and the supporters of the abolition of slavery pass a runaway slave from city to city throughout the length and breadth of the Union, until—perseverance and good-luck aiding—he is finally enabled to set his foot on British territory, and set at defiance the law and the authority which would again make him captive. In most, if not all American cities, there is some male or female philanthropist, some member of the Society of Friends, or some merely philosophic friend of man, who, looking upon slavery as a crime and a curse, makes it a point of duty to assist the negro in escaping a bondage which he believes to be an individual no less than a national disgrace. All these persons are acquainted with, and correspond with each other, though their existence may be unknown to the authorities and principal persons of the cities in which they reside. By degrees they have organized a system, in conformity to which they shelter and feed the runaway, and provide him with the means of passing from one city to another, until he is safely beyond the reach of all pursuit from the law officers of the central government, or from the officious interference of local functionaries or busybodies. Such is the underground railway. Canada is its usual terminus; for there, and there alone, is safety. Unfortunately, however, for the negroes, they do not find always either a welcome or the means of subsistence in their new home. Canada, besides, is somewhat too frosty for the negro blood; and the fugitives not unfrequently leave it in despair, to return to captivity and punishment in the more genial South, where, whatever may be their moral state, their physical wants are better supplied, and with less cost and exertion to themselves than in the more wholesome and more invigorating North.

But it is not every negro, who, in the heat of passion for real or imaginary wrong inflicted upon him by master or mistress, escapes from thraldom, that hopes, or even attempts, to reach Canada. The way is too long; the dangers are too many; and, moreover, it is not one negro in a thousand who knows where Canada is, and who, even when inspired by the love of freedom, would attempt such a journey. The nearest refuge of the negro of Louisiana, Mississippi, and Alabama is the Swamp, and thither the runaways betake themselves on the rare occasions when they quarrel with their masters, or appeal to them in vain from the tyranny or maltreatment of their overseers. The overseers, it should be stated, are seldom Southern men, but mostly "Yankees" from the New England States, or indubitable Scotchmen, gaining their first footing in the world by a mode of life to which their poverty rather than their Calvinism or their education reconciles them. Once in the Swamp and well armed, the fugitive, if not pursued too rapidly by his master or the overseer with the blood-hounds on his track—by no means an uncommon occurrence—succeeds, sooner or later, in joining a band of unfortunates like himself, and in penetrating into the jungle deeply enough to elude or defy pursuit. Bands of forty or fifty negroes, and sometimes in larger numbers, have been known to haunt the remote swamps of Louisiana and Mississippi, and to make their retreats inviolate, partly by the aid of the pestilential climate, and partly by the terror inspired by their ferocity and desperation. They have even been known to clear portions of the wilderness, and plant it with maize or Indian corn for their subsistence, and to levy, like the "merry men" of Robin Hood or Rob Roy, a very considerable black mail and tribute upon the pastures of the planters within two or three days' reach of their fastnesses. When powder and shot fail them, they have recourse to the more primitive implement—the bow, and thus provide themselves with subsistence from the spoils of the forest. At night they light large fires with the superabundant timber of their hiding-places, not dreading, so far from the white men, that their pursuers will dare to break in upon them in such dangerous places, or trusting, if they do, that their superior knowledge of the ground will enable them, if not to capture, at least to elude whatever force, public or private, may be sent against them.

The day will come, if not within the lifetime of this generation, yet in a short period compared with the history of civilization, when all these swamps will be drained, and when all this jungle will be cut down to make room for the cultivation of cotton and sugar. But at present the cultivated land of the Southern States is but a margin and border on the great rivers. Beyond these narrow strips lies on either side the great interior country, equally rich and fruitful. But the white population in these regions, unlike that in the north and west of the Union, and unlike that in Canada, grows by its own natural growth. It has no aid from immigration. The white race increases but slowly. The black races increase rapidly—so rapidly that, in default of that immigration from the Old World, and from the already over-populated states of New England, which is such a constant source of wealth, power, and dominion to Ohio, Indiana, Illinois, Iowa, Wisconsin, and Michigan, and which will be the same to Kansas, Nebraska, and scores of other states and territories not yet settled, the negroes will ere long outnumber the whites. What may result when this takes place, and when the fact is known to the negro population, it is not for any one now living to predict:

"But forward though we canna look,
We guess and fear."

CHAPTER XXI.

FROM LOUISIANA TO ALABAMA.

Montgomery, Alabama, March 2.

FAREWELL to the pleasant and sunny city of New Orleans! Farewell to its warm-hearted people of Creoles, both French and Anglo-Saxon! Farewell to the St. Charles Hotel, that perfect epitome of Southern life when it escapes from its enforced solitudes in the plantations of Louisiana, and mixes in the gayety of this "Petit Paris" of America! Farewell to the busy, picturesque, swarming levee, with its negroes and its Irishmen, its cotton, its sugar, its pork, its corn, its whisky, and its huge white steam-boats, with their tall black funnels, two to each! Farewell to its fruit-shops, luscious and bursting over with oranges and bananas, freshly gathered from the tree! Farewell to the bowers of roses and jessamines on the banks of the Mississippi! And farewell to that great River Mississippi itself, fit for every thing except to drink and to wash in, winding, and twisting, and pouring to the sea its majestic tide for upward of two thousand miles, receiving into its bosom, from tributaries scarcely inferior to itself, the drainage of an area sufficient to feed and lodge one half of the human race! And farewell, too, to the sweet South, where by a little manœuvre and change of plan I had contrived to evade the frost and snow, and to make Spring follow immediately upon Autumn! I was now bound for Mobile, in Alabama, and turned my face northward, traveling with the Spring. Hitherto New Orleans had been to my imagination a weird city, a city of the plague, a city that London life-assurance offices would not allow their clients to visit unless upon payment of a premium for the extra risk; but for the future it was to be associated in my mind with all pleasant fancies and ideas—of beautiful women, beautiful flowers, beautiful skies, and balmy breezes.

From the St. Charles Hotel to the Lake Pontchartrain railway station is a distance of less than a mile. The hack fare demanded of each passenger on this occasion was one dollar. London cab-drivers, who are not allowed by the law or the police to extort as much as they please from the fear, the ignorance, or the indolence of the public, might advantageously expatriate themselves to Louisiana, or, indeed, to any other state in the wide dominion of "Uncle Sam." Were the American hack-drivers all white men, it might not unreasonably be supposed that they had immigrated from the European side of the Atlantic, to revenge themselves for deprivation of the liberty of cheating in the Old World by the exercise of an unbounded license of extortion in the New. But this theory does not hold in the South, where at least one half of the hack-drivers are negroes. Yet five hundred London cabmen, the very worst and most insolent that London could spare, might effect a social revolution in this department by coming over to America. If they demanded no more than four times the legal London fares they would get abundance of custom, for, even at these rates, they would be able to do the work at half the price of the American Jehus, native or imported. From the railway dépôt to Lake Pontchartrain is six miles, and the fare was a quarter of a dollar. From Lake Pontchartrain, by the fine mail steamer the *Cuba*, the distance is 165 miles, and the fare on this occasion was precisely the same as the hackney-coach fare, one dollar. The accommodation afforded included supper, a night's lodging, and breakfast in the morning. But let no future traveler imagine that such a rate is a permanent institution. There was on that day an opposition boat on the line; and, to vanquish and overwhelm the opposition, it was contemplated, if the ruinous rate of one dollar would not effect the purpose, to reduce it still farther to half a dollar. The consequences were, as might have been expected, that the boat was inconveniently overcrowded, and that there was a ferocious scramble at breakfast-time for seats at the table. It must be admitted, however, that the cuisine was as liberal as if the full price had been demanded. For my part, it was not without a compunctious throb and qualm of conscience that I was lending myself to a robbery, that I condescended to eat either supper or breakfast.

We left New Orleans at four in the afternoon, and steamed all night through the two sea lakes of Pontchartrain and Borgne, and along the inner shore of the Gulf of Mexico—inner, because protected from the outer gulf by a breastwork of islands. At nine the next morning the *Cuba* was safe in the Mobile River, discharging her freight and passengers at the levee. The population of Mobile is about 25,000, free and slave, who all, either directly or indirectly, live and thrive by the cotton trade. Mobile and Liverpool are, in different ways, as closely connected by interest and business as Liverpool and Manchester, and their transactions are annually on the increase. The wharves and levee, like those of New Orleans, are covered with cotton bales. The gutters, when it rains (and the rains of Mobile are floods), bear down waifs and strays of cotton to the river, and the river is studded and flecked with cotton-drift floating about on its surface like so many nautili. The thoughts of the merchants of Mobile are of cotton. They talk of cotton by day, and dream of it by night. When news arrive from Europe, they turn instinctively to the Liverpool cotton report. A rise or fall of a farthing per lb., or even of one eighth of a farthing, may make the difference between ease and embarrassment—between riches and poverty—between a good speculation and a bad one.

"Cotton is in their steps, cotton is in their ears;
In all their actions, enterprise and cotton."

Next to the State of Mississippi, Alabama is the greatest cotton state of the Union, and produces from 500,000 to 700,000 bales per annum, at an average value of from forty to fifty dollars (£8 to £10) per bale.

Mobile was founded by the French in 1700, when they were the possessors of Louisiana; but the name, though it resembles a French word and suggests a French origin, is said by the natives to be Indian. It was ceded to England in 1763, and, seventeen years afterward, was made over to Spain.

It bears but few traces either of its French or its Spanish founders, and some of its most enterprising citizens are English and Scotch, attracted to it by its business connections with Liverpool and Glasgow. As a city Mobile offers few attractions to the traveler. It has no public buildings of any importance, and only one street (Government Street) which has any pretensions to beauty, and those are derivable more from its width, and the luxuriant tropical beauty of the trees which shade it on either side, than from its architecture. Should any of the surplus population of London cabmen, already alluded to, bethink themselves of coming to the United States, they will do well to consider the advantages which Mobile offers to them. My traveling companion, for going to and coming from an evening party at a gentleman's house within a distance of a mile and a half from our hotel, had to pay one driver the sum of eight dollars (£1 12s.); and for escorting two ladies to the theatre " on a raw and rainy night," a distance of less than half a mile, he had to pay six dollars (£1 4s.) But those who do not keep carriages of their own in Mobile seldom or never ride. If it be fine, they walk; if it be wet, they stay at home; so that, after all, the hackney-coach business may not be so prosperous as might be supposed from such an unconscionable tariff.

The great charm, beauty, and attraction of Mobile is its famous Magnolia Grove. The drive for about three miles is over an excellent plank road, through the bowery avenues of which are to be attained at every turn most picturesque glimpses over the Bay of Mobile, and far beyond it on the verge of the horizon, of the Gulf of Mexico, and the mysterious springs and sources of that great Gulf Stream which works its tepid way across the Atlantic to make green the fields of Ireland and England, and to soften the climate of the Hebridean Isles of Skye and Lewis and the fiords of Norway. On entering the grove, the magnificent magnolias, tall and umbrageous as the chestnut-trees of Bushy Park, are seen growing to the very edge of the sea, interspersed with equally magnificent pines and evergreen oaks. The combination of these stately trees presents the idea of perpetual summer. The magnolias were not in bloom so early (the 25th of February), but the wood violets were out in rich though inodorous luxuriance; the jessamines were unfolding their yellow blossoms, redolent of perfume; and the bay-spice displayed on every side its gorgeous crimson flowers and glossy aromatic leaves. Amid all these and a variety of other trees, the wild vine, that had not yet put out its tender shoots, wreathed and twined itself, suggesting the fuller beauty that would burst upon the land when the mocking-bird would trill its delicious notes, the magnolia woo the "amorous air" with its profuse white pyramids of flowers till the breeze became faint with excess of odor, and the vine itself, with its full drapery of verdure upon it, should festoon together all the trees of this exuberant wildwood.

Walking out by myself, and meriting neither then, nor at any other time, the anathema of Cowley, who says,

> "Unhappy man, and much accursed is he
> Who loves not his own company,"

a beautiful little spring by the wayside in the Magnolia Grove suggested to me, sitting on a fallen tree, and basking in the sunshine, the following lines:

THE WAYSIDE SPRING IN ALABAMA.

> "Bonnie wayside burnie,
>   Tinkling in thy well,
> Softly as the music
>   Of a fairy bell;
> To what shall I compare thee,
> For the love I bear thee,
>   On this sunny day,
> Bonnie little burnie,
>   Gushing by the way?
>
> "Thou'rt like to fifty fair things,
> Thou'rt like to fifty rare things,
> Spring of gladness flowing
>   Grass and ferns among,
> Singing all the noontime
>   Thine incessant song;
> Like a pleasant reason,
> Like a word in season,
> Like a friendly greeting,
> Like a happy meeting,

Like the voice of comfort
　　In the hour of pain,
Or sweet sleep long vanished,
　　Coming back again:

"Like the heart's romances,
　　Like a poet's fancies,
Like a lover's visions
　　Of his bliss to be;
Like a little maiden
　　Crowned with summers three,
Romping in the sunshine
　　Beautiful to see;
Like my true love's accents
　　When alone we stray,
Happy with each other,
　　Through the meads of May,
Or sit down together,
　　In the wintry weather,
By the cheery fire,
　　Gathering in that circle
All this world's desire,
　　Hope, and love, and friendship,
And music of the lyre.

"Bonnie little burnie,
　　Winding through the grass,
Time shall never waste thee,
　　Or drain thy sparkling glass;
And were I not to taste thee,
　　And bless thee as I pass,
'Twould be a scorn of beauty,
'Twould be a want of duty,
'Twould be neglect of Pleasure—
So come, thou little treasure!
　　I'll kiss thee while I may,
And while I sip thy coolness,
　　On this sunny day,
I'll bless thy gracious Giver,
Thou little baby river,
　　Gushing by the way."

We were detained at Mobile no longer than three days, and then, once more taking passage upon a steam-boat, we steamed up, and not down, a great American river. The Alabama is not so great as the Mississippi or the Ohio, but is still a great and a noble stream. It is formed by the junction of the Coosa and the Tallapoosa, and is navigable by large steam-boats from Mobile to Wetumpka, a distance of about six hundred miles. About forty miles above Mobile it is joined by a river with the somewhat cacophonous name of the Tombigbee, and from the point of junction downward is sometimes called the Mobile River. The river runs for two or three hundred miles right through the middle of the State of Alabama, of which it is the broad, the silent, and the beautiful highway, and then slopes to the east toward Georgia. But this reminds me that I am speaking, not of nature, but of the map, and committing an error similar to that of a newly-appointed postmaster of Mobile, who wrote to a clerk in his department at the farther end of the State of Alabama asking him how far the Tombigbee ran up. The reply was that the Tombigbee did not run up, but down: a truth and a witticism which cost the sharp clerk his situation by the fiat of the offended functionary, who, if he had sense to see the joke, had not magnanimity enough to pardon it.

From Mobile to Montgomery, by the windings of the stream, tracing it upward, is a distance of nearly five hundred miles, and the voyage usually occupies about forty-eight hours. Between these two points the only towns of importance are Selma and Cahawba, towns which in England would be called villages, but which in America are called cities. To steam up this lonely and lovely river, fringed to the water's brink with apparently interminable wildernesses and swamps of cane and cypress—the cypresses heavy and gloomy with the banner-like beards of the tillandsia—was like steaming into the aboriginal forest for the first time. So still and dream-like was the landscape, so bright a moon shone on the fairy solitude of wood and flood, that it seemed as if we had passed the uttermost confines of civilization, and were tempting the unknown waters of an unknown land, where the savage still prowled, where the war-cry still resounded, and where the uplifted tomahawk might still glitter in the moonlight over the scalp of the too adventurous white man rushing recklessly into danger. For forty miles at a stretch we traveled onward —ever onward—without seeing any trace of a human habitation, though occasionally we stopped at a lonely corner where negroes, bearing torches, suddenly appeared, to receive a barrel of corn, or pork, or other commodity with which we were freighted. There were cotton plantations within easy distances, though not always visible from the river. In the downward voyage of the steamers the owners of these plantations load them with cotton for Mobile, but in the upward voyage to Montgomery the freight is usually of such articles as the planters require for themselves and their slaves. Alabama finds cotton production more profitable than any other. It grows but little corn, raises but little pork, and carries on no manufactures. There is, in consequence, a continual exchange of cotton for every other commodity and thing which the free man's luxuries and his slaves' necessities require.

Alabama is not yet totally free of the Indian tribes, and portions of them come annually down to Mobile to sell their fancy bead-work, and the little ornaments of bark which the women make in the winter. The women, young and old, are often to be seen in Mobile with bundles of fire-wood on their backs, which they sell in the streets, crying with a melancholy intonation, "Chumpa! chumpa!" the only word resembling English which they speak, and somewhat more musical than "chumps," which it signifies. The Alabama River was the scene of many romantic and many horrible incidents of the early warfare between the white and red races, and many stories are told of the encounters of the hardy pioneers of civilization with the equally hardy but more luckless aborigines who resisted their invasion, and of which the Alabama, its swamps and bluffs, was the scene even so lately as the year 1830. Among the Indian heroes, one, "General" Mackintosh, the son of a Scotchman by an Indian mother, stands conspicuous for his chivalry and bravery, and for the influence which he exercised over all the Indian tribes of Alabama. The river is almost as intimately associated with his name as Loch Lomond is with that of Rob Roy, or the caves of the Island of Skye with the memory of Prince Charlie.

Montgomery is the capital of the State of Alabama, and carries on a considerable business in the forwarding of cotton and other produce to Mobile. Its population is under 10,000.

It offers nothing to detain the traveler, and has nothing remarkable about it except the badness of its principal hotel. Among the numerous eccentricities of this establishment may be mentioned the fact that it contains no bells in its rooms. By this economy the traveler is compelled, if he want any thing, to go to the top of the stairs and use his lungs, or, if that be disagreeable or unavailing, to help himself, which is, perhaps, his most advisable mode of getting out of the difficulty. Another peculiarity of this remarkable hostelry is (or was) that nothing is (or was) to be had on a Sunday evening after six o'clock. Having dined by compulsion of the custom of the place at one o'clock, I sought out a negro waiter about nine o'clock, and asked for some refreshment. There was nothing to be had—no tea, no milk, no meat, not even a crust of bread. "Is the bar open?" I inquired, with a faint hope that that department might prove more hospitable, and afford a hungry traveler a "cracker" (the American name for a biscuit, and for a Southern rustic) and a glass of beer or wine. The hope was vain; the bar-keeper had shut up at six o'clock. It was a case of starvation in a land of plenty; and, to make the matter more provoking, it was starvation charged in the bill at the rate of two dollars and a half per diem. I made a friend of the negro, however, and he borrowed a crust of bread for me out of doors somewhere, and managed to procure me a lump or two of sugar; a worthy Scotchman at Mobile had, when I left that city, filled me a pocket-flask with genuine Islay whisky from the "Old Country;" and, with these abundant resources, and a tea-kettle, I was enabled to be independent of the landlord of the bell-less, comfortless, foodless hotel of Montgomery, Alabama.

CHAPTER XXII.

SOUTH CAROLINA.

Charleston, South Carolina, March 5, 1858.

Two days after our pleasant voyage up the Alabama River the weather suddenly changed. A "norther" (a wind as much dreaded in the sunny South of this continent as is the kindred "bora" by the inhabitants of the sloping hills of the Adriatic from Trieste to Zara) swept over the states of Alabama and Georgia, and in less than two hours the thermometer fell forty degrees. In the morning it was a luxury to breathe the balmy airs from the Gulf of Mexico, redolent of fresh flowers and all the wealth of early spring; in the afternoon the weather was raw and bleak, and suggested Siberia or Greenland. The unhappy wayfarer, unaccustomed to the clime, was fain to betake himself to his thickest robes, or to sit in stifling proximity to that greatest of all abominations, an American stove, glowing at a red heat with anthracite coal. Nor was it strangers alone who suffered. The natives are no more inured to these abrupt changes of temperature than travelers are. The men think it unsafe to leave off their overcoats in February days that seem to an Englishman as hot as the days of mid-June; and the ladies—more susceptible of cold than any ladies I ever met with in the Old World—will not venture their fair noses or their fair finger-tips beyond the warm privacy of their boudoirs or bed-rooms when there blows a breeze from the east or north.

While steaming up the Alabama, and for twenty miles running a race with another boat, which, greatly to my satisfaction, parted company with us at the junction with the Tombigbee, I could not help reflecting on the numerous fires, wrecks, and explosions for which the rivers of the South are notorious. I inquired whether it was the recklessness of the captains, or whether it was that of the passengers, who but too often incite captains to race with rival boats, *pour passer le temps* and to beguile the monotony of the voyage, that produced such accidents. Then I debated whether there could be any stimulating influence in a Southern atmosphere which acted upon the human brain and organization so as to make men more thoughtless and impulsive than they are in the steadier and soberer North; or whether it was a want of care in the manufacture or the management of the machinery; or whether all these causes might not combine more or less to render life more insecure in the Southern railways and rivers than it is in other parts of the world? Altogether I was so gloomily impressed with the idea of impending calamity, that I looked carefully and anxiously around to weigh the chances of escape if our boat should be the victim either of misfortune or mismanagement. The prospect was not particularly pleasant. The river had overflowed its banks, and the trees on each side, as far as the eye could pierce through the intricacies of the primeval forest, stood three or four feet deep in the stream. There was nothing to be seen but a waste of water and a tangled forest-growth—the haunt of alligators and rattlesnakes. There was this comfort, however—it was too early in the year either for alligators or rattlesnakes, both of which hibernate in these regions until the beginning of May. I ultimately came to the conclusion that, if the *St. Charles* (such was the name of our boat) took fire or burst her boiler, the most reasonable and promising chance of safety would be to seize a life-belt, to plunge into the water and make for the jungle, where, perched on the branch of a tree, I might await with all the fortitude at my command the mode and the hour of deliverance. On retiring to rest for the night, having made sure of a life-belt (and one is placed in every berth to be ready for the worst), I speedily forgot my forebodings in the blessed sleep " which slid into my soul." Next afternoon, safely landed at the pretty but inhospitable city of Montgomery (only inhospitable as far as its principal inn is concerned), I exchanged the perils of the river for the perils of the rail. Let me not be considered an exaggerator or an alarmist. *All* traveling is in the South more perilous than it is any where else. The " reason why" is difficult to tell on any other supposition than that the climate is too relaxing to the body and too stimulating to the brain of the Anglo-Saxon races, and that they become reckless and careless in consequence. But I must leave this point for the consideration of physiologists, assuring them that, like the shake of Lord Burleigh's head in the play, "there may be something in it," and proceed with my story.

After leaving Montgomery, and traveling all night through the long, weary, and apparently illimitable pine forests of Georgia, in the upper branches of which the night wind made a perpetual moaning, our train arrived at nine in the morning in the beautiful little city of Augusta. Here an hour was allowed us for breakfast, and hither the electric telegraph conveyed to us from the Tombigbee and Alabama Rivers, the announcement of one of the most heart-rending steam-boat calamities that had ever occurred, even in Southern waters. The newspapers put into our hands at breakfast narrated the circumstances in the curtest, dryest, and baldest manner, but I learned the details afterward from a variety of sources. These details, doubtless, made a stronger impression on my mind than they might otherwise have done, from the strange presentiment of evil which I had experienced on the river, and from the similarity of some of the circumstances that actually occurred to those which my fancy had conjured up on the lovely moonlight evening when our vessel had pierced the silent wilderness of "the beautiful river."

Before leaving the "Battle House" at Mobile I noticed a large steamer at the levee called the *Eliza Battle*, and wondered whether she were so named after one of the Battle family, from whom the Battle House, or Hotel, had taken its appellation. This elegant steamer, a floating palace, as most of these river boats are, was suddenly discovered to be on fire in her voyage from Mobile up the Tombigbee. She had a large freight of dry goods, provisions, and groceries, which she was taking up to the plantations in part payment of the cotton bales which she had brought down, and upward of fifty passengers, of whom about twenty were women and children.

How the fire originated is not known; but, as already narrated, the night was intensely cold, and water spilled upon the deck froze almost immediately. Large icicles hung on the inside, and oozed through the wood-work of the paddle-boxes; and even the negro stokers, who fed the furnaces with wood, were cold at their work. The machinery, furnaces, and boilers of these boats are on the lower deck, open to all the winds of heaven, and are not inclosed like the machinery of English boats, so that, even in feeding the furnaces with logs of greasy pine and looking at a roaring fire, the workmen may feel cold. Whether the negroes piled on the wood too fiercely and overheated the funnel, or whether sparks from the chimney fell on some of the more combustible freight upon the lower deck, is not, and possibly never will be known; but at one hour after midnight the fearful cry of "Fire!" was raised in the *Eliza Battle*. The flames made rapid progress, and all efforts to extinguish or subdue them were unavailing. Amid the shrieks and frantic prayers of agonized women—some moved out of their beds at a moment's notice, and rushing on to the deck in their night-clothes, some of them grasping their terrified little children by the hand, or clasping them to their bosoms, ready to plunge into the river as the less fearful of the two forms of death which menaced them—the voice of the captain was heard giving orders, and urging all the passengers to keep to the ship. In one minute he promised to run her ashore among the trees. Husbands consoled their wives with the hope of safety; and all the passengers, male or female, tacitly or openly agreed that the captain was right, and that their only chance of safety lay in obedience to his orders.

The captain was at his post. The wheel obeyed his hand, and in less than a minute the ship was aground on the riverbank, her upper deck high amid the branches of the oaks, cottonwood, and cypress. How it was managed my informants could not tell, but in a few minutes between forty and fifty human creatures—white and black, free and slave, male and female, young and old—were perched upon the strongest boughs to the leeward of the flames, a motley and a miserable company. Soon after, the burning vessel drifted down the stream with the bodies of many of the passengers and of the negro crew; how many, none at that time could tell, nor have I ever been able to ascertain.

Then a new horror became visible and palpable, and grew more horrible every hour. In this desolate situation, the tender women and children, without clothes to shelter them, were exposed to the pitiless breath of a "norther," the coldest wind that blows. Some of them were so weak that strong-handed and kind-hearted men stripped themselves of their under garments to cover their frailer fellow-sufferers, or tied women and children — by stockings, cravats, pocket-handkerchiefs, and other contrivances—to the branches, lest their limbs, benumbed by the cold, should be unable to perform their offices, and they should drop, like lumps of inanimate matter, from the trees into the dismal swamp below. Hour after hour, until daylight, they remained in this helpless condition, anxiously looking for assistance. They listened to every sound on the water with the faint hope that it might prove to proceed from the paddles of a steam-boat coming to their deliverance, or the plashing oar of a row-boat from some neighboring plantation, whose owner had heard of their calamity and was hastening to the rescue. Even the cry of a water-bird gave them courage, lest the bird perchance might have been startled by an approaching boat; but no boat appeared. There was no help within call. The cold stars shone alone upon their misery. The night wind rustled and shook the dead leaves of last year upon the trees, and the ripple of the river, flowing as calmly to the sea as if human hearts were not breaking, and precious human lives ebbing away upon its dreary banks, were the only sounds audible except their own prayers and lamentations, and the wailing cry of a young child dying in its mother's arms. After a couple of hours, one little baby, frozen to death, dropped from the hands of its young mother, too benumbed to hold it, and, falling into the swamp below, was lost from sight. After another short interval, the mother also fell from the tree into the swamp alongside of her child. A husband, who had tied himself to a tree and held his wife and child close to his bosom, discovered that both wife and child were dead with cold, and kept kissing their lifeless forms for hours, until he, too, felt his hands powerless to hold them, and they dropped from his nerveless grasp into the same cold receptacle. And when morning at last dawned upon their sufferings, it was found by the sad survivors, on counting their numbers, that twenty-eight were missing, and had only escaped the fearful but quick death of fire to perish by the still more fearful, because more lingering, death of cold. Surely in all the annals of shipwreck there has seldom occurred a more affecting incident than this!

With this story in full possession of all my sympathies, I saw but little of the landscape between Augusta and Charleston—nothing but a wilderness of pine-trees—amid which, every time the engine stopped to take in water, I could hear the low wind moaning and sighing. Pine-trees—nothing but pine-trees—such is the landscape of Georgia and the Carolinas.

CHAPTER XXIII.

SOUTH CAROLINA.

Charleston, March, 1858.

THERE is a class of very small critics in America who are continually on the look-out for the errors, great or small, that may be made by English travelers in their description of American scenery, manners, or institutions. There is another class of persons who make it their pleasure to mystify, bamboozle, and hoax strangers, and who palm off upon them, with grave faces, lies of every magnitude, great and petty, mischievous and harmless. There is another class, composed to some extent of persons belonging to the snarlers and *mauvais farceurs* already mentioned, but including many honest and estimable people, who think that no person from the Old World can understand the New, and that America is, and must be, a mystery to all but Americans. Some of my letters published in England from time to time have more or less excited the attention of these persons. The first—in spying out and commenting upon small mistakes, in which the obvious errors of the printer were set down to the writer—attempted to prove that the leaven of one unimportant misstatement leavened the whole lump. The second tried their best and worst, but were guarded against, and, to use their own jargon, they did not "sell the Britisher." For the benefit of the third and of the first class of objectors, and to show them what a difficult animal to catch is a fact, and what a slippery tail it has, even when you think you have got safe hold of it, a little story relative to Boston, in Massachusetts, may not be inappropriate or useless, inasmuch as it may convince some of them that the most conscientious and painstaking of travelers may involuntarily fall into mistakes, and that, in some instances at least, these mistakes may be traced to the incapacity or carelessness of those who answer questions, and not to the incapacity or carelessness of those who put them. Being in the office of a gentleman who had resided thirty years in the city of Boston, he informed me that in the street next to his own Benjamin Franklin was born.

"Does the house exist?"

"No, it was pulled down some years ago, and a large store or pile of buildings was erected on the site."

"Is there no inscription to state that here was born Benjamin Franklin?"

"None whatever."

"I am surprised at that. The birthplace of a man of whom Boston and all America is so justly proud—one of the great fathers of American liberty—of a man who, next to Washington, is the American best known throughout the world, ought to have been designated by some inscription or memorial."

"Well, I agree with you that there ought to have been something of the kind, but there is not."

Ten minutes afterward I passed through the street of Franklin's birthplace, looked from the opposite side of the way to the large building erected on the site of the humble cottage where the great man first saw the light, and there, on the top of the building, in large letters, "that those who run might read," was the inscription which the old inhabitant ignored, or was unaware of, stating the fact that in that place was born Benjamin Franklin. A traveler might well have been excused for taking the not very important fact, or no fact, on such respectable authority as that from whom I received it, but yet the traveler would have been wrong, and might have been yelped at for his inaccuracy by all the angry curs of half a dozen little Pedlingtons.

But this has nothing to do with Charleston in South Carolina except as far as it may serve to bespeak the charitable indulgence both of those who do and of those who do not know how difficult it is to catch fast hold of a fact, large or small, and what amount of the errors of a traveler may be fairly attributed to those with whom the traveler may be brought into contact, and who lead him astray without intending to do so.

Charleston, the greatest city of South Carolina, but not its capital, is pleasantly situated between the Rivers Ashley and Cooper, at their junction with the sea. These names were given to the two streams by an early English governor of South Carolina, who sought in this manner to perpetuate his own patronymics in the New World; but there is a disposition at present to revert to the original Indian appellations, and to call the Cooper the Ettiwan, and the Ashley the Chicora. The population of Charleston is variously estimated from 50,000 to 60,000, of whom at least 20,000 are slaves. The city, founded in 1670, was laid out on a plan sent from England, and does not present the monotonous rectangularity of streets which characterizes American cities of a later growth. The original Constitution of South Carolina was framed by no less a person than the philosopher John Locke; and the principal church of Charleston, that of St. Michael, is affirmed by the citizens and by tradition to have been built from the designs of an architect no less renowned than Sir Christopher Wren. King Street and Queen Street were named after Charles II. and his consort, names which have been retained by the Charlestonians in spite of attempts made to change them during periods of war with England. Thus Charleston has reminiscences of the "Old Country," and is proud of them. The society of South Carolina and of Charleston is polished and aristocratic, and the principal citizens love to trace their descent from Englishmen, or from old Huguenot families driven to America by the Revocation of the Edict of Nantes. Charleston covers a large space of ground. To look at it from the top of the tower of St. Michael, or to steam into it either from the ocean or from the arms of the sea, which percolate through the Sea Islands extending along the coast from Savannah, the traveler might imagine it to contain a population of at least a quarter of a million. The great attraction of Charleston is the Battery, at the extreme point of land where the Ashley and the Cooper (or the Ettiwan and the Chicora) mingle their waters. Upon the Battery, which is laid out in walks and drives, are situated some of the finest mansions of the city; and here, in all seasons, the inhabitants congregate in the afternoon and evening to walk or ride, and inhale the fresh breezes of the Atlantic. It is their Hyde Park, their Prater, and their Champs Elysées, and they are justly proud of it.

South Carolina is called the "Palmetto State," from the abundance of palmettos that flourish in the Sea Islands along the coast—the Sea Islands that produce the cotton so much in request in England for the manufacture of the finer descriptions of muslins and cambrics. In East Bay Street, nearly opposite the office of the *Charleston Courier*, stands, carefully guarded by a fence, a magnificent palmetto in full luxuriance of growth, and in the gardens of the citizens the same tree flourishes in almost tropical beauty. The piers of the wharves at Charleston are made of palmetto wood—for the worm that consumes all other available timber spares the palmetto. The wharves of Charleston, though not so busy and bustling as the levee of New Orleans, present an animated spectacle, and the port is filled with vessels, principally from Liverpool and Greenock, taking away cotton in huge and multitudinous bales for the mills of Manchester and Glasgow, and bringing in exchange for the white freight which they carry home the black freight of the English and Scottish collieries. Coal for cotton or rice is the ultimate barter into which the commerce of Charleston often resolves itself, to the mutual advantage of all concerned.

Charleston had at one time a bad name for its inhospitable treatment of colored seamen who came from Great Britain,

France, or the free states of America into the port. It was the rule, rigidly enforced, that such seamen, whether British subjects or not, should, as soon as the vessel arrived in the harbor, be conveyed ashore and locked up in prison until such time as the captain should notify to the authorities that he was ready to depart, when his men were restored to him under strong escort, and safely deposited on board without having been permitted to exchange a word with any inhabitant of Charleston, black or white. This law led, as a natural consequence, to frequent misunderstandings, and often to reclamation, on the part of the British authorities. The rigor of the rule has lately been somewhat relaxed, chiefly, if not entirely, through the exertions of Mr. Bunch, the present British consul for North and South Carolina. Thanks to his exertions, the colored seaman, instead of being treated as a felon, is allowed to remain on board of his ship in the harbor provided he or his captain can procure bail or security that he will not attempt to go on shore. If a free colored seaman presume, in defiance of this law, to walk in the streets of Charleston, his bail is forfeited, and he is marched off to prison as a felon. It will be seen, although the system is an improvement on that which previously existed, that the people of Charleston are still too much alarmed at the idea of the consequences which might result from the admixture, even for a short period, of free negroes among their slaves, and from the interchange of ideas between them, to do justice either to themselves, to their port, to free black men, or to the maritime nations of Europe with whom they trade. But slavery is a sore subject in South Carolina and in Charleston, though not, perhaps, more so than it is in Louisiana, Alabama, Mississippi, Tennessee, Arkansas, and Georgia. Every night at nine o'clock the bells of St. Michael's ring as a signal to the negroes to return to their homes. A quarter of an hour is given them to wend their way to the abodes of their masters; and any negro, male or female, young or old, who is found in the streets after that hour without a written permit or warrant from his owner, is liable to be led off to prison and locked up until the morning.

And, while upon the subject of slavery, I may be permitted to mention the universal anxiety which prevails at the South that strangers, and especially Englishmen, should see the social operation of the system at the plantations and elsewhere, and judge for themselves as to the condition of the negroes. The slave-owners, who, as far as my observation has extended, appear to be very urbane, polished, gentlemanly, and estimable persons, imagine, from the exaggerations which have been circulated respecting negro slavery, that Englishmen who have never been in America are predisposed to look upon them as monsters of ferocity and oppression; as tyrants who maim and scourge, harass and persecute the black race, and as positive ogres of lust and cruelty. When they prove, as they may easily do, that they treat their slaves with kindness, and that, as a rule, slaves are better clad, fed, and cared for than the agricultural laborers of Europe or the slop tailors and seamstresses of London and Liverpool, they imagine that they cover the whole ground of objection to slavery.

The writers in the slave interest love to draw a contrast between the "hireling" of Europe and the "slave" of America, in which they give all the advantage to the latter. They dilate upon the certainty of subsistence in return for his labor which the slave enjoys, and upon the uncertainty that attends upon the life and the struggles of the free man, or, as they contemptuously call him, the "hireling." They assert that the free man is only of value while he can work; that if he is sick and unable to labor he must starve, unless for public or private charity; but that the slave is subject to no such hazards; that his subsistence is secured from the cradle to the grave, and that he is happier than the free man, from the absence of all care for the morrow. They refuse to argue the question upon higher ground than that of the mere animal well-being of the human cattle whom they buy and sell, and breed for profit. They seem to be satisfied if they can convince the stranger from a far country that they treat their poor dependents and immortal chattels with common humanity.

A few of them go still farther, and justify slavery not only by expediency and necessity, but by social and economic considerations—by philosophy and ethnology, and even by religion. They support it by the Old Testament and by the New, by the Pentateuch and by the Book of Revelations, by Moses and by St. John the Evangelist. Some of them go so far as to assert that it is impious to attempt to abolish slavery, inasmuch as at the end of the world—at the opening of the Sixth Seal (Revelations, chap. vi., v. 15)—there will be slavery in the world, because it is written that "every bondman and every free man" will at that day hide himself in the dens and rocks of the mountains from the wrath of God. They support it by their attachment to the doctrines of Christianity, and allege that in their opinion slavery would be a good thing in itself, if for no other reason than that it made the benighted African conversant with the great truths of the Gospel, which he could not otherwise have known, and that it raised him from the condition of paganism in his own land to that of Christianism in another.

At Charleston a book was put into my hand setting forth in glowing language the happy condition of the slave in America and the unhappy condition of the free working man in England, France, and Germany. One of the chief arguments of the author was employed to demolish the logic of a writer in the *Westminster Review*, who had cited among other objections to slavery that it demoralized the slave-owner far more than it did the slave, and that slavery was to be condemned for the very same reasons that induced the British Legislature to pass a law against cruelty to animals—cruelty which was not only objectionable, and worthy of punishment because it inflicted wrong upon the inferior creation, but because it brutalized and degraded the human beings who were guilty of it. "Very true," said the pro-slavery writer in a tone of triumph, "very true; but did the British Legislature, in its zeal in this cause, ever go so far as to decree the manumission of horses?" And, as if this argument were a triumphant answer to all objections, he left the Westminster reviewer, without deigning to take farther notice of him, crushed under the weight of such tremendous logic!

The slave-owners, as a body, are not cruel, and many of them treat their slaves with paternal and patriarchal kindness; but they are blinded by education and habits, as well as supposed self-interest, to the real evils of a system the horrors of which they do their best to alleviate. In my next letter, without entering into any argument *pro* or *con*, I shall describe my visit to a very large rice plantation near this city, where upward of two hundred slaves are employed, and where the system is in full operation.

CHAPTER XXIV.

A RICE PLANTATION.

Charleston, South Carolina, March, 1858.

IN visiting a rice plantation, my object was not so much to satisfy myself that the slave-owners of America are kind to their negroes, as to satisfy the public opinion of Charleston that English travelers are not prejudiced against Southern proprietors, and that they are willing to be convinced, by ocular demonstration, that humanity and generosity toward the negro race may exist in the bosoms and sway the actions of men who hold property in their fellows. So much exaggeration has entered into the descriptions of negro life in the South, which have been given to the world by writers who have earned for themselves the title of "malignant philanthropists," that the slave-owners actually think they have sufficiently vindicated slavery when they have proved, as they easily can, that they do not scourge, disfigure, maim, starve, or kill their negroes, but that, on the contrary, they feed them well, clothe them well, provide them with good medical attendance for the ills of the flesh, and spiritual consolation for the doubts and distresses of the soul. They will not stand on higher ground. But far different is the case with those educated in the different moral atmosphere of Europe. On my first arrival at New Orleans I lingered for a few moments at the open door of a slave dépôt, without daring to go in, lest I should be suspected of espionage or of idle curiosity, and expelled. But seeing among the company an eminent merchant of New York, whose friendship I had been fortunate enough to make, and whom I knew to be no slave-dealer or supporter of slavery, I walked in and joined his party, drawn thither, like myself, by curiosity. On one side of the room the male slaves, with clean linen, and shining new hats and boots, were arranged, and on the other the females were disposed in their best attire, most of them exceedingly neat, but some bedizened with ribbons of colors more flaring and tawdry than elegant or appropriate. I was immediately beset with entreaties to purchase.

"Achetez-moi," said a young negress in French; "je suis bonne cuisinière, et couturière. Achetez-moi!"

"Buy me," said another, in the same language; "I am accustomed to children, and can make myself useful in the nursery."

I felt a sensation something similar to that of the first qualm of sea-sickness to be so addressed by my fellow creatures—a feeling of nausea, as if I were about to be ill. I told the poor women that I was a stranger who had not come to buy. But they were incredulous; and, when at last convinced, they returned to their seats with a sigh and an expression of deep disappointment on their dark and good-humored features. I entertained at that moment such a hatred of slavery that, had it been in my power to abolish it in one instant off the face of the earth by the mere expression of my will, slavery at that instant would have ceased to exist.

I then walked to the male side of the slave mart, where I was beset by similar entreaties, urged in every variety of tone and manner, and by almost every variety of laborer and handicraftsman. Some were accustomed to the cotton, and some to the sugar plantation; some were carpenters, some gardeners, some coachmen, some barbers, some waiters; but all were equally anxious to be sold. One man—who, to my inexperienced eyes, seemed as white as myself, and whom I at once put down in my own mind as an Irishman, of the purest quality of the county of Cork—got up from his seat as I passed, and asked me to buy him; "I am a good gardener, your honor," said he, with an unmistakable brogue. "I am also a bit of a carpenter, and can look after the horses, and do any sort of odd job about the house."

"But you are joking," said I; "you are an Irishman?"

"My father was an Irishman," he said.

At this moment the slave-dealer and owner of the dépôt came up.

"Is there not a mistake here?" I inquired. "This is a white man."

"His mother was a nigger," he replied. "We have sometimes much whiter men for sale than he is. Look at his hair and lips. There is no mistake about him."

Again the sickness came over me, and I longed to get into the open air to breathe the purer atmosphere.

"I would like to buy that man and set him free," I said to my friend from New York.

"You would do him no good," was the reply. "A manumitted slave has seldom any self-reliance or energy. Slavery so degrades and cripples the moral faculties of the negroes that they require the crutch, even in freedom, and can not walk alone. They find it impossible to compete with the free whites, and, if left to themselves, sink into the lowest and most miserably-paid occupations."

"You are an Englishman and a traveler," said the slave-dealer, "and I should be much obliged to you if you would put any questions to the negroes."

"What questions?" said I. "Shall I ask them whether they would prefer freedom or slavery?"

"I don't mean that," he replied. "Ask them whether I do not treat them well? whether I am not kind to them? whether they do not have plenty to eat and drink while they are with me?"

I told him that I had no doubt of the fact; that they looked clean, comfortable, and well fed; but— And in that "but" lay the whole case, though the worthy dealer of New Orleans was totally incapable of comprehending it.

As already mentioned, I had received many invitations while in the South to visit plantations of cotton, sugar, and rice, that I might see the slaves in their homes, and watch them at their labors in the field or the swamp, and judge for myself whether they were well or ill treated, and whether their owners were men of the patriarchal type, like Abraham of old, or of the type of Blunderbore in the child's story—ogres of cruelty and oppression. I was unable to accept any of these invitations until my arrival in Charleston, when I gladly availed myself of the opportunity afforded me by the courteous hospitality of General Gadsden to visit his rice plantation at Pimlico. The general is known both to Europe and America as the negotiator of the famous Gadsden Treaty with Mexico, by means of which a portion of the large province of Sonora was annexed to the already overgrown dominion of Brother Jonathan. His estate at Pimlico is situated about twenty-seven miles from Charleston. The general owns on this property between two and three hundred slaves, but only resides upon it for a small portion of the year, having possessions in Florida and other parts of the Union, and being compelled, like all other men of European blood, to avoid, in the warm weather, the marshy regions favorable to rice cultivation.

From Charleston the railway for twenty miles runs as straight as an arrow's flight through a forest of primeval pine. These melancholy trees form the most conspicuous feature of the landscape in the two Carolinas and in Georgia. Often for whole days, and for hundreds of miles, the traveler sees no other vegetation but this rank, monotonous forest growth. Here and there a clearing, here and there a swamp, here and there a village, dignified with the title of a town or of a city, and one unvarying level of rich but uncultivated land—such is the general characteristic of the "sunny South" as the traveler leaves the sea-board and penetrates inward to the great valley of the Mississippi. In less than an hour and a half our train stopped at a station at which there was neither clerk, nor check-taker, nor porter, nor official of any kind. Having descended, luggage in hand, we saw our train dart away into the long-receding vista of the forest, and awaited in solitude the vehicle which had been ordered from Pimlico to convey us to the plantation. We being before, or the negro-driver after the appointed time, we had to remain about a quarter of an hour at the station, and amuse ourselves as best we might. Though the station itself was deserted, a small log hut and inclosure almost immediately opposite swarmed with life. A whole troop of ragged children, with fair hair and blue eyes, played about the clearing; a donkey browsed upon the scanty undergrowth; cocks crowed upon the fence; hens cackled in the yard; and lean pigs prowled about in every direction, seeking what they might devour. The loneliness of the place, with the deep, thick pine woods all around it, and the shiny lines of rail stretching as far as the vision could penetrate in one unbroken parallel into the wilderness, suggested the inquiry as to who and what were the inhabitants of the log hut. "The pest of the neighborhood," was the reply. "Here lives a German Jew and his family, who keep a store for the accommodation of the negroes." "And how a pest?" "The negroes require no accommodation. They are supplied by their owners with every thing necessary for their health and comfort; but they resort to places like this with property which they steal from their masters, and which the men exchange, at most nefarious profit to the Jew receiver, for whisky and tobacco, and which the females barter for ribbons and tawdry finery. Wherever there is a large plantation, these German traders—if it be not a desecration of the name of trade to apply it to their business—squat in the neighborhood, build up a wooden shanty, and open a store. If a saddle, a coat, or a watch be lost, the planter may be tolerably certain that it has been bartered by his negroes at some such place as this for whisky or tobacco. The business is so profitable that, although the delinquent may be sometimes detected and imprisoned, he soon contrives to make money enough to remove with his ill-gotten gains to the Far West, where his antecedents are unknown and never inquired after, and where, perhaps under a new name, he figures as a great merchant in the more legitimate business of a dry-goods store."

A drive of five miles through the forest, in the course of which we had to cross a swamp two feet deep with water, brought us to Pimlico and its mansion, pleasantly embowered among trees of greater beauty and variety than we had passed on our way. Among these, the live or evergreen oak, the cypress, the cedar, and the magnolia, were the most conspicuous. The mansion, like most of the houses in the South, where trees are abundant and stone is scarce, was built of wood, and gave but little exterior promise of the comfort and elegance to be found within. Here we fared sumptuously, having our choice of drinks, from London porter and Allsop's India ale, to Hock and Claret, and Catawba and Isabella, of Longworth's choicest growth. The food was of every variety, including fish with names unknown in Europe, but of most excellent quality, and game in an abundance with which Europe can scarcely claim equality. The greatest novelty was the small turtle called the "cooter," similar to, but smaller than the "terrapin," so well known and esteemed in Baltimore, Philadelphia, and Washington. The "cooter" is, it appears, a perquisite of the slaves. They will not themselves eat it, looking upon its flesh with loathing and aversion, but in their leisure moments they seek it in the water-courses and trenches, or at the borders of the streams, and sell it to their masters. Among other privileges which they are allowed may be here mentioned that of keeping poultry on their own account, the profits of which enable them to buy tobacco for themselves and finery for their wives.

In the morning we sallied over the plantation, under the guidance of the general, and saw the whole art and mystery of rice cultivation. At high water, the river, which gives the estate its value, is five feet above the level of the rice-ground, so that by means of sluices it is easy to flood the plantation, or any part of it, and just as easy to let off the water as soon as the growing crop has received a sufficient steeping. The rice is submitted to three several floodings before it is fit to be harvested. The first, in the early spring, is called "the sprout flow;" the second, or intermediate, when the green stalks have acquired a certain strength and height, is called "the long flow;" and the last, "the harvest flow."

Between each "flow," the slaves, male and female, are employed in gangs, under the superintendence of the overseer (or "boss," as the negroes always call a master of any kind), in hoeing among the roots. In this occupation we found about a hundred and fifty of them in different parts of the estate. They were not asked to rest from their labor on our arrival. They were coarsely but comfortably clad, and wore that cheerful good-humored expression of countenance which seems to be the equivalent and the compensation granted by paternal Providence for their loss of freedom. Measured by mere physical enjoyment, and absence of care or thought of the morrow, the slave is, doubtless, as a general rule, far happier than his master. His wants are few, he is easily satisfied, and his toil is not excessive.

Rambling along the raised dikes and sluices, the strangers of the party were surprised to see the immense flocks of birds which suddenly rose from the ground or from the low bushes that fringed the stream, and which sometimes settled upon a tree in countless thousands till the branches seemed to bend beneath their weight. They were declared to be blackbirds; but a boy of about twelve years of age, the adopted son of the the general, who had been out all the morning with his gun making havoc among them, having brought one for our inspection, it was found to be very different from the blackbird of Europe. It wanted the golden bill and the glowing plumage, and had, instead of them, a white bill and a breast speckled like that of the English thrush. It was too early in the season for the alligators to make their appearance; but they swarm in the river in the months of June and July, and commit sad depredation, not only among the fish, but among the ducks and geese, or wild-fowl that frequent the stream. Alligators are said to be quite equal to the Chinese in their partiality for dogs and cats when they can get hold of them; but cats are proverbial for their dislike of water, and dogs are too knowing to treat themselves to the luxury of a bath in any stream where the alligator is found, so that the poor alligator seldom enjoys the dainty that he most loves. But the bark of a dog excites him as much as the sight of a live turtle does a London alderman; and you have but to bring a dog to the brink of a river and make him bark, when the alligators, unless they suspect mischief, will pop their long noses out of the water, and yearn for the delicacy which hard Fate has denied them.

From the rice-grounds our party proceeded to the negro village where the slaves resided. Most of the occupiers were at work in the fields; but we entered some of the tenements, and found nothing to object to on the score of comfort. To each hut was attached a plot of ground for a garden; but none of the gardens were cultivated, or gave the slightest promise of a flower. In one there was a luxuriant peach-tree in full bloom —a perfect blaze of crimson beauty—but, as a general rule, the negro has either no love of gardens, or no time to attend to their cultivation. From all I could gather here and elsewhere, and as the result of my own observation, the former and not the latter reason explains the neglect of this beautiful and innocent means of enjoyment which both climate and circumstances place within the reach of the black population.

In the village there were a hospital, an infirmary for the sick, a chapel, where twice every Sunday Divine service was performed by a missionary, allowed to have access to the slaves upon condition of not preaching freedom to them, and a nursery, where the young children, from the earliest age upward to fourteen, were taken care of during the absence of their parents in the fields. The elder boys and girls were made useful in nursing the infants; and the whole swarm, to the number of nearly seventy, were drawn up by the side of the road, and favored us with several specimens of their vocal powers. The general declared them to be "hominy-eaters" and not workers; and they certainly looked as if hominy agreed with them, for a plumper and more joyous set of children it would have been difficult to assemble together in any country under the sun. Their songs were somewhat more hearty than musical. The entertainment was concluded by the Methodist hymn, "And that will be joyful, joyful," which the vociferous singers contrived unconsciously to turn into a comic song. But this feat, I may as well mention, is not peculiar to little negroes, for some obstreperous free Americans on board of our outward-bound steamer favored their fellow-passengers with a similar exhibition, and even managed to make a comic song out of the "Old Hundreth."

We were next introduced to "Uncle Tom"—such was the name by which he had been known long before the publication of Mrs. Stowe's novel—a venerable negro who had been fifty years upon the plantation. His exact age was not known, but he was a strong hearty man when brought from the coast of Africa in the year 1808. "Tom" had been sold by some petty African king or chief at the small price of an ounce of tobacco, and had been brought over with upward of two hundred similar unfortunates by an American slaver. He was still hale and vigorous, and had within a few years married a young wife belonging to a neighboring planter. He was told by the general that I had come to take him back to Africa; an announcement which seemed to startle and distress him, for he suddenly fell on his knees before me, clasped his hands, and implored me in very imperfect and broken English to let him stay where he was. Every one that he had known in Africa must have long since died; the ways of his own country would be strange to him, and perhaps his own countrymen would put him to death, or sell him again into slavery to some new master. He was much relieved to find that my intentions were neither so large nor so benevolent, though malevolent would perhaps be a better word to express the idea which impressed itself upon his mind in reference to my object in visiting him. The old man was presented with a cigar by one of our party, and with a glass of whisky by the general's orders, and he courteously drank the health of every one present, both collectively and individually. Drinking to a lady, he expressed the gallant wish that she might grow more beautiful as she grew older; and to the donor of the cigar, he uttered his hope that at the last day "Gor Almighty might hide him in some place where the devil not know where to find him."

On this plantation I have no doubt, from what I saw, that the slaves are kindly treated, and that the patriarchal relation in all its best aspects exists between the master and his poor dependents. But I do not wish to depict this one as a sample of all, but confine myself to a simple narrative of what I saw. Slavery has many aspects, and upon some future occasion I may be enabled to state some other facts, less patent, which may throw light upon its operation not only upon the fortunes and character of the white men who hold them in bondage, but upon the future destinies of the United States of America.

CHAPTER XXV.

SAVANNAH AND THE SEA ISLANDS.

March, 1858.

From Charleston to Savannah by sea is a distance of one hundred miles; by land—there being no railway communication, except by traversing two sides of a triangle—the distance is about two hundred. A direct coast railway is in course of construction; but at present most travelers, except those who are very bad sailors, prefer the sea passage. As I had already gone over a considerable portion of the land route, through the pine forests of Georgia and South Carolina,

> "Where, northward as you go,
> The pines forever grow;
> Where, southward if you bend,
> Are pine-trees without end;
> Where, if you travel west,
> Earth loves the pine-tree best;
> Where, eastward if you gaze,
> Through long, unvaried ways,
> Behind you and before,
> Are pine-trees evermore;"

I preferred the sea, as offering more comfort, as well as more novelty, than the land route. Taking my passage in the tidy little boat, the *St. Mary's*, bound for the St. John's River in Florida, and touching at Savannah, I found myself in comfortable quarters. The crew consisted entirely of negro slaves; the only white men on board, the passengers excepted, being the captain and the clerk. There are two routes to Savannah by sea—one the outer, and one the inner—and the *St. Mary's* being more of a river than a sea boat, only ventures on the outer passage when the weather is calm. Such being the case on this particular day, we made a short and pleasant passage, leaving the harbor of Charleston at nine in the morning, and arriving at Savannah before seven in the evening. It was not until we arrived at the mouth of the Savannah River, and began to steam up for eighteen miles to the city, that the scenery offered any attractions. On each side was a low, flat, fertile country, with reeds twenty feet high—the summer haunts of the alligator—growing upon the bank, and the land studded with palmetto trees, rice plantations, and negro villages. As the night darkened the blaze of a burning forest lit up the whole of the landward horizon, and gave lurid evidence that man was at work, and displacing the wilderness to make room for rice and cotton. The flocks of wild-fowl upon the Savannah positively darkened the air, and, when the birds descended to feed or rest, it seemed as if black clouds, moved by their own volition, had taken refuge among the reeds and canes. The Savannah River divides the States of Georgia and South Carolina for a portion of its length. It is navigable for sea steamers only as far as the city of Savannah, and for steamers of a smaller draught as far as Augusta, the second city of Georgia, 230 miles inland.

Savannah was founded in 1732 by the celebrated General Oglethorpe, and is the chief city of Georgia, though not the capital, that honor being conferred, as is usual in the States, upon a more central place, of very inferior importance. Milledgeville, the political capital, contains a population of about 3000 persons, while Savannah, the commercial capital, has a population of upward of 30,000, of whom about one half are slaves. Of all the cities in America, none impresses itself more vividly upon the imagination and the memory than this little green bowery city of the South. It stands upon a terrace about forty feet higher than the river, and presents the appearance of an agglomeration of rural hamlets and small towns. If four-and-twenty villages had resolved to hold a meeting, and had assembled at this place, each with its pump, its country church, its common, and its avenue of trees, the result would have been a fac simile of Savannah. Twenty-four open spaces, as large as, or larger than Bedford Square, with a pump in the middle, a church or a bank at one side, and neat wooden and stone houses around, the open spaces being laid out into walks and drives, and thickly planted with trees, among which the flowering China-tree or pride of India, the œlanthus, and the evergreen oak are the most prominent—such are the component parts and general aspect of Savannah. The soil is so loose and sandy that a good road is a luxury to be read of and imagined by the people, but not to be enjoyed for want of stone and every other material of sufficient hardness. There is, it is true, about a mile and a half of shell road leading toward the lovely estate of Bonaventura on which a carriage can roll with a moderate amount of comfort. This road gives so much satisfaction that the people are determined to extend it, and to imitate it in other directions by such means as fortune and circumstances have placed within their control. Like all Americans, whether of the North or the South, the inhabitants of Savannah, rich or poor, free or slave, consume immense quantities of oysters. For breakfast, for dinner, and for supper, oysters, in one form or another, are sure to be supplied to all above the poorest classes of the population; and here there are few who can be called as absolutely poor as their compeers in Europe. The result is, according to the calculation of a notable inhabitant, that Savannah consumes in a year a sufficient quantity of oysters to leave shells enough for the construction of one mile of road. But at present the roads are no exception to the general badness of American thoroughfares. They are dusty and rutty in the fine weather, muddy and rutty when it rains.

The view from the Custom-house and Exchange, and from the street occupied by the stores, offices, and warehouses of the merchants, and which skirts the river for a mile, extends to the distant horizon over a low, flat country, covered for the most part with rice plantations and marshy ground. A gentleman of this city who had filled a diplomatic appointment in Turkey and Egypt, and whose courtesies at Savan-

THE CEMETERY OF BOYATZKEUI.

nah I gratefully remember, declared that he often thought he was looking at Egypt when he looked at this portion of Georgia. There were the same climate, the same atmosphere, the same soil, the same cultivation, and a river offering the same characteristics as the Nile. But of all the scenery in and about Savannah, the Cemétery of Bonaventura is the most remarkable. There is nothing like it in America, or perhaps in the world. Its melancholy loveliness, once seen, can never be forgotten. Dull indeed must be the imagination, and cold the fancy of any one who could wander through its weird and fairy avenues without being deeply impressed with its solemnity and appropriateness for the last resting-place of the dead. One melancholy enthusiast, a clergyman, weary of his life, disgusted with the world, with a brain weakened by long brooding over a disappointed affection, happened in an evil moment to stray into this place. He had often meditated suicide, and the insane desire took possession of his mind with more than its usual intensity as he lingered in this solemn and haunted spot. For days and nights he wandered about it and through it, and at last determined in his melancholy phrensy that to die for the satisfaction of being buried in that place would be the supremest happiness the world could offer. He wrote his last sad wishes upon a piece of paper, left it upon a tomb, and leaped into the Savannah River. His body was discovered some days afterward; but—alas for the vanity of human wishes!—his dying request was not complied with, and it was decided by the authorities that he should be buried in the city of Savannah. So he died as he had lived—in vain.

And why is the Cemetery of Bonaventura so eminently beautiful? Let me try to describe it. The place was formerly the country seat of an early settler named Tatnall, one of the founders of the colony of Georgia. This gentleman, though he came to a forest land where trees were considered a nuisance, admired the park-like beauty around the great country mansions of the nobility and gentry in his native England, and, while every one else in the colony was cutting down trees, made himself busy in planting them. Having built himself a house on the estate of Bonaventura, he planted an avenue or carriage-drive leading up to its porch, and the tree he chose for the purpose was the evergreen oak, next to the cypress and the magnolia the noblest tree in the Southern States of America. In due time, long after the good man's death, the trees attained a commanding height, and from their boughs hung the long, feathery festoons of the tillandsia, or Spanish moss, that lends such melancholy beauty to all the Southern landscape. In the shadow of the wild wood around this place the Tatnalls are buried; but the mansion-house, which was of wood—as nearly all the rural dwellings are in Georgia and the Carolinas—having taken fire one Christmas evening, when a large party were assembled, and being utterly destroyed, with the sole exception of the chimneys and a little brick-work, the then owner took a dislike to the place, and never rebuilt the dwelling. The estate was ultimately sold, and now belongs to Mr. Wiltberger, the proprietor of the Pulaski House at Savannah, who, finding the tombstones of the Tatnalls and others in the ground, had a portion set aside for the purposes of a public cemetery. Never was a place more beautifully adapted by nature for such an object. The mournful avenue of live oak, and the equally mournful glades that pierce on every side into the profuse and tangled wilderness, are all hung with the funereal drapery of the tillandsia. To those who have never seen this peculiar vegetation it may be difficult to convey an adequate idea of its sadness and loveliness. It looks as if the very trees, instinct with life, had veiled themselves like mourners at a grave, or as if the fogs and vapors from the marshes had been solidified by some stroke of electricity, and hung from the trees in palpable wreaths, swinging and swaying to every motion of the winds. Not unlike the effect produced by the tattered banners hung from the roofs of Gothic cathedrals as trophies of war in the olden time, or to mark the last resting-places of knights and nobles, is the effect of these long streamers pending from the overarching boughs of the forest. Many of them are so long as to trail upon the ground from a height of twenty or thirty feet, and many of the same length, drooping from the topmost branches of oak and cypress, dangle in mid air. What adds to the awe inspired by the remarkable beauty of this parasitic plant is the alleged fact that wherever it flourishes the yellow fever is from time to time a visitant. It grows plentifully on the shores of the Lower Mississippi from Cairo to New Orleans, and throughout all Louisiana, Alabama, Mississippi, Tennessee, Georgia, and South Carolina. In North Carolina it is not so common, and disappears altogether in Virginia. In New Orleans it has been converted into an article of commerce, and being dried and peeled, it is used instead of horsehair—which in this condition it much resembles—for stuffing mattresses and cushions for chairs and sofas.

As I had determined to return to Charleston by sea, I gladly awaited at Savannah the return of the *St. Mary's* from Florida. It was not until thirty hours after her appointed time that the little steamer, with her white captain and her black crew, reappeared in the river. She had met with strong head winds at sea, and, the bad weather still continuing, the captain determined to try the inner instead of the outer passage. This arrangement was in every way to my taste, as it would afford me the opportunity of sailing through the countless and picturesque mazes of the Sea Islands. These islands extend from Charleston downward to Savannah, and as far south as the great peninsula of Florida, and are famous for the production of the fine staple so well known and esteemed in all the cotton markets of the world—from New Orleans, Mobile, and Charleston, to Liverpool, Manchester, and Glasgow—as the "Sea Island cotton." In the summer this region is not habitable by the whites, but in the early spring there is neither fog nor fever, and the climate is delicious. Though the storm raged in the outer sea, the weather was calm, sunny, and beautiful as the *St. Mary's* threaded her way for a hundred and fifty miles through the narrow channels amid these low and fertile islands, some as large as the Isle of Wight or the Isle of Man, others as small as the islets of Venice.

At times the water-way was like that of a noble river, broad as the Mississippi, but without its currents, and at others not wider than the Regent's Canal, or the New River at Islington. So narrow was it at times that we could have jumped ashore from either side of the deck; but the feat, though possible, and indeed easy, was not inviting; for, had any one been frolicsome enough to do so, he would have found himself up to the middle, or perchance to the neck, in soft bog and swamp. We had often to twist and turn in places where it seemed quite impossible that a steam-boat could pass, and the negroes had continually to push us out of difficulties by means of sturdy poles ten or twelve feet long—an exercise in which some of the passengers seemed delighted to take part. The tall rushes and reeds grew up to the height of the deck; and, had it been midsummer, we might have disturbed many an alligator as we wound our way, north and south, east and west, far into the bowels of the land, and then out again toward the sea, in this intricate navigation. Twenty times at least the *St. Mary's* seemed fast aground, and as often did stalwart negroes launch the ship's boat and row ashore, to affix a tow-rope to a stake left amid the vegetation in previous voyages, to enable us to be manœuvred off again. The whole voyage was one constant succession of novelties of scene and adventure.

From the deck we could look over a large expanse of country, studded with cotton-fields, with the white mansions of the planters, with negro villages, and with here and there a stretch of pasture land in which the cattle were feeding. Amid the swamp the palmetto, sometimes singly, sometimes in clusters, raised its graceful branches, while on the higher grounds, and sometimes on the bank of the channel, were clumps of pines and evergreen oaks, all hung with the graceful but melancholy drapery of the tillandsia. At one turn we came suddenly upon a negro village, and several little "darkies," from the ages of three to ten, some entirely and others partially naked, who were upon a dungheap, set up a shout of delight on our arrival, which speedily brought forth the sable elders of the place, as well as the dogs, to take a look at us; the adults grinning and showing their white teeth, the dogs and the children vying with each other who should make the most noise in our honor. Many of the planters' houses which we passed were large and commodious, and surrounded by groves of oak, cedar, and magnolia, giving the place the leafy attractions of an English midsummer all through the winter.

There is throughout all this country a very considerable population engaged in the cultivation of the Sea Island cotton, and the villages as well as country mansions were numerous as we passed. Here, for four or five months in the year, the planter lives like a patriarch of the olden time, or like a petty despotic monarch, surrounded by his obedient subjects, with a white "oikonomos," or overseer, for his prime minister, who, on his part, is condemned to endure the climate the whole year, that the slaves may be kept in order, while the master himself hurries away with his family to the far North—to New York or to Newport, and very often to London and Paris—to spend the abundant revenues of his cotton crop. We passed one considerable town or city—that of Beaufort, the capital of the Sea Islands, and pleasantly as well as imposingly situated—and then, steaming through the broad channel of the Whapoo, reached Charleston after a long but by no means disagreeable passage of forty-eight hours.

CHAPTER XXVI.

FROM SOUTH CAROLINA TO VIRGINIA.

March, 1858.

AWAY again through the eternal pine forests for hundreds of miles! The railway was as straight as an arrow's flight or a mathematical line, and we had to travel for thirty hours without other stoppages than an occasional ten minutes or quarter of an hour for breakfast or dinner. The country was unpicturesque, the railway the reverse of comfortable, and sleep, if wooed, was difficult to be won in "cars" or carriages where there was no support for the back or the head of the unhappy traveler; where there was not even a place to stow away a hat, a stick, an umbrella, or a bag; and where about sixty persons of all ages and conditions of life, including half a dozen young children, and at least twenty people who chewed tobacco and spat, were closely packed in an atmosphere deprived of all its moisture and elasticity by the red heat of the anthracite stove that glowed and throbbed in the middle of this locomotive den. Behind the stove, on the side of the car, in large letters, was the following inscription:

GENTLEMEN
ARE REQUESTED
NOT TO SPIT
ON THE STOVE.

And here, as well as at any other point of his journey, let a European, unaccustomed to the odious practice of tobacco-chewing, and its concomitant and still more odious practice of spitting, so disgustingly prevalent in the Southern and Western States, and to a minor extent in the Northern, disburden himself upon the subject, and have done with it. Before witnessing the extent and prevalence of this filthiness, I imagined that the accounts given by preceding travelers were exaggerations and caricatures, intended to raise an ill-natured laugh; but observation speedily convinced me that all I had previously read upon the subject fell short of the truth, and that it would be difficult to exaggerate the extent of the vice, and the callousness with which it is regarded even by people of education and refinement. Americans who have traveled in Europe do not seem annoyed that strangers should take notice of the practice and be offended by it; but custom so dulls even their perception of its offensiveness that they consider the fault-finders as somewhat squeamish and over-sensitive. Once, at Washington, I found myself the centre of a group of members of Congress, two of whom were among the most expert and profuse spitters (I was going to write expectorators, but the word is not strong enough) whom it was ever my fortune to meet with, when, the conversation having turned upon the military prowess and skill of several gentlemen who had distinguished themselves in the Mexican war, I was suddenly asked by one of them—who cleared his mouth, for the purpose, of a most portentous flood of tobacco-juice—who, in my opinion, and in that of Englishmen who studied American politics, was the greatest general in the United States? The reply was, General SPIT. "Well," said the senator, "I calculate you are about right; and though you, as a Britisher, may say so, I should advise you not to put the observation into print, as some of our citizens might take it as personal." On another occasion, an eminent lawyer, who had filled some of the highest offices of the state, a man to whom ancient and modern literature were equally familiar, who had studied European as well as American politics, whose mind seemed to have run through the whole circle of human knowledge, and who could converse eloquently on any subject, though, while he spoke, the tobacco-juice oozed out of the corners of his mouth, and ran down upon his shirt-front and waistcoat, took a large cake of tobacco from his side-pocket, and courteously offered me a chew. The cake, I should think, weighed about half a pound. I asked him if he had ever calculated how many gallons of spit such a cake represented? "Well," he said, putting the cake back again into his pocket, "it *is* a disgusting habit. I quite agree with you. I have made several attempts to break myself of it, but in vain. I can not think or work without a chew; and, although I know it injures my stomach, and is in other respects bad for me, I am the slave of the habit, and will, I fear, be so to the end of my days." Even in the presence of ladies the chewers and spitters do not relent; and ladies seem almost, if not quite, as indifferent to the practice as the other sex. In theatres and lecture-rooms are constantly to be seen inscriptions requesting gentlemen not to spit in the boxes or on the stoves; and in all places of public resort the spittoon is an invariable article of furniture. Spittoons garnish the marble steps of the Capitol at Washington; spittoons are in all the reading-rooms, bars, lobbies, and offices of the hotels; spittoons in every railway-car; and in the halls of every State Legislature which I visited, the Parliamentary spittoons seemed to be as indispensable as the desks and benches of the members. If the American eagle were represented as holding in his or her claw a spittoon instead of the thunderbolt of Jove, the change might not be graceful or poetical, but would certainly not be inappropriate. But enough on this subject, which I would gladly have omitted to mention if I had not hoped, as I do, that the concurrent testimony of all travelers will ultimately produce some effect, and that, sooner or later, gentlemen addicted to this form of intemperance—for there are many gentlemen among them—will be shamed out of a habit so loathsome in itself, and so prejudicial to the health, bodily as well as mental, of all who indulge in it.

But do Europeans come into court with clean hands when they accuse Americans of the abuse of tobacco? Are not Englishmen in some respects almost as filthy? And is it, in reality, more disgusting to chew tobacco, than it is to walk in the streets, with or without a lady—but more especially with a lady—smoking either a cigar or a pipe in her presence? Is it not, in fact, as vulgar for any one to smoke as it would be to eat in the street? And is it more offensive in men to chew than it is in boys and youths to smoke? These are but questions of degree, and in some respects the American chewer is less offensive than the English street-smoker. The chewer poisons his own mouth, it is true, but he poisons no one's else, which is more than can be said for the smoker, who pours his pestilential fumes into the wholesome atmosphere, which belongs quite as much to his inoffensive fellow-mortal, the non-smoker, as to him, and which he, the smoker, has no legal, moral, or natural right to contaminate, to the annoyance or the injury of his neighbor.

The first night brought us to a place called Florence, whence, after a stoppage of twenty minutes, we started—sleepy, but sleepless—through the pine woods once again. At morning dawn we were in the State of North Carolina, and still amid the pine woods, stretching, vast and apparently illimitable, on every side. Most of the trees on our line of travel were tapped for their precious juice, and at every station were to be seen barrels of turpentine, the staple produce of North Carolina, waiting for transport to the coast, and thence to all parts of the civilized world. We made no stay in this ancient commonwealth, which the "smart," "go-ahead" people farther north have chosen to designate, after the well-known personage in Washington Irving's story, as the "Rip Van Winkle State," to express thereby their opinion of the somnolent, unprogressive character of the people. All day our train wheeled through its forests, and at night we expected to enjoy the luxury of a bed in the renowned and beautiful city of Richmond, in Virginia. But this was not to be. The limit of our train was at the city of Petersburg, twenty-two miles from Richmond, where we were to "connect" with another that was to carry us to our destination. But our train was two hours behind its time. The connecting train had started to the appointed minute, and there was no help for it but to remain in Petersburg and make the best of it. And we made the best of it, and certainly did not fare badly. We found an excellent hotel—fish of names unknown in Europe, and most deliciously cooked; Catawba, both Still and Sparkling, of Longworth's best; and reasonable charges. Petersburg is the third city in Virginia in point of population and importance; is situated on the Appomattox River, a tributary of the James, by which it has communication with the sea; and contains nearly 20,000 inhabitants. There is nothing of interest to be seen here, and, if there were, weary travelers such as we, who had not slept for thirty hours, and who had to rise the next morning at three o'clock, were not likely to start in the evening on any visits of exploration to the wonders of nature or the curiosities of art. So to bed we went, and had half a night's rest, being rewarded for the short allowance of sleep by the full enjoyment of a more gorgeously beautiful sunrise than often falls to the lot of any one to behold. We crossed at early morn the railway-bridge over the sparkling and foaming rapids of the James River, and entered Richmond, the capital of the Old Dominion, and the metropolis of the F. F. V.s.

The reader may ask what is the Old Dominion? and who or what are the F. F. V.s.? The Old Dominion is the name affectionately given to Virginia by its inhabitants, proud of its ancient settlement in the days of Queen Elizabeth; and the F. F. V.s. are the First Families of Virginia. "Who is your master?" said I to a negro-driver in Washington. "He is an F. F. V.," was the reply. "And are you working out your freedom?" "Yes," he replied. "And when you have got it, what will you do?" "Stay in Washington, and have all my earnings to myself."

Richmond is picturesquely seated on a hill, overlooking the windings of the James River, and is said to have received its name from its resemblance to Richmond in Surrey. But this resemblance is difficult to discover; for the landscape seen from Richmond, in Virginia, is almost bare of trees, while that from our English Richmond is a paradise of verdure and beauty. The Capitol, or Parliament House, stands on the crown of the hill, and, seen from a distance, gives the city an imposing and imperial air, as if of a city destined to command; but at nearer approach the illusion vanishes, and the Capitol dwindles into an insignificant-looking edifice, without either beauty or proportion. Lest the Virginians should object to the criticism of a stranger on the principal edifice of their state, I quote from a local hand-book the following description: "The Capitol is a Græco-American building, having a portico at one end, consisting of a colonnade, entablature, and pediment, whose apicial angle is rather too acute. There are windows on all sides, and doors in the two longer sides, which are reached by high and unsightly double flights of steps placed sidewise, under which are other doors leading to the basement. The view from the portico is extensive, various, and beautiful."

The "General Assembly"—such is the name given to the Parliament of this Commonwealth—was in session on our arrival, and the speakers of both the upper and lower House did me the honor of admitting me to what is called "the privilege of the floor." I had thus an opportunity of listening to the debates, and of observing the easy, decorous, and expeditious manner in which the public business is transacted. But far more attractive was the library, containing the original draught of the Constitution of Virginia by George Mason—a man of whom Virginia is, and ought to be proud; and the lower hall of the Capitol, containing the celebrated statue of Washington—most illustrious of Virginians as of Americans —by Houdon, a French artist. The statue, of the size of life, is represented in the costume of an American general, worn by the hero, and bears about it all the unmistakable but undefinable signs of being a true portrait. Stuart's portrait of Washington—taken in his later years, when he wore false teeth, badly made, that gave an undue and unnatural prominence to his lower jaw—is the one by which he is generally known. It is difficult to look upon that portrait, even if ignorant of the circumstances under which it was taken, without forming a hope that it is not a true resemblance. Houdon's statue is very different; and my first impression on beholding it was an instinctive belief that this was the real Washington —this the identical patriot—this the man who founded what is destined to be the greatest empire in the world. I was not a little gratified to learn, some days afterward, that when Lafayette visited Richmond, a few years before his death, he affirmed this to be the only likeness of Washington that did him justice. "Thus he stood," he said, "and thus he looked. This is Washington! This is my friend! This is the very man!"

The statue stands on a pedestal four feet and a half high; and no pedestal ought to be much higher, if it be desired that the countenance of the person honored or apotheosized should be seen by the public, to excite whose emulation it is erected. The pedestal bears the following honest, simple, and eloquent inscription:

"The General Assembly of the Commonwealth of Virginia have caused this statue to be erected as a monument of affection and gratitude to

GEORGE WASHINGTON,

who, uniting to the endowments of the Hero the virtues of the Patriot, and exerting both in establishing the Liberties of his Country, has rendered his name dear to his Fellow-citizens, and given the world an immortal example of true Glory. Done in the year of

CHRIST

one thousand seven hundred and eighty-eight; and in the year of the Commonwealth the Twelfth."

The citizens of Virginia had, a few months before my visit, just inaugurated, on the hill of the Capitol, another and a larger statue of Washington, executed by the eminent and lately deceased sculptor Crawford. It is a noble equestrian statue of bronze gilt, but, to my mind, not equal as a work of art to the pre-existing statue of Houdon, and somewhat injured in its general effect by the undue height and disproportionate narrowness of the pedestal on which it is elevated eighteen feet into the air. Around the base are to be ranged six other statues of illustrious Virginians, only two of which are as yet completed —one of Jefferson, and the other of Patrick Henry. Both of these are infinitely superior as works of art to any statues which London can boast. But as this of itself would be but poor praise, it may be added that these two figures are so dignified, so truthful, and so nearly perfect as to cause a feeling of regret that they should serve as accessories and adjuncts to a larger statue instead of standing by themselves.

Richmond contains a population of about 30,000 souls, of whom nearly 10,000 are slaves. It carries on a very large export trade in wheat and flour, has extensive flour-mills, and is noted as the great dépôt of the well-known tobacco for which the State of Virginia is celebrated, and in the growth and manufacture of which it principally employs its slave population.

CHAPTER XXVII.

FROM RICHMOND TO WASHINGTON.

March 24, 1858.

WEARY of the rail and all its nuisances—mental, physical, and olfactory—it was with pleasure, after a ride of seventy-five miles from the pleasant capital of Virginia, that I found myself at Aquia Creek, on the banks of the Potomac, and took a place on board the mail-steamer bound up the river for the City of Washington.

The Potomac at this place is a noble stream, apparently from two to three miles in width, and far more picturesque than any other river I had seen in North America, with the sole exceptions of the Hudson and the St. Lawrence. The wooded heights and undulating hills on the eastern and western shores slept in a haze of golden sunlight. The broad bosom of the river, unruffled by the slightest breath of wind, reflected the landscape like a mirror; and numerous flocks of canvas-back ducks—vagrants from the luxuriant marshes of Chesapeake Bay, where they breed in countless myriads—floated on the smooth water like tiny argosies. But Baltimore is the city *par excellence* of the canvas-back duck—one of the greatest delicacies of America; and what is to be said upon that subject shall therefore be reserved for its proper locality.

In natural beauty the Potomac is rich, but there is no place of any historic or even legendary interest on its banks between Aquia Creek and the capital, except one; but to every traveler, whatever his nation, that one is the most interesting spot in the United States. But *interesting* is too weak a word to express the feeling with which it is regarded by all the citizens of the Great Republic, young or old, male or female. It is their Mecca and their Jerusalem—hallowed ground, consecrated to all hearts by the remembrance of their great hero and patriot—the only one whom all Americans consent to honor and revere, and whom to disparage, even by a breath, is, in their estimation, a crime only second to blasphemy and parricide. Mount Vernon, the home and tomb of George Washington, is the sacred spot of the North American continent whither pilgrims repair, and on passing which every steam-boat solemnly tolls a bell, and every passenger uncovers his head, in expression of the national reverence. Our boat did not stop to allow us to visit the place—a circumstance which I have since much regretted, as I never had another opportunity; but in the summer season, when travelers are more numerous, sufficient time is usually allowed for the purpose on the downward trip from Washington. But the bell on the upper deck tolled its requiem for the departed, and captain, crew, and passengers took off their hats and remained uncovered until Mount Vernon was left behind, and the home and grave of the hero were hidden from sight among their embowering verdure.

The Americans, as a people, are accused of being utterly without reverence. A recent French tourist, more famous for music than for philosophy, declared them to be "*une nation railleuse et moqueuse;*" while others have asserted that they love and respect nothing but the "almighty dollar." The deep homage paid to the memory of Washington is sufficient to exonerate the Americans from such a sweeping censure. They certainly treat their living statesmen with little respect. They set up a president only to attack and vilify him, just as some African savages make an idol that they may kick and cuff while they pretend to pray to it; and the abuse which they at times lavish upon some of the ablest, noblest, and purest-minded of their statesmen is such as to afford some grounds for the belief that veneration is not the organ which is most largely developed in the American brain. But this view of the matter is a superficial one. There are no living men to whom they owe loyalty, or toward whom they can feel it; for it is they who make, and who, if need be, can unmake presidents, governors, and members of Congress. It is they who are the only source and the sole agents of power. They are so courted and flattered by knaves, at all sorts of elections, for all sorts of offices, from that of president down to that of door-keeper in a court of justice, and so besmeared with fair words, which mean nothing, by intriguers who put their tongues in their cheeks almost before their fine speeches are ended, that they value their public men at exceedingly little. Perhaps they treat their great authors, painters, and sculptors with more regard; for literary men and artists do not, as such, canvass for votes, or stand upon platforms to flatter a mob, but rely solely upon their genius, to be appreciated or not, as the people please. In this respect the universal homage rendered to the venerable Washington Irving, and the affection with which the mention of his name is every where received; the pride with which all people of every party speak of such writers as Prescott, the able historian and accomplished gentleman, and of many others who have made American literature illustrious in our day, is a proof that, beyond the sphere of politics and the bitter question of slavery, the Americans can render ample justice to their living greatness. Yet, if ungrateful to men in public life, and especially to politicians, they make amends to the memory of the illustrious dead, and prove abundantly that they have both loyalty and veneration in their nature by pouring them around the name of Washington, and in a minor degree around those of other early heroes and founders of the republic, such as Franklin, Hamilton, Jefferson, Mason, Adams, Patrick Henry, and, in more recent times, those of Clay, Calhoun, Andrew Jackson, and Quincy Adams. And, as regards living statesmen, before we accuse the Americans of want of veneration for authority, let us ask ourselves who can be better abused than a prime minister of England, or a leader of the House of Commons?

Mr. J. A. Washington, the present representative of the family of Washington, and proprietor of the Mount Vernon estate, to whom I had the honor of an introduction, at the hospitable table of Mr. G. P. R. James, the British consul at Richmond, had incurred considerable odium at the time of my visit—odium which, whether deserved or not, was more than sufficient to show that the loyalty of Americans was not rendered to a mere name, but was jealously reserved for individual services and glory. A lady of Richmond, Miss Pamela Cunningham, weak in body, but strong in mind, bedridden, but able to wield an eloquent and persuasive pen, entertained, with many others, the idea that the tomb of Washington ought to belong, not to any individual proprietor, even though his name were Washington, but to the American people. Miss Cunningham may not, perhaps, have been more strongly imbued with this idea than others; but it is certain that she gave more effect to her feelings than any of the persons who may have shared the conviction before she gave it life and palpability. From her sick-bed she wrote and dictated letters to the newspapers to stir up the sentiment and enthusiasm of the country. Her appeals—earnest, simple, and eloquent—answered their purpose. She summoned the ladies of America to unite with her, as statesmanship and Congress would do nothing to aid them, and to form an association for the purchase of Mount Vernon by the voluntary subscriptions of the American people. In the course of a few months she found herself burdened with an amount of correspondence to which that of a Secretary of State was a trifle. The ladies responded cordially to the appeal from every part of the Union, and gave not only their names, but their time and talents to the work. Madame Le Vert, of Mobile, wrote a book of her travels in Europe, and handed over the profits to the Mount Vernon Association. Other ladies painted pictures, composed music, established fancy bazars, got up balls and concerts, and all for the purchase of Washington's tomb. Others, again, who objected to such aids to a good cause, and who had influence, marital or filial, over popular preachers, enlisted them in the subscription, until there was scarcely a church or chapel in the land of which the congregations had not subscribed to the fund. And last, but by no means least, Mr. Everett, the most eloquent of living Americans, was brought into the service. He was persuaded by some of these fair enthusiasts—whether by Miss Cunningham, by Mrs. Le Vert, or by Mrs. Ritchie (so well known and greatly admired in London as Mrs. Anna Cora Mowatt), or whether by these three graces in combination, it is difficult to say—but, by the happy thought of some insinuating fair one, he was induced to travel from city to city throughout the Union, and to deliver his celebrated oration on the "Life and Character of Washington," for the benefit of the fund. By his exertions alone upward of £5000 sterling had at an early period of the year 1858 been secured toward the purchase of Mount Vernon, and there was every probability that by these and other agencies the whole sum requisite would be obtained within one year, or at most two, and Washington's tomb, with a few acres of land adjoining, handed over to the perpetual guardianship of the ladies of America. At the commencement of their patriotic agitation they were incorporated for the purpose by solemn Act of the Legislature of the Commonwealth of Virginia, confirmed by the still more solemn fiat of the General Congress of Washington.

And here it will perhaps be asked why and whence the odium thrown upon Mr. J. A. Washington? The charge made against him chiefly by the press, was, that he had asked too much of the ladies of America, and that he had "trafficked in the bones of his illustrious relative." But in a country where, above all others,

> "The value of a thing
> Is just as much as it will bring,"

and where the pursuit of wealth is carried on with an eagerness elsewhere unparalleled, the charge appears ungracious, if not unnatural. The representative of the Washingtons is far from wealthy; he has a large family, principally of daughters; in the opinion of impartial persons, he did not ask a cent more for the acres than they would be likely to sell for by private contract to any one who desired to possess them, and less, perhaps, than they would fetch by public sale; and, moreover, the committee of the Ladies' Association have publicly declared, with their names appended to the declaration, that nothing could be more straightforward, manly, honest, and liberal than the conduct of Mr. Washington in the whole course of the transaction. It is to be presumed, judging from the temper displayed in the discussion, that nothing would have satisfied the objectors to Mr. Washington except his free donation of the property; and that any sum he might have asked would have been carped and caviled at by people determined to be displeased. Surely it was unreasonable to expect from a man, even though he bore a great name, that he should have sacrificed his interests to the manes of his illustrious predecessor, and done in his own person what the state ought to have done? If honor were to be paid to the memory of Washington by the purchase of his burial-place, and its dedication forever to the reverence of the American people, the central government, representing all the states of the Union, or even the government of the Commonwealth of Virginia, should have drawn upon the public purse for the funds necessary to purchase the property. As the purchase of the nation, both the tribute would be greater than if it proceeded from the pocket of any individual, whether his name were

Washington or any other less renowned. If the rich nation declined to act in the matter—a nation so rich that it does not know what to do with the public money—why should Mr. Washington, who is not rich, be blamed for not taking upon himself a task that was not his by any natural or national compulsion, and which, moreover, he could not undertake without injustice to those who were nearest and dearest to him, and who, if he had reduced them to penury, might have asked in vain for a dollar from the national bounty?

Under all the circumstances, it is more creditable to the American character that the purchase should be effected by the voluntary effort of the people than by any other means. The ladies of America have done a noble deed in a graceful and gracious manner, and nobody is the poorer for it—except, perhaps, Miss Cunningham, who has well-nigh exhausted the energies of a frame that was never powerful by the labors consequent upon so great an organization. But her name upon the records on the Mount Vernon Association, and on the book that will, doubtless, lie upon Washington's tomb, setting forth how it became the property of the public, will be to her a sufficient reward. And that, at least, will be hers as long as America shall revere the name of Washington.*

* In reference to this subject, the following memorandum has been received from Mr. Everett:

"It is intimated that I was enlisted in the Mount Vernon cause by the ladies named in your letter. This is inexact. I have been most proud and happy to co-operate with those very estimable ladies in this excellent cause; but I commenced delivering my 'Washington Lectures' at Richmond for the benefit of the Mount Vernon Fund as a volunteer, without the suggestion of any man or woman. I made the offer to do so before I had made the acquaintance of Miss Cunningham or Mrs. Ritchie, and without any previous communication on the subject with either of them, or any other human being."

CHAPTER XXVIII.

THE SOCIAL AND POLITICAL ASPECTS OF SLAVERY.

Washington, March 25, 1859.

No traveler in the United States, who desires to record his free, unbiased opinions, can give the go-by to the question of slavery. That question has long been a sore in the bosom of the Great Republic, but has not pressed at any time for immediate solution. It has been a difficult and complicated, as well as an exasperating subject. It has been the battle-ground of parties—the touchstone of political life—the theme of the senate, the platform, the pulpit, and the press; but it has involved too many personal and national interests, and been of too vital an importance to the integrity of the Union to be driven even by the most zealous friends of negro freedom to such a point as to force a deliverance. If, on the one hand, there were slavery to be abolished, there was, upon the other, the union of the thirty-two republics which lend a star each to the banner of the states to be maintained inviolate. Many abolitionists have been prepared for the *fiat justitia*, but not for the *ruat cœlum;* and the few able and earnest men who have avowed themselves ready to confront all consequences, however ominous or fatal, have been in such a minority as to render their action hopeless for the present, and to adjourn it into the indefinite future, where all hopes grow, and where all theories gradually transform themselves into facts.

In the District of Columbia slavery is not offensive in its outward manifestations; and Washington contains a large number of free negroes. But the fact that slavery is permitted to exist within the district is made a particular grievance by the abolitionists of the free North. "You have slavery in you own states," they say to the people of the slave-holding South, "and, unfortunately, we have not the power to interfere with you; but we know of no right that you have to introduce the objectionable and criminal system into Columbia and the City of Washington, which belong to the whole Union, and not to the South, and to us quite as much as to you." The South has replied by insisting on as much right to maintain slavery as the North has to abolish it; that possession is nine points of the law, and that, being in possession, they are determined to remain so. Several attempts have been made by the abolition party to carry a law through Congress to free the national capital and its small surrounding district from the " domestic institution" of the South, but hitherto in vain. The fact, however, suggests the opportunity to say a few words on the social and political aspects of this great question, not simply as affecting the national metropolis, but as affecting both the white and the black races in every part of the Union.

It was intended by the original framers of the Declaration of Independence that all the United States should be free. Wiser at this time than the monarchy, whose yoke they so gallantly threw off, they thought to repudiate slavery, and all that appertained to it. It was their wish to set an example to the world. They desired to proclaim that "a man was a man for a' that," and that the accident of his color made no difference in his rights or his responsibilities. But a timid and unwise conservatism, even at this early stage of American history, was permitted to prevail, and because slavery *was*, it was allowed *to be*. At a later period, the parent monarchy, impelled by the irresistible impetus communicated to its actions by the people, abolished slavery in all its forms and phases. The republic profiting, or fancying that it profited, by the evil thing, and not only tolerating, but loving it, because it was established, refused to follow the noble example. Thus it sowed dragons' teeth over more than half of the fairest dominion that ever in all recorded history fell to the lot of an energetic and intelligent race. The result is what we now see, and what all the friends of human liberty deplore. The dragons' teeth have grown up into giants. Frankenstein has made his monster, and the monster puts poison into the cup of prosperity, and keeps his master in constant terror of a day of retribution. Slavery, that might have been easily eradicated half a century ago, has assumed such formidable dimensions that it is hard to say which is the more difficult thing to do—to put up with it, or to abolish it; and which course is fraught with the most danger—to give the slaves their freedom, or to allow them to increase and multiply in bondage. But the history of such model states as Massachusetts—one of the most respectable and wise communities in the world—and, indeed, of all the New England States, together with New York and Pennsylvania, and the commonwealths of the West, which are gradually spreading themselves to the bases of the Rocky Mountains, is a proof not only of the far-sighted philanthropy, but of the worldly wisdom of the men who, at the earliest period of American history, washed their hands of the shame and guilt of slavery. The free states are not only the most populous, the most wealthy, and the most energetic in the Union; but by the activity of their intellect, the exuberance of their literature, and the general vigor—public and social, as well as private and commercial—of their citizens, they give the law and the tone to the whole of the Union. Massachusetts, Vermont, New Hampshire, Rhode Island, Connecticut, and Maine—small in extent, and, with the exception of Maine, as finely cultivated and almost as densely peopled as that Old England from whose shores their early founders emigrated, in disgust with the political and religious tyranny of their time—are the great hives that supply the fruitful and all but illimitable West.

The emigration from Ireland, from Germany, and from Norway, great as it is, would not keep the great West in healthful and progressive motion, were it not for the Yankees of New England. It is these who drift off from their parent establishments in these elderly states—for Massachusetts, as a commonwealth, is older than many European kingdoms, and not much more juvenile than Prussia—and who found mills, banks, stores, newspapers, churches, chapels, and universities in the wildernesses of the Upper Mississippi and Missouri. Every now and then, when their numbers have sufficiently increased by European and other immigration, they "thunder at the gates of the capital," and claim admission for the new territory which they have wrested from desolation or from the Indians as a sovereign state and component part of the greatest confederation in the world. The non-existence of slavery within their bounds is one of the causes of their unparalleled growth and prosperity. The poor white man—the ragged, half-starved Irishman—with nothing to offer in exchange for his food, lodging, and raiment but the unskilled labor of his brawny arms; the frugal German and Norwegian, desirous to gain a few dollars by hard manual labor, and to invest the results in the purchase of an acre or two of the virgin earth—will not settle in large numbers in the slaveholding states. In the South they would enter into competition with the slave, and the slave, as far as mere labor goes, is master of the position. In the ruder operations of the field and plantation, where no particular intelligence is required, and where a horse is almost as good a laborer as a man, he is cheaper than the white race; and the white man, with higher aspirations than to be always a hewer of wood and a drawer of water, naturally betakes himself to regions where negro labor does not come into competition with his own, and where he will not be kept by capitalists, either of land or money, at a lower level than he believes to be his by right of his superior mind.

The free states are progressive, and, to use the regular Yankee word, "go-a-head-ative." They see far before them. They do not stand continually upon the ancient ways. Like Englishmen and Scotchmen, with whom they have many points of resemblance, they are "look-a-head-ative" as well as "go-a-head-ative," if I may imitate themselves so far as to coin an ugly but expressive word for the occasion; and, seeing that the whole continent requires to be settled and cut up into commonwealths; thinking little of distance and of time, and scarcely considering either as impediments to any work which they may undertake, or to any design on the accomplishment of which they have set their hearts; knowing no superiors to themselves, politically or socially, and being fired with the ambition not simply to become rich, but to be eminent and powerful, they manufacture states for the Union as

SOCIAL AND POLITICAL ASPECTS OF SLAVERY. 235

well as fortunes for themselves. They give their names to towns, cities, and counties, and do, in this advanced age of the world, and by a different process, what the early Saxons and Danes did twelve hundred years ago for the British Isles. The people of the free states have an immense work yet before them. Maine is the only one of the six New England States that exists to any considerable extent in the condition of the primeval wilderness. The other five are finished. Their roads are made, the tree-stumps have been long ago removed, the original forest has disappeared, except where it has been allowed to remain, here and there, in small patches, for its beauty and amenity. The log hut is not often to be seen; but the neat, elegant, comfortable white house, the church, the chapel, the bank, are every where to be met with. There is no trace of squalor or of misery, but over the whole land there is an air of refinement and of high civilization. But the other free states have not yet arrived at the same high culture. Large portions of the "Empire State" of New York are still in a state of nature, and, though the Red Man has long ago disappeared, the bear and the wolf are in possession of districts not a day's journey by rail from the mighty city of Manhattan, and almost within sound of the paddle of the monster steam-boats that ply upon the Hudson. With capabilities of soil and climate, and with natural resources more than sufficient to feed a population of ten or twelve millions, the State of New York, though constantly invaded by the Saxon, Celtic, and Scandinavian immigration, has a resident population of less than four and a half millions. Though the most populous state in the Union, and absolutely much richer, both in wealth and in men, than England was in the days when Henry VIII. first began to make England a power in the world, and almost as populous as when Cromwell first made his country to be feared and respected throughout Europe, still, New York is but half peopled. Pennsylvania, another large and flourishing commonwealth, with agricultural and mineral wealth all but inexhaustible in its soil, is not more populous than Scotland; and Ohio, one of the noblest of all the free states, and able to support as large a population as England, numbers upon its fruitful bosom little more than two millions of people, or a million less than London and its circumjacent boroughs.

Indiana—which an intelligent old Scotchman, who had cultivated his farm in it for upward of ten years, declared to me, with an expression of sorrow in his rough, honest countenance, to be an unwholesome place for a man of northern blood to live in—might contain and feed the whole population now existing in the United States, and be all the better for the burden, does not number above a million and a half of people. I asked the Scotchman what was his objection to Indiana? "Objection," he replied, with a strong Highland accent; "objection, did ye say? There is no objection but to its overfruitfulness. The soil is so rich, the climate so delicious, that the farmer has no adequate inducement to work. The earth produces its fruits too readily. The original curse presses too lightly. The sweat of a man's brow is to be read of, but not to be experienced here; and the very air is balmy and sleepy. Idleness is the affliction that we have to struggle against; and idleness leads to drinking, and to quarrelsomeness, and all other evil. Satan is to be fought with hard work, and that will conquer him better than preaching. Na, na," he added, shaking his head, "if I had my life to live over again, and know what I know now, I would settle in a ruder soil and in a colder climate. Men whose ancestors are from the cold North—the wholesome North, I say—require frost to bring out their virtues. Heat is fatal to the true Scotchman, and, for that matter, to the true Englishman also. Men of our blood thrive upon difficulties. We grow rich and fat upon toil and obstruction; but here, in Indiana, Illinois, and away to the West as far as you can go, man gains his bread too easily to remain virtuous. This is a matter," he continued, "which people do not sufficiently consider. The Southern and Middle States will in time deteriorate for these reasons, but the North—the North—*that* will be the country. And as for Canada, no one can describe, without being accused of extravagance, the greatness and the glory of which it may be made capable." In this respect, if my Highland friend was right—which I firmly believe he was—Wisconsin, Iowa, Kansas, and the large territories of Nebraska, Oregon, and Columbia, large enough to be made into fifty commonwealths of the extent of Massachusetts, may share with Canada the advantages of a climate that makes men hardy, enterprising, and strong. It certainly seems to have been of some effect in stimulating the energies of the "Yankees," and in making them, all things considered, the sharpest, smartest, and most eminent people in the Union—a people little loved, perhaps, but very much respected.

In the Southern States, partly, perhaps, from the influence of the climate, but more probably in a still greater degree from the operation of slavery upon the life, character, and feeling of the whites, there is nothing like the same social, commercial, and literary energy that exists in the North. The contrast between these two sections of the Union is in this respect most remarkable. Between Massachusetts and South Carolina, between Vermont and Arkansas, between Connecticut and Alabama, there exists almost as great a difference in every thing, except language and the style of dress and architecture, as there does between Scotland and Portugal, England and Naples, Wales and the Ionian Islands. The cities in the free " Far West" double, treble, and quadruple their population in twenty, sometimes in ten years. The cities of the slave states, and the slave states themselves, either remain stationary or increase disproportionately. In the free states all is bustle and activity; in the slave states there is elegant and drowsy stagnation. The railways in the North are well conducted. Populous towns, villages, and manufactories swarm and glitter along the line; but in the South the railways are for the most part ill-served and ill-regulated. The land is imperfectly cultivated, and the primeval forest is more extensive than the farms and plantations. The great rivers Missouri and Mississippi run for nearly two thousand miles through a comparative wilderness; the reclaimed land on either side occupies but a very narrow belt and border of the illimitable dominion that man has yet to rescue from the wild animals, and from the super-exuberant forest and the deadly swamp. Even in Virginia, ancient enough to have been called by the same name when the empire now known as Russia was called Muscovy, and whence the swamp and the wilderness have long since disappeared, there is an air of non-progressiveness, if not decay and desolation.

The traveler from New England and the other free states no sooner penetrates into the slave-land than he sees all around him the proofs that slavery is omnipresent; not in the mere appearance of negroes at every turn and in all places, for they are to be found every where in America, but in the slovenly cultivation, the want of drainage, the absence of towns and villages in the rural districts, and the paucity of population even in the largest cities. Competition—the very soul of progress—is scarcely to be found. Where it exists at all it is only among the retail tradesmen. Thought is not free. You may talk of the dissolution of the Union as desirable and probable, abuse the president and his ministers, speak ill of Congress collectively and individually, be profane or immoral in your speech or life, but you must not say a word against the sanctity of the "Domestic Institution." Rome itself, with its *Index Expurgatorius*, does not act with an effect more blighting and deadly upon intellectual activity than the South does when it forbids the expression of opinion on this subject. No doubt it would be dangerous to allow of free discussion; as dangerous as it would be in Rome to allow Protestant divines to dispute publicly with priests and cardinals on the vital truths of Christianity, or the comparative merits of Luther and Pope Hildebrand. Slavery being an admitted fact and an established institution, it is not to be supposed that those who are educated in the belief that they profit by it can do otherwise than forbid, within their own jurisdiction, the calling of it in question, either by zealous and malignant philanthropists among themselves, or by interlopers from New or Old England, but the fact remains that thought is not free. Consequently, the wings of the Angel of Knowledge are clipped, so that he can not soar into the empyrean or sit upon the clouds. Literature, which can not attain its full development under any system of restriction or impediment whatsoever, whether it be theological, political, or social, attains but a stunted and imperfect growth. It loses its most generous inspiration, the sense of absolute liberty. It becomes conventional instead of natural. It "gives up to party what was meant for mankind;" and, as a necessary consequence of its thraldom, finds it impossible to compete with the universal literature which knows no such restrictions, and appeals to the wider audience of all humanity. The slave states have produced some excellent lawyers, some admirable orators, and some consummate politicians and statesmen, but they have produced no great poet, no great novelist, no great historian, no great philosopher or metaphysician; nay, as far as my knowledge extends, they have not brought forth even one great or eminent preacher. They have produced a few pleasant and fanciful rhymers and versifiers, both male and female, and one or two novelists and essayists of some ability, but no writer in any walk or department of literature whom the most adulatory partisanship or local preference can conscientiously compare with such names as Bryant, Longfellow, Whittier, Holmes, and Lowell in poetry; such historians as Prescott, Bancroft, and Motley; such novelists as Washington Irving and Hawthorne; or such a philosopher as Emerson—all of whom are Northern, and the greater number New England men or Yankees. The leading spirits in the slave states are aware of the deficiency without being aware of the cause, and can not as yet see that there are many things which can be obtained without liberty; but that a great, and wholesome, and fructifying literature, which can speak trumpet-tongued to all mankind, and move the universal heart of nations, is not among the number.

One characteristic of both the slave states and the free, which has been partially noticed by all travelers, though few, if any, have attempted to account for it on philosophical principles, is the intensely aristocratic sentiment, or, it may be called, instinct of the native-born Americans, of the Anglo-Saxon, and generally of the white race. It was the eminent statesman and orator, John C. Calhoun, who first enunciated the dogma, which has, since his time, been openly accepted by the whole South, and more tacitly and partially by the

North, that there is not such a thing as a democratic republic; that there never was such a thing in ancient or modern times; and that there must, of necessity, be an aristocracy of some kind or other to keep the frame-work of society together, under a form of government so delicate and so complicated as a republic. That there may be a monarchy and a despotism without an aristocracy is proved by Asiatic as well as by European experience; and we need not travel forty miles eastward from the English coast to find a striking proof of it; but Mr. Calhoun held a strictly democratic republic to be impossible, and appealed to Greece and Rome, to Venice and Genoa, for corroboration. He declared that the only possible aristocracy in the United States was the aristocracy of color and race. He may, to some extent, have undervalued or ignored the aristocracy of wealth and genius, which always, in every society, whatever may be its form of government, assert and maintain their own claims to pre-eminency; but there can be no doubt that, as regards the aristocracy of color, avowed or unavowed, he was perfectly right in the fact. As regards the political conclusions which he drew from it, opinions will probably differ. The North, which will not tolerate slavery, shows its participation in this aristocratic notion by refusing to tolerate the social equality of the "nigger." "We shall not make the black man a slave; we shall not buy him or sell him; but we shall not associate with him. He shall be free to live, and to thrive if he can, and to pay taxes and perform duties; but he shall not be free to dine and drink at our board—to share with us the deliberations of the jury-box—to sit upon the seat of judgment, however capable he may be—to plead in our courts—to represent us in the Legislature—to attend us at the bed of sickness and pain—to mingle with us in the concert-room, the lecture-room, the theatre, or the church, or to marry with our daughters. We are of another race, and he is inferior. Let him know his place, and keep it." This is the prevalent feeling, if not the language of the free North. A negro must not ride in the public omnibuses nor in the railway cars; he must not, however wealthy, sit in the boxes or in the pit of a theatre; and if he

SOCIAL AND POLITICAL ASPECTS OF SLAVERY. 241

desires to go to church, he must worship with those of his own color, and not presume to taint the atmosphere of the pure whites by the odors that exhale from his impurer epidermis. The whites in the North object to a negro not alone for moral and political, but for physical reasons. They state that he smells, and that it is almost as offensive to come near him as it would be to fondle a skunk. The words of a pretended hymn — made for the negroes, but not by one of them, although it is sometimes asserted that the author had a dark skin—are often quoted to those who are incredulous as to the odors that exhale from the black man:

> "De Lord He lub de nigger well,
> He know de nigger by de smell;
> And when de nigger children cry,
> De Lord He gib 'em 'possum pie."

I attended a negro church, and heard a negro preacher at Richmond, in Virginia; and, though I have as sensitive a nose as most people, and a more sensitive one than many, I was quite unconscious of any unpleasant effluvium, or of any effluvium at all, proceeding from the persons of the seven or eight hundred black men and women there assembled to worship their Creator. I mentioned the fact to the Virginian gentleman who accompanied me. He replied that it was quite true that there was at that time no smell, "but then," said he, "the month is March. In June or July the odor would be perfectly intolerable, and I, for one, should not have ventured to have done myself the honor of accompanying you." But, whatever may be the fact as to the physical discomfort said to be produced by the odors of the black men on the olfactory nerves of the whites, it is evident that in the South, where, if any where, this peculiar unpleasantness would be more likely to be offensively demonstrative than in colder climates, there is no such repugnance to the persons of the black population as there is in the North. In the South, the slave-owner not only cohabits with the more youthful and beautiful of his female slaves, but seems to have no objection whatever to the close proximity of any negro, young or old, male or female; though the Northern men, who talk so much of liberty, and

L

of the political equality of all men, turn up their scornful noses at the slightest possibility of contact with an African. Negro women are not only the favorite and most fondly-trusted nurses of white children, but often, and, indeed, generally, entertain for the infants of their masters and mistresses, whom they have reared and tended in their helplessness, a life-long and most devoted affection. They inspire the same feelings in the bosoms of their young charges. Black women nurse the little white girl in her babyhood—wash her, dress her, and adorn her—take her to school in her girlhood—and share in all the joys and sorrows of her youth. They are, besides, the honored, though humble confidants of their wedded life and maturity, and would scorn to accept of a freedom that would separate them from the objects of this disinterested and ungrudging affection. In the South, the negro may ride in the omnibus without offense; his proximity to the white creates neither alarm nor disgust; and the faithful slave, looked upon as a friend, receives the familiar and affectionate title of "uncle" or "aunt," as sex may dictate. If the master or mistress be young, and the "uncle" or "aunt" old, the negroes exercise the right of advice, authority, and control in every thing that relates to personal comfort and domestic ease; and the superior race is gratified by the control, and the interest which it presupposes. If the Northern states and the Northern people would only show half or a quarter as much social kindness to the negro as is shown in the South, the question of negro slavery would be deprived of one of its greatest difficulties. But, while Northern men talk of the political rights of the negro—while they oppress and degrade him socially, although they may neither buy nor sell him—their anti-slavery speeches, books, and resolutions savor of hypocrisy and false pretense. More than this, they harden the hearts of the slave-owners, who can see through a false pretense quite as readily as the Yankees, and tend to deprive the question of the abolition of slavery of the grace, the force, and the impetus that are derived from an uncompromising and thoroughly sincere conviction.

Another proof of the aristocratic feeling which pervades

the white democracy of the United States is the repugnance which native-born Americans almost universally entertain to domestic service. As is well known, a domestic servant of American birth, and without negro blood in his or her veins, who condescends to help the mistress or master of a household in making the beds, milking the cows, cooking the dinner, grooming the horse, or driving the carriage, is not a servant, but a "help." "Help wanted," is the common heading of advertisements in the North, where servants are required. A native American of Anglo-Saxon lineage thinks himself born to lead and to rule, and scorns to be considered a "servant," or even to tolerate the name. Let negroes be servants, and, if not negroes, let Irishmen fill the place; but for an American, an Englishman, or a Scotchman to be a servant or a waiter is derogatory. Such people consider themselves of superior breed and blood. They are the aristocracy of the New World; and if poverty fall upon one of this class, as it may do upon many a noble-minded fellow, and compel him to tend sheep, wait in a shop, or, worse than all, to stand behind a chair at table, he is a help, not a servant. But the negro is not a help; he is emphatically a servant. And the Irishman is seldom long in America before he too begins to assert the supremacy of his white blood, and to come out of what he considers the degrading ranks of "service." The negroes, both free and slaves, have generally a great dislike to the Irish, whom they were the first to call "white niggers." A very poor white man—such as an Irishman generally is when he arrives in America, and struggles hard to compete with the negro for the lowest kinds of occupation—is looked upon with pity and hate by Sambo. "A white Buckra" is the most opprobrious epithet that a negro can make use of; for, in his eyes, wealth, authority, power, and white blood should always be found together. The Irish women fall willingly at first into domestic service, but the public opinion around them soon indoctrinates them with the aristocratic idea that black men and women are the only proper servants; that white men ought to trade and cultivate farms, and that white women are their proper helpmates, and should scorn to serve, save in their own households, and in behalf of their own husbands and children.

But to return to slavery, which is, in reality, far more of a white man's than of a black man's question, and of which the aristocratic tendency, as regards the white, is but one feather out of the multifarious plumage of the subject—it is well to consider what effect it has upon the whole policy of the United States among men, both of the North and South, who care no more for the negro, as a negro, than they do for their horse or cow, but who use him, or abuse him, as suits the higher political purpose which sways their actions. And here we come to the very core of the political differences which separate the free from the slave states of the Union. These differences are many and serious, and are, besides, embarrassed and exasperated by numerous complications of interest and policy quite unconnected with slavery. Free America is ultra-protectionist, and Slave America is strongly in favor of the widest freedom of trade. The free states are alarmed at the increase of British manufactures, while the slave states are not only not alarmed, but gratified, and desire to profit by British industry to the fullest possible extent, in the cheapening of clothes for themselves and their slaves, and of all articles of domestic use and luxury, which Great Britain can furnish better and more cheaply than the manufacturers of the North. But this is the least of their differences. The unfortunate provision in the Constitution which allows a slaveholder to possess votes for the House of Representatives—not one vote simply in his individual right as a free white man, but several votes in proportion to the number of the black population—makes a Southern white of more integral political importance than the Northern. He is a heavier weight in the political scale, and, individually, is of more power and consequence than any ordinary white man can be, unless the other add to his personal vote the influence always derivable from eloquence and genius in swaying the opinions of his fellow-men. The struggle between the North and South, of which the negro is made the pretext, is, as all the world knows by this time, a struggle for political power and ascendency—for the patronage of the re-

SOCIAL AND POLITICAL ASPECTS OF SLAVERY. 245

public, and of the several commonwealths which compose it. The men of the North and of the West—whether they be the old and staid conservatives of such states as Massachusetts and Connecticut, or the hardy pioneers of Michigan, Wisconsin, and Kansas, or those equally hardy and more adventurous and far-sighted "go-a-heads" who look to Nebraska, Oregon, Columbia, and even cast a longing look to the arable land of the Hudson's Bay Company, as the scene of their future operations in the art and industry of state-making—may ask why individually, and man for man, they should be of less account than the slave-owners and slave-breeders of the South, who vote in right of their slaves, but do nothing to extend the boundaries of the Union, unless by aggression upon the dominions of independent European and American powers? And this is the main difference between the two great sections. The Southern States desire to annex, and to increase the territories of the Union, but they have no means of doing so unless by war, just or unjust, against Mexico and Spain, and the effete, ridiculous, and perishing republics of Spaniards, half-breeds, and quadroons, that vegetate southward of Mexico as far as Panama. The Northern States, on the contrary, in sending out their pioneers, come into contact with no European powers. The wilderness is their natural inheritance, and neither to them nor to their forefathers has the Red Man been an invincible or even a formidable obstruction. It has always been possible to deal with him without doing much violence to the consciences of those who traded or fought with him. Philanthropy, very like misanthropy in its results, gave him trinkets and fire-water, that he might "civilize himself off the face of the earth;" and the Puritan or the peddler stepped into his broad acres, and made himself, like Alexander Selkirk or Robinson Crusoe, the autocrat of every circle bounded by the horizon. The North is compelled by nature, instinct, policy, and calculation to send forth its superabundant children to subdue and replenish the fruitful earth not otherwise preoccupied. The South has no such chances. It sees a territory farther south which is already subdued and replenished, though by an inferior race, and must either take that territory, *per fas aut nefas*, from its present possessors, or consent to be outnumbered, outweighted, and conquered by its rivals for power and office at Washington. To Europeans it sometimes appears strange that the United States—as an aggregate, already sufficiently large—should have such an insatiable lust of territory as to invade Mexican, Spanish, and other independent territories in this ruthless and unconscionable fashion; but, fairly and dispassionately looked upon, it seems as if the "manifest destiny" of which they speak were no dream, but a reality. They are doomed to "annex" by the necessities of their social politics. Like Robespierre, they must cut off heads or lose their own. Mexico is tempting, and Cuba is more tempting still; yet the prizes are costly. As for the little republics carved out of the weakness of Spain, which lengthen and spin out their useless lives in the latitudes between Mexico and Panama, no power on the earth, even if it can, will be so foolish as to interfere to prevent the inevitable consummation either of their absorption into the American Union, or of their annexation, in some more dependent form, to the great confederation. Were it not that the Constitution of the United States had made no provision for any increase except by the normal form and force of agglomeration and accretion, the Spanish republics or empires (for these moribund states change from one political condition to another with kaleidoscopic rapidity) would long ago have been absorbed into the ever-gaping and yawning maw of Uncle Sam. And herein exists a difficulty for the Union, all consequent upon slavery, and the antagonism which it excites at the North. Foreign conquest appears to be imperative; but, if it be undertaken, how will the North, which only wars with the Indian, with desolation, and the wild beasts of the forest, be affected by a state of affairs alien to the intentions of the founders of the Constitution, and to the whole spirit of the most populous and energetic portion of the republic? The answer to the question is in the future. No one can foresee the ultimate pattern which the moving of the shuttles and rollers will produce, or whether the whole machine will not ultimately break into pieces. The strength of a chain cable is but the strength of its weakest part. The strength of the American Union is the strength of slavery. It is that question which bears the whole strain of the mighty ship; and, if it prove strong enough, the ship may defy all other dangers, and ride triumphantly upon all seas and into all ports. But if that link be weak or broken, and have no supports in nature and necessity, and no links in the heart of humanity, it will drop sooner or later, and then the world will see a new shifting of the kaleidoscope. The focus may be symmetrical, but the component parts will be differently disposed; and the Northern States may make one pattern, the Southern a second, and the Californian or Pacific sea-board a third. There is room enough and to spare for all of them.

CHAPTER XXIX.

PRO-SLAVERY PHILOSOPHY.

THERE was a time, not very remote, when the slaveholders of the South and their supporters, driven into a corner by the arguments of the abolitionists, were content to rest their case upon the existence of slavery as a great fact—"a chiel that wadna ding"—and which it was useless to dispute. They agreed that *per se* slavery was wrong, and not to be defended upon philosophical or religious grounds; but they insisted that to abolish it would be to produce far greater calamities, both to the slave and his master, than to permit its continuance, with such modifications as circumstances might allow. Virtually they gave up the controversy, and made an appeal *ad misericordiam* to the vulgar common sense of mankind, to the conservative feelings of many, who would rather submit to old evils than run risks of new experiments, to the general laziness and selfishness of the masses, who are content to endure the existence of afflictions that do not come home to themselves; and they strengthened all these arguments in favor of the *status quo* by many economic considerations of trade and commerce, and the supposed necessity that lay upon England to manufacture cotton under the penalty of revolution, and the equally strong necessity to produce it, under the similar penalty of ruin, that weighed upon the Southern States of the Union. The easy politicians of the Middle and Northern States, from Pennsylvania to Maine, and from New York to Wisconsin, who cared a great deal more for the Union than for the "rights of man"—and especially of that portion of the race which happened to have black skins—were quite contented to rest the existence of slavery upon arguments such as these; while in favor of freedom in the abstract they postponed into the indefinite future all attempts to realize it. "After this generation let the deluge come, but let us not be disturbed in our time." Such was their prayer and such their policy. Imbued with these motives, they strengthened the "peculiar institution" which they affected to condemn, and allowed the black man to be a man theoretically, but not a man politically or socially. In their refusal to eat, or drink, or pray with him, or to allow him the civil rights which they claimed for themselves in virtue of their white skins, they treated him, in effect, as if he were only a superior kind of horse, or perhaps of monkey; a docile, useful, agreeable, affectionate brute; to be kindly treated, but still a brute; and no more fit to serve upon a jury, to sit upon the bench, or to be governor of a State, than Gulliver was to give laws to the Houyhnhnms, or Cæsar's horse to be a consul.

But within the last two or three years a change has come over the philosophy and the tactics of the slaveholders. The North is weary of the "Nigger question;" and the South, feeling the weakness of a position dependent upon the toleration of its foes, has ceased to make the appeal *ad misericordiam*. Not only justifying slavery as an established fact, they have gone one step lower (or an infinite number of steps lower), and asserted it to be a reasonable, a benevolent, and a divine institution—an institution entirely in the order of nature, and one far better for the slave than freedom; better for the master, better for the workman and for him who profits by the work, and who calls himself a shopkeeper or a merchant: a system that is not dependent upon the color or race of those who are enslaved, but which may conduce to the advantage of a white slave quite as much as to that of the black. In one sentence they allege slavery to be the normal and only proper condition of society. Instead of being defendants in the great court of the world's opinion, they have assumed the position of plaintiffs. They have intrenched themselves upon their rights, and accuse all that portion of the European world which condemns slavery as being false not alone to morality and religion, but to the true principles of trade and to the philanthropy of social science. ' In short, the slaveholders—worried, vexed, perplexed, and exasperated—have, like a dying stag in the wilderness, done desperate battle with their opponents. They have taken up a position with their backs to the rock, and defied all onslaught. Over any foes who will recognize things so totally distinct, but in their minds so homogeneous as the authority of the Bible, the right of Labor and its adequate reward, the superiority of intellect to animal strength, and the distress and misery of European laborers, they claim a logical, a political, a philosophical, and a religious triumph. They assert themselves to be students and neophytes no longer, but doctors of the law. They speak no more with bated breath, as if they were afraid of somebody, but bellow and thunder *ex cathedrâ*, calling upon the whole world to listen to a philosophy as old as history and as indestructible as human society. "Slavery is no evil," they say; "so far from its being a wrong, or the curse of humanity, it is the proper condition of the masses of mankind, and better than the freedom in which they pine and starve, and—if they do not go to the grave before their time—in which they breed revolution and war. The black man is necessarily the first slave, because he is the stupidest, the least valuable, and most easily captured; but the white laborer with nothing to give to the world on whose bosom he was born but the unskilled labor of his brawny arms, in a slave *de facto* in every part of the earth, and were he a slave *de jure*, would be happier and more comfortable than he can ever hope to be under the system prevalent in Europe and in the free states of America."

Such is the trumpet-blast blown in loud and saucy defiance by the new generation of Southern writers and politicians. Among these, one of the ablest and most conscientious—a man who writes as if he believed himself to be the preacher and the apostle of a new science which is to enlighten the darkened, and reform the corrupted world—is Mr. George Fitz Hugh, of Virginia. This gentleman boldly enunciates the theory that free society is a failure; and that the best, if not the only hope of civilization, unless it would fall the prey of stronger and honester barbarism, is the re-establishment of slavery, independently of color and race, in every part of the world. Although the Gospel be preached, the rails be laid, and locomotives run—although the electric telegraph sends its messages, and the printing-press is in constant activity, disseminating ideas—he holds his system to be fully adapted to such a state of circumstances. There are many other writers, both in prose and verse, who have taken up this principle as the social religion of the South, but Mr. Fitz Hugh is the one who has gone most systematically and philosophically into the discussion, and laid down authoritatively a system of slavery pure and simple. He would not only enslave the negroes, but the poor Irish and German immigrants as fast as they arrive in New York, and either send them off to till the ground in the cotton and sugar regions, or sell them at Charleston or New Orleans by public auction to the highest bidder. "Liberty is for the few—slavery, in every form, is for the many!" That is the maxim of which he attempts to justify the universal relevancy by history, by philosophy, by religion, and by the "eternal fitness of things."

It may be thought that Mr. Fitz Hugh and the other doctrinaires of slavery write in jest. On the contrary, they write in grim earnest, and as if they were the founders of a new or the restorers of an old religion. But their arguments, when not supported by or drawn from the Old Testament, and the "bondage" known among the Egyptians and the Jews, or from the negative support they derive from the absence of an express denunciation of slavery in the New Testament, and the more positive authority which they imagine they have discovered in the book of Revelations, when, at the opening of the sixth seal, the free man and the "bond" are to call upon the rocks to cover them from the wrath of the Almighty, are chiefly devoted to the one point upon which they make the whole question to revolve, the superiority of the physical condition of the slave to that of the free laborer in Europe. The poets of the South attempt to sing of the happy Arcadia where the planter, like the patriarch of old, sits under the shadow of his vine, and treats his slaves as if they were the members of his own family, the sharers in all his gains, his faithful and affectionate dependents, who are provided for by his care, who enjoy all the benefits of his prosperity, but never suffer from his adversity; who work for the common good when they are hale and well, and who, when they are old and sick, or from any cause unable to work, are tended quite as affectionately as if they still contributed to the common stock. Philosophers like Mr. Fitz Hugh, while painting the same sunny picture, and holding up the condition of the slave as if it were the *summum bonum* of human bliss, dive deeper than the poets into the social causes of the state of things of which they so highly approve, and demonstrate, to their own satisfaction and that of all the South, that the few must be lords and the many slaves, and that the lordship on the one side and the slavery on the other are equally right and mutually beneficial. And from this peculiar point of view their arguments are sound. If the sole aim, end, and enjoyment of the bulk of mankind be to eat and drink, to be clad and housed, and to have no care for the morrow—no moral responsibilities—no harassing duties, that make them prematurely old, not so much with labor as with anxiety, then the condition of the slave in the Southern States of the American Union is superior to that of the free laborer in Europe. To the argument that "man shall not live by bread alone"—that his moral, intellectual, and religious nature—of infinitely greater importance than his merely physical well-being—can not only not be cultivated and developed, but must deteriorate in a state of slavery—these writers reply with scorn: "The customary theories of modern ethical philosophy, whether utilitarian or sentimental," says Mr. Fitz Hugh, "are so fallacious, or so false in their premises and their deductions as to deserve rejection, and must be replaced by others founded on a broader philosophical system and on more Christian principles." "The world will fall back on domestic slavery when all other social forms have failed and been exhausted. That hour may not be far off." "I treat of slavery as a positive good, not a necessary evil." Such is the new doctrine.

Mr. Fitz Hugh draws a contrast between what he calls the white slave-trade and what others call the black slave-trade very much to the disadvantage of the former. He defines the white slave-trade to mean the employment of white men at low wages, regulated rather by the keenness of their own competition with one another than by the intrinsic value of their labor, and their non-sustenance, as soon as they become impotent and unfit to work, by those employers who made the most of them when they were strong. He alleges it to be far more cruel than the black slave-trade, "inasmuch as it exacts more from the workers, and neither protects nor governs them." He asserts that when the abolitionists, or enemies of slavery, proclaim that white labor is cheaper than black, they destroy their own case; and, so far from leading men of sense to give the blacks their freedom, they merely lead the true philanthropist and the wise philosopher to govern, employ, protect, and enslave the whites. The whole theory is thus stated in the first chapter of Mr. Fitz Hugh's treatise:

"The profits made from *free labor* are the amount of the products of such labor which the employer, by means of the command which capital or skill gives him, takes away, exacts, or exploitates from the free laborer.

"The profits of *slave labor* are that portion of the products of such labor which the power of the master enables him to appropriate. *These profits are less, because the master allows the slave to retain a larger share of the results of his own labor than do the employers of free labor.*

"But we not only boast that the white slave-trade is more exacting and fraudulent than black slavery, but that it is more cruel, in leaving the laborer to take care of himself and family out of the pittance which skill or capital have allowed him to retain. When his day's labor is ended he is free, but overburdened with the cares of his family and household, which make his freedom an empty and delusive mockery. But his employer is really free, and may enjoy the profits made by other people's labor without a care or trouble as to their wellbeing. The negro slave is free too when the labors of the day are over, and free in mind as well as in body; for the master provides food, raiment, house, fuel, and every thing else necessary to the physical well-being of himself and family. The master's labors commence when the slave's end. No wonder white slaveholders should prefer the slavery of white men and capital to negro slavery, since the white slaveholding is more profitable, and is free from all the cares and labors of black slave-holding."

Here is the picture drawn in support of the first part of the principle: "The negro slaves," says Mr. Fitz Hugh, "are the happiest, and, in some cases, the freest people in the world. The children and the aged and infirm work not at all, and yet have all the comforts and necessaries of life provided for them. They enjoy liberty, because they are not oppressed either by care or labor. The women do little hard work, and are protected from the despotism of their husbands by their masters. The negro men and stout boys work on the average, in good weather, not more than nine hours a day; the balance of their time is spent in perfect *abandon*. Besides this, they have their Sabbaths and holidays. White men, with so much of license and liberty, would die of *ennui;* but negroes luxuriate in corporeal and mental repose. With faces upturned to the sun, they can sleep at any hour, and quiet sleep is the greatest of human enjoyments."

This is the picture drawn in support of the second: "The free laborer must work or starve. He is more of a slave than the negro, because he works longer and harder for less allowance than the slave, and has no holidays, because with him the cares of life begin when its labors end. He has no liberty, and not a single right. We know it is often said that air and water are common property, in which all have equal right to participate and enjoy. But this is utterly false.

The appropriation of the lands carries with it the appropriation of all on or above the lands, *usque ad cœlum, aut ad inferos*. A man can not breathe the air without a place to breathe it from, and all places are appropriated. All water is private property 'to the middle of the stream,' except the ocean, and that is not fit to drink.

"Free laborers have not a thousandth part of the rights and liberties of negro slaves. Indeed, they have not a single right or liberty except the right or liberty to die.

"Where a few own the soil, they have unlimited power over the balance of society until domestic slavery comes in to compel them to permit this balance of society to draw a sufficient and comfortable living from *terra mater*.

"Free society asserts the right of a few men to the earth. Slavery maintains that it belongs in different degrees to all.

"The slave-trade is the only trade worth following; slaves the only property worth owning. All other is worthless, a mere *caput mortuum*, except in so far as it vests the owner with the power to command the labor of others; in other words, *to enslave them*. Give you a palace — ten thousand acres of land, and you are poorer than Robinson Crusoe if you have no slaves — either to capital or domestic slaves. Your capital will not bring you an income of a cent, nor supply one of your wants without labor. Labor is indispensable to give value to property. If you owned every thing else, and did not own labor, you would be poor. But fifty thousand dollars mean, and are, fifty thousand dollars' worth of slaves. You can command, without touching on that capital, three thousand dollars' worth of labor per annum. You could do no more were you to buy slaves with it, and then you would be cumbered with the cares of governing and providing for them. You are a slaveholder now to the extent of fifty thousand dollars, with all the advantages, and none of the disadvantages and responsibilities of a master.

"Property in man is what every body is struggling to obtain. Why should we not be obliged to take care of men, our property, as we do of our horses and our hounds, our cattle and our sheep? Now, under the delusive name of liberty, the free laborer is wrought from morn to eve, from infancy to old age, and then turned out to starve."

It will be seen from this abstract how bold the assertion, how weak the argument, and how great the fallacy that underlies the whole. To horse, bullock, or dog—to white man or to black—such reasoners apply the same rule; for horse, bullock, dog, and man are only different varieties of the worker—to be all tended and taken care of, as their natures require—all unfit, though in ever-varying degrees, to take care of themselves. But, without personal disrespect to Mr. Fitz Hugh, who is evidently a sincere and an accomplished man, or to any others who have preceded or followed him in the enunciation of his doctrine, may we not ask him and them to consider in what condition he or they would have been in at this moment if the principles of the philosophy they uphold had been acted upon in the case of white laborers in England, or Europe generally, at and subsequent to the period of the discovery and colonization of America? Perhaps two out of three of the white population now flourishing in the South— the owners and rulers of the soil of the most fertile portions of the United States—are the descendants of laborers—men of mere arms and sinews—men born to till the earth, and having no skill or knowledge of any other art but that of agriculture in its rudest forms. Had their progenitors been made slaves of then—as they ought to have been, if the theory be good for any thing—their descendants, and perhaps Mr. Fitz Hugh among the rest, would have been slaves also, and, according to his argument, far better off, physically, than they can hope to be under the *régime* of personal liberty. But what would have been the progress of the great continent of America? Who would have fought with Washington for the independence of a noble nation? Who would have covered the land with railroads, and sent ships to every sea? Who would have built such cities as New York, Washington, Cincinnati, St. Louis, and San Francisco? And where would be the great republic that, young as it is, holds up its head among the mightiest powers of the earth, and treats with them as equal to equal?

The basis of this philosophy—if it be not a desecration of the name so to apply it—is the grossest sensualism. Better be a sleek horse, or a corpulent pig snoozing upon a dunghill, than a lean man overburdened with anxiety. Such is the ultimate element into which all such reasoning resolves itself. And no doubt there is many a pig which is happier than a man. To suffer, and to elevate ourselves by suffering, is our great privilege as human beings. To endure and to grow is in the essence of the immortal mind. Were it not so, the gradations of happiness would extend downward, and not upward. The happy pig would be less happy than the oyster; and the oyster itself would be a miserable creature compared with the monad, and still more miserable compared with a stone. We should either wallow in the styes of sensualism, or take refuge in the Brahminical philosophy—that annihilation is supreme bliss. We should live lives of despair instead of hope, and cry in our blank misery, with melancholy Byron,

> "Count o'er the joys thy days have seen;
> Count o'er thine hours from anguish free;
> And know, whatever thou hast been,
> 'Tis something better not to be."

But it is not necessary to argue out to its ultimate deductions a system like this, upon which many readers may perhaps be of opinion that too much has already been said. It was, however, necessary to say thus much, to indicate, for the better comprehension of English readers, the new phase into which the slavery and anti-slavery controversy has entered. The friends of slavery act no longer on the defensive. They have outgrown their early timidity. They no more walk warily, as if upon rotten ice, but step out boldly, as if upon the rock and the solid earth.

Slaves, in a certain sense, all men are. We are slaves to the law of gravitation and to the laws of health; slaves to hunger and thirst; slaves to our passions and our affections; slaves to our prejudices; slaves too and prisoners of the earth, from which we can not escape under the penalty of death. We are slaves to capital also—as Mr. Fitz Hugh asserts—unmistakably slaves to it; and the capitalist, also, is the slave of the laborer, without whom, as he says, all his capital is worthless. But Mr. Fitz Hugh, and all the Southern reasoners, who look upon him as the apostle of the new faith which is to end all controversy with those who maintain that a black man is not a chattel, must go far deeper into first principles before they can convince one human being, out of the narrow circle of Southern society, that they have either made a discovery, or that their discovery is of the slightest value. The white laborer is a slave, and is often a slave ill paid and ill tended, with none to care for him, and with nothing oftentimes but Christian charity to depend upon for his life when he is old and sick, and unable to toil any more; but he had this consolation in toiling, that no man could come to his cottage or his hovel, and take away the wife of his bosom, and sell her into bondage in a strange land; that none could take his children forcibly away, so that he might see them no more; and that none could lay hands upon himself, and make him toil upon the land, when he preferred to toil upon the water, or treat him with the same unconcern as a dog or a horse. Any one powerful enough to carry off Mr. Fitz Hugh and sell him into bondage, might apply to him the arguments he uses to negroes and to white slaves; and if he remonstrated, say to him, "Foolish fellow! why do you complain? You shall not labor more than nine hours a day. You shall have Sundays and holidays. You shall have the comforts and necessaries of life. When you are sick, you shall be tended. When you are old, you shall be taken care of. Go away! Do your work, and be happy. When you have done it, make your mind easy, and sleep; for sleep is the greatest of all blessings. And pity me, your unfortunate master, who am compelled to take care of you, to think for you, and to protect you." If such arguments are good for black men and white men alike, why not for white philosophers?

Are not a crust and a draught of water in the pure fresh air, with liberty of locomotion and the privilege of looking at the sunshine, better than turtle soup and choice wines in a dark dungeon? Let the advocates of the new faith decide. But Mr. Fitz Hugh is a slave already—a slave to his theory.

CHAPTER XXX.

DECLINE OF THE SPANISH RACE IN AMERICA.

Washington, March, 1858.

As Greece was to Persia, and as Rome was to Carthage in ancient days—as England was to France within the memory of living men—so are the United States to the Spanish races on the North American continent, and more especially to the Mexicans. There is deadly and traditional enmity between them, and a growing conviction on the part of the Anglo-Saxon race, strengthened by prejudice, by passion, by interest, and by a vague and nameless, but powerful antipathy, that, sooner or later, Mexico must be invaded, conquered, and annexed. And not only Mexico, but the whole continent as far south as Panama, is doomed in the popular mind to a gradual incorporation into the great republic. The star-spangled banner has now but thirty-two stars to glitter on its folds, or one for each state; but, should that day ever arrive, it will have to place at least one hundred and fifty stars upon it, or adopt a new symbolism for a power so magnificent. Nor is this a mere dream of ambition confined to the warm South and the teeming fancy of Southern politicians, who, by the supposed necessities of the institution of slavery, imagine that, as they can not extend to the great West, or keep pace with the growth of the free states by any other means, they must perforce annex Cuba, and the vast, ill-governed, miserable, but beautiful and fertile regions lying between the frontiers of Texas and the two oceans that all but mingle at Panama. The feeling is shared by many soberer men and cooler politicians, who deplore, while they assert the necessity that impels them. They consider it the "manifest destiny" of the Saxon, Anglo-Saxon, and Scandinavian race—for these are but one in their origin—to drive out the degenerate Spaniards, and descendants of Spaniards, who are about as unfit to develop the country as

DECLINE OF THE SPANISH RACE IN AMERICA. 259

the Red Indians, and utterly unable to establish any thing like a free or a firm government. And every year, things, instead of mending, become worse. The Spaniards intermarry with the Indians, and produce a mixed race, with all the vices of both breeds, and none of the virtues of either. By their indolence, rapacity, and lawlessness, they come into constant collision with Yankees and other adventurous spirits of the United States, who push south to trade and speculate, and at the least real or supposed indignity or injustice, clamor lustily for the interference of the government at Washington, glad of an occasion for quarrel, and panting for the spoils of a race whom they despise, and of a country which they covet.

The last war against Mexico, which ended in the annexation of California, was one of the most popular ever undertaken by any nation. The spirit of the whole country was aroused. Farmers left their farms, lawyers their desks and courts, tradesmen their stores, students their colleges, and members of Congress their seats in the Legislature, to fight against the Mexicans. Not only the youth, but the middle age of the Southern and some of the Northern States were in arms, burning for glory and for annexation. Men of fortune shouldered the rifle, and went through all the hardships of the campaign in the capacity of private soldiers; and the number of volunteers was so great, that the government had to repress, rather than encourage, the martial ardor of the citizens, and to throw every imaginable impediment in the way of their enthusiasm. Should there be any new cause of quarrel with Mexico leading to a war, the same ardor would indubitably be aroused, and not all the sobriety and *vis inertiæ* of New England, nor all the prudence of all the statesmen that the Union possesses, would be sufficient to cool the martial spirit, or prevent farther conquest and the annexation of at least another province.

The popular favor enjoyed by General William Walker, the famous filibuster and invader of Nicaragua, is but one out of many proofs of the feeling with which the people of the United States regard their effete Southern neighbors. This personage, who is as familiar in Pennsylvania Avenue and in the purlieus of Congress as any public man in Washington, and who has just left, accompanied by his second in command, a General Henningsen, formerly connected in some capacity with the press of London, was brought to this capital in custody of the United States marshal for having infringed the laws of the United States in his late attempted invasion of Nicaragua. But his imprisonment was a mere sham. He was free to go hither and thither as he pleased; and he was ultimately released even from that nominal captivity and surveillance without even a caution as to his future behavior. In fact, Walker, though, by the law of nations, a vulgar pirate and outlaw, was a popular person even in Washington, and in New Orleans and Mobile was the honored recipient of enthusiastic ovations. Though his conduct was disavowed and condemned by the federal government, the public feeling was strong that it was his failure, and not the attempt itself, which was distasteful to men in power. "To go in and win" would have been admirable; but to be foiled and beaten was disagreeable to the government. Failure brought inconvenient remonstrances and remarks from foreign powers, and placed the executive in a false position. Walker has identified himself for the time being with this particular movement; but Walker is but a straw upon the wind, and there are hundreds of others ready to supply his place, should fortune play him false, and give him the pirate's death instead of the victor's laurel, and a high gibbet instead of Nicaragua.

The present condition of Mexico, and of all the Central American republics, and the probable future that awaits them in consequence of their own tendency toward disorganization and the rapid increase in population, trade, and moral power of the United States of America, are questions quite as pertinent to Englishmen as to the rest of the civilized world. The growth of the United States is merely one of the forms of the development of that political and industrial civilization of which England was the birthplace, and of which Englishmen and Scotchmen are still the leaders, and which is founded upon the greatest personal freedom, consistent with order and organization, and the untrammeled liberty of individual en-

DECLINE OF THE SPANISH RACE IN AMERICA. 261

terprise. Addressing itself to the elevation of man through the development of his material interests, which must always precede, to a greater or less extent, the development of a higher form of civilization, Anglo-American progress is fated to exercise a powerful influence over the decaying communities of Spanish America.

Impressed with the general bearing of these truths, but having no means of making a personal investigation into the actual circumstances of all these quasi republics and anarchies —as showing how far the instinctive notion of their irretrievable decay which is prevalent in the United States was founded on facts—I requested Mr. Thrasher, of New York, a gentleman who passed some years in Cuba and in Mexico in a high official position, to put into writing the results of his experience. I was favored shortly afterward with the following *résumé* of the subject, which, though it may happen to be tinctured with the American sympathies of the writer, is none the less interesting from the information it conveys, and from the political warnings which may be drawn from it:

"In taking a succinct view," says the writer, "of the political and social condition of the Spanish-American republics in North and South America—though South America is of little importance in the inquiry—it is necessary to keep in view the fact that they have constantly endeavored to imitate the political example of the United States, in which they have as constantly failed. In this must be sought the causes of failure—causes which may easily be found. Whenever a nation is constituted by the separation of itself from that of which it formed a part, it necessarily receives a political impulse, the direction of which it is apt to follow ever after. When the distinct, and, to some degree, discordant British colonies of North America severed their connection with the crown, their first impulse was to create a common centre of action. The result was the erection of the federal power; and the involuntary political tendency of the United States has ever been to increase the influence of the federal executive and of the federal Congress. In the Spanish colonies of America the reverse of this took place. Under the rule of the mother country, the form of government was a thorough centralization; and the old viceroyalties of Mexico, Peru, and Buenos Ayres, as well as the captain-generalcies of Guatemala, New Granada, Venezuela, and Chili, were divided into provinces, or intendencies, as they were called, merely for the purposes of local administration. In the struggles which gave birth to them as independent nations, the political impulse which they received was toward decentralization, and the advocacy of the principles known in America as the doctrine of States' Rights. The involuntary political tendency of these countries has ever been to diminish the influence of the central or federal government.

"Thus movements seemingly identical in their origin produced directly opposite results; for while in the United States the power of the federal government to repress domestic rebellion continually increased, and was never stronger than it is at present, that of the federal power in the Spanish-American States continually diminished, and was never more impotent to suppress revolt and rebellion than it is to-day. Other circumstances have also contributed to the political decay of the Spanish-American States, among which their readiness to adopt the ideas of the first and last French Revolution, and to place the individual above the state, holding that the state owes him an obligation greater than he owes to the state, has been, perhaps, the most prominent.

"While, under such influences as these, the political fabric in Spanish America has exhibited a constant decay, the changes in social organization have been equally great. The line of separation between the discordant, unequal, and inferior races that constitute the population, and which, under the rule of Spain, was kept in constant view, has been destroyed, and all the old Spanish laws for the organization of labor have been repealed without the substitution of any thing in their place. Mexico may be taken as the type of the result; for the same thing, with slight modifications, has occurred in all those countries. The political and social inducements to the white race to preserve its purity and integrity having been removed, it has gradually amalgamated with the inferior races; and the latter, possessing a numerical superiority of seven millions to one million of white inhabitants, has nearly swallowed up the white race in the course of the one generation that has elapsed since the era of their independence.

"The consequence of all these causes is, that the northern states of Mexico have lost nearly all their white population, and that the unorganized native communities are unable to resist the attacks of the savage Apaches, Comanches, Seminoles, and other Indian tribes, who are driven southward from their old hunting-grounds by the westward march of Anglo-Saxon civilization. In the beautiful province of Sonora, the rule of Mexico is reduced to a few towns, such as Guaymas, Ures, and Hermosilla; in Chihuahua constant sallies of the government troops are necessary to protect the scattered rural population; in Durango the Indians roam, in small parties, unmolested over the whole state, and the civilized inhabitants have been compelled to concentrate in the cities and large towns for mutual protection. The grazing districts of Coahuila, Leon, Zacatecas, and Sinaloa are a constant prey to small parties of savages, who drive off the cattle, and carry the women and children into captivity amid their mountain fastnesses.

"In the southern part of Mexico a similar state of things exists. General Alvarez, who, although he boasts a Spanish name, is a cross between the negro and the Indian, has long ruled the State of Guerrero with despotic sway. But he has ever given a lip-obedience to the federal government, and has kept the Pintos, as the preponderating native race is called, in subjection. His own recognition of the federal government, and the influence of his name, have hitherto kept the other native races in the south to their allegiance; but lately they have revolted; and now, at the age of eighty years, he is engaged in a war of doubtful issue with the Indians of Chilapa and Oajaca, who are hounded on by priests and plotters, who refuse to recognize the present federal government of Mexico. The course of Alvarez in this question has produced dissatisfaction among his own people, the Pintos, which will doubtless break out into open revolt after his death. In the eastern and peninsular state of Yucatan the savage tribes of the interior have recovered possession of nearly the whole territory, and the quasi whites are driven into the cities of Merida, Sisal, and Campeachy, the capital (Merida) having been frequently menaced by a large force of Indians.

"Amid all this disintegration and political decay, the federal power has grown constantly weaker, until its influence has become too powerless to reach the more distant portions of the republic. In the south, Alvarez has long held supreme power; in Sonora, the Gandara family ruled for many years, until recently overthrown by Pasquiera, who likewise pays little heed to Congress or the President. Vidaurri, in the north, has annexed the State of Coahuila to that of Nuevo Leon, where his will is law; and endeavored, a little more than a year since, to perform the same act with the State of Tamaulipas. In Central Mexico a more formal obedience is rendered to the federal authority, but one that is practically of little import; and, amid all their party divisions, two great principles emerge. The first asserts that the national decay is owing to the decentralization of power, and the other that power is still too much centralized. The one principle triumphs, and brings back Santa Anna to the Dictatorship, as in 1853, to be overthrown in 1855 by a plan of Ayutla, which installs a new Constitution in 1857, decentralizing the federal power still more, and placing it entirely in the hands of a single representative chamber, that is to sit permanently, either of itself, or through a committee of one representative for each of the states. This, again, is immediately superseded by the establishment of the Dictatorship of Comonfort, which may be overthrown between the writing and the publication of these remarks.

"Under these circumstances, the remnant of the white race in Mexico is seeking new blood and a reinvigoration by an infusion from abroad. When the army of the United States held Mexico, General Scott, the American commander-in-chief, was tendered a bonus to himself of two hundred thousand pounds if he would resign his commission and accept the supreme power in Mexico. At this time he aspired to the presidency of the United States, and he declined the offer. When Santa Anna returned to power in 1853, he drew around him a large number of Spanish officers from Cuba, but took with him no troops. It is said that he looks forward now to an early return to Mexico, and that he will seek to create several regiments composed entirely of Spaniards. On the other hand, Comonfort has turned his eyes toward the United States, and anticipated receiving aid from the ambitious and restless spirits that abound here. The experience of the past, as shown in the expeditions of Lopez to Cuba, Walker to Lower California and Central America, Carvajal to Tamaulipas, and Raousset de Boulbon and Crabbe to Sonora, leads to the belief that, though these have failed, they will be followed by others that will succeed in the future, sustained as the spirit of American filibusterism is by what is called Saxon "pluck" and tenacity of purpose.

"But let us follow the process of political disintegration southward. The former Republic of Central America, obeying the political impulse it received at its birth, soon destroyed the federal power it had created in imitation of the United States, and broke up into the five independent states of Guatemala, San Salvador, Honduras, Nicaragua, and Costa Rica. In Guatemala, after years of successive revolutions, the Indian races asserted their supremacy, and elevated Carrera, a half-bred Creole cattle-driver, to supreme power. He rules something as Montezuma and Atahualpa may be supposed to have ruled, but with some of the forms of a civilized organization. In parts of the state the government still decrees what proportions of the land shall be sown in wheat, what in maize, and what in other productions of the soil. Carrera has centralized power in Guatemala, and peace reigns for the time.

"In San Salvador, Honduras, and Nicaragua internal discord has been the rule for many years, and in the struggle the white race has gradually died out or been absorbed, until now it does not possess a single representative man. The native and mixed races have triumphed under the leadership of the half-breeds. Santos Guadiola, the President of Honduras, partakes largely of the Indian; and Martinez, the new president of Nicaragua, is a dark mulatto. Costa Rica, having a larger infusion of white blood, and few negroes or Indians, has kept the races more distinct, and the rule of the whites is represented by the family of Mora. This state has exhibited less intestine disorder than any of the others of Central America.

"The condition of Southern America, in as far as it is occupied by the Spanish races, is equally suggestive of approaching change.

"First in geographical order on the southern continent comes the former republic of Colombia, founded by Bolivar, the hero of South American independence. Before his death he was driven from power, and the state followed the political impulse of its creation, breaking up into the smaller republics of New Granada, Venezuela, and Ecuador. The first of these, New Granada, held until quite recently a centralized form of government, in which the white race, settled upon the slopes of the three Andean ridges that run through it, retained the political power. But the rule of centralization now prevails, and during the present year a federation of states has been formed on the model of the North American Union. In the tropical regions of the coast and the riverine provinces, the Sambo, or mixed race of whites, negroes, and Indians, preponderate; but in the temperate regions of Antioquia, Socorro, and Cundinamarca the white population hold political and social sway. Under their rule, the several revolutions that have been attempted by the mixed races have never succeeded, and the republic has exhibited a political stability and material development equaled only by that of Chili among the Spanish-American nations.

"Venezuela, whose territory consists mostly of vast tropical grazing plains, inhabited by negroes and mestizos on the coast, and roving white and Indian herdsmen in the interior, has followed a political course similar to that of Guatemala. The Monagas family, by ingratiating themselves with the mixed and black population, have centralized political power in their own hands, and kept the country quiet for several years. The same struggle exists there, however, as in the other states; and General Paez and many others are in exile, watching an opportunity for a new revolution. Ecuador, being one of the Spanish colonies upon the Pacific, received less slave importation than the others which possessed ports on the Caribbean Sea, and consequently has less of the negro element in its population. But the want of white immigration from Europe, and the gradual absorption of this race by the native, are rapidly bringing the latter into power, and even now the communities of the interior are assimilating to the pure Indian.

"Peru contains more of the negro and mixed races on the coast, but the whites still preserve, in a great measure, their former political and social influence. But in the interior there exist many native communities that do not recognize the rule of the government at Lima, and who not only preserve the memory and the traditions of the Incas, but make continual forays upon the settlements of the Christian native races. The same decentralizing tendency exists, as is seen in the new Constitution issued recently by the Convention at Lima, which body has now been three years in continual session. The possession of the valuable guano islands on her coast has given the white rulers the means of maintaining their sway, and at the same time afforded a constant provocative to revolutionary attempts to get possession of the government. In Bolivia, Belzu succeeded for a time in becoming absolute master, after the manner of Monagas in Venezuela, and Carrera in Guatemala, supporting his power by a monopoly of the valuable trade in quina, or Peruvian bark. A revolution is now raging there—the attempt being made to place Linares in power instead of Cordova, a relative of Belzu, who is president.

"Chili lies in a more temperate zone than the tropical countries we have just reviewed, and has received less of the negro element from the slave importation than other Spanish colonies. Besides this, the Araucanian Indians of the south have always maintained their independence and a hostile attitude toward the whites. Chili, for a variety of reasons, has exhibited more material progress and intellectual development than perhaps any other of the Spanish-American republics.

"The old viceroyalty of Buenos Ayres, so long the scene of the despotisms of Rosas and Dr. Francia, presents nearly the same political and social features as the rest of Spanish America. Lopez has succeeded Francia in Paraguay, and Urquiza wields a portion of the power that Rosas held in Buenos Ayres; but the political tendency there is also toward decentralization, and the Argentine Confederation is the result. The Guachos of the Pampas have a large portion of the Indian, with something of the negro blood in them, and entertain the greatest dread of the savage tribes on the southern, western, and northwestern frontiers. A line of forts has been erected to protect them, and travelers across that portion of the continent to Chili still pursue the path opened by the Spaniards more than a century ago. So great is the fear of the mixed races, that the inhabitants of the northwestern provinces, near the eastern slopes of the Andes, have never dared to descend the water-courses of the Bermejo, Salado, and other large rivers until the present year. The expedition of the United States' steamer *Water Witch*, under Captain Page, two years ago, to examine these rivers, has stimulated the desire for fluvial navigation, and some foreign houses are sending small steamers up the Bermejo and Salado. General Taboada is at this moment receiving great praise in the Argentine Confederation for having dared to cross the wilderness with a party of one hundred men, to meet the steamer on one of the rivers.

"I have endeavored to present only a succinct view of the political and social retrogression of Spanish America, without touching some other questions of great importance that are being developed there. I can not, however, refrain from mentioning one prominent fact to be observed in all these countries, and that is the decay of the Roman Catholic Church. Every where in Spanish America the temporal organization of the Church is a point of attack. A spirit of rationalism, somewhat of the French and somewhat of the German school, is pervading the more intelligent portion of the rising genera-

DECLINE OF THE SPANISH RACE IN AMERICA.

tion, while the more ignorant are relapsing into uncouth religious practices that savor of paganism.

"Under the operation of political, social, and religious decay, the immutable law of races plays its part in the great drama. The race which largely preponderates in number swallows up the others, and thus the aboriginals of Spanish America are reassuming their ancient sway. This fact is giving rise to movements in America for which there is no parallel in Europe. There moribund civilization is seeking for support by an infusion of new vigor through white immigration, and assistance from Europe and Northern America. In the Argentine Confederation an active immigration from Spain and other portions of Southern Europe is already established, and the distance of those countries from the United States will no doubt protect them from the Saxon overflow from North America, and will possibly enable the renewed European element to work out the problem of its future without interference. Whether it possesses the requisite qualifications to insure success I shall not stop to examine. But Mexico and Central America lie too near the busy, enterprising, and ambitious elements that swarm in the United States to justify the opinion that they will be left to die quietly. Already the paths of American intercourse between the Atlantic and Pacific Oceans are laid in many places across the territories of those republics, and the natural result that has followed the footstep of the Anglo-Saxon in all parts of the world must follow it there. The policy of the United States government, thus far, has been to avoid all concessions from those countries, except the absolute transfer of territory from Mexico, about one half of whose former dominion is now incorporated in the American Union; and the Bulwer-Clayton Convention, now existing, with Great Britain, precludes any farther settlement or occupancy. But, before the great necessities of nations, policies change and treaties become inoperative, so that there is little doubt that, either through the action of the government or that of filibusterism—which some friends of General Walker and General Henningsen designate by the more courteous appellation of 'private enterprise'—

the disintegrating communities of Mexico and Central America will receive their new life from the Anglo-Saxons of North America. The manner and time of this operation who shall undertake to predict?"

The Mexican pear has, since these observations were written, been ripening and rotting. Brother Jonathan need not pluck it, for it will drop into his mouth; and then, the greatest of all the troubles of the Union—slavery alone excepted—will begin.

CHAPTER XXXI.

BALTIMORE AND MARYLAND.

Baltimore, March 27, 1858.

MARYLAND is one of the original thirteen states of the Union, and the most northern of the slaveholding communities. But slavery does not flourish upon its soil. In such a climate as it enjoys, white men can perform all kinds of agricultural labor with as much pleasure and impunity as in the British Isles. Consequently, the labor of the negro becomes unprofitable, and white men are gradually displacing the black from all employments except those of the waiter, the barber, and the coach-driver. The same state of things has resulted, in a greater or less degree, in Virginia, North Carolina, Kentucky, and Missouri, where slavery, though still maintained as a "domestic institution," is proving itself every day to be a social and economic failure. These states, and more especially Maryland and Virginia, having no purpose to which they can profitably devote slave labor, have become mere breeders of negroes for the rice, cotton, and sugar plantations of South Carolina, Alabama, Mississippi, Arkansas, Tennessee, and Louisiana. In states like Maryland, slavery exists in its most repulsive form; for the owner, having no use for the superabundant negroes, seems to acknowledge no duties or responsibilities toward them, but breeds them as he would cattle, that he may sell them in the best market. Farther south, the owners of slaves, who employ them in the cultivation of the soil, establish what they call the "patriarchal relation," and seldom or never think of selling them, of separating families, or of treating them otherwise than kindly. But not so in the tobacco and corn growing states. As slaves are not wanted, and are a burden to maintain, the owners have little compunction in selling the wife without the husband, or both without the children, according to the caprice or wants of the purchaser.

It is constantly repeated in America—by those who, without any strong feelings on the subject, are nevertheless of opinion that slavery is wrong, and that it would have been better for the Union if it had never existed—that, had it not been for the extreme violence of the ultra-abolitionists, it might long ago have been peaceably abolished in the five states just named. They urge that abolitionism has become more of a political than a philanthropic movement; and that the people in these Middle States have clung to slavery, even when it has ceased to be profitable, because they would not by its abolition weaken or dissever the Union, or overthrow the balance of power so as to place it completely in the hands of the North. The Northern abolitionists are almost invariably protectionists. They would give freedom to the black man, but they would put shackles upon commerce for the benefit of the Northern manufacturers. In the South the case is exactly the opposite. The Southern planters would—some of them say—abolish slavery if they were not goaded and exasperated to it, and if they saw or could invent the immediate means of doing so without ruin both to themselves and the negro; and they are free-traders almost to a man.

The first British settlement in this part of the continent was made in 1634, by Leonard Calvert, brother of Lord Baltimore. The country was granted to Lord Baltimore by charter of King Charles I., and is said to have been named Maryland in honor of Henrietta Maria, queen of that monarch. But this has been denied, and the honor claimed on behalf of Mary Calvert, wife of Lord Baltimore. Virginia, the neighboring state, was named in honor of Queen Elizabeth; and Maryland, taken possession of in the preceding reign, but not settled or colonized so early, is by others asserted to have taken its appellation from the ill-starred lady known to Protestant tradition as "Bloody Mary." But, however this may be, Maryland was not ambitious to rival the character of such a sovereign, but took a course on religious matters which entitles its early founders to grateful mention in the history of the world. By an act passed in 1639 it granted entire freedom of religious faith and practice to all creeds, sects, and denominations whatsoever within its boundaries.

Baltimore, though not the capital, is the principal city of this state, and contains a population of upward of two hundred thousand, taking rank as the largest city in the slaveholding states. It was founded in 1729. Its growth, however, has not been rapid. Cincinnati, not yet forty years old, has outstripped it; and Chicago, still younger, has a population nearly as great. But cities like these last mentioned are fed by the great stream of immigration from Europe, which invariably stops at the frontiers of slave states, and spreads its fructifying waters only in the lands of the free. Should the day ever come when Maryland shall abolish slavery, the growth of Baltimore will doubtless be more steady. Philadelphia, its free sister, has a population approaching to half a million; and there seems to be no reason, except slavery, why Baltimore should not become as rich and populous as the capital of the Quakers.

Baltimore, famous for the beauty of its women, is seated on the Patapsco River, at about twelve miles from its junction with Chesapeake Bay, and has harbors for the largest merchant vessels. It is called by its admirers "The Monumental City," but why it should have received so flattering a title is not very obvious. Of the three or four monuments on which its only claim to this distinction can be founded, there is but one worthy of the name, and that is the column erected to the great hero of America. "The Washington Monument" is a noble Doric pillar of pure white marble, one hundred and sixty-six feet in height inclusive of the basement, surmounted by a colossal statue of the *pater patriæ*. It stands in the centre of a square, on a terrace one hundred feet above the level of the Patapsco, and, seen from the river, or from any part of the neighboring country, forms an imposing and picturesque object. Of "Battle Monument," erected to the memory of those who fell in defending the city against the British forces in the war of 1814, the less said the better. A basement of twenty feet, surmounted by a column of only eighteen, surrounded by houses three or four times as lofty, looks ludicrously small; and, however much we may respect the motives of its builders, is more suggestive of a pencil-case standing upon a snuff-box on a drawing-room table than of a piece of architecture. In other respects Baltimore deserves the name of a fine city. It possesses many elegant public buildings; its streets are wide, long, and full of life and activity, and seem, if the traveler may judge by the names on the shop-doors, to partake largely of the Irish element. Its principal trade is in tobacco, and, next to the home consumer, its principal customer is Great Britain.

I was "under the weather," as the Americans say, when I arrived in Baltimore, and had caught so violent a cold from sitting in a draught between two windows in a railway-car, preternaturally heated by a fierce cast-iron stove, glowing red with anthracite coal, that I found it comfortable, if not necessary, to retire early to bed. My name had not been entered in the hotel books above an hour, and I was just preparing myself for slumber, when a negro waiter knocked at my door, and, entering, handed me the card of a gentleman who desired to see me on very particular and important business. The card bore this inscription: "The Eccelentisssimo Herr Alphonso G——r, Prince of Poets of the United States of America, to the Right Hon. Charles Mackay, Prince of Poets of England."

"Surely," said I to the negro, "this man must be mad?"

"Don't know—nebber see him before, massa."

"Tell him I'm sick, and in bed; say that he must write his business, and call again to-morrow."

"Yes, massa."

I turned round in bed, and was trying to forget the untimely visitor, when the negro again appeared.

"He won't go away, massa."

"Tell him that my name is Brown, or Jones—that he has made a mistake. Tell him that I've got the smallpox, or the yellow fever—any thing to get rid of him."

It was evident that the negro did not quite understand me. I fancied, moreover, that I heard the "Eccelentissimo Herr" and "Prince of Poets" close behind him. And, as a last resource, I got out of bed, told the good-natured negro to be gone, and barred and bolted the door. This was sufficient security for the night, and I soon forgot all about the interruption; but next morning, just as I was putting on my boots, there came a gentle tap at the bedroom door. Oblivious of the "Eccelentissimo Herr" and "Prince of Poets," I said, "Come in;" and in walked a young man, with a very dirty shirt, very dirty hands, very shabby garments, very wild eyes, and very loose, discolored teeth. He smelt very strongly of tobacco, and held in one hand a roll of paper, and in the other a card. The card was a fac-simile of the one I had received on the previous night. I knew my fate. I knew that I was in the presence of a lunatic. There was madness in every line of his countenance, in every movement of his limbs and body, nay, in every thread of his attire. Having rung the bell, I desired him to sit down, that I might make the best of him, and get rid of him with all possible celerity.

"I was determined to see you," he said, in very good English, but with a German accent that betrayed his origin. "I have been watching your arrival for three months. You came over in the *Asia*. I saw it announced. You dined with the President. You should not have done that. Excuse me, but 'Old Buck' is not the right man. He knows nothing of poetry. But let him slide! I am glad to welcome you to Baltimore."

I endeavored to look pleased; and as politely and as blandly as I could, I thanked him for his courtesy, and asked him his business.

"You are a prince of poets," he said. "So am I. I am the greatest poet of America—perhaps the greatest in the world. Now I want you to do me a favor."

Here the bell was answered, and a negro entered. "Wait

a minute or two," said I. "I will attend to you when I have done with this gentleman." "And what is the favor?" I inquired.

"To read this MS.," he said, "and give me your opinion of it. It is poetical, musical, philosophical, and astrological. It is the grandest work ever written on this continent. But, sir, the editors here are utter fools: there is not one of them fit to clean my boots. They refuse to look at my poems. And the President of the United States is no better than they are. He knows no more of poetry than a pig; and as for music, sir, I don't believe he knows the difference between a grunt and a psalm."

The Eccelentissimo Herr here proceeded to unfold his MS., which was very dirty and spotted with tobacco-juice. It was covered all over with hieroglyphics, astrological signs, musical notation, algebraic formulæ, and odds and ends of sentences, partly in German and partly in Italian text; sometimes written across the page, and sometimes down, in Chinese fashion.

"I am very sorry," said I, "that I can not read your composition; I am too ignorant—too utterly uninstructed in the symbols you use."

"Oh, that will not signify," he replied; "I will read it for you. In fact, I have come on purpose. It is an oratorio as well as a poem, and some of the best passages will have to be sung. Would you like to hear them?"

I fancy that I must have looked alarmed at the probability of such an infliction, for he said with great good-nature, "Not now, if it will distress you, or if you are busy. But I must absolutely have your opinion within a day or two. The work, I am sure, is magnificent; and, if you will only have the kindness to say so publicly, all Europe and all America will believe you. You are going to Europe soon?"

I nodded assent.

"That is lucky; I will go with you; and then I shall be able to read my poem to you on the passage. When we get to London I shall ask you to introduce me to the queen. I have heard that she is very fond of poetry, and has given Mr.

Tennyson a pension out of her husband's pocket-money, and that she often sends him a bottle of wine."

"I have not the honor of being personally known to her majesty," I replied; "and if I had, I could not introduce you. The American embassador in London would be the proper person."

"I don't believe in embassadors. They are all humbugs. They know nothing except how to tell lies. But did you say that you were not personally known to the queen?"

"I have not that honor and privilege."

"Excuse me, stranger," he said, slowly and emphatically, "when I say that won't do. You can't sell Brother Jonathan in that manner."

"I really do not know the queen, nor does the queen, as far as I am aware, know me."

"What! the Queen of England not know all about the poets of her own country? Does she not give Mr. Tennyson wine? And has she never given you any? I am certain the Queen of England knows me—the 'Prince of Poets of America.'"

"Quite certain?" said I.

"Oh, quite certain," he replied. "I have written to her about my oratorio, but she never answered the letter. But I shall go to England and see the queen. Music and poetry are properly rewarded there; and you shall introduce me to her, to Lord Palmerston, and the Archbishop of Canterbury, and all the rest of them."

"What does massa please to want?" chimed in the negro waiter, who had been listening all the time with very little comprehension of our discourse.

"I want you to order me a carriage; I have a very particular engagement."

"Excuse me," I added, turning to the Eccelentissimo Herr Alphonso, Prince of Poets, "if I am obliged to go away. I shall, perhaps, have the pleasure of seeing you again—next week."

"Do you stay a whole week in Baltimore? Then I shall make it a point to call upon you every day. You will thus have an opportunity of hearing my poetry and my oratorio. There is nothing like them in the whole world. Stupid America! and still stupider Baltimore! But, after all, it is not so much the fault of Baltimore or of America as of the dough-faced editors. But you, sir, must know me better. Look here!" And he again spread forth his greasy, tobacco-spotted manuscript, and pointed to a passage which it was utterly impossible to decipher. "Look here! and tell me if the man who wrote that is not worth a thousand dough-faced editors?"

He looked so wild as he spoke that I thought it good policy to coincide in his opinion touching dough-faced editors. If he had been the Prince Consort of Great Britain or Emperor of all the Russias, I could not have treated him with greater courtesy and deference. He was evidently pleased.

"Come again another day," I said.

"This evening?" he asked.

"No; I am particularly engaged."

"To-morrow morning?"

"I shall be very busy."

"To-morrow evening?"

"I will write to you whenever I can conveniently fix the time."

"Ah!" he said, with a deep sigh, "I am afraid you are no better than the dough-faces. You do not want to read my poetry?"

I was in a dilemma. I did not wish to tell him so disagreeable a truth. There was no way of getting out of the perplexity unless by humoring him till the carriage was ready—a carriage that I did not want, but for the arrival of which I began to grow impatient.

For ten minutes, that seemed to have lengthened themselves out to ten hours, I had to play with this lunatic, to watch every change in his countenance, and to be constantly on the alert, lest his madness should take a turn unfavorable to my safety, for he kept fumbling with his right hand under his waistcoat in a manner that suggested the possibility of a concealed bowie-knife or revolver, or, perhaps, another oratorio longer than the first. But by dint of assumed unconcern and great politeness, I managed to parley with him without giving him offense or exciting his suspicions. When the carriage was announced, he walked with me through the lobbies and hall, saw me safely into it, kissed his hand to me, waved his manuscript in the air, and said, "To-morrow!"

On my return, I took especial care to arrange with the landlord for my future freedom from all intrusion on the part of the Eccelentissimo Herr and Prince of Poets, and was informed that, though very troublesome, he was harmless; that he went every day to the hotels to ascertain the arrivals by inspection of the hotel books, and that, if he found a name of which he had ever before heard, whether in politics, literature, music, or the drama, he sought out the distinguished stranger, and requested his attention to his poem and oratorio. He raved more particularly about the Queen of England, and imagined that if he could see her his merits would be acknowledged by all America, and especially by the Baltimore editors, all of whom he pronounced to be "dough-faces," "muffs," and "white niggers." I saw no more of him; but he called at least a dozen times, and finally declared his solemn conviction that I also was a "white nigger," a despiser of poetry, and one not worthy to be known to a person like the Queen of England, who had the good sense to send wine to Mr. Tennyson; but that when M. Thalberg (then expected) came to Baltimore, he would find a man of true genius to appreciate his oratorio.

Baltimore is celebrated for the canvas-back duck, one of the greatest delicacies of the table in the New World. The canvas-back feeds and breeds in countless myriads on the waters of Chesapeake Bay, that great arm of the sea which extends northward into Maryland for upward of one hundred and twenty miles from the Atlantic. Among the wild celery which grows on the shores of the shallow waters, the canvas-back finds the peculiar food which gives its flesh the flavor so highly esteemed. Baltimore being the nearest large city to the Chesapeake, the traveler may be always certain during the season, from November to February, of finding abundant and cheap supplies. Norfolk, in Virginia, at the entrance of

Chesapeake Bay, is, however, the chief emporium of the trade, which is carried on largely with all the cities of the Union, and even to Europe, whither the birds are sent packed in ice, but where they do not usually arrive in such condition as to give the epicure a true idea of their excellence and delicacy. "There is," says a writer in the *American Sportsman*, "no place in our wide extent of country where wild-fowl-shooting is followed with so much ardor as on the Chesapeake Bay and its tributaries, not only by those who make a comfortable living from the business, but also by gentlemen who resort to these waters from all parts of the adjoining states to participate in the enjoyments of this far-famed shooting-ground. All species of wild-fowl come here in numbers beyond credence; and it is necessary for a stranger to visit the region if he would form a just idea of the wonderful multitudes and numerous varieties of ducks that darken the waters. But the great magnet that makes these shores the centre of attraction is the canvas-back, that here alone acquires its proper delicacy of flavor. The sportsman taxes all his energies for the destruction of this one species alone, regarding all others as scarcely worth powder and shot." The best places on the bay are let out as shooting-grounds to companies and individuals, and appear to be as strictly preserved as the grouse-shootings in Scotland. If steam shall ever shorten the passage across the Atlantic to one week, Europe will doubtless be as good a customer for the canvas-back duck as America itself.

CHAPTER XXXII.

FROM BALTIMORE TO NEW YORK.

April 3d, 1858.

IN proceeding from Baltimore, in Maryland—the last of the slave cities—to Albany, the political capital of the State of New York, the train by which I traveled made a short stoppage at Philadelphia. On purchasing a newspaper from one of the venders who at each great "dépôt" make their way into the cars, I was somewhat surprised and amused to read the denunciations hurled against myself by an irate editor. This personage called upon the stones of the streets to rise, and the tiles of the roofs to fall down, in judgment against me if I ever presumed to revisit Philadelphia. And what, the reader may ask, was the dire offense which had been committed? Not much of an offense. I had expressed an opinion slightly adverse to the claim of Philadelphia to be considered the most eminently beautiful of all the cities of America. I had alleged that its long rectilinear and rectangular streets, kept in a continual drench by the squirtings of water on the legs and feet of wayfarers at all hours, from sunrise to sunset, by Irish maid and negro man servants, were neither to be commended for their architectural amenity nor for their external pleasantness. For this want of taste or appreciation the vials of editorial wrath were uncorked against me. I was declared to be a person without knowledge or judgment—a prejudiced Britisher, who had come to America to inflame international animosities, and a person meanly jealous, as all Englishmen were, of the glory and the power of "our great country" and its "free institutions."

It appeared from some of the allusions of this angry editor that a controversy had been raging on the subject in several of the Philadelphia newspapers for at least a week previously, and that some gentleman in the *North American*—one of the most influential and best-conducted papers in the Union—had been endeavoring to do battle in my behalf, to show that there was some modicum of truth in what I had stated, and that, whether right or wrong in my opinions on this not very important matter, I had not overstepped the limits of courtesy. My champion was almost as scurvily treated as myself. All that I could gather from the hullabaloo was another proof, in addition to many more, of the extreme sensitiveness of public opinion in America on the reports of English travelers. French and Germans may condemn, and nobody cares what they say; but every editor seems to care about the expressed opinions of an Englishman, and to take an unfavorable verdict as a personal affront.

A native-born American may abuse his country as much as he pleases, and say the bitterest things imaginable of its climate, its institutions, its cities, its villages, its men, its women, and even of its habits and characteristics. No one is at all surprised or offended. But if a "Britisher" says the gentlest word, or makes the faintest hint that is not of thorough and uncompromising approbation, he is forthwith brought by the press to the bar of outraged nationality, and adjudged to be either a knave or a fool. Previously he may have been hailed as a hero, a wit, a statesman, or a poet; but as soon as he has published a word, correctly or incorrectly, in disparagement of any thing American, these writers ignore or deny all his good qualities. What was heroism becomes poltroonery; the wit collapses into drivel, the statesmanship into folly, the poetry into doggerel; and the unhappy wayfarer, who meant no offense, and who only spoke to the best of his judgment and to the extent of his opportunities for forming it, may think himself fortunate if he be not accused as a public enemy, or, at the best, as no gentleman.

Nor is it always as safe to praise as it is unsafe to condemn. Agree with an ultra-American recently imported or of native growth that his country "beats all creation," and that, as Governor Walker, of Kansas, once affirmed, New York will, in twenty years hence, be the political, financial, and commercial centre of Christendom, and he will put on a grave face and accuse you of "poking fun at him." The truth seems to be that Americans really desire to stand well in English opinion. They care little for the good word of any other nation under the sun. It is their over-sensitiveness in this respect which leads them to attach undue importance to what English travelers may say; which causes them to wince under censure, to mistrust praise, and act like those people in private life who, not being assured of the reality of their own position, find enmity where none is meant, and see covert depreciation even under the guise of the most flattering speeches.

On arriving at New York I took a few days' rest—much needed after a journey, since I left it three months previously, of upward of six thousand miles, principally by railway, and inclusive of fourteen hundred miles down the Mississippi, and through all its manifold perils of fire, flood, and snags. Here, at the New York Hotel, in the upper part of Broadway—a palace for travelers, to be highly recommended to all strangers who value choice fare, excellent wines, comfortable accommodation, moderate prices, and courteous attention—I prepared myself for a new course of travel to the noble St. Lawrence, the Great Lakes, and the loyal British colony of Canada.

New York, which, when I left it, was in a state of commercial depression consequent upon the un-ended panic of 1857, had recovered all its confidence. A leading journal no longer thought it necessary to denounce gentlemen who gave dinner-parties or ladies who gave balls as public enemies, who mocked the miseries of the people. Every thing had resumed its natural course; and beyond the fact that a few commercial firms, once of high repute, had disappeared altogether from business, and were known no more in Wall Street, there was little or nothing to show that the country had so recently passed through a severe financial crisis.

It was estimated during the panic, by those whose knowledge of the subject entitles them to form an opinion, that British capital to the amount of $450,000,000, or nearly £90,000,000 sterling, was invested in American securities. The whole gold coinage of the United States put into circulation from the year 1793 to the 1st January, 1856, is stated, on the authority of the *American Almanac*, to be only $396,895,574; the silver coinage circulated during the same period is placed at $100,729,602; and the copper coinage at $1,572,206; the three together making a total of $498,197,383.

It will be seen from this statement that the difference between the sums invested by Englishmen in American stocks and the whole metallic circulation of the United States is but little more than $38,000,000, or £7,500,000 sterling. Thus it is obvious, if these figures be true, that all the gold in the United States would not suffice to pay back to British capitalists the sums they had invested in American railroads and other stocks, with the hope of larger dividends than similar enterprises yield in their own country; and that more than half the silver, in addition to the whole of the gold, would be required for the purpose. The Duke of Wellington once said that "high interest was but another name for bad security;" and the late panic in New York, and the suspension of cash payments by nearly all the banks throughout the Union, was but another proof, added to thousands of others in European as well as in American history, of the wisdom of the apophthegm.

The railroads in the United States, the depreciation in the stock of which so largely increased the panic, extend over 22,259 miles of territory; and are thus classified, according to the several commonwealths in which they have been constructed. The State of Arkansas is omitted, no return having been made:

	Miles.		Miles.
Maine	472.70	Brought forward	12,830.31
New Hampshire	479.96	Alabama	397.00
Vermont	493.04	Mississippi	92.00
Massachusetts	1,451.30	Louisiana	296.00
Rhode Island	65.50	Texas	57.00
Connecticut	618.55	Tennessee	592.00
New York	2,749.85	Kentucky	195.00
New Jersey	479.41	Ohio	2,695.00
Pennsylvania	1,777.00	Indiana	1,533.00
Delaware	94.00	Illinois	2,285.50
Maryland	545.00	Michigan	678.80
Virginia	1,132.00	Iowa	94.00
North Carolina	653.00	Wisconsin	348.00
South Carolina	677.00	Missouri	145.00
Georgia	1,142.00	California	22.00
Carried forward	12,830.31	Total	22,259.61

These roads are managed by no less than 202 companies, of which the names and titles figure at full length in the official records, and by a large and unknown number of smaller companies, not designated, but classified in the statistics of each state as "other roads." The paid-up capital of scarcely any of these roads has been found sufficient to construct and work them. The amount of the paid-up capital, and debts of the greater portion of them, have been published. Taking a few of the most important, and beginning with the richest and most indebted—the two words have of late years come in some quarters to signify the same thing—it appears that the New York and Erie, running 445 miles, has a paid-up capital of $10,023,959, and a debt, funded and floating, of $25,902,540; the Illinois Central, with a paid-up capital of $2,271,050, has a debt of $19,242,000; the New York Central, a paid-up capital of $24,000,000, and a debt of $14,000,000; the Baltimore and Ohio, a capital of $13,000,000, and a debt of $9,700,000; the Vermont Central, a capital of $5,000,000, and a debt of $4,900,000; the New Albany and Salem, a capital of $2,535,000, and a debt of $5,282,000; the Western, a capital of $5,966,000, and a debt of $10,495,000; the Philadelphia and Reading, a capital of $11,000,000, and a debt of $9,200,000; the Philadelphia, Wilmington, and Baltimore, a capital of $5,600,000, and a debt of $8,022,000; the Virginia and Tennessee, a capital of $2,500,000, and a debt of $3,000,000; the Kentucky Central, a capital of $1,300,000, and a debt of $2,235,000; the Central Ohio, a capital of $1,521,000, and a debt of $3,485,000; the New Jersey Central, a capital of $2,000,000, and a debt of $2,266,000; the Michigan South and North Indiana, a capital of $6,929,000, and a debt of $6,319,000. All the American railroads are constructed at a much cheaper rate than those of Great Britain. Land is cheap, law is cheap, and no show is made by the erection of monster stations in the cities, or of stations with the least pretense to architectural beauty in the minor towns or villages. The cars are all first-class, but of a construction very little superior to second-class carriages in England, and much inferior to second-class carriages in France and Germany. Yet the competition among the various lines is so keen, that fares are, in a great number of instances, reduced far below the remunerative point.

Another and very important reason why American railroads do not pay, notwithstanding their cheapness of construction, is not sufficiently known in England to the capitalists who have advanced their money to make them; it is, that there appears to be no sufficient, or any efficient check upon the accounts. The stations, or stopping-places, are not walled in as with us; the taking of a ticket is not imperative upon the traveler, though he who enters a train without a ticket has to pay ten per cent. excess to the conductor. The great fault is that there is no check upon the conductor. He travels with the train all the way, collects the tickets and the money, and if he be dishonest can put into his own pocket all the cash that has come into his hands. A conductor of this kind was threatened with dismissal by the directors of a line. "You are foolish to dismiss me," he replied. "I have got my gold watch, my chain, my diamond pin, and my fair lady. If you turn me away, the next man will have to get these things at your expense. Better let me stop."

To turn to the Banks. At the end of the year 1855 and the beginning of 1856 the number of Banks in the States of the Union was 1396, whose conditions and operations at that time are thus stated:

Capital	$343,874,272
Specie Funds	19,937,710
Specie	59,314,063
Circulation of Notes from one dollar upward	195,747,662
Loans and Discounts	634,183,280
Stocks (Railroad and other)	49,485,215
Real Estate	20,865,867
Other Investments	8,822,516
Deposits	12,705,662

A few additional figures, without comment, will show what a vast amount of wealth is produced in America, and how soon such a country will be enabled to right itself after a financial squall. Its exports, under the several heads of "Productions of the Sea," "The Forest," "Agriculture," and "Manufactures," amounted in the year 1852 to $192,368,984, and in the year 1855 to $246,708,553. The imports from foreign countries in 1855 amounted to $261,468,520. The American tonnage engaged in the foreign trade, and entered in American ports for that year, was 3,861,391 tons, and the foreign tonnage, 2,083,948 tons. In the same year the United States exported 1,008,421,610 lbs. of cotton, at the average price of 8.74 cents ($4\frac{3}{4}d.$) per lb.; 52,250 tierces of rice; 150,213 hogsheads of tobacco: and breadstuffs to the value of $38,895,348. In the year 1855 there were built and launched from American ports 381 ships and barks, 126 brigs, 605 schooners, 669 sloops and canal-boats, and 243 steam-vessels: a total of 2024 vessels, with a tonnage of 583,450 tons. Of the whole tonnage of the United States, 770,285 is engaged in steam navigation, 186,773 in the whale fishery, 102,928 in the cod-fishery, 2,491,108 in the coasting trade, and 21,265 in the mackerel fishery. The crews of American vessels entered in the same year were 137,808, of whom only 557 were boys; and of foreign vessels, 100,807, of whom 916 were boys. The sales of public lands by the United States government, principally in the West, the great resort of emigrants from the "Old Country," as it is fondly called, has greatly fluctuated within twenty years. In 1836 the sales amounted to upward of twenty millions of acres, the price received by the government being twenty-five millions of dollars. In 1837 the sales dropped to 5,600,000 acres. The years from 1851 to 1855 inclusive show the following results:

	Acres sold.	Dollars.
1851	1,846,847	2,390,947
1852	1,553,071	1,975,658
1853	1,083,495	1,804,653
1854	7,035,735	9,000,211
1855	15,729,524	11,248,301

These figures will suffice to throw some light, to those who attentively peruse them, on the present as well as on the future of the United States, which have within them all the elements of power, greatness, and prosperity in a far greater degree than any other empire, Great Britain not excepted.

By the seventh and last census of the United States, taken in 1850, the total white population of the thirty-two states, the District of Columbia, and the territories not yet admitted as states into the Union, was 19,533,068. In addition to these were 433,643 free blacks, and 3,204,347 slaves, making a total population of 23,171,058.

In 1790 the total population was 3,929,872, or, in round numbers, 4,000,000. In 1850 it was upward of 23,000,000, as above stated, or a more than five-fold increase. In 1790 the slaves amounted to 697,897, and in 1850 to 3,204,313, or rather under a five-fold increase. But when we take into account that the white population, within the last twenty years, and especially for the two or three years preceding 1850, was augmented by a vast immigration from Europe, from Ireland and Liverpool alone amounting to upward of 1000 per day, and that during that period the slave population was only augmented by its natural increase, we must come to the conclusion that the black race thrives better than the white in America.

CHAPTER XXXIII.

AMERICAN LITERATURE, ART, AND SCIENCE.

New York.

THE British races, transplanted to America, had scarcely concluded their earliest wars with the aborigines when the literary spirit began to manifest itself among them; and although the struggle for independence so gallantly fought and so nobly concluded was unfavorable to any other literature than that of the newspaper and the political pamphlet, the United States produced some authors of repute even while they were yet colonies of Great Britain. The most noted, if not the best English grammar ever written, and which has not yet been superseded on either side of the Atlantic—that of Lindley Murray—was the work of an American of that early period; and Franklin was a name both in literature and in science before it became a name in politics and diplomacy.

The progress of Time and the consolidation of civilization in the elder commonwealths of the Union, such as Pennsylvania, Massachusetts, Connecticut, and the New England States, together with the diffusion of education among the whole people—not as a charity and as a dole, but as the inherent and sacred right of every American child—led naturally to the growth of a literary taste and to the encouragement of literary genius. Though for a long period the Americans were too bountifully supplied with the literature of England to bestow adequate encouragement upon the authors of their own land, and though American booksellers flourished too luxuriantly upon the brains of English genius to give any thing but the cold shoulder and the averted look to any native talent that claimed to be paid, a change was gradually wrought.

For the last quarter of a century the United States have produced as many eminent poets, historians, philosophers, and essayists as Great Britain herself. In every department of literature Americans have entered the lists of Fame, and competed for the prizes, and no one can say that they have competed in vain, or failed to pay back to England a portion of the delight and instruction which our modern as well as our ancient literature, like a beneficent fountain on the wayside, has afforded to all who chose to drink of her gushing waters. In their poetry, which was formerly but little more than a faint echo of the poetry of the old land, the Americans have imbued themselves with the color and with the spirit of their own clime, and, in growing more national, have become more original. And it will show alike the newness of the poetic genius of the United States, and how much has been done in a short time, if we recall the fact that all the great poets whom America has produced are living men, and some of them still in the prime of their lives and the vernal efflorescence of their powers. Bryant, Longfellow, Dana, Lowell, Halleck, Whittier, Emerson, Holmes, Stoddard, and others, as familiar by their names and writings to Englishmen as to Americans, are still in the land of the living; and even the Nestor of the choir, Bryant, has not wholly ceased to sing. All these poets, it may be observed, are men of the free North.

The South, with its lovely climate, its balmy skies, its magnolia groves, and the abundant leisure of its aristocratic white population, has not yet produced any poet whose name is worthy to be enrolled among those above cited; or if it have, he blushes unseen, and his merits are unknown to the reading public both in the Old World and the New. It is not, however, to be asserted without qualification that slavery is the cause of this. But it is, at all events, singular to remark, that, except in the literature of their newspapers, the slave states do not compete with the literary genius of the North, and that they have as yet but few authors, and that these few are not of the highest class.

America is even more distinguished for its great historians than for its poets. Such men as Prescott, Bancroft, Ticknor, Motley, and Washington Irving have not only conferred honor upon the land of their birth, but on the language in which they have written. The same may be said of such novelists and essayists as Cooper, Hawthorne, Emerson, and Channing; and, indeed, of many more whose names will readily suggest themselves to all who are conversant with the current books and intellectual activities of our age. And, under every aspect of literature, America is bravely doing its part to maintain the ancient reputation of the language which it is its privilege to have inherited; that noble language which, above all others now spoken or written in the world, gives expression to the best hopes and highest aspirations of mankind. British and American literature are twin branches of the same lordly and wide-spreading tree, under the shadow of which every man can not only speak, but print and publish his free thoughts. There is no other language spoken either in Europe or in America which has a living literature, unless it be the literature of the brothel, as in France, and that of metaphysics and theology, as in Germany.

In the English language only can the great thoughts with which the heart of the world is heaving be freely expressed, and those searching inquiries into all subjects of human thought and speculation — political, philosophical, and theological—which signalize our time, be carried on to any available purpose. Without the enfranchisement of the people from the pestilential thraldom and blight of irresponsible despotism, it is utterly impossible for a wholesome and fruitful literature to take root. The languages of France, Italy, and Spain, once so prolific in poetry, history, biography, romance, and philosophy, retain the works of by-gone authors; for tyrants fortunately, however tyrannical and mighty they may be, can not destroy a book that has once been published; but these languages produce nothing new for the delight of the world. They are left in arrear with the intelligence of the age, and can only keep pace with the progress of a more generous and expansive literature by translations of such masterpieces of genius as appear in the English language.

Where treason may lurk in a song, where heresy may leaven a history or a romance, and where a logical argument subversive of the illogical arguments upon which a throne may have been founded may be traced in a treatise upon electricity, in a grammar, a sermon, or even a dictionary, and where the caprice or the passion of one fallible or perhaps insane man, and not law or justice, has to decide what is treason, what is heresy, and what is sound philosophy, how is it possible for poetry, history, romance or philosophy to exist? The horses of Apollo's chariot can neither draw the state carriage of an autocrat nor the omnibus of a vulgar crowd. The winged steeds are free, and to submit them to thraldom is as fatal as to send them to the knacker's. Without liberty poetry becomes mere jingle, history a lie, romance the pimp and the pander of licentiousness, metaphysics practical atheism, and theology the text-book of superstition.

Having so great a language and such great ideas and duties in common, it is much to be deplored that the two kindred nations on the east and the west of the Atlantic should not yet have devised the means of establishing an identity of interest in the productions of contemporary literature. The federal government, as if it were actuated by the thoughts, the feelings, and the calculations of a trader and dealer in books, and not with those of the living and dead men without the exercise of whose genius there could be no such things as books, has hitherto evaded, in a manner the reverse of brave and noble, the question of an international copyright. It has either forgotten, or has not chosen to admit, that the authors of a nation, more largely than any other class of men, build up the glorious fabric of the national renown, and that these men, like all others, require to eat, to be clothed and housed, and to provide for their families. But on these men not a thought has been bestowed if they have happened to be Englishmen.

Much has been said of the scandal and disgrace that would attach to both if son and father should ever go to war; but thousands who thus speak and write do not consider what a peace-maker literature is, and that if an American author had a legal copyright in England and an English author a legal copyright in America, the very best and wisest men of both nations would be peace-preachers and peace-makers, and fuse in the mighty alchemy of their genius all the heterogeneous ideas that would militate against the perpetual friendship of two great states with a bond like this to unite them.

It is to be hoped that the day will come when the federal government will be bold enough to look at this question in its proper light, and cease to make itself the mere partisan of piratical booksellers, and of the very lowest and most mercenary influences of the shop. But as it is beginning to be apparent in America that American authors would gain quite as largely in England as English authors would gain in America by the establishment of a system worthy alike of the civilization and the relationship of the two countries, the probabilities increase that the bookselling interest will be made to know its true place, and that the author, both British and American, will receive his due. And let no one undervalue the importance of the question, or affect to treat it as one in which authors alone are interested. On the contrary, it is a question affecting, more or less, the whole policy of both nations, and one which, if carried, would be of more real and enduring efficacy than any treaty of peace and friendship which diplomatists could frame or governments establish. It must be observed, too, in reference to this subject, that no impediment exists on the part of the British government. All the opposition to justice on this plea comes from America.

In considering, in however cursory a manner, the literary developments of the United States, it is impossible to avoid some mention of that great and growing power, the newspaper press. It can not be said, by any one who knows them both, that the press of America, as a whole, is equal to the press of London, or of the British Isles generally. In Great Britain newspapers are comparatively few. It was not until the recent repeal of the newspaper stamp duty that such populous towns and cities as Manchester, Birmingham, Liverpool, and Edinburgh bethought themselves of having daily newspapers of their own. Until that time, a man who advocated the establishment of a daily paper out of London was considered a crack-brained enthusiast, born before his time, a candidate for Bedlam or St. Luke's. In Glasgow, the only place where the experiment was previously tried, the results were not such as to make men of business in love with it. Had these towns and cities been in America instead of in Great Britain, they would each have had five or six, or perhaps a dozen daily newspapers, besides weekly newspapers too numerous to count; and the daily papers, instead of being things of yesterday, would perhaps have been thirty or forty years old. In the United States, every town of 20,000 inhabitants, or even less, has generally one, if not two daily newspapers to represent its politics and clamor for its advertisements. In laying out a new city in the West, the hotel, the mill, the bank, the church, and the newspaper-office are often in existence before the streets have any other claims to identity than such as are derived from the plans of the architect and surveyor. The natural consequence of this universal demand for newspapers is that there are by far too many of them; and that pressmen and compositors, or other persons having even less connection with literature than these, establish newspapers in the merest villages, and are their own editors, their own reporters, their own cashiers, and their own publishers; nay, actually shut up the shutters of their own shop, sweep the office, or take "a turn at case," as necessity may dictate. In such great cities as New York, Boston, Philadelphia, Baltimore, Washington, Cincinnati, Louisville, St. Louis, New Orleans, and in many minor cities of the New England, the Southern, and the Western States, a different state of things prevails, and the newspapers are conducted by competent and highly accomplished editors and writers; but, as a rule, and in consequence of their multiplicity, the newspapers of the United States are far below the European average. Of late years a marked improvement has been visible in the daily press of the great cities of the Union; and New York, New Orleans, and Washington more especially, have newspapers which might challenge comparison, not alone in commercial enterprise, but in literary ability and incorruptible honesty with those of London.

One distinguishing characteristic of the American press, considered not with reference to any particular city or state, but in its broadest aspects, is the personality—sometimes ill-natured, and often very good-natured—in which its editors and reporters indulge. Every one lives in a blaze of publicity in the United States; and English snobbery, which records who dined with the Duke of This and the Marquis of That on such a day—details gathered by penny-a-liners and Jenkinses from footmen and butlers, and not communicated by the "noble lords" themselves—is outdone by the snobbery of America. There being no nobles to fasten upon, it makes a grip at political or literary notoriety in the male, and at wealth and beauty in the female sex, and retails unblushingly what we in England would consider the most sacred secrets of life. In England, Jenkins tells us who dined with such a duke, marquis, or earl, and who were present at the ball of the Duchess of Rosewater or the Countess of Dash, but he indulges in names only; and if he have any descriptive power, he displays it upon the furniture, the millinery, or the supper. Not so the Jenkins of America. He goes farther and deeper, and presumes to describe, and even to criticise, the female beauty that falls under his notice. He is gossiping, familiar, and gallant, but sometimes ungallant, and writes as if it were the most natural and proper thing in the world— of the eyes, the hair, the lips, the teeth, the shape, the smiles, the accomplishments, and the fortune, nay, of the very age of maids, wives, and widows. He criticises a fashionable beauty as he would a book — with the name in full, and the address also. In short, there is nothing like the same privacy in America that there is in England. Doubtless the principal cause of this vulgarity is the keen competition among newspapers, which has gradually broken down the barriers of propriety, and accustomed the public to a favorable and unfavorable personality, which, under no circumstance, can be reconciled to good taste or gentlemanly feeling. Something of the same kind, though less virulent, has become observable in the provincial papers of England since the abolition of the newspaper stamp; but, with few and base, and no doubt ephemeral exceptions, it has not yet tainted the press of the metropolis. Let us hope that it never will.

One peculiarity of second and third rate newspapers in all countries is the number of advertisements of quack medicines which they contain. In this respect the United States seem to beat the whole world. To judge from the announcements in all the journals, America must be the very paradise of medical and non-medical impostors, and the people the most credulous or the most sickly under the sun. These announcements, always offensive, sometimes disgusting, and often indecent, render the journals that publish them unfit to be introduced into private families. But it does not appear that they lose in circulation what they gain in advertisements; and that the business of compounding and puffing such frauds upon the public credulity, if not upon the public health, must be highly profitable, we know by the experience of England. I doubt, however, if it be carried on to any thing like the same extent in England as in America.

Two other peculiarities of the American press may be noted, not for any importance attaching to them, but as showing the difference of manners in the Old World and the New. In a land where liberty is supreme, fortune-telling, astrology, and necromancy, under the old names, and not disguised under the veil of clairvoyance and spiritualism, appear to be recognized and lawful professions. The *New York Herald* publishes almost daily a string of advertisements under the head of "Astrology."

The following, taken from the first number of that journal that I could lay hands on after beginning to write upon the subject, and from which the names and addresses have been purposely excluded, will serve as specimens. The fourth in the list, who "feels confident she has no equal," would speedily, if she carried on her swindle in England, make an intimate acquaintance with the interior of the House of Correction:

"ASTROLOGY.

"ASTROLOGY AND CLAIRVOYANCE.—M. B—— CAN BE CONSULTED AT her office, —— Street, second block east of the Bowery, up second stairs, first door, where she has astonished thousands with her truth in the line of astrology and clairvoyance. Fee 50c."

"CLAIRVOYANCE.—MRS. H——, THE BEST MEDICAL CLAIRVOYANT IN the world. Mrs. H—— has restored thousands to health when all other remedies have failed, and the patient left to die. Long doctor's bills and life saved. Let the wise consider. Rheumatism cured. Residence, B—— Street."

"NOTICE.—MRS. F——, CELEBRATED FOR HER SCIENCE, GIVES MEDICal advice, and can be consulted on business, marriage, etc., at her office, B—— Street. She speaks French, English, and German. N.B.—She cures consumption and rheumatism."

"N. B.—WHO HAS NOT HEARD OF THE CELEBRATED MADAME P——? She has been consulted by thousands in this and other cities with entire satisfaction. She feels confident she has no equal. She tells the names of future wife or husband, also that of her visitor. If you wish truth, give her a call, at ——, opposite B—— Street. Ladies 50 cents, gentlemen 1 dollar."

"FIVE THOUSAND DOLLARS REWARD IS OFFERED TO ANY PERSON who can surpass Madame C—— in the art of clairvoyancy and astrology. She warrants to cure any disease in its worst form, particularly rheumatism, affection of the throat or lungs. N.B.—Madame C—— is the only natural clairvoyant in the United States. All who are afflicted, in trouble, or unsuccessful in business matters, call and see this naturally gifted lady."

"ASTROLOGY AND CLAIRVOYANCE.—M. B——, THE MYSTERIOUS VEILed lady, can be consulted on all events of life, and has also a charm to bring people together who are unhappy, at G—— Street, second block east of the ——, second stairs up, front door."

"CLAIRVOYANCE.—MRS. S——, No. —— S—— STREET, THE MOST SUCcessful medical and business clairvoyant in America. Consultations day and evening on sickness, business, absent friends, etc., and satisfaction guaranteed always, or no pay taken."

"MADAME L—— CAN BE CONSULTED ABOUT LOVE, MARRIAGE, AND absent friends: she tells all the events of life; she has astonished all who visit her. If you wish truth, give her a call at M—— Street, in the rear. Ladies, 25c.; gentlemen, 50c."

The second peculiarity, not so much of American newspapers as of American society, is that, while marriages and deaths are invariably announced in their journals, births are excluded. On asking for an explanation, the answer of one person was that there was no reason except ancient custom, while a second informant explained that it was considered indelicate to parade such matters before the public; but how a birth could be more indelicate than a marriage or a death was not stated.

The progress of America in art has not been by any means so striking or so rapid as its progress in literature. But the taste for art is on the increase, and many of the most wealthy of the merchants and bankers in New York, Washington, Boston, and Philadelphia have fair collections both of ancient and modern pictures.

The Century Club—one of the most agreeable of all the places of resort in New York to which a stranger can be introduced—was established and is supported for the purpose of bringing together the wealthy inhabitants who love art and literature, and those who cultivate art or literature as a profession. Here every night may be met in social intercourse with men of wealth and enterprise the principal living artists of rising or established fame. These, instead of being ignored or depreciated by their countrymen because they are Americans, are the more highly esteemed on that account; not only because they are good artists, but because the natural vanity is flattered by the proof which their talents afford that Americans are able to compete with Europeans in a walk of genius hitherto considered above the stage of civilization to which the United States have attained.

Among the most deservedly celebrated of American artists may be cited Mr. Kensett in landscape, and Mr. Darley in delineation of life and character. In figure drawing Mr. Darley is perhaps the greatest artist that America has yet seen. His outline illustrations to "Margaret" are equal, if not superior, to "Retch's Faust;" and his designs for bank-notes, descriptive of American scenery, incident, trade, and character, are unrivaled for breadth and facility of touch, and for admirable truth to nature.

Mr. Darley, unfortunately for the art of which he is an ornament, has been too fully employed by the banks of America in making designs for their notes to have leisure for more ambitious performances; but no one who has seen his drawings can doubt that his pencil rivals that of Horace Vernet in breadth of effect, and that of John Gilbert in facility.

But it is in sculpture that the artistic genius of America is seen to the best advantage. Sculpture—grand and severe, and dealing with the gigantic as well as with the lovely—seems to suit the taste and the capacities of a people who have so vast a continent to subdue and replenish, and which appeals strongly to the primitive feelings of men who know they have a great work to do and are determined to do it. Hiram Powers has made himself a name throughout Christendom by his Greek Slave, though as a work of art it must be considered somewhat meretricious. Miss Hosmer has worthily competed for the laurels of sculpture, and won them. Crawford, cut off prematurely in the meridian of his genius, has endeared himself to all America by his statue of Washington at Richmond, in Virginia, and by many other excellent works. Hart, who does not disdain to make geometry an aid to portrait sculpture, is one of the best moulders of busts known in our age; and Palmer, of Albany, in the State of New York, in a higher degree than any of these, promises to be the great sculptor of America. This gentleman renders the female figure in immortal stone in a manner that not even our own E. H. Baily, who gave the world "Eve at the Fountain," has excelled. This artist seems not to have derived from Greece or Italy, but from natural intuition and patient study at home, the mental conception and the manual dexterity which have already enriched his native land with many admirable pieces of sculpture. His figure of a Puritan girl, the daughter of one of the early settlers, stripped and tied to the stake preparatory to her cremation by the savages—a figure in which innocence, modesty, beauty, supplication, and horror are inextricably blended—haunts the memory of all who have seen it —a joy and a sorrow forever.

In science the United States have long since established their claim to high rank among nations. It was Benjamin Franklin, an American, who first "tethered the lightning to a wire." It was on the Hudson or North River, under the auspices of Fulton, that the first steam-boat paddled through the waters. It was Lieutenant Maury, of Washington, who first made a chart of the currents of the ocean. It was Morse, of New York, who first promulgated the daring idea—not yet brought to working perfection—of an electric telegraph from the Old World to the New; and, if farther proofs than these were required of the scientific taste and proficiency of the

American people, they are to be found in the Patent-office, at Washington, where there are models of every kind of invention and of reinvention, betokening alike the mechanical ingenuity and the scientific mind of the people. To walk through these long and well-filled rooms of that great Museum of Invention—to which few, if any nations can offer a parallel—is to be impressed with a deep feeling of respect for the practical genius of the Americans, and to anticipate many greater triumphs of science at their hands. And although many of the models exhibited are but the dreams and crotchets of clever men, and others are but the reinventions by uninformed and self-taught genius of contrivances previously well known, if not in full operation, it is impossible to look without interest and admiration upon the skill, the perseverance, and the philosophic penetration displayed in their construction. Doubtless it would be easy to turn into ridicule the misplaced energy and perverted talent of too many of the patentees whose models are here exhibited; but to the philosophic mind even the aberrations of talent are worthy of respect. The steam-engine was not brought to perfection in a day; and many failures must be incurred by many men before the one man, more fortunate than his predecessors, and knowing how to take advantage of their shortcomings and mistakes to build up the edifice of his own success, vaults into the high places which they could not reach, and makes himself a name among the benefactors of his race.

Much as the United States have done in literature, art, and science, they have as yet done nothing in music. England, erroneously and stupidly said to be a non-musical country until Mr. Chappell, in his painstaking and highly valuable work, "The Popular Music of the Olden Time," knocked the absurdity on the head and killed it forever, seems to have transmitted no portion of her musical genius to her children in America. Though "Yankee Doodle" inflames the patriotism of Americans abroad and at home, and is remarkable for the spirit of bravado and "pluck" which made the nation adopt a song of ridicule and reproach, and transform it into a chant of glorification and triumph, the air is not American, but old English; and the poetry, if it be not a desecration of the name to call it so, is below contempt, both in its English and its American version. Their one great national song, "Hail Columbia," above the average as a poetical composition, has also been wedded to music which is not American. "When Bibo thought fit from this World to Retreat," a roistering old English ditty, of the days when to get drunk after dinner was supposed to be the mark of a gentleman, furnished the air to which these vaunting lines are sung. The "Star-spangled Banner," another patriotic song, is sung to an English tune; so that the United States, even in so sacred a matter as the national glory, remain without a melody. The airs called "negro melodies," concocted for the most part at New York, may seem, at first glance, to militate against the theory that the Americans have no music. But, on the contrary, they serve, in the minds of those who have studied the subject, to prove the truth of the assertion. The tunes are neither negro nor American. The negroes have no capacity whatever for the composition of music, and their pretended melodies, as any one skilled in music, who will take the trouble to investigate, will speedily discover, are but rifacimenti of old English, Scotch, and Irish melodies altered in time and character. "Buffalo Gals" is an old Christmas carol; "Sailing Down the River on the Ohio," "Bobbing Around," and many other alleged negro melodies, are all built upon English and Scottish foundations; and, so far from being genuine and unconscious perversions on the part of negroes, are the handiwork of white men well known in Broadway. Certainly there is no reason why the United States should not produce first-rate musical composers as well as poets, orators, historians, and sculptors; but the fact is worth mentioning that, up to the present period, no such composer has established a claim to the highest honors of musical art. An opera, by an American gentleman connected with the press of New York, was produced at the Academy of Music, with considerable success, in the spring of 1858, and it is possible that hereafter the claim then put forward may be substantiated. But as yet the United States are without a national composer. Until they produce one worthy of the people, they must be content with their fame in literature, science, and art, and not ask for it in music.

CHAPTER XXXIV.

PARTIES AND PARTY TYRANNY.

New York.

THERE being no great and self-supporting forces in social and public life in the United States to balance and trim each other, no hereditary privilege, no aristocracy of rank, no preponderating church, no overshadowing families, alike illustrious by their descent, powerful by their wealth, and historical by their services, to compete with and to rival public opinion, mainly expressed through the newspapers and by the orators of the local and general Legislatures, elected by universal suffrage, it results that, in many important respects, the great American republic is not a country where there exists as much political freedom for the individual as we enjoy in England. The whole course and action of public life in the republic go to prove that political freedom may exist in the aggregate without being permitted in the segregate, and in the body corporate without extending to the individual members. The press, having no rival except the senate, is a greater power than it can ever become in an older country, where its rivals are many, and enjoys a liberty for itself which it does not always care to extend to those who differ from its opinions or refuse to share its passions. This despotism is mainly shown in party organization, and in the exaction by party as a body of duties real or supposed from its individual members, which are incompatible with the right of private judgment. Party and the press act and react upon each other, and between them both they establish a political tyranny, none the less unscrupulous and effectual because it is unsupported by bayonets, cannon balls, and dungeons, or the other agencies of despotism employed in Europe.

Universal suffrage is not only the substratum on which the whole political edifice rests, but the supreme arbiter in all

PARTIES AND PARTY TYRANNY. 301

cases; and the intricacy of the system of government—firstly, as regards the separate states, and, secondly, as regards the federation—is such that the appeal to its arbitration is incessant. Scarcely a day passes in which the popular vote is not required, sometimes for the election of merely municipal officers or the appointment of judges, at others for the election of members of the local Legislatures, some of which have but one and some two houses. But it is the still more important election of members of Congress, with representatives elected for two and senators for six years, and the quadrennial election of the President, which call the life of the country into periodical activity, and create a perpetually recurring source of political agitation.

All elections whatsoever are party questions, and, as such, are contested with a bitterness which might astonish the most experienced burgesses of our own Eatanswills and Little Pedlingtons, and make our oldest and astutest electioneering agents blush for the littleness of their own field and scale of operations. Though there have never been more than two great and well-defined parties in the United States in existence at any one time, their nomenclature, as well as their objects, have always been so shifting and uncertain as to puzzle the English student and observer to understand exactly the principles which they profess, and the strict line of demarkation between them. To add to the difficulty, these parties have at times assumed names which are preoccupied in England, without reference to their original meaning. Thus, in England, and in Europe generally, a Democrat and a Republican are terms which are well-nigh convertible. But in the United States the Democrat and the Republican are quite as distinct and antagonistic—as far as office and its emoluments are concerned, if not in principle—as Whig and Tory, or Liberal and Conservative are in the British Parliament. A Whig in America means, or used to mean—for the party that once existed under this venerable cognomen is either defunct or denies its name—an ultra-Conservative, or what in England would be called a Tory of the old school. In a country where all are Republicans, to be called a Republican is to be called by a designation that one half of the country would repudiate; and in a purely democratic government, a large portion of the electors indignantly object to being called Democrats.

At the present time, the two great divisions into which the whole politics of the American Union resolve themselves are the two just named—the Democratic and the Republican. The existing President, Mr. Buchanan, is a Democrat, and came in on what is called the Democratic ticket. By Democrat seems to be understood, at present—though possibly the word had not always the same meaning—one who is opposed to the anti-slavery and the free-soil agitation—one who would refrain from abolishing, or attempting to abolish, slavery in any of the Southern or Middle States, but who is not committed to the policy of extending it beyond those bounds, and who would not aid in its reintroduction into any state by the Constitution of which it has already been abolished.

The Democrats desire to see the end of the anti-slavery agitation in all its forms and phases, believing that the statesmen of the Union have something better to do and think of than to be always, as they phrase it, "talking about niggers." But as the slave states, by an unfortunate political necessity, and to maintain the balance of power, must annex territory to the south of the existing limits of the Union, and by the acquisition of Cuba—by fair means or by foul—the Democratic party is obliged to give more countenance to slavery than it has always cared to confess. The slave states have no chance of keeping up their equality of numbers with the free states, which are always adding to the votes of their party in the Senate and in the House of Representatives by the creation of new states in the great wildernesses of the Far West—wildernesses that are capable of being cut up, in time, into at least twenty new commonwealths, and all free of slavery except by Southern immigration. Hence the Democratic party is composed of two sections: one which loves slavery for its own sake; and another which neither loves nor hates it, but is quite content to tolerate it, and even to extend it for the sake of political power, which might otherwise slip from its grasp. The Republicans, on the other hand, are opposed to slavery on principle, and look with some alarm upon its growth within its own recognized boundaries, and with still greater alarm upon its extension into such territories as Kansas, or any other states which may hereafter be formed to the north of the latitude formerly known as the Missouri Compromise Line. There are some minor and some important differences between these two great parties on other points—the Republicans, whose stronghold is in the manufacturing North and New England, being for the most part ultra-Protectionists, while the Democrats are occasionally more inclined to look favorably upon those doctrines of Free Trade, of which British policy, since the repeal of the Corn-laws, has set the world so great an example.

In all civilized countries, and more especially in those where there is any degree of popular liberty, there must be a party which desires to move, and a party which desires to stand still; a party which would reform abuses, and a party which would retain them as long as possible, for fear lest in removing them some great bulwark of wise liberty, as distinguished from irrational license, might be carried away along with them. These two parties have always existed in the United States, although universal suffrage would seem to leave nothing for the advanced Liberals to desire, and had defined their principles, with more or less of perspicuity and sharpness, long before the recognition of the republic by Great Britain. In the days when Washington was President, the two great parties in the States were the Federalists and the Democrats. Washington was himself the leading spirit of the Federalists, as his great opponent, Jefferson, was of the Democrats. The Federalists desired a strong central government, that it might present a bold front against foreign aggression, and hold up its head as equal to equal among the greatest powers of the earth. The Democrats, on the other hand, while not wishing to oppose the end, objected to the means, and were fearful that, if power too extensive were given to the central government, the liberty of the people in the several states and commonwealths of the Union would be impaired and ultimately destroyed. The Federalists disappeared from the arena of politics after the last war with Great Britain in 1812-14, but began to reappear afterward under the newer name of the "National Republicans." The same party, with some minor shades of difference, appears to have sprung into renewed activity in 1831-32, under the revived name of "Whigs," when the Northern manufacturers, alarmed at the progress of the cotton and woolen, as well as of the iron and metal manufactures of England, began to clamor more lustily than before for protection to native industry. Thus a new source of antagonism between parties, in addition to slavery, Federalism, and what are called State Rights, was introduced. It would be useless to detail all the nicknames which the two great factions of the Outs and the Ins, and the slave and the free, the Protectionists and the Free Traders, have accepted either from their friends or their enemies—names which lasted their little day, and are almost forgotten even in Washington and New York. But among these may be mentioned the Nullifiers, the Free-soilers, the Locofocos, the Know-nothings, and the Native Americans. Some of these would exalt the particular state at the expense of the Union, and some the Union at the expense of the state. Some would annex territories for the sake of slavery, and some for the sake of abolition. Some would welcome the immigration from Europe, and give it political rights as soon as it arrived, and some would acknowledge no political privilege but in men born on the soil, and would keep all the political good things of America entirely for the Americans.

It is not for modes or principles of government that American parties are arrayed against each other. They have established universal suffrage, the ballot, short Parliaments, paid membership—all the points upon which our English Chartists insist as necessary to political salvation, but they have not entered on the political millennium, or secured good or cheap government. But they have secured a tyranny of party and opinion, to the violence and stringency of which the annals of British constitutional strife can offer no parallel. In public life in the United States a man is not allowed to exercise a right of judgment in opposition to his party; if he do, it is at his peril. He must go with his party in all that the leaders in public meeting assembled consider to be necessary or expedient. He must accept the whole "platform," whether he like it or not. He must not presume to take one "plank" out of the structure, and adhere to that alone, as independent judgment is treason to the cause. If he be guilty of it, he is lost as a politician, and is solemnly "read out" of the ranks, to become a mere aerolite, revolving in his own orbit, but having no farther connection with the greater planetary body of the party except to be dashed to pieces should he ever come within the sphere of its attraction. The utmost discipline and obedience are enforced. As party selects its men not only for Congress and the central government, but for the several state governments and Legislatures, as well as for municipal offices, all of which act together and fit into each other like pieces of one machine, beginning with the town or city, and, through the medium of the individual commonwealth, acting upon the United States government at Washington, it is easy to see how vast is the ramification, and how complicated the cranks and wheels that are set in motion. At the recent nomination of a mayor for the city of New York, which threatened to produce a split in the Democratic ranks, and a serious defalcation from the party, it was openly avowed and insisted upon by Democratic organs in the press, and by Democratic speakers at Tammany Hall—a celebrated place of meeting, to which political slang gives the name of the "Wigwam," and to the principal speakers at which it gives in like manner the name of the "Sachems"—that if the party proposed the devil himself for mayor of New York, member of Congress, or President of the republic, no member of the party would have a right to exercise any judgment as to the propriety of the nomination, but must support the devil by vote and influence, or leave the party. And in the United States, the rewards of party service are not only much more numerous than in England, but the opportunity of giving and receiving them occurs regularly every four years on the nomination and election of a new President. It is not simply the ministers and heads of departments, but all the officials, clerks, and even supernumeraries in their employ, who go out of office with the President—not only embassadors and consuls, but every person, high or low, great or small, in receipt of a salary from the state. That such a system leads to corruption, and to making the most of opportunities while they last, to peculation and to jobbery of all kinds, and that it can not lead to good, efficient, honest public service, few Americans deny. But none can see a remedy which would not, in general opinion, be worse than the disease. To extend the presidential term to eight or ten years is one remedy that has been suggested, rather for the sake of showing its impracticability than for any other reason. Such a president, if an able man, might become too powerful for the Constitution, and seek to overthrow it; and if engaged in a foreign war, in which he was gaining victories and territories, and thus flattering the national vanity and feeding the national passions, might, by a *coup d'état*, render his position permanent or hereditary, and so make an end of the republic.

Another remedy which has been suggested is that of leaving the president to go out of office every four years, but appointing for life the minor officers of the state. But this proposition has excited almost as much opposition and jealousy as the other, and armed against it all the multitudinous aspirants to office; all the classes who have not energy enough for successful trade and commerce, but greediness enough to look with wistful eyes upon the public money; all the classes who are more fitted to obey than to command, and to be subordinates than principals; and all that still more numerous class in America who think that the honors and emoluments of public life are due to those who organize victory for the candidates of their party, and that the triumph of the party ought to be followed by the personal advancement of every one prominently connected with it. The United States are overrun with placemen and functionaries; and as the members of the local Legislatures as well as the members of Congress are paid for their services, politics has become a recognized profession, to which men are regularly trained, and by which they expect to gain their subsistence or make their fortunes. The consequence is, that party is as strict in its rules and discipline as the clerical, the medical, the legal, the military, and the naval professions are in Great Britain with regard to the conduct of those who are once admitted within the circle. As in England there are offenses in a clergyman which the bishop or archbishop can not overlook; as there is conduct in a barrister for which he may be disbarred, and in a military man for which he may be tried by court-martial, so, in America, the party politician must adhere to the rules of his party, follow the proper lead, and vote and act as the party require, or be brought to judgment, and, if found guilty, be drummed out of the regiment, and lose all right and title to the loaves and fishes, as well as those honors with which the president elected by the party might in other circumstances have rewarded him.

And it is held, moreover, that this condition of affairs is not only proper in itself, but absolutely necessary to the efficient conduct of public business. The obvious tendency of government in the United States is to be weak and to be weakened. Lawmakers there are more habitually law-breakers than in older communities; and men, especially in the half-settled districts and in the slave states, are but too much inclined to be judges, jurors, and executioners in their own cause, and to supersede all other judgeship by the decisions of that very famous and expeditious judge, whose court is in the highway and the by-ways, whose instruments are the passions of the people, from whose decisions there is no appeal, and whose name is LYNCH. To prevent this tendency to the disintegration of power consequent upon the fact that every man considers himself a sovereign, a judge, and a lawgiver by virtue of his inherent and indefeasible right to a vote, it is found necessary to set up a counter jurisdiction to that of the individual, in the jurisdiction of the party, and to fuse, as it were, the million chaotic, heterogeneous, and conflicting tyrannies of the mass into the two larger and more manageable tyrannies of the expectant Outs and the complacent Ins. Universal suffrage for the mere choice of a ruler, and for nothing else, may lead to a strong government, as in France; but universal suffrage extending not only to the choice of the chief magistrate, but to the whole course of his policy, and to the whole *personnel* of his appointments, leads inevitably—as in America—to a weak government; so weak that the tyranny of party becomes absolutely necessary to keep life and soul together, and to prevent that disintegration which is political death.

Party strife and its results in Great Britain indirectly affect the whole people, inasmuch as they affect the course of the national policy at home and abroad; but it is only a small section of the governing class and its immediate dependents who are directly interested, and whose personal positions and fortunes are palpably involved. With us the battles of party kill only the officers, and leave the rank and file unscathed. In the United States the whole army takes the chances of war, and when the generalissimo goes, his lowest soldier goes with him. And there is this defense for the American system—it is a natural conclusion from the premises. Granted a pure democracy; and party tyranny is the necessary result. Every man is eligible to the presidency. Every man thinks himself as good or better than the President; and if the President has any thing to give away, why not give it to his political equal who helped to elect him? And when the President goes, it would seem to be a depreciation of the dignity and value of the humblest *employés* in Custom-house or Post-office whom he appointed if they did not follow him into retirement. And they go accordingly, and remain in opposition for another four years, until a new turn in the wheel brings their party back again into office, and themselves into advancement.

In Massachusetts and some other states, the judges are appointed for life by the Senate and the governor, and are thus placed above the turmoil of party politics, to breathe a serener atmosphere, more suitable to a due administration of justice than the murky and lurid air which chokes those lower valleys where the combatants meet. But, with the exception of such local judges, and those of the Supreme Court, there is scarcely a functionary in the Union that has held the same office above four years; and perhaps the most ancient of all as a functionary is the honest Enniskilliner, named M'Manus, well known to all the City of Washington, and to every body who has official business there, who holds the position of door-keeper at the White House or President's mansion. For no less than three presidential terms has M'Manus—as great in his own way as any Gold or Silver Stick, Black Rod or Polonius in Europe—kept his position. Presidents, like comets, have sailed into the political heaven with their portentous tails, and passed out of sight, but he has remained in his appointed sphere, to introduce any one to the President with or without a card, or at any time; to be " Hail, good fellow, well met!" with senators, representatives, governors, embassadors, and judges; to wait behind the presidential chair, or usher the guests to dinner, or hold a conversation on the politics of Europe or America in the ante-room ere dinner is announced. Partly a lord-chamberlain, partly a Gold Stick, partly a lord in waiting, partly a door-keeper, partly a butler, partly a footman, and entirely a citizen, M'Manus is himself an institution—an important and urbane personage, and one who has probably had more real enjoyment in the possession of the White House than any president who ever went in or came out of it.

CHAPTER XXXV.

ALBANY.

April, 1858.

FROM New York to Albany was a short journey; but, ere starting, the interesting question—to one who had not beheld the magnificent scenery of the Hudson—was how to undertake it—by rail or steamer? The weather and time of year decided me in favor of the rail. The ice upon the Hudson had not sufficiently cleared away to enable steam-boats to recommence their usual passages. Though at a later period I was enabled to see this great river in all the glory of spring—to sail past the Palisades, through the Tappan Zee, and up to Albany (when I found abundant reason to agree with the most enthusiastic of Americans that no river in Europe, unless it be the Clyde, surpasses the Hudson in natural beauty, and that the Rhine itself, deprived of its ruined castles, could not stand a comparison with this splendid stream), I saw nothing of it on this occasion but a few stray glimpses of its surpassing beauty as the train shot rapidly along. Traveling thus on the left bank of the river for upward of one hundred miles, I arrived at Albany, and betook myself to " Congress Hall," in the upper part of the city. This hotel was recommended to me as an establishment much frequented by members of the two houses of the Legislature, who here, in the capital of the " Empire State," undertake the local government of a Commonwealth almost as large as England, and nearly double as populous as Scotland. I found no reason to repent my choice, and during a residence of ten days was enabled to see the senators in *déshabillé*, and to learn something of the mode and the agencies by which public and private bills are brought in and carried through Parliament in an ultra-democracy. I also got some insight into the art and mystery of what the Americans very aptly call " lobbying."

Albany—beautifully situated on ground rising steeply from the banks of the Hudson—contains about fifty thousand inhabitants, and is one of the most attractive, cleanly, well-ordered, and elegant cities of America. Though overshadowed by the commercial greatness of New York, which in this respect it can never hope to rival, it is, next to Washington, the greatest focus of political life within the limits of the Confederacy. Between the commercial and the political capitals of this great state, which it has recently been proposed to call Ontario instead of New York, there is a great contrast. New York city is busy, unscrupulous, energetic, ill-governed, full of rowdyism and of the most violent manifestations of mob-law and mob-caprice; but Albany is staid, decent, and orderly. The tone of society is quiet and aristocratic, and the whole appearance of the place gives the traveler an idea of wealth and refinement. Farther acquaintance only tends to confirm this impression.

State Street—at the top of which, in the Park, a beautiful

open space adorned with noble elms and maples, stand the Capitol and other principal public buildings—rises steeply from the water's edge to the crown of the hill. It is a broad and busy thoroughfare, and at various points commands a picturesque view over the Hudson to the lofty green hills beyond. Albany is a place of considerable trade and manufacture. It produces very excellent cabinet-work of all kinds, and is particularly celebrated for its stoves, grates, and ornamental iron-work. It has two, if not three daily newspapers, and a flourishing literary and scientific institution. The Roman Catholic Cathedral is internally one of the largest and most magnificent ecclesiastical edifices in America. Here high mass is sometimes performed with a splendor and completeness, orchestral and vocal, not to be excelled even in Paris or Vienna, and to which London, as far as I know, can make no pretensions. Albany is the proposed site of what promises to be the noblest Observatory in America, to the foundation of which the public spirit of a private citizen (if the term be applicable to a lady) has contributed the sum of $80,000.

Albany, which is memorable as having been the seat of the great Convention held in 1754 for the purpose of bringing about a confederation of the thirteen original states and colonies for their mutual defense and general benefit, was called Fort Orange by the Dutch at the time when New York was known to the world as New Amsterdam. The Albanians, as the people of this city are fond of calling themselves, though to European ears the name sounds oddly, and is suggestive of Greece rather than of America, do not seem to be generally aware that the word Albany springs naturally from that of York; that the Dukes of York in the "Old Country" are Dukes of Albany; that Albany is an ancient name for the kingdom of Scotland, and that the dukedom of Albany was the appanage, by right of birth, of the heir-apparent of the Scottish crown.

Up to this point, and no farther, sailed the adventurous Hendrik Hudson in search of the western passage to China; and here, and all the way up from the Palisades—still dreaming that he was on the highway to Cathay and all its fabulous and scarcely-to-be-imagined wealth—he held intercourse with the simple-minded natives, and exchanged his petty gewgaws with them for the spoils of the forest. It was not until the year 1609—long after the discovery of America—that Hudson, in his ship the *Half Moon*, entered the Narrows, and pronounced the shores on either side to be "a good land to fall in with, and a pleasant land to see." On the 11th of September in that year he began to ascend the noble stream which now bears his name, and on the 19th he anchored off the spot where now stands the city of Albany. At the place now called Castleton he landed and passed a day with the natives, finding them kind and hospitable. He would not, however, consent to pass the night away from his ship; and the natives, thinking in their unsophisticated innocence that he was afraid of their bows and arrows, broke them into pieces and threw them into the fire. Little did honest and unfortunate Hendrik Hudson know what an empire he was helping to establish! Little did the poor Indians dream what an empire was passing away from hands no longer fitted to hold it, and what omens of downfall and ruin lay in every flap and flutter of the sails of that strange ship! Had they foreseen that their race was doomed to melt away and disappear in the fierce light of those pale faces like the ice of the winter before the sunlight of the spring, their gentle courtesies might have been converted into hatred as unrelenting as that with which the white strangers were received elsewhere, and which looks, in the light of subsequent history, as if it were prompted by the instinct, which so often transcends reason. No trace of the Indians now remains in all the wide territories of the State of New York except a few stunted, miserable stragglers and vagabonds in the wildernesses of Lakes Champlain and Niagara—wildernesses which will speedily cease to be wildernesses, and in which the Red Man in a few years will no longer find a resting-place for the sole of his foot, and where he will even cease to be regarded as a show and a curiosity. What an enormous change in less than half a century! At St. Louis there are men still living who had to fight hand to hand with the Indians for their lives, and whose hearts palpitated many a time in the silent watches of the night, when the war-whoop sounded in their ears, lest ere the break of day the tomahawk should flash before their eyes, and their scalps should hang as trophies at the girdles of the savages.

From the polite art of scalping to the politer art of lobbying is a long leap, but both are suggested by Albany past and present. Lobbying is one of the great results of equality, universal suffrage, and paid membership of Parliament. Where the profession of politics is pursued, not for love of fame or of honor, or from motives of patriotism, but simply as a profession offering certain prizes and privileges not so easily attainable in law, medicine, art, or literature; in a political scramble, where the man with "the gift of the gab," the organizer of public meetings, the marshaler of voters, the ready orator of the mob, is provided with a seat in the Legislature and a respectable salary at the same time, it is not to be wondered at that men of more ambition than intellect or virtue should aspire to and attain parliamentary power. There are brilliant exceptions, no doubt—men of fortune and intellect, who serve, or try to serve their country from purely patriotic motives; but these do not form the bulk of the State Legislatures of the Union, or even of that more dignified Congress which sits at Washington. The three, four, or five dollars per diem which the members receive in the local Legislatures is but too often their only source of subsistence; and no one who knows any thing of the internal working of American politics will deny the fact that such members are notoriously and avowedly open to the influence of what is called "lobbying." In our ancient Parliament strangers have but scant and sorely-begrudged admission to the debates, and none whatever to the body or floor of the House; but in the American Legislatures the privilege of the floor is, if not indiscriminately, very freely granted. Governors, deputy governors, and ex-governors, ex-members, judges, generals, newspaper editors, and a whole host of privileged persons, can enter either chamber, and mix familiarly with the members, sit with them on their seats, and be as free of the House for every purpose, except speaking and voting, as if they had been duly elected by the people.

This easy and familiar intercourse leads, in the case of private and local bills, to an immensity of jobbery, and has made "lobbying," in most, if not all the states, a recognized art and science among the prominent outsiders of political life. Nor can it well be otherwise, the preliminary conditions being granted. All the local business as regards public works and improvements of the great city of New York is transacted at Albany, which is the Westminster without being the London of the " Empire State." And how is it to be expected that a needy and ambitious lawyer without practice, having nothing but his three or four dollars a day, and upon whose single vote the fortunes of a project costing millions to carry into effect may absolutely depend, shall not be open to the influences of those who "lobby" him? No farther disquisition upon the morality or propriety of such a state of affairs is necessary. It may be noted, however, for the guidance of such of the "advanced politicians" of our own country who think or argue that if a thing be established in America it would be well to give the same thing a trial in England, and who, for this reason, advocate paid membership of Parliament among ourselves.

CHAPTER XXXVI.

THE FUTURE OF THE UNITED STATES.

In traversing this great republic—so vast in extent, so rich in resources, not one tithe or one hundredth part of which is yet developed or thoroughly known—it is impossible for any traveler of ordinary intelligence, whatever be the bent of his mind, to avoid indulging in some degree of speculation as to its future destiny. If now, with a population not equal to that of the British Isles, but with a territory capable of employing and feeding ten or twenty times the number, it holds so high a place in the polity of nations, what will be its power and influence abroad and its happiness at home when its fruitful valleys, its teeming hill-sides, and its magnificent prairies are all brought under cultivation; when its coal, its copper, its iron, its lead, its silver, and its gold mines shall be all adding their tribute to the national wealth; when the smoke of countless factories shall darken the air in districts where the primeval forest yet stands; and when it shall produce within its own boundaries all the articles of necessity and luxury that it now draws from Europe? Inhabited by the noblest and most intelligent races on the earth; starting fair and free in the great competition; utterly untrammeled by the impediments which have retarded the progress of the same peoples in our older hemisphere, to what uses will they turn their unparalleled advantages? Will they be able to solve the great problems of government which have puzzled sages and philosophers, kings and statesmen, students and men of business since the world began? And will they secure, as they grow older and more thickly peopled, that which all governments profess to desire—the greatest happiness of the greatest number? Shall practice and theory be found compatible with each other? And shall republicanism be able to justify itself in the eyes of all men, as not only the most equitable and workable, but the most beneficial and convenient form of government for the masses of mankind? And, above all the rest, will the union of perhaps a hundred commonwealths, instead of only thirty-two, as at present, be permanent? Or will the increase of population lead to difficulties which are now lightly felt—if felt at all—in consequence of the immensity of elbow-room which the wilderness allows discontent to emigrate to and to thrive in? And will those difficulties —aided by time, aggravated by circumstances, and rendered different in degree as well as in nature in the South and in the North, and on the Pacific Sea-board, by the operation of climate upon the life, character, and brain of the race—become so irreconcilable as to dissever the glorious fabric, and re-enact in America the melancholy drama of Europe and Asia?

Americans who bring the knowledge acquired by European travel to the study of their native politics, past and present, do not conceal their opinion that a dissolution of the Union is among the possibilities and even probabilities of the future; but, as they do not anticipate such an event while the population is under fifty millions, or even under a hundred, it gives them no great anxiety. The deluge that is to burst over the earth in a hundred years is a deluge which, even if positively certain to come and impossible to prevent, gives little trouble to the existing generation. Many persons in the United States talk of a dissolution of the Union, but few believe in it. At intervals, some fiery orator or editor of the South, exasperated by the taunts of equally fiery and unreasonable abolitionists and Free-soilers in the North, and feeling, at the same time, that he is taxed in his wearing apparel, his household furniture, and in every article of luxury for the supposed benefit of Northern manufacturers, calls for a Southern confederation of slave states, and insists that they could maintain themselves against the free north either by their own unaided energy and resources, or by means of a commercial and free-trade alliance with Great Britain, their best customer for all their agricultural produce of sugar, rice, and cotton. Sometimes a Northern orator or editor endeavors to retaliate upon the South, to show it that without the North they could not subsist, and that the North, with three times their population, and all composed of free men, could reannex the South in a summer campaign, even without raising the cry of freedom to the negroes to exasperate and to shorten the struggle. Another section of the North, not so warlike in tone, is sometimes driven to make the assertion that, if it could get rid of its enforced participation in the sin of slavery by any other means than disruption, it would welcome disruption as a boon. But all this is mere bravado and empty talk. It means nothing. The Union is dear to all Americans, whatever they may say to the contrary; and if any one not an American presumes to reiterate the belief—which may, perhaps, have been instilled into his mind by American arguments—that the Union will be disrupted, he is either told that he knows nothing about the matter, or that, being filled with a mean jealousy of American greatness, " the wish is father to the thought."

Whatever may happen in future, there is no present danger

to the Union, and the violent expressions to which over-ardent politicians of the North and South sometimes give vent have no real meaning; and those who would truly understand the feeling of Americans in this respect must remember that the North and the South have not all the arguments to themselves, and do not compose the whole Union. The largest portion, and one which promises to be hereafter the richest and most prosperous of the whole Confederation, is the West. The "GREAT WEST," as it is fondly called, is in the position even now to arbitrate between North and South, should the quarrel stretch beyond words, or should anti-slavery or any other question succeed in throwing any difference between them which it would take revolvers and rifles rather than speeches and votes to put an end to. General Cass, who in early life was United States Commissioner for the Indian Territory west of the Ohio—a territory at the borders of which now stands the large city of Cincinnati, and which is covered for hundreds of miles beyond that point with cities, towns, and villages, and all the stir of a busy civilization—expressed at a recent railway meeting in Cincinnati the prevalent idea of his countrymen on this subject: "I have," said he, "traversed this Western region when it was a wilderness—an almost unbroken forest from this point to the Pacific Ocean—a forest inhabited only by the wild Indian and by the wilder animals which God gave him for his support. Where I then followed the war-path I now pass up the railway. I have in the interval visited the most highly civilized nations of the Old World, and I have returned, I think, a better citizen and a wiser man. I say that there is not on this earth, from the rising to the setting sun, a more prosperous country than the United States, a better government, or a happier people. You, my fellow-citizens of the West, hold the destinies of this magnificent republic in your hands. Say to the North or to the South, or to any quarter whence comes a threat of disunion, 'Peace, be still!' We in the West have the power to preserve this precious work of our fathers, and we *will* preserve it! The Hebrews of old had their pillar of cloud by day and their pillar of fire by night to guide them through the desert to the promised land; and since the memorable day of our exodus from the bondage of England we have had guides—pillars by day and night—which have led us through many trials and dangers, till there is now no one to injure us but ourselves, and nothing to fear but the just judgments of God. Let us pronounce, then, with one voice, 'Withered be the hand that is stretched out to touch the Ark of the Union. The mighty West will defend it, now and forever!'"

And no doubt this is the feeling of Americans of all parties wherever they reason calmly upon the subject, and are not betrayed into petulance by the slavery question. As the venerable statesman truly observes, the United States incur no danger from foreign aggressions; there is no one to injure them but themselves; and they have nothing to fear but "the just judgments of God." But this is only a portion of the subject, and the questions still remain, Will they not injure themselves? And will they not incur the judgments of God by contravention of his moral laws, and by their lust of territory, bringing them into collision with foreign powers? That the people will increase, and multiply, and replenish the whole continent, no one can doubt; and that, in the course of ages, North America will be as populous as Europe, and reach a far higher civilization than Asia ever attained even in the pre-historic ages, which have left us no other records but their marvelous architectural ruins, it would be a want of faith in the civilizing influences of freedom and Christianity to deny. But, in speculating upon the future of a people, the mind clings to the idea of empire and government, and we ask ourselves whether empire in this noble region will be one or many, central or local, imperial or republican? Whether the great republic shall exist undivided, or whether it will fall to pieces from its own weight and unwieldiness, or from some weakness in the chain which shall be the measure and the test of its strength? Or whether, for mutual convenience and by common consent, these Anglo-Saxon commonwealths, when they have doubled, trebled, or quintupled their numbers by the subjugation of the entire wilderness, shall not rearrange themselves into new combinations, and form a binary or a trinary system, such as the telescope shows us in the heavens? Or whether, in consequence of internal strife, some new Alexander, Charlemagne, or Napoleon of the West shall arise to make himself lord absolute and hereditary, and at his death leave the inheritance to be scrambled for and divided by his generals? Though it may be folly to attempt to look too far into the future, or for a statesman to legislate with a view to what may or what may not happen a hundred and fifty years hence, still true wisdom requires that men charged with the destinies of great nations, and having the power to influence the course of events by their deeds and their opinions, should not confine themselves to the things of to-day, but calculate by aid of the experience of history, and by knowledge and study of human nature, how the deeds of to-day may influence the thoughts of to-morrow, and how the thoughts of to-morrow may produce deeds in endless succession through all future time.

That the Union may be disturbed or disrupted at some period near or remote, is an idea familiar to the mind of every inquirer and observer; and were it not so, the very threats of the North or South, meaningless as they may be at the present time, would serve to make it so. Mr. Buchanan, the actual president, whose perceptions have been enlarged by European travel and residence, and whose mind is not entirely inclosed within an American wall, as the minds of some of his countrymen are, is among the number of statesmen in the Union whose eyes are opened to the dangers which it may incur hereafter when population has largely increased, and when the struggle for existence—now so light in such a boundless and fertile region—has become as fierce and bitter as in Europe. It is, after all, the hungry belly of the people, and not the heads of legislators, that tries the strength of political systems; and when all the land is occupied, and has become too dear for the struggling farmer or artisan to purchase; when the starving man or the pauper has a vote equally with the well-fed and the contented proprietor; and when the criminal counts at an election for as much as an honest man, what may be the result of universal suffrage on the constitution of the republic and the stability of the Union?

In a letter apologizing for non-attendance at the centennial celebration of the capture of Fort Duquesne, the President uttered these memorable words:

"From the stand-point at which we have arrived, the anxious patriot can not fail, while reviewing the past, to cast a glance into the future, and to speculate upon what may be the condition of our beloved country when your posterity shall assemble to celebrate the second centennial anniversary of the capture of Fort Duquesne. Shall our whole country then compose one united nation, more populous, powerful, and free than any other which has ever existed? Or will the federacy have been rent asunder, and divided into groups of hostile and jealous states? Or may it not be possible that, ere the next celebration, all the fragments, exhausted by intermediate conflicts with each other, may have finally reunited, and sought refuge under the shelter of one great and overshadowing despotism?

"These questions will, I firmly believe, under the providence of God, be virtually decided by the present generation. We have reached a crisis when upon their action depends the preservation of the Union according to the letter and spirit of the Constitution, and this once gone, all is lost.

"I regret to say that the present omens are far from propitious. In the last age of the republic it was considered almost treasonable to pronounce the word 'disunion.' Times have since sadly changed, and now disunion is freely prescribed as the remedy for evanescent evils, real or imaginary, which, if left to themselves, would speedily vanish away in the progress of events.

"Our Revolutionary fathers have passed away, and the generation next after them, who were inspired by their personal counsel and example, have nearly all disappeared. The present generation, deprived of these lights, must, whether they will or not, decide the fate of their posterity. Let them cherish the Union in their heart of hearts—let them resist every measure which may tend to relax or dissolve its bonds—let the citizens of different states cultivate feelings of kindness and forbearance toward each other—and let all resolve to transmit it to their descendants in the form and spirit they have inherited from their forefathers, and all will then be well for our country in future time."

The President, although it may seem presumptuous in a stranger to say so, seems to mistake the feelings of his countrymen on "disunion." He appears to believe their transitory anger to be the expression of a deep conviction. From his high position as an American, he does not adequately understand or clearly see that what Americans say to Americans in the heat of conflict is not what they say in cooler moments to Europeans. As husband and wife often hurl words of bitterness and scorn to one another, which they would be very sorry that any one else should hurl or even whisper against either of them; in like manner, the Americans speak of the rupture of the Union "en famille." "They skin their skunk" in their own domain, and wish no foreigner to be within reach of the bad odor. And although the present Constitution of the Confederacy be a Constitution for fair weather, often unworkable and coming to a dead lock, and no more suitable for stormy weather than one of the elegant and commodious Hudson River steam-boats is for the swell and tempest of the Atlantic Ocean, it is clear from their own past history, recent as it is, that the Constitution can be amended, and be made elastic enough to meet all ordinary contingencies of wind and weather.

The real dangers of the Union do not spring from the inelasticity of the Constitution or from the quarrels of the North and South, from slavery or anti-slavery, or from any domestic question likely to arise, so much as they do from lust of territory on the one part, and from political and social corruption on the other. Both of them are peculiarly the vices of republics. The first leads to war; war produces warriors; warriors, if brilliantly successful, become ambitious; and ambition tempts to the overthrow of the political system that will not allow it scope. The Alexanders and the Bonapartes are a class which has more numerous representatives than the Washingtons. The United States have had one pure patriot, and will be both unfortunate and fortunate if they have another to equal either his purity or his renown—unfortunate in the civil commotions and difficulties which can alone produce such a man, and fortunate, should a hero of equal courage and fortune emerge out of civil strife, if he do not turn his victories to personal account, and aggrandize himself at the expense of the liberties of his country.

But a greater danger even than this—the most formidable of all the rocks that are ahead—is the growth of peculation and corruption, and the decay of public virtue. A republic is, theoretically, the purest and most perfect form of government, but it requires eminently pure men to work it. A corrupt monarchy or despotism may last for a long time without fatal results to the body politic, just as a man may live a long time, and be a very satisfactory citizen, with only one arm, one leg, or one eye. In despotic countries the people may be virtuous though the government is vicious; but a corrupt republic is tainted in its blood, and bears the seeds of death in every pulsation. And on this point Mr. Buchanan seems to have a clearer vision than many of his countrymen. The presidential chair, like the tripod of the Pythoness, gives an insight into things. He knows by the daily and hourly solicitations of political mendicancy—by the clerkship demanded for this man's son or that man's cousin—by the consulship required for this brawler at a meeting, and the embassadorship to London or Paris, or a place in the ministry claimed by this indomitable partisan or that indefatigable knocker and ringer at the door of promotion, how corrupt are the agencies at work. He knows, too, what personal humiliation he himself had to undergo before reaching the White House, and which he must daily suffer if he would please his party. He knows, as every President must know, no matter who or what he is, or what his antecedents may have been, what a vast amount of venality has to be conciliated and paid, one way or another, before the hungry maw of Universal Suffrage can be fed and satisfied, and the wheels of the great car of the republic be sufficiently greased. In reference to this fever in the blood of the state, he thus solemnly warns the citizens in the letter from which quotation has already been made:

"I shall assume the privilege of advancing years in reference to another growing and dangerous evil. In the last age, although our fathers, like ourselves, were divided into political parties which often had severe conflicts with each other, yet we never heard until within a recent period of the employment of money to carry elections. Should this practice increase until the voters and their representatives in the state and national Legislatures shall become infected, the fountain of free government will be poisoned at its source, and we must end, as history proves, in a military despotism. A democratic republic, all agree, can not long survive unless sustained by public virtue. When this is corrupted, and the people become venal, there is a canker at the root of the tree of liberty which will cause it to wither and to die."

For the utterance of truths like these, and as if to prove, without intending it, and by a very round-about method, that they are truths, although unpalatable, Mr. Buchanan has been held up to ridicule by his party opponents, condemned as an "old fogy," and proclaimed to be too slow for the age in which he lives. But if corruption have attained its present growth with a population so scant, in a country by the cultivation of which ten times the number could live honestly and independently, if they trusted to hard work, and not to intrigue, for the means of subsistence, what will be the extent of corruption fifty years hence? Shall a despotism attempt a remedy worse than the disease? Or will the patient be warned of the evil of his ways, and amend his life in time? But if these may be considered the views of a Pessimist, what shall the Optimist make of the picture? Grant that no foreign war brings into the field a European coalition against the United States —a coalition that would infallibly make the Americans a far more warlike people than they are, and compel them to turn their thoughts to pipe-clay and the rifle, and to the admiration of generals rather than of statesmen and orators; grant, also, that public virtue becomes of the true republican standard of ancient days, pure gold without alloy; grant, moreover, that slavery is peaceably abolished, or dies out and ceases to trouble the men of the twentieth century, is there no danger to the cohesion of the Union, resulting entirely from its physical magnitude? It is not likely either by fair means or by foul to annex Canada, for the Canadians feel that they have a destiny of their own to accomplish, and that they start without the great burden of slavery to impede their progress; but the United States will certainly annex to themselves all the moribund republics between Texas and Panama, including, of course, the whole of Mexico. The Union already extends to the shores of the Pacific, though the intervening spaces are not filled up. It takes a representative for California three times as long to reach Washington as it takes a New Yorker or a Bostonian to visit Liverpool, London, or Paris. Is there no danger in this? Is not the prospective unwieldiness of the Union a reason why it may be expected to break up into compartments a little more manageable, and resolve itself into at least three or four federations instead of one? The time may come when the New England States, weary of participating in the slavery which they can not abolish, may seek to effect a legislative union with Canada; when New York and the Middle and Western States may form another constellation of republics; and when the South, extending to Panama, may cultivate its "domestic institution" and cotton at the same time, defying North or West, or the whole world to trouble it; and when California and the other commonwealths on the Pacific sea-board, from mere considerations of distance and locality, may set up in business for themselves. That such a result would be injurious to the cause of liberty and progress in the United States, there is not the slightest reason to believe. On the contrary, by diminishing the chances of collision, by segregating the incongruities caused by climate, character, and education into related but not identical systems; and by rendering the prizes within the reach of military ambition less glittering and valuable than they would otherwise be, it is possible that the pacific dissolution of the Union, for reasons as cogent and as unimpassioned as these, would be greatly for the advantage of the Anglo-Saxon races in America. A binary, trinary, or quadrinary system of republics, having the same language, literature, laws, and religion, might preserve their identity as republics, and yet be able to establish and consolidate among themselves a balance of power, by means of which no one of the number could, under any circumstances, be permitted to declare war against another, just in the same way as, by the present Constitution of the United States, Maine can not declare war against Louisiana, Maryland against Ohio, or New York against Oregon; or, as in England, Kent can not take the law into its own hands to remedy any grievance it might chance to have against Pembroke or Merioneth. So far from the indivisibility and inviolability of the Union tending to the happiness or advancement of the race by whose energy and enterprise it has been established, it would seem, on the contrary, as if its very bulk would lead it into mischief, independently of those other causes of evil which wise and prudent statesmanship, looking beyond to-day at the possibilities of tomorrow, may endeavor to remove. The United States of America are but the first step in a great progression, of which the next may be the "United Republics of America." Why not? And yet it is vain to ask, for the present age can give no answer to the inquiry. But the men of the present age may, at all events, be allowed to calculate the chances of the next; and that this is one of the most important of them, no one who looks intelligently at the actual condition of Christendom can permit himself to doubt.

CANADA.

CHAPTER XXXVII.

FROM ALBANY TO MONTREAL.

April, 1858.

From Albany to Montreal, the commercial metropolis of the Canadas, is a ride of 254 miles; a long distance if measured by time, for the express trains upon American railways, so far from equaling the speed attained in England, seldom average more than twenty miles an hour. Leaving Albany late in the afternoon, our train halted, after having made ninety miles, at Rutland, in Vermont, where the passengers had to sleep for the night. In this distance an incident occurred, of no particular importance in itself, but interesting to a stranger and worth recording, as showing the free-and-easy manner in which some public affairs are managed in America, and how much more of a leveling institution the railway is sometimes made to be in the New World than it ever can be in the Old. I had taken my place in the car at the extreme end, where there is but room for one person on the seat, but with accommodation opposite for two. A traveler shortly afterward deposited his overcoat upon one of these seats to retain possession. In about three minutes afterward a stout, burly personage entered the car, leading in a white man and a negro, fettered, and manacled together. This was the first time during my travels in the States that I had ever observed a colored man in a public vehicle. Approaching my place, the burly individual in charge, whom I supposed to be a constable, but who called himself the sheriff, coolly threw upon the floor the coat left by the intending traveler, and directed his white and black prisoners to take possession of the two seats. I told him that one of the seats was engaged. "I can't help that," he replied; "it's doubly engaged now by my prisoners." Not desirous of such close proximity either to a white or a black felon, I looked around the car in search of more agreeable accommodation, but all the seats were filled. Resolving to make the best of a disagreeable business, I took refuge in the perusal of a book, and hoped that I should soon be relieved from such uncomfortable companionship by the arrival of the captives at their place of destination.

"What have these chaps been a doin', sheriff?" said a traveler to me, turning his quid in his mouth.

"I am not the sheriff," I replied. "If I were, I think I should travel with my prisoners somewhere else than in the public carriage."

"Well, it a'n't pleasant," he rejoined, "especially when one of 'em's a nigger. What have you been a doin' on, Sambo?" he added, turning suddenly to the negro.

"Nuffin at all, massa," was the reply. "I'm innocent, and did nuffin, and am got two years for it."

The white prisoner made no observation; and, the real sheriff making his appearance at this moment, my interlocutor assailed him with a cannonade of inquiries, and elicited the whole of the circumstances. The white man—a well-formed youth, scarcely twenty years of age, with a countenance by no means unprepossessing—had committed a desperate highway robbery, and, after having nearly killed a man, had rifled him of all his money, amounting to no more than seventy-five cents, or three shillings. For this crime he had been sentenced to ten years' imprisonment. The negro had been implicated, with a woman of bad character, in robbing a sailor of thirty dollars, and had been sentenced to two years' imprisonment. The negro was loud in his complaints of the injustice of his punishment, but the white man refused to enter into any conversation upon the subject; not because he was dogged or obstinate, but apparently because he knew that his sentence was just, and that the less he said about it the less there would be of hypocrisy in his behavior. He was exceedingly gracious to his black companion, and several times took a large cake of chewing-tobacco out of a side-pocket of his coat and offered it to the negro. The two chewed together in sympathy of sorrow, and contributed quite as largely as any two freemen present—perhaps a little more so—to the copious saliva upon the floor. The "sheriff," in this respect, kept them company, and condescended to accept from the highwayman the luxury of a chaw.

"Will he have any of that in prison?" I inquired.

"No, poor devil!" said the sheriff; and, as if that were the most grievous part of his sentence, "no, not for ten years."

Next morning, on starting from Rutland for Montreal, I secured a seat at a distance from the officer of the law and his prisoners, and saw no more of them. Our train sped near or through the cities of Vergennes, Burlington, and St. Albans, and amid the beautiful scenery of the Green Mountains. The weather, though it was the second week of April, was exceedingly cold, and the tops and slopes of the Green Mountains were covered with snow; but in the valleys the neat white cottages and villas, and still neater white churches of the descendants of the ancient Puritans, built of wood, but painted to imitate stone, gleamed cheerily in the sunshine. But the farther north we went the thicker lay the snow; and, on arriving at the shores of Lake Champlain, not one of the largest, but perhaps the most beautiful of all the American lakes, we saw innumerable blocks of floating ice upon the water. From Whitehall, at its southern extremity, where it is no wider than a river, to Rouse's Point, at its northern termination, Lake Champlain extends for nearly 150 miles. In some parts it is twenty miles in width, and in other parts varies from one mile to ten or twelve. In the summer it is traversed by numerous fine steam-boats, but at this early period of the year they had not commenced their trips, and the only mode of conveyance was the dreary rail and the suffocating car. Before arriving at Rouse's Point the rails cross Lake Champlain twice, the transit on each occasion affording to the passengers magnificent views over its beautiful expanse.

At Rouse's Point I took my farewell of the territory of the United States, and entered into the dominions of her majesty Queen Victoria. This important station ought to have belonged to Canada, and would have done so if Lord Ashburton, dispatched by our government in 1846 to settle the Oregon and Maine boundaries, then in dispute between the two nations, had been any thing like a match in intellect, in dexterity, in logic, or in purpose to the astute lawyer, Daniel Webster, against whom he was pitted. But the British lord, half an American in heart, and perhaps allied too closely to the trading interests of the great house of Baring Brothers to see things in their true light as regarded either Great Britain or Canada, was of no more account than a piece of red tape or a stick to be whittled in the hands of the great Yankee lawyer and orator. Not only Rouse's Point—a place of great strategical importance—but the larger portion of the State of Maine, and with it the free access of Canadian traffic to the ocean in mid-winter, when the St. Lawrence is closed up by the ice, were thus lost to Canada, and all because Great Britain, ignorant of Canada and of its vast importance, sent a good-natured and incompetent lord to make himself agreeable to Brother Jonathan, and settle a business which neither he nor the home government understood any thing about, except that it was troublesome. Let all true Englishmen fervently pray that war between the United States and Great Britain will never arise to make the Canadians rue the day when their interests were so grossly sacrificed by a man who knew so little about them, and by a government that scarcely deserved to retain so splendid a colony.

From Rouse's Point the rail stretches to the Canadian village of Caughnawaga, on the St. Lawrence. This village is inhabited wholly by the Indian tribe that forms almost the sole remnant of the once-powerful Iroquois. These Indians, who have a strong family resemblance to the Gipsies of Europe, and who pretend to tell fortunes in the same manner by palmistry, are the sole recognized pilots of the Rapids. To the emoluments which they derive from this source they add the profits gained by the manufacture of moccasins, leggins, bead purses, and other fancy work, in which their women more particularly excel. Here our passengers had to leave the rail and embark on the steamer to cross the St. Lawrence to Lachine. This place is situated near the celebrated Rapids of the same name. Here the loud cry of "All aboord!"—universal in America—summoned us to take our places once more in the railway cars; and, after a journey of some miles, we arrived at the venerable, picturesque, and flourishing city of Montreal.

In the United States the towns are so much alike in their architectural and general appearance as to cease very speedily to have much interest for the traveler beyond that inspired by history, or by the remembrance of the kind friends who reside in them. The only prominent exceptions within the compass of my experience were New Orleans and Boston—far apart, it is true, but suggesting reminiscences of Europe, either by the crooked picturesqueness of their streets, or, as in New Orleans, by the foreign names and costume of the people, and the style of building. But Montreal combines, to European eyes, all these sources of interest, and has features of its own which give it a character quite distinct from that of any other place on the American continent except Quebec. Let me not be accused of narrowness of mind and sympathy, or of an undue and unwarrantable feeling of nationality, if I avow that I experienced a sensation of pride and satisfaction, after a six months' tour in a country where I was made to feel that I was a "foreigner," on once again setting my foot upon British territory, upon seeing the familiar standard of England floating from the public buildings, and noticing the well-known red coats of the British soldiers who were doing duty in the streets. To pass from Rouse's Point to Canadian soil was like crossing the Atlantic in the difference which it made in my patriotic sentiments—or prejudices, if they deserve the latter name. I felt almost as much at home in Montreal as if I had landed in Liverpool. To me the Canadians were Englishmen, not Americans. And one of the most noticeable things in Canada, with which a stranger can scarcely fail to be impressed before he has been a week in the country, is not exactly the antipathy, but the estrangement which has sprung up between the people of the United States and those of the British possessions. During the last twenty years the line of moral and political demarkation between the two seems to have been gradually lengthened and strengthened. The explanation is, that the less heavily the yoke of the mother country has been allowed to bear upon the colony, the more affectionately the colony has clung to the old land, from whose best blood she has sprung, and by whose gentle example she is governed. So far from expressing a desire for annexation to or incorporation with the United States, the Canadians insist in the most fervid manner upon their separate and irreconcilable nationality. Not unfrequently, when hard driven by ultra-Republican orators of the "Spread Eagle" school, they declare it to be far more probable, if ever a split take place in the Union, or a war break out betwixt the United States and Great Britain, that Vermont, Maine, Connecticut, Rhode Island, and Massachusetts will claim incorporation with the Canadas, than that the Canadas will claim incorporation with the Republic of the Stars and Stripes, and so inherit the heavy responsibilities of slavery, without deriving any real advantage from association with the North. When an overzealous American so far forgets his manners as to talk of annexation in the company of Canadians, the reply not unfrequently takes the somewhat contemptuous turn that the Hudson is the natural boundary of Canada, and that, if annexation be either necessary or desirable, Canada may some day take the initiative, and seize upon Maine and the harbor of Portland. I have witnessed more than one Yankee so taken aback at the daring of the suggestion as to give up the struggle without any farther parley, except, perhaps, between two chaws or two whiffs, such slang phrase as "I guess that's coming it strong — rayther!" or "Brother Jonathan's not green enough to be done."

Montreal, generally pronounced Montre-all, is one of the most ancient cities of North America, having been founded in the year 1642. It contains a population of about 70,000. It is beautifully and solidly built of stone, and wears a general air and aspect of strength befitting the climate. By the French Roman Catholics, who form nearly one half of the population, it is called affectionately the "Ville Marie," or town of the Virgin Mary, and the names of its principal streets, derived from those of the saints in the Romish calendar, bear witness alike to the fervency and to the faith of its founders. The original Indian name, or rather that of the village on the site of which it is built, was Hochelaga, a name still given to it by poets, and by orators who desire to speak grandiloquently. Its French and British name of Montreal is derived from that of the large island in the St. Lawrence, on the southern base of which it is built, and in English ought properly to be Mount Royal. Its gray limestone embankments on the St. Lawrence—its long, substantial quays and wharves—its noble cathedral with the two tall towers (the most imposing-looking ecclesiastical edifice on the North American continent, unless Mexico offer exceptions)—its stately Market-hall of Bon Secours, a prominent object either in near or remote views of the city—its elegant public edifices, banks, nunneries, monasteries, and churches—and, above all, the Victoria Tubular Bridge, the most gigantic work of science and enterprise on the habitable globe—all combine to render Montreal either important or picturesque, and to give it an enduring place in the memory of all who visit it.

The island of Montreal, or the Royal Mountain, is about thirty miles long, and in some parts eight or nine wide, and rises in the centre to a height of about 900 feet. It has been called from its fertility the Garden of Canada, but whether the compliment be deserved is matter of dispute among scientific agriculturists. Against the northern shore of the island beats the strong and turbid current of the Ottawa; and against the southern shore, where Montreal rears its busy streets, rushes the stronger and clearer current of the St. Lawrence. These powerful streams unite about eighteen miles westward of the city, but refuse to commingle their waters until they have traveled beyond the mountain isle in their progress toward Quebec. The bases of the mountain are gradually being occupied by the houses and villas of the wealthier inhabitants of Montreal. In Rosemount—one of these—it was my good fortune to enjoy for three weeks the generous hospitality of the Hon. John Young, late one of the representatives of Montreal in the Canadian Parliament, and Minister of Public Works, and to obtain through his good offices a greater insight into the real condition of Canada, and of the city of Montreal, than I could have procured without such aid in a much longer sojourn in the country. The view above Rosemount, toward the summit of the mountain, stretches over a wide expanse of fertile country, and away to the Green Hills of Vermont and the State of New York, the St. Lawrence rolling its majestic tide through the valley, and sounding a music from the Rapids of Lachine, nine miles distant, far louder than the roar and rumble of the adjoining city. Its carrying and forwarding trade, as a port competing with New York for the European commerce of the Far West, constitutes the principal business of Montreal. As such it possesses few manufactures; but it has a growing trade in potash and pearlash, and one more recently established in those luxuries—so dear to the Anglo-Saxon—bitter ale and porter. Its average exports of potash and pearlash amount to about £300,000 per annum; and in the year 1857 they reached £400,000. The farmers in the back woods, and in newly-cleared or half-cleared lands, add considerably to their resources by the sale of this portion of their produce. For the testing of the strength of these two valuable commodities, inspectors are appointed by the government. By the courtesy of one of these gentlemen, I was shown over the establishment whence all this agricultural wealth is distributed over the world, and initiated for the first time into the previously unsuspected mysteries of burnt timber and boiled ashes.

The brewery and distillery recently established at Montreal, where there are no excisemen to interfere with the manufacture and increase the cost of the articles, are under the superintendence of proprietors who learned the mysteries of their art in London and Burton-upon-Trent, and who have succeeded in producing bitter ales far superior to the lager beer of the United States, and almost, if not quite, equal to the ales of Messrs. Bass or Allsop.

Much has been done of late years to develop the capabilities of the harbor of Montreal, and when the Victoria Tubular Bridge—already the pride and chief ornament of the city—shall have been opened for the traffic of the Grand Trunk Railway, it will become, to a larger extent than it is at present, the rival of New York and Boston. The idea of bridging the St. Lawrence River at Montreal is of older date than is generally known. The Honorable John Young was, perhaps, the most zealous and untiring in his endeavors to bring the subject prominently before the world. More than one engineer of eminence in America was referred to and consulted by him before any steps were taken to bring the subject before the public. Surveys, examinations, and various reports resulted from these—differing, of course, somewhat in their details, but generally recommending timber structures similar to those invariably resorted to in the United States for bridging the great rivers. Nothing in connection with the Tubular Bridge had ripened into maturity until the project of the Grand Trunk Railway had been propounded and urged on by the provincial government in 1852. The Honorable Francis Hincks (being then prime minister and inspector-general of Canada) and Mr. Young (being at the same time a member of his administration), after several fruitless endeavors to interest the imperial government to aid in furthering their objects, which had in view the accomplishment of an international railway, extending from Halifax to the western extremity of Canada, ultimately resolved to invite private English capitalists to undertake the great work of the Grand Trunk Railway in so far, at least, as Canada was concerned. For this purpose the province undertook to provide thirty per cent. of the capital required, and with this impetus the Grand Trunk Railway assumed in due time the proportions of a palpable and beneficial fact.

In July, 1853, Mr. Stephenson, the engineer, visited Canada for the purpose of finally fixing the most eligible site, and determining the dimensions and general character of the Tubular Bridge; and, having communicated his ideas to Mr. A. M. Ross, who, in accordance with them, prepared and arranged

THE VICTORIA TUBULAR BRIDGE.—MONTREAL.

all the information required, the result, in a very little time, was the adoption of the structure now far advanced to completion, and which promises to be the greatest triumph of engineering skill of which either the Old World or the New can boast.

CHAPTER XXXVIII.

TO THE TOP OF BEL ŒIL.

Montreal.

LOOKING southward from Rose Mount, on the sunny slope of the great hill of Montreal, the most conspicuous object in the distant landscape is the mountain of Bel Œil, commonly, but erroneously called Bel Isle. To scale its heights, and visit the lake near its summit, was an expedition which I fancied might be easily performed on foot, and back again in one day. The idea was no sooner mentioned than scouted by my excellent host. Near though the mountain looked, its apparent proximity was the effect of the pure Canadian atmosphere upon the eyes of one not accustomed to measure distances through such a transparent medium. Instead of being no more than nine or ten miles from the city of Montreal, as I had calculated, the nearest point of approach to Bel Œil was at the railway station of St. Hilaire, seventeen miles from Longueil, on the opposite shore of the St. Lawrence. The river itself being nearly two miles wide, and Rose Mount being two miles from the Montreal shore, the distance to St. Hilaire was, according to all methods of computation, European or American, twenty-one miles. From St. Hilaire to the centre of Bel Œil was nine miles more, or thirty altogether from point to point. Thus it was clearly out of the question to make the excursion on foot. Thirty miles out and thirty miles in, even if we had taken two days to the excursion, were too many for pleasure. But the difficulty was overcome, as most difficulties may be, by a little management. The Grand Trunk Railway of Canada kindly placed a special train to and from St. Hilaire at our disposal, and our party of three,

Mr. Young, Mr. Andrew Robertson, solicitor and barrister (for legal gentlemen combine both branches of the law in the United States and the colonies), and myself, started to dine *al fresco* on the top of the mountain. The weather was propitious, and Canada is not in this respect like the Old Country. When a day begins favorably it ends favorably in ninety-nine instances out of a hundred, so that a preconcerted picnic is not likely to be disturbed in Canada, as it is almost certain to be in any part of the British Isles.

Our hamper, thanks to the provident thoughtfulness and liberal reckoning up of our wants, which only a kindly-hearted woman could have so well appreciated, was abundantly stored with bread, biscuits, cheese, sandwiches, tongue, chickens, and beef, besides pale ale, pale brandy, Champagne, and Sparkling Catawba. Not the smallest minutiæ were forgotten. Even tumblers, salt, and a corkscrew were included in the repertory. We had to cross the St. Lawrence in a wherry, with two oarsmen, for it was a holiday, and the only morning steamer across to Longueil had taken its departure an hour before we were ready. It is only necessary to say of the passage across that we had to make it diagonally, and so to double the distance, to allow for the strength and rapidity of the current; and that any one who should advise a future traveler to miss the steam ferry-boat for the chance of any pleasure derivable from this more primitive method of passing the great river, would be a *mauvais farceur* and a false friend. Arrived at Longueil, we found the steam up and our train ready, and in less than three quarters of an hour were safely deposited at St. Hilaire, at the base of the mountain which loomed large before us, and promised us from its steep top a prospect to be enjoyed, and an appetite to be earned by hard exercise. Both of these blessings were duly appreciated at their appointed season. The road lay all the way from Longueil through the flats of the St. Lawrence, and of its tributary the Richelieu, the northern outlet of Lake Champlain. The country is as level as Lincolnshire, and so thickly studded with farms and villages as to look as if it maintained a population of at least half a million. But these appearances are deceptive. The subdivision of the land, each family on its own plot, with the house in the centre, gives the idea of a population twenty times denser than it is; and the soil itself, a hard clay, has been impoverished and well-nigh exhausted of what original fertility it ever possessed by the bad farming of the *habitans*, consequent upon the perpetual parceling and reparceling of the land, and the non-employment of either capital or science to renew its over-taxed capabilities. It is Old France repeated over again in New France. The ignorant husbandry; the unwise attachment to the paternal nest, or pig-hole, as the case may be, in preference to better spots of earth at a hundred, fifty, or even twenty miles distance; and a limpet-like contentment with poor diet, and the enjoyment of the good that Fate and Chance provide on the original rock, in preference to a greater good to be found afar off, all seem to combine to keep the country poor, and to prove the ineradicable tendencies of race and religion. Of late years there has been a slight improvement, a few Scotch and English farmers having found their way into the valley, and introduced a better system of husbandry. But, owing to the smallness of the farms, and their constant tendency to grow smaller from generation to generation, the good example has not been of the efficacy that might have been expected under other circumstances; yet, superficially considered, a congeries of happier-looking communities than those which occupy the valley of the Richelieu is not easily to be found. Socialism without communism; contentment willing to sink rather than exert itself; a poor lot on earth cheered by the hope of a happier lot in heaven—such seem the characteristics of the place, and of the good, docile, honest, and amiable people. Their great defect is that they lack above all things what the homely Scotch proverb calls "a spice of the devil in them to keep the devil out."

Arrived at St. Hilaire, our first difficulty was how we should manage to carry our provisions to the top of the mountain. The road was rough, steep, circuitous, and long; and though the crest of Bel Œil seemed but two miles off, it was, in reality, near upon nine. To carry the provender ourselves would have been to make too much toil of a small pleasure, and a stout guide fit for the duty, and willing to undertake it upon a saint's day and a holiday, was not easily to be found in a country where such festivals were highly venerated and greatly enjoyed. After nearly an hour's inquiry we heard of an old farmer who had a cart and a pony, who would drive up as far as the lake—an ancient Jean Baptiste, as Norman in his dress, his speech, his aspect, and his ideas as if we had fallen in with him in one of the remote villages beyond Rouen or Caen. But we took him and were glad of him, not for the sake of our legs, for we preferred walking to riding, but for the sake of the provisions, which we could not otherwise convey. Besides, his pony was lame, and his cart had no springs; and so, by walking, we were not only merciful to his beast, but to our own bones. The road skirted the basis of the hill, and the ascent was gradual for three or four miles, in the course of which we passed a great number of small but comfortable-looking farm-houses, many gardens and orchards, principally of apple-trees, bearing the famous *pommes grises* of Canada. We also passed many groves of wild maple, the finest trees by the road-side, having each the well-known wounds, and the rude trough on the ground to catch the juice that flows in the early spring when they are tapped, and of which the *habitans* manufacture a very excellent sugar for home consumption. Indeed, in most of the Northern and Western States of the Union and throughout Canada, the maple is extensively used for this purpose, and is not only one of the most abundant and useful, but most beautiful trees of the country. It is lovely alike in spring, summer, and autumn. In autumn more especially it glows and glitters with its gold and crimson leaves, illuminated by the first touch of frost, and lights up the whole landscape with a glory of color unknown in Europe.

Leaving Jean Baptiste, his cart, his pony, our hamper, and two dogs, which had persisted in following us all the way from St. Hilaire, to await our return on the shore of the lake, we started alone through the pine woods for about a mile and a half to the summit of the mountain. The lake, which is about two miles in circumference, and discharges its overflow in a small brook that runs down the side of the mountain toward St. Hilaire, fills the hollow of what seems to have once been the crater of a volcano, and, though shallow on its banks, is said to be of great depth in the centre, and to abound with very excellent trout.

The grass had not begun to show itself, and there were considerable drifts and wreaths of snow in the pine woods and in the shaded recesses of the hills, but in the glades where the sunshine could penetrate, and wherever there was a southern aspect, the anemones were peeping out among the pine spiculæ and the dead leaves of the last autumn. As we clomb higher and higher, we left the pine woods behind us for the bare, hard rock, and at last stood upon the wind-beaten summit of Bel Œil. Here, in the clear sunshine, we indulged our eyes with a goodly prospect. We were in the centre of a circle of at least 100 miles in diameter, and could see on the far horizon a majestic panorama of a thousand hills, the indented rim of the great basin, in the hollow of which pierced up our mountain top, a solitary cone. To the south and west stretched the green hills of Vermont, and the higher peaks of Lake Champlain; and to the north and east the long Laurentian range which forms the only bulwark between Lower Canada and the polar blasts that sweep from Hudson's Bay and the Arctic Circle. The broad St. Lawrence wound its way through the prospect like a river of gold, joined by the Richelieu, a smaller but equally brilliant thread in the mazy web of beauty. Montreal, with the twin towers of its cathedral, and the tin roofs and spires of its numerous churches and ecclesiastical buildings, glittered like a fairy city at the base of its own mountain, while at every point in the nearer prospect on which the eye happened to rest might be caught the shimmer of a tin-covered spire, and underneath and around it a village, seemingly no larger than a wasp's nest or an anthill. It seemed from that height, looking over a country rather bare of trees, that here was the abode of a civilization as ancient as that of China, and that the population in those countless hamlets, bourgs, and villages, too numerous to subsist only by agriculture, must have long ago had recourse to trade and manufactures to provide themselves with the means of subsistence. But the standard of living is not every where so high as in our bread, beef, and beer consuming England. The French Canadian can live happily on a diet upon which an Englishman would either starve or become a Red Republican. But if the Englishman can conquer the world upon his high diet, he does not always conquer that which is still better—as all philosophers inform us—a contented mind.

Reflections connected with man or his works were, however, not those which were predominant in my mind after the first impression of the scene had worn away. As I stood on the mountain top, looking up and down the course of the St. Lawrence, I could not refrain from carrying my imagination back to the day when the peak of Bel Œil was a small island in the middle of as large a lake as Ontario, and when that great system of inland seas, commencing at Superior, and ending with Ontario at the Thousand Isles, extended to Quebec; when the Falls of Niagara did not exist; and when the level of Lake Erie was the level of the waters all the way to the Gulf of St. Lawrence.

It is scarcely possible to look down from Bel Œil upon the immense flat alluvial basin from which it rises in solitary grandeur without coming to the conclusion that, at an early period in the history of our planet, the Laurentian range on the one side, and the hills of Lake Champlain and Vermont on the other, were the landward barriers of a lake nearly 300 miles in length and seventy or eighty in breadth, and of which the shores all round were on the level of Goat Island at the Falls of Niagara.

After descending from the crest of the hill, and winding our way back through the pine woods to the lake, at the shores of which we had left our car, we found Jean Baptiste keeping watch and ward over our provisions. We selected a sheltered spot for our picnic on the bank of the little stream that carries the overflow to the valley, and here having spread our cloth and unpacked our hamper, we commenced operations. A few stragglers gathered about us to learn what we were going to do; but when they saw the solemnity and importance of the business that was to occupy us, they politely withdrew, and Jean Baptiste along with them. Not so the two dogs which had followed us from St. Hilaire. They knew by a sense keener than that of sight that there were fowls and beef in the hamper, and were contented to take their chance of the bones if nothing better offered. Neither of these animals understood a word of English, but their comprehension of French was perfect. The one of them was tolerably well fed, and manifested his contempt of bread and biscuit by a perfect immobility of every part of his body, his tail excepted, which wagged, "*Non, je vous remercie*," quite as intelligibly as a tongue could have spoken it. The other dog had not only no contempt for bread, but an insatiable love of it. To him bread or bare bone was alike acceptable. He was as lean as if he had tasted nothing for a month, and his behavior during our repast, contrasted with that of his companion, afforded us an amount of amusement greater than any farce upon the stage could have given us. To throw a piece of bread into the stream, and to see the lean dog leap after it and chase it down the current, while the fat dog looked on with philosophic contempt; to throw him the skeleton of a fowl, and see him gulp bone after bone with one sharp and decisive crunch, as if it had been firm flesh; and to give him a piece more than usually large, and watch him jump with it over the stream, and retire into a corner under a tree, about twenty yards off, to devour it in the seclusion of private life, were but a few of the varieties of recreation which the good dog afforded us, his companion all the while looking at him with lazy but undisguised contempt. But the crowning absurdity, at which we laughed till the tears actually trickled down our cheeks, was when, in despair of satisfying the cravings of the animal by any thing smaller than a half quartern loaf, we solemnly presented him with that article uncut. He eyed it for a moment wistfully, and then suddenly turning round with a low howl of sorrow, mingled with indignation, that he should be so insulted, leaped over the stream, and took his station within sight, but far off, where he barked and howled as if his heart were broken. We whistled to him and called to him in vain. His pride was hurt. He was not to be soothed or conciliated. At last we threw him half the leg of a fowl as a peace-offering. He accepted it, and came back to us gayly, as if nothing had happened. Three or four small slices of bread were next given to him and taken, when, as an experiment upon his canine nature, we for the second time presented him with a whole loaf. The result was the same as before. He was offended at the idea that we should consider him so gluttonous as to accept it, and bounded off with a reproachful moan to his former place of penitence and seclusion, where he howled dolefully, and refused to be comforted even by the wing of a chicken.

Jean Baptiste shook his head. "You have given that dog food enough in one day to last a man for a week;" and as he himself up to this time had had no share in the repast, his criticism was doubtless intended as a reminder. Whether or not, it was so received. Jean Baptiste had his full share of the solid contents of our hamper, and half a bottle of Champagne to boot—a liquor which he declared he had never tasted before. When told that it came from France, he held up his withered hands and exclaimed,

"*Le cher pays! que je ne verrai jamais!*" He begged to be allowed to keep the empty bottles as souvenirs of our excursion, and especially the bottle that had come from France. "That," said he, "shall have the place of honor on my mantel-shelf, *là bas à St. Hilaire.*"

And so we returned as we came, the two dogs following us to the village, and the lean one looking as lean as ever, frisking sometimes before and sometimes behind, the happiest dog that day in all Christendom.

CHAPTER XXXIX.

THE ST. LAWRENCE.

FORSAKING the Grand Trunk Railway for the beautiful scenery of the St. Lawrence—most magnificent of all the rivers of North America—and having engaged our state-rooms on board the steamer *Napoleon*, we—that is, myself and Mr. Young—left that city for Quebec on a lovely afternoon in early May. In compliment to the French Canadians, whose sympathies with France are not yet utterly extinct, one of the two principal vessels on this line has been named the *Napoleon*, after the Emperor of the French. The other, in compliment to their liege lady and mistress—under whose mild and beneficent sway they enjoy an infinitely greater amount of freedom than could ever have fallen to their lot under the domination of their mother country, which, continually changing its form of government from a limited monarchy to a limited republicanism, and finally to an unlimited despotism, has always escaped what it most desired, a rational and well-defined liberty—has been named the *Victoria*. The *Napoleon*, on which we steamed, was an admirable boat; and there being neither snags nor sawyers in the St. Lawrence, nor a reckless captain, and a still more reckless negro crew to work her, we had no such fears for our safety as those who travel on the Mississippi, the Alabama, or the Ohio must always entertain, more or less. From six o'clock, when we embarked, until midnight, when we turned into our berths, the time passed both pleasantly and profitably, for my companion knew all the intricacies, all the history, and all the beauty of the St. Lawrence, and had done more by his single energy to improve its navigation, deepen its shallows, and make it the first commercial river of the continent, than any other man in America. As we left Montreal, the tin-covered domes, steeples, and roofs of its cathedrals, churches, convents, and monasteries gleamed brightly in the rays of the setting sun; and when evening fell, as if by one stroke, upon the landscape, without the intervention of that lingering twilight to which Englishmen are accustomed at home, the whole firmament was suddenly irradiated by the coruscations of the Aurora Borealis. It was so vivid in its brightness, and so rapidly changeful in its hues—from green to red, amber and purple, and back again through the whole gamut of color, that the scenery of the river was for a while eclipsed by the grander scenery of the skies. By that glorious light our voyage down the St. Lawrence became a kind of triumphal procession, in which the heavens as well as the earth and the waters seemed to bear their part.

The Canadians on board paid no particular attention to the magnificence of the spectacle, which was doubtless too familiar to their eyes to excite the wonder and delight which it created in mine, that had never, in the more watery clime of England, beheld such splendor. It seemed as if the banners of eternity were waved in the clear blue firmament by angelic hands, and as if aerial hosts of seraphim and cherubim were doing battle in some great undefinable cause of liberty and right; or perhaps—for imagination was unusually vagrant at the time, and roamed whither it pleased—these electric ebullitions were but the tentaculæ of the great Earth-Monster floating in the Ocean of Space, as the medusæ float in the clear waters of the Western seas. Nay, might they not be the respirations of that sublime Mother and Bona Dea, upon whose epidermis man is but an insect, and his proudest works but the scraping and piling up of the exudations of her cuticle?

But after a time—for admiration, however great, requires novelty to feed upon—the sublime spectacle did not take such entire possession of the mind as to shut out altogether that of the majestic river on whose bosom we floated, nor cause us to forget that its never-changing current, rolling rapidly to the sea, was the drainage of the larger portion of a continent. The river, which is from a mile and a half to two miles wide, is studded with many islands, some of them large and fertile.

At every three leagues on either shore, in a prominent position, to be easily seen of all who pass up or down the river, is built a church of the well-known style of architecture so familiar to all who have ever traveled in France, the only difference being the invariable tin spire or dome, which gives such peculiar picturesqueness to the ecclesiastical buildings of Canada. These churches indicate the religious zeal and piety of the French Roman Catholic colonists of early times, who made the most ample provision for the religion of the people when they first took possession of the country. They called it New France, and endowed the Church with broad lands and ample revenues, upon the model and example of old France, ere the plowshare of the Revolution passed over the land, half burying the Church and wholly burying the aristocracy. The farms of the *habitans*, and their neat white houses, are thickly strewn on both banks of the river; and the lights from the windows, shining in the darkness as we journeyed rapidly along, conveyed the idea that we were passing through a densely-peopled and highly prosperous country —an idea far different from that which takes possession of the traveler on the Mississippi, who by night or by day sees more frequent signs of the rude, untrodden wilderness and the dismal swamp, than of the abodes of free men and the haunts of an active commerce.

As regards the St. Lawrence itself, familiarity with it breeds no contempt. On the contrary, the more it is known the more it is admired. Without exaggeration, it may be called the chief and prince of all the rivers of the world. If it be presumed that its real sources are to be sought in the multitudinous and often nameless streams that rise in the wildernesses of the Far West, and that have poured the rainfall and the thaws of thousands of years into the three great hollows which form the Lakes of Superior, Michigan, and Huron, we shall find the true commencement of the St. Lawrence at the place where the combined waters of these inland seas force their passage to the lower levels of Eastern Canada on their way to the ocean. This is at Sarnia, in Canada West, at the southern extremity of Lake Huron. The stream at this point is called the St. Clair River. After running a course of about forty miles under this name, it discharges itself into the small Lake of St. Clair; whence, again seeking an outlet, it takes the alias of the Detroit River. Running for about twenty-five miles farther, it fills up another great hollow in the earth, and forms a fourth inland sea, called Lake Erie, 18 fathoms deep and 564 feet above the level of the ocean. At the eastern extremity of this lake, the overflow, hastening ever onward to the Atlantic, finds a channel which is called the Niagara. The stream, flowing swiftly but equably for fifteeen miles, froths up suddenly into the rapids as it approaches the celebrated falls, and thence dashes itself in foam and spray into the noblest cataract in the world. After its precipitous descent of 160 feet, it rushes for three miles so furiously that at one part of the narrow channel, a little below the Suspension Bridge, the middle of the stream is ten feet higher than its two sides—a veritable mountain of waters. Growing calmer as it runs, and as the channel widens, it discharges itself into a fifth great hollow, which it fills, and thus forms Lake Ontario. It is only at its outlet from this magnificent sheet of water, which is 100 fathoms deep and 235 feet above the level of the sea, that it receives at the "Thousand Isles" the name of the St. Lawrence, by which it is known in all its future course of 750 miles.

Including the chain of lakes by which it is fed, the course of the St. Lawrence is upward of 2500 miles. Its chief affluents, besides the myriad streams that originally formed the gigantic bulk of Lake Superior, are the Genesee, which falls into Lake Ontario; the Ottowa, which mingles with it to the southwest of Montreal; and the Saguenay, a deep, dark river, with high, precipitous banks, which unites with it below Quebec. The lakes, the rapids, the falls, and the islands of the St. Lawrence add to the multifariousness of its attractions, and render it immeasurably superior to the Mississippi, the Missouri, or any other river of North America for grandeur and beauty. Indeed, there is no aspect under which a river may be regarded in which the St. Lawrence is not pre-eminent. But, like every thing else in the world, it has its imperfections. In the first

BREAK-UP OF THE ICE ON THE ST. LAWRENCE.

place, it is liable to be closed for half the year by the ice. A disadvantage such as this, man's energy and skill are, unfortunately, not able to remedy. Its remediable defects commence at the extremity of Lake Erie, where it overflows into Lake Ontario, to the lower level of its future course. The Falls of Niagara, which render it so beautiful in the eyes of the lover of Nature, give it no charm in those of the merchant, who seeks his way to a profitable trade in agricultural produce with the great corn and wheat growing states of the American Union that border upon the great lakes of the West. But this commercial defect has been partially remedied. The Welland Canal, twenty-eight miles in length, has been constructed, and through its narrow channel a corn-laden vessel from Chicago has already made the whole voyage from that city to our English Liverpool without transhipment of cargo. For vessels of 400 tons the Falls of Niagara are virtually non-existent. The question remains, and will speedily have to be decided, whether they can not be rendered non-existent, commercially, for vessels of 1000 tons burden and upward. The solution of this question is the deepening and widening of the Welland Canal—a costly work, no doubt, but one which must be accomplished if Canada is to derive all her rightful advantages from her admirable geographical position, or to hold up her head on an equality with the United States. The cost will be large, but will be met either by private enterprise or government encouragement, unless the whole trade of this vast region, seeking its market in Europe, is to be permitted to pass over the Erie Canal and through the United States, instead of through Canada and the St. Lawrence, its natural outlets.

The next obstruction to the navigation occurs at Dickenson's Landing, 120 miles beyond Kingston and the Thousand Isles, at the first rapids. The beauty and grandeur of these and the whole series of rapids between the Thousand Isles and Montreal will be more particularly described hereafter. At this place the rapids run for nearly twelve miles, and the difficulties they place in the way of the up-stream navigation have been surmounted by a canal from Dickenson's Landing to Cornwall, at the head of an outspreading of the river called Lake St. Francis. The next interruption occurs at the rapids between Lake St. Francis and Lake St. Louis, to surmount which the Beauharnois Canal has been constructed. From this point to the third and last series of rapids at Lachine, within nine miles of Montreal, no difficulty occurs. The Lachine Canal admits vessels of a burden much greater than the Welland Canal can accommodate. The remaining obstruction to the navigation arises from a totally different cause, the shallowness of the river, where it widens out to the Lake St. Peter. This lake, which in one place is nearly fifteen miles broad, acted, until the works for its improvement were undertaken, as an effectual bar to the direct ocean commerce of Montreal, except by transhipment. In the year 1843 the Canadian government commenced the construction of a ship canal through the centre of the shallows. The work was continued until 1847, when it was temporarily abandoned. In 1850 the Harbor Commissioners of Montreal, impressed with the importance of the work, applied to the Government for authority to complete it. The power was granted, and the necessary legislative provision made for the cost and maintenance of the improvements. In five years the channel throughout the whole length of the lake was deepened five feet; and in the summer of 1857 a depth of seven feet greater than the original bed of the lake had been attained. "The magnitude of the work," says the Hon. John Young, on behalf of the Montreal Harbor Commissioners, "will be seen when it is considered that the deepening extends over a distance of eighty miles; that dredging has actually been done over twenty-four miles, the width of the channel dredged being nowhere less than 300 feet; and that about 4,250,000 cubic yards of excavation have been removed from the bed of the lake and river, and carried off and dropped at distances averaging more than a mile." The object of all these works is to afford free egress from and ingress to the St. Lawrence and Lake Ontario, and the great lakes of the West, to vessels drawing twenty feet of water—a work which, when accomplished, will not only divert from New York a vast amount of trade

THE ST. LAWRENCE. 353

that now finds its way thither, but which will largely aid in developing the resources of Iowa, Wisconsin, Minnesota, Michigan, Canada West, and the yet almost desert and untrodden regions of the Red River and the Saskatchewan.

But how to avoid or overcome the impediments to trade and navigation caused by the climate, and the imprisonment of the great current of the river under the ice of an almost Siberian winter? That difficulty is not to be entirely conquered. There is no remedy that man can apply. But the difficulty does not affect the St. Lawrence alone, for it extends even to the Hudson River and to Lake Champlain, which are nearly, if not entirely, valueless to commerce during the greater part of the winter and early spring.

But even here the same far-sighted wisdom which has been the cause of such improvements in the St. Lawrence — improvements advocated and carried on amid every kind of discouragement and difficulty—has seen the opportunity of aiding in the development of the country. The Hudson and Lake Champlain are less affected by the frosts than the St. Lawrence. From Caughnawaga, nine miles west of Montreal, and nearly opposite to Lachine, to the northern extremity of Lake Champlain, is a distance of no more than twenty miles. A corn-laden vessel from the rich lands around Lake Superior, if prevented by the severity of the weather from proceeding beyond Montreal, might have the chances to a later period of the year of sailing down Lake Champlain, and thence to the Hudson and to the ocean, provided there was a ship canal from Caughnawaga to Rouse's Point. The State of New York—wise enough to see not only the importance of connecting the Hudson with Lake Erie by means of the Erie Canal, but with Lake Champlain — constructed a canal some years ago, effecting the junction at the southern end of the lake. This canal is sixty-five miles in length, but only admits vessels of eighty tons. But the link between Caughnawaga and the northern extremity of the lake, in British territory, would more effectually unite the St. Lawrence, and consequently Lake Ontario, with the Hudson. This project has been put prominently forward by Mr. Young, and, there being no engineering impediments, the only real objection raised against it is the expense. But this objection will disappear; and it is all the more important that it should, not only for the sake of the trade of the St. Lawrence, but for that of all Canada, deprived by geographical circumstances of the Erie Canal, and, by the easy, good-natured ignorance of the late Lord Ashburton, of the harbors in the territory of Maine, which, by every consideration of geography, trade, politics, and natural right, ought to have belonged to it.

How necessary it is for Canada and the friends of Canada to stir in all matters relating to the improvement of the St. Lawrence and to the harbor of Montreal may be understood by the instructions to Messrs. Childe, M'Alpine, and Kirkwood, the civil engineers appointed by the Harbor Commissioners of Montreal to examine and report on the subject; "Although the magnificent canals on the St. Lawrence are in perfect order, and have been in operation since 1849, with a system of railways also in operation for two years, running from Quebec, and connecting with all points south and west, yet, up to the close of 1856, the St. Lawrence route had only succeeded in attracting fifteen per cent. of the Western Canadian and Western United States' trade, eighty-five per cent. of that trade passing through the Erie Canal and over the railways of the State of New York."

All these matters, and many others, I studied that night upon the St. Lawrence. At seven in the morning, with a clear, bright sky above us, we arrived within sight of Cape Diamond and the imposing fortifications of Quebec. By half past seven we had passed Wolfe's Landing and the Heights of Abraham, where the battle was fought that decided the fortunes of America, and at eight were safely landed in the quaintest and most remarkable city of the New World.

CHAPTER XL.

QUEBEC.

May, 1858.

To Quebec belongs the distinction of being the most antique, the most quaint, the most picturesque, and in many respects, both historical and strategical, the most important city on the North American continent; and, before attempting either to describe it or to record the reflections excited by its singular history, a few words on the very doubtful point of the origin of its name may neither be uninteresting nor inappropriate. The names both of Canada and of Quebec have long puzzled etymologists, and, rampant, fiery, and ungovernable as may be the etymological hobby—a very Pegasus careering through all the sciences, and through all knowledge, sacred and profane, ancient and modern—it can not be denied that inquiries into the derivations of words and names of places, if fairly conducted, may conduce to instruction, and throw new light upon old subjects, both in the highways and by-ways of history and literature.

The name of Canada is supposed by one class of etymologists to have been derived from the Spaniards, and by a second from the native Indians. Father Hennepin, a Jesuit writer, states that the Spaniards first discovered Canada—a very doubtful point, however—and that, finding nothing on the coasts that came up to their expectations or excited their cupidity, they called it the "Capo di Nada," or "Cape Nothing," whence, by abbreviation, Canada. Charlevoix, a later French writer, repeats the story, and adds that the natives of Gaspé, on the St. Lawrence, were in the habit of repeating to the French navigators of the days of Jacques Cartier, the real discoverer of the St. Lawrence and of Canada, two words which they had picked up from the Spanish adventurers of an earlier date, "Aca nada," or "Nothing here;" and that the French mistook their expression, and imagined that the name of the country was Acanada, or Canada. The French have laid no claim to the word, though it may be mentioned as singular that in the Walloon country of Belgium, and in the neighboring French territory, where the same dialect is spoken, a potato is called a canada. But the Indian derivation seems the most probable. Both on the Canadian and the New York side of the St. Lawrence occur Indian names of places of which the word Caugh is the leading syllable. Thus, opposite Lachine is Caugh-na-waga, or the Village of the Rapids, Caughna-daigha, or Canandaigua, in the county of Genesee, in the State of New York; and Onon-daugha, or Onondaga, in the same state. Caugh-na-daugh, pronounced by the Iroquois Indians Cah-na-dah, signifies a village of huts, or a town; and the word seems to have been adopted by the French in the time of Jacques Cartier. Wherever they found an Indian village in their intercourse with the natives from Gaspé to Sault St. Louis, they asked its name, and were invariably answered Caugh-na-daugh, and thence believed that the word was the name of the whole country.

Whether this be or be not the true solution, is now difficult, and perhaps impossible to decide; but it seems fortunate that so large and fine a country has a good and sounding name of its own, whencesoever it may have been derived. In this respect, as well as in some others, Canada has an advantage over the "United States of America"—a phrase which designates, but does not name, the country. And equally difficult is it to know whence came the name of Quebec. The Iroquois Indians called the place Staugh-Daugh-Cona, or Stadacona; and the Hurons, a small remnant of whom still lingers in the neighborhood, called it Tia-ton-tarili, or the "place of the narrows." Champlain, who has given his own name to the large and beautiful lake that lies between the St. Lawrence and the Hudson, says that the word Quebec is of Indian or Algonquin origin, and signifies a "strait." Charlevoix, who wrote nearly a century after Champlain, repeats the statement; but the Indians themselves deny that there is any such word in their language or dialects, and universally agree that it is of French origin. La Potherie, who wrote on the discoveries of Jacques Cartier, relates that the Norman crew of that distinguished navigator, on catching the first glimpse of the imposing promontory of Cape Diamond, on which the citadel of Quebec now stands, exclaimed " *Quel bec !*"—what a beak ! or promontory—and hence the name. But, although this derivation seems improbable, if not absurd, it leads inquiry toward Normandy, and to the early settlers in New France, as Canada was then called, as to the true source of the word. As there is a town called Caudebec on the Seine —as there is the Abbey of Bec-Hallouin, in Normandy—may there not have been some hamlet, bourg, fief, or castle named Quebec, of which the name was transferred to the New World by some immigrant Norman adventurer and native of the place? This supposition was at one time greatly strengthened by the discovery of a mutilated seal of the famous William de la Pole, Earl of Suffolk, in the reign of Henry V. of England. This seal, engraved in *Edmonstone's Heraldry*, bears in the legend the distinct syllables " Quebec" and " Suffolchiæ;" and, as the greater portion of the legend is broken off, the gap was thus conjecturally supplied : SIGILLUM WILLIELMI DE LA POLE, COMITIS SUFFOLCHIÆ, DOMINUS DE HAMBURY, ET DE QUEBEC. " This," says the writer in Hawkins's excellent "Picture of Quebec," published in that city in 1834, " proves *beyond doubt* that Quebec was a town, castle, barony, or domain, which the powerful Earl of Suffolk either held in his own right, or as governor for the king in Normandy, or some other of the English possessions in France." But, though there was no doubt in the mind of the local historian, there would, perhaps, have been a very considerable doubt had he consulted " Dugdale's Baronage" for the titles of William de la Pole. In vol. ii., page 186, of the folio edition of 1675–6, occurs the following passage: " In 4 Henry V. this William was retained by indentures to serve the king in his wars of France with thirty men-at-arms, whereof himself to be one, five knights, twenty-four esquires, and ninety archers. * * * In remuneration of which and other services, he then obtained a grant to himself and the heirs male of his body of the Castles of HAMBOR and BREQUEBEC, with their appurtenances, as also of all the fees and inheritances which Sir Fulke Pagnell, Knight, possessed within the duchy of Normandy, being then of the yearly value of three thousand and five hundred scutes."

Thus it appears that William de la Pole was Lord of *Brequebec* and not of *Quebec*, and this explanation suggests that on the mutilated seal the first syllable (Bre) may have been broken off. Brequebec, or, as it is now called, Bricquebec, is a village eight miles from Valognes, in Normandy, between Cherbourg and St. Malo, and possesses the ruins of an ancient castle, with a lofty donjon keep eighty feet high. It was taken from the family of Paynell, Paganel, or Paisnel, after the battle of Agincourt, and bestowed by Henry V. on the Earl of Suffolk, as stated in Dugdale. So the etymology founded upon the authority of the imperfect seal must fall to ground; and we must either look for some other French town, castle, or bourg named Quebec without the "Bre" or the "Bric," or discover a more probable derivation.

It appears that an early French writer, Le Père du Creux, writes the word in Latin, Kebeccum; and that, in Major Wally's "Journal of the Expedition against Canada under Sir William Phipps in 1690," the place is called Cabeck. Is not the last-mentioned the real clew, after all, to the difficulty? The western extremity of the long promontory of which the citadel of Quebec forms the eastern termination is called Carouge, an abbreviation of Cap Rouge; and may not Cabeck be in the same manner derived from Cap Bec? The name, said to have been given to it by the sailors of Jacques Cartier, was Bec, or promontory, whence the transitions to Cape Beck, Cap Bec, Cabeck, Kebbeck, and Quebeck, are so simple as to require even less than the usual amount of etymological stretching to make them fit. But if the name of the cape have been given to the city, as seems most probable, the cape itself has lost its original designation, and is now called Cape Diamond.

I had not been many hours in Quebec before I stood at the wall of the citadel, overlooking the river from a dizzy height of three hundred feet—the standard of Great Britain floating over my head, the red-coated soldiers of my native land pacing their rounds, and suggesting, by their arms, their dress, their accoutrements, their whole look and bearing, the dear old country from which I was separated by so many thousand miles of ocean, and on the soil of whose noblest colony I stood.

And the panorama, stretching on every side, had all the elements of grandeur and loveliness to impress itself vividly upon the memory and the imagination. The wintry snows, though it was in the second week of May, had not entirely disappeared from the landscape, but glittered in the distance in patches like the white tents of some immense army; or lingered, in still larger wreaths, on the high banks of the opposite side of the St. Lawrence, though on the Quebec side, having a southward aspect, they had long since disappeared. The sky was beautifully clear, and distant objects seemed closer to the eye than in the mellower and hazier atmosphere of home. At the feet of the spectator, one hundred yards in perpendicular descent, and closely huddled against the rock, lay the old city—picturesque, narrow, and crooked—a transatlantic Edinburgh—with its castle-crowned height and bristling citadel; but possessing an advantage over Edinburgh in the broad and majestic river at the base of the precipice. To the west were the Heights of Abraham, and the path up the rocks to the Plains, famous in history as the battle-field where Wolfe, the young and immortal general of thirty-two, gained Canada for Great Britain and wrested from the French their American empire. Opposite were the Heights of Pointe Levi and the town of New Liverpool. Away to the east was the beautiful island of Orleans, where Jacques Cartier landed on his second voyage, and called it the island of Bacchus for its beauty and fertility, and the number of wild grapes he found growing there; an island thirty miles long, dividing the broad St. Lawrence into two currents; while the river itself, blue and beautiful, and studded with vessels of all sizes, wound its majestic way to the ocean. The white sails of the ships and boats gleamed in the sunshine, and gave both beauty and animation to the scene; while, close to the edges of the stream, the "booms," in which the "lumber" or timber, which forms so large a portion of the wealth of Canada, was inclosed previous to its shipment for Europe and the United States, suggested the idea that Quebec was not merely a war citadel and fortress, but the important centre of a lucrative and increasing commerce.

Even had the spot been unassociated with the historic and heroic incidents that have made it one of the most memorable on the surface of the globe, it would be difficult for any cultivated mind to refuse the homage of admiration to its natural advantages, and its romantic loveliness. Within the citadel is a monument erected to the memory of Wolfe and Montcalm—a small obelisk, bearing the names of the mighty dead: Wolfe on one side of the tetragon, Montcalm on the other; and recalling by their juxtaposition in death and in history, as well as on the monument, the lines of Sir Walter Scott on two very different heroes:

> "The solemn echo seems to cry,
> Here let their discord with them die;
> But, search the land of living men,
> Where wilt thou find their like again?"

And if their rivalry, just one hundred years ago, had taken another turn, what would have happened? If Montcalm had vanquished Wolfe, or Wolfe had failed to scale the Heights of Abraham, and drag up his one gun to the Plains, what—if we are justified at all in entering into such inquiries—would have been the condition of North America at the present time? Nay, what would have been the condition of our ancient Europe? Wolfe's victory, and the fast following conquest of Canada were, there can not be a doubt, among the most powerful of the reasons which induced the French monarchy to lend its aid to the revolted subjects of the British colonies in America, and which brought to George Washington the chivalrous aid of Lafayette, and procured for the United States that independence of England which under other circumstances they might not perhaps have enjoyed to this day. And that noble struggle, in which Lafayette and his Frenchmen played so distinguished a part, had its influence in Europe, and wrought so powerfully upon the minds of the French people as not only to predispose them for the events of 1789, but to exasperate and impel them. American liberty was the mother of the French Revolution. It was the example of Washington and Franklin that helped to raise up the early zealots of 1789 to attempt in the Old World what was so splendidly accomplished in the New. If Montcalm had been the conqueror instead of Wolfe, and if Canada had remained French, Louis XVI. might not have lost his head on the scaffold; no Robespierre and Danton might have proved themselves the fanatics of liberty; no Napoleon Bonaparte might have arisen like a fiery meteor to illumine and affright the world; and the mighty republic of the United States might have been what Canada now is—a free and a prosperous colony of the British crown. It is difficult in such a spot as Quebec—the military key to North America, and where the great event associated forever with the name of Wolfe was decided—to avoid indulging more or less in reflections of this kind. Such trains of thought are the homage demanded by the *genius loci*, and he who does not pay it may be as wise as an owl, and possibly as insensible.

Quebec has greatly outgrown its original limits; and the large suburb of St. John's, stretching far beyond the fortifications of the citadel toward the Plains of Abraham, contains a population which considerably exceeds that of the city proper. The whole population is estimated at about 40,000. The aspect of the old town is essentially French, while the suburb partakes more of the Anglo-Saxon character, but not so much so as to destroy the predominant French element. The monasteries, convents, churches, and cathedrals vindicate by their architecture the country of their founders, and are the main ornaments of Quebec. Indeed, it may be said that, without exception, the ugliest building in the city—the wharves on the river side excepted—is the English Episcopal Church, or perhaps it should be called Cathedral, as it boasts an English bishop. The Roman Catholic churches have more pretensions to architectural beauty, and the tin roofs of the numerous spires and cupolas, glittering in the clear sunlight of the clime like burnished silver, add greatly to the picturesque beauty of the town, and aid in impressing it upon the memory of the traveler.

From the rising ground of Mount Pleasant, forming the eastern ledge of the Plains or Heights of Abraham—where I was lodged in the hospitable abode of one of the principal merchants—the view over the valley of the Charles River to the long, straggling village of Beauport was suggestive, like that of the panorama of the St. Lawrence, of a densely-peopled and highly cultivated country. The whole land seemed to swarm with life, and to be cut up into little farms—each farm-house in the centre of its own square, like a pawn upon a chess-board. The French Canadians, like the French at home, have divided and subdivided the land *ad infinitum*, until they have well-nigh exhausted the fertility of the soil. Instead of spreading out into the wilderness as population increased, they have preferred to remain upon the narrow strips on the banks of the river where their forefathers first effected a settlement, while for miles beyond them lies the virgin forest, ready for the axe and the plow, and capable of maintaining a numerous population both of agriculturists and traders. But Jean Baptiste, as the *habitant* is called, is a quiet, good soul, strongly attached to his paternal four acres, or one acre, as the case may be, and has not the restless spirit of enterprise within him that carries the Yankee or the Englishman into the busy world to carve himself a fortune. He loves to linger around the church, and would rather live upon a small pittance within its shadow than quintuple his income, or rise to wealth in a new and ruder district. In the still busy and fertile valley of the Richelieu, on the opposite shore of the St. Lawrence, already described, the same feeling and practice prevail, and the same results have ensued. The land is so subdivided and exhausted that a district which once annually exported large quantities of wheat now scarcely grows enough for the consumption of its own inhabitants. This defect in the character of the people appears to be ineradicable, and threatens to produce in Canada a state of things, though with a difference, such as that which existed in Ireland prior to the famine and plague of 1847-8-9, and which made the government of Ireland the greatest difficulty with which the crown of England ever had to contend. The New World, with its boundless agricultural resources, would seem, at the first glance, to be too large for pauperism; but it must be confessed that the past history and present condition of the French colonists of Lower or Eastern Canada justify the fear that this plague of Europe may be introduced into America, and that, as was the case in Ireland, the social disease may be aggravated by questions of race and religion. Yet when the evil attains its climax there will doubtless be a remedy; and the *habitans*, pushed into the wilderness by a necessity from which there will be no means of escape, will not have so far to travel in search of new fields and fresh pastures as their fellow-sufferers of the Green Isle. If those who see or suggest the possibility of such a growth of circumstances be not open to the accusation of looking somewhat too far into the uncertain future, should not those who have it in their power to direct public opinion in Canada, and especially among the descendants of the early French, warn the people while it is yet time? A rich Church and a poor, contented, and simple-minded people form one sort of Arcadia, but it is not the Arcadia of Englishmen, or of any branch of the Anglo-Saxon family; neither is it an Arcadia for the perpetuation of which they are likely to contribute any portion of their own hard-won earnings.

Every visitor to Quebec, unless his heart be utterly ossified by the pursuits of trade and deadened to all sentiment, pays a visit to the Plains of Abraham, to the spot where Wolfe fell, marked by an obelisk, and to the steep path up the cliff from the shore, at the place now called Wolfe's Cove. The drive over the Plains to Cap Rouge would well repay the visitor by the beauty of the scenery, even were there no such history attached to the ground as to hallow it by the reminiscences of patriotic heroism and glorious death. The road runs parallel with the St. Lawrence from cape to cape, and the river bank is studded with the villas of the merchants of Quebec, each with its surrounding groves and gardens. The cultivated and inclosed ground has gradually occupied the battle-field and its approaches, so that it is now difficult to trace the actual scene of the conflict; but in the very heart of the battle, on the spot where Wolfe fell mortally wounded, a stone was erected in 1834—seventy-five years after the event—bearing the following simple and eloquent inscription:

HERE DIED

WOLFE,

VICTORIOUS.

Better in 1834 than never; but it was not creditable to the British government that three quarters of a century should have been suffered to elapse ere this tribute was paid to the gallant soldier and man of genius, who won for Britain so splendid a prize as Canada, and sealed the purchase with his blood. In the history of this great struggle it should always be remembered, to the enhancement—if that be possible—of the pure fame of Wolfe, that he and his army of Britons scorned to accept the murderous aid of the Indian tomahawk, and that, as far as Great Britain was concerned, it was a fair fight with fair weapons. When Montcalm was told that Wolfe had landed above the town, and made good his footing on the Plains, he refused to give credence to a fact so unexpected and alarming. "It must only be Wolfe and a small party," he said, "come to burn a few houses, look about him, and return." When no longer able to doubt that Wolfe, with a goodly force of British troops, and the Grenadiers burning to wipe off the stigma of a previous repulse at Montmorenci, were in actual military possession of the Plains and of the approaches to Quebec, "Then," said he, "they have got to the weak side of this miserable garrison; therefore we must endeavor to crush them by our numbers, and SCALP them all by twelve o'clock." Montcalm, though he did not hesitate to employ the Indians and their scalping-knives, was perhaps allowed no discretion in the matter by his superiors at home, and was not otherwise an ungenerous foe. He, too, lost his life in the struggle; and, ere dying, paid the British forces and Wolfe—who expired several hours before him—this magnanimous compliment: "Since it was my misfortune to be discomfited and mortally wounded, it is a consolation to me to be vanquished by so brave and generous an enemy. If I could survive this wound, I would engage to beat three times the number of such forces as I commanded this morning with one third the number of British troops."

It is difficult to decide which of these two great soldiers is most beloved by the existing generation of Lower Canadians. There is sympathy for the fate, and glory for the name of both. It is no longer bad taste for an Anglo-Saxon to praise Wolfe in the presence of a French Canadian, or for a French Canadian to glory before a British settler in the deeds and character of Montcalm. Time has effaced all jealousies, and to the victor and the vanquished are alike accorded the tribute of history and the love and respect of posterity.

Quebec possesses the beautiful public cemetery of Mount Hermon, two miles from the city, on the road to Cap Rouge. From every point of the grounds is to be obtained a fine view of the St. Lawrence, rolling far beneath the feet of the spectator the abundant current of its waters. Seen from that height, it seems to repose as calmly as the bosom of a mountain lake, and gives no evidence of the strength and majesty with which it sweeps to the Atlantic. The grounds of Mount Hermon are very tastefully laid out and planted; and, while sufficiently near to the city for convenience, are too distant to justify the fear that any possible increase of Quebec will ever render the cemetery intramural. Here, at the extremity of a leafy avenue, lies, under a handsome monument, erected by the liberality of his sympathizing countrymen, the body of John Wilson, the once-celebrated Scottish vocalist, who died of Asiatic cholera in Quebec in 1849. But the solitudes of Mount Hermon possess a more melancholy and a more interesting grave than this. In one long trench, two deep, one above the other, buried with their clothes on, as they died, lie no less than two hundred and sixty-two persons of all ages. Here are grandfathers and grandmothers, sons and daughters, husbands and wives, brothers and sisters, and little children, who all perished in the burning of the steam-ship *Montreal*, bound from Glasgow to Montreal, in June, 1857. The sad calamity excited a painful sensation throughout Canada, as well as in Scotland, from which nearly all the emigrants came. They were all of the best class of farmers and mechanics, mostly strong young men, with their wives and families, who had saved a little capital by prudence and thrift in the Old Country, and came hither in all the pride of health and strength, and in the flush of hope and enterprise, to try their fortune on a new soil. They had passed in safety through all the perils of the Atlantic, and for upward of six hundred miles through the Gulf and River of St. Lawrence, with the land of their adoption within an arrow's flight on either side of their ship. As the noble vessel passed Quebec on her way to Montreal, the people on the wharves and on the fortifications turned out to look at her; and one who had been a sailor, and had a keen eye for all the appurtenances of a ship, remarked to a comrade, "That vessel is on fire!" And so it proved. She had not steamed two miles past Wolfe's Cove when the flames burst out; and the captain, as the only chance of safety, drove her on shore on a narrow ledge of rock between Wolfe's Cove and Cap Rouge. Unfortunately, there were ten feet of water on the landward side of the ledge, and the distracted people, listening to no counsel, in their terror to escape from the dread enemy, Fire, leaped by scores and hundreds into the water, knowing nothing of its depth, and hoping to be able to wade ashore. Out of upward of four hundred souls, only about eighty were rescued; the remainder, including many hapless mothers and their little children, and many beautiful young girls, were drowned within sight—and, had they remained quiet and self-collected for a few moments longer, within reach—of deliverance. And here they lie in one long grave, their very names unknown, save, perhaps, to their sorrowing relatives in Scotland; and, in some instances, where whole families perished together, unknown to living man. Few of the survivors of the calamity remained in Canada. There seemed to their minds to be a curse upon the country, and they returned to the old land in despair. The loss to Canada was great. They were the very class of emigrants the most needed and the most useful; and their combined capital, and the use they could have made of it within four or five years, represented at least half a million of pounds sterling. The Canadians came forward on the occasion with a generosity that did them honor. The Scotch particularly distinguished themselves by the liberality of their subscriptions for the relief of the survivors. Quebec, Montreal, Toronto, Hamilton, and other cities contributed large sums to the fund. It seemed to me, when standing upon the spot, that few graves could be more affecting. The mounds raised over heroes slain in battle, or the trenches into which are thrust the victims of a plague, may appeal strongly to the sympathies of those who in the presence of Death remember humbly and reverentially their own humanity; but the grave of hope, of health, of strength, of youth, and of infancy, all mingled together by the accident of one moment—by one tick of the great pendulum of Fate—appeals still more potently both to the heart and the imagination.

Closely adjoining Mount Hermon, and on the same Heights of Abraham, is Spencer Wood, the summer residence of the Governor General of Canada, through the pleasant grounds of which our party strolled at will for upward of an hour ere we proceeded to an equally pleasant though smaller villa, where an English gentleman, retired from the British army to cultivate a Canadian estate, awaited our coming, and gave us a hospitable welcome.

But, though the Heights of Abraham and the road to Cap Rouge are among the first drives or walks taken by every visitor to Quebec who has time at his command, they are not the only excursions that should be made by those who have an eye for the picturesque, and who desire to enjoy the beauties of a land that is pre-eminently the land of torrents and waterfalls—a land that is even more musical with the voice of streams, than Scotland or Switzerland, and that possesses, in addition to the world's wonder, the great Niagara, such splendid cataracts as those of Montmorenci, Lorette, and the Chaudière. The ride to the Falls of Montmorenci, and that equally picturesque to the village and Falls of Lorette, can not be omitted by any traveler who dares to say, on his return to Europe, that he has been to Quebec. The ride to

Montmorenci, through the long village of Beauport, is only interesting from the glimpses which it affords of French Canadian peasant life. The fine church, the mean cottage, and the cross by the wayside, are all familiar objects to him who has traveled in Europe; but Beauport possesses characteristics of its own, which are due to the climate rather than to the people. The village (the head-quarters of Montcalm in 1759) extends nearly the whole distance from Quebec to Montmorenci, straggling on both sides of the way, each house presenting itself to the road diagonally, with a sharp corner. The front door is reached by a high flight of steps; both arrangements being essential to the comfort of the people in the long and severe winters of Canada. The cornerwise implacement of the houses allows the wintry winds to carry to the rear the snow which might in other circumstances be drifted to the front; and the high door is necessary for the safe egress and ingress of the people to their homes in seasons when the accumulated snowfall is often ten or twelve feet in depth. The windows of nearly every one of these cottages were so profusely filled with flowers as to challenge a stranger's attention not only to their beauty and choiceness, but to the elegant taste of the wives and daughters of the *habitans*, of whose love of floriculture they afforded such pleasant proofs.

The Montmorenci River discharges itself into the St. Lawrence over a high, precipitous bank of nearly two hundred feet—a very noble cataract. The winter seldom lays its icy touch upon the waters with such severity as to arrest the current, but every year the spray cast upward by the torrent is frozen ere it falls, and sprinkles the banks and the ice of the lower stream with showers of show, which form a cone or hill at a short distance from the fall. In cold weather this cone often rises as high as the upper level of the rock from which the river leaps. It is a favorite diversion of the citizens of Quebec, when the winter forbids all business, and nothing is to be thought of unless it be pleasure, or the balancing of the gains and losses of the previous spring and summer, to make excursions to Montmorenci, and give the young folks or the ladies a slide down the cone in cars constructed for the purpose. At the time of my visit, though the spring was far advanced, the cone still remained about forty feet in height, and the river, at the base of the fall, was thickly coated with ice. From one point of the rock, on the eastern side of the gorge, a fine view of Quebec, glittering at a distance of seven miles to the west, is to be obtained; while eastward stretches the island of Orleans, with its superabundant wild grapes, its sunny shores, and its fertile hills and valleys.

There is within the limits of the British Isles one spot from which a view equally grand and extensive is to be had, and that is at the very summit of Strone Point, in the Frith of Clyde; a place seldom visited, but which may be recommended to all pedestrians and lovers of the grand and romantic in scenery who find themselves on a summer day at Greenock, Kilmun, Dunoon, or any other of the beautiful watering-places for which the Clyde is celebrated, and who may wish to see at small effort, and without the necessity of crossing the Atlantic, a resemblance to the most romantic scenery of Canada.

The Falls of Lorette are not so picturesque as those of Montmorenci, but are well worthy of a visit, not only for their own beauty, but for their close proximity to the Indian village of Lorette, where resides the last scanty remnant of the once powerful tribe of the Hurons, the former lords and possessors of Canada. Paul, the chief or king of the tribe, is both the most exalted and the most respectable member of the tribe, and carries on with success, by means of the female members of his family, a trade in the usual Indian toys and knickknacks which strangers love to purchase, and in his own person cultivates a farm in a manner that proves him to be a skillful and thrifty agriculturist. His aged mother and her sister, the "Queen of the Hurons," received us hospitably in their neatly-furnished cottage; and the latter, eighty years of age, whom we regaled with a quart of Bass's pale ale, which she relished exceedingly, and drank off at two draughts, showed us a silver medal which she had received from Alderman Garratt, Lord-Mayor of London, in 1825, when she and her late husband, the "king," had visited London, to urge some claim of territorial right upon the British government. The old lady, in return for the interest I had expressed in her, and perhaps, also, to show her gratitude for the bitter ale, obligingly told my fortune by looking at my palm, and refused to receive fee or reward for her pains. What the fortune predicted was, and whether it has come true, need not be told farther than it was just as favorable and just as true as that with which any Gipsy nearer home could have flattered me; and any one more like a Gipsy than the "Queen of the Hurons" I never saw. I could not help believing, when I looked upon her, and as I do when I recall her to my mind, that the Red Men of the New World and the Gipsies of the Old are one people; the same in their features, build, and habits; in their restless and wandering mode of life; in their claims to the power of divination; and in their incapability of enduring continuous hard labor, or reaching any high degree of civilization.

CHAPTER XLI.

TORONTO.

From Montreal to Toronto by the Grand Trunk Railway is a long day's journey of 333 miles. The line passes by or near the towns of Cornwall, Prescott, Brookville, Kingston, Belleville, Coburg, Port Hope, Bowmanville, Oswaka, and others, of which the populations vary in numbers from 1800 at Port Hope, to 16,000 at Kingston. By taking the rail, the traveler misses all the scenery of the St. Lawrence, the Rapids, and the Thousand Isles, but as these are seen to greater advantage in descending the river, and as there is no possibility of shooting the rapids except with the current, the rail is the most expeditious mode of traveling from Montreal westward, and the steamer by far the best and most agreeable for travelers going east. I therefore left unvisited until my return the Thousand Isles and the Rapids, and, bidding a temporary farewell to the pleasant city of Montreal, started for Toronto at seven in the morning. The scenery after we lost sight of the

TORONTO.—CANADA WEST.

hills of Montreal, and the glistening spires and cupolas of the city, soon ceased to be picturesque, and all the way to Kingston, a distance of 173 miles, was flat and monotonous in the extreme. Our train was composed of five long cars of a construction precisely similar to that of the comfortless traveling kennels used in the United States; and the method of taking the tickets, and of allowing to the conductor the entire control over moneys received from the passengers who enter at the principal or at the intermediate stations, without the preliminary purchase of tickets, was exactly the same. Soon after leaving Kingston, our course for upward of 150 miles skirted the shore of Ontario. The lake was on this occasion roughened by a storm, that made its broad expanse far more picturesque than the flat, unvarying panorama on the landward side; from whence, ever and anon, as our train stopped, we could hear the load croaking of multitudes of frogs, which, from their power of lung, must have been of a considerably larger species than the largest bull-frogs of the Old World. I was informed by a passenger that these were the "veritable nightingales of Canada," and that their croak sounded uncommonly like the words "strong rum, strong rum." Our train reached its destination in little more than fourteen hours and a quarter, arriving at twenty minutes past nine in the evening, only five minutes after the advertised time. Such punctuality as this it was never before my good fortune to witness on any railway in America, and the speed, nearly twenty-nine miles an hour, including stoppages, was greater than the average rate of traveling in the States. Having taken up my quarters at the Rossin House, a monster hotel—the largest in Canada—conducted by an American on the American principle, I sallied out in the morning to take my first look at the legislative capital for the time being of the two Canadas.

The contrast between Toronto and the cities of Canada East was so marked and striking, that it was some time before I could persuade myself that I was not back again in the United States. In Montreal and Quebec, the solid, substantial aspect of the houses, the streets, the churches and public buildings, continually suggests the idea of Europe. Every thing seems to have the slow growth of centuries, as in France, Germany, and England. The streets seem to have arranged themselves to the wants of successive generations, and to have been made straight or crooked, wide or narrow, according to the need or caprice of the moment, and not in pursuance of any pre-devised plan. But Toronto, a thing of yesterday, a mere mushroom compared with the antiquity of Montreal and Quebec, though rivaling the one, and exceeding the other in trade and population, is built upon the American principle, which loves the economy of straight lines, asserts the necessity of system, prefers the chess-board to the maze, and the regularity of art to the picturesque irregularity of nature. It is first the plan and then the city; not the city in the first instance, to grow afterward, or to cease to grow as it pleases, as was the case with all cities more than two hundred years old.

The streets are long and straight. There is no more crookedness in them than there is in Philadelphia; and they all run at right angles to the lake; and one of them—York Street—is supposed on the map to stretch away—straighter than an arrow's flight—to Lake Simcoe, nearly forty miles distant. There is a Yankee look about the whole place which it is impossible to mistake; a pushing, thriving, business-like, smart appearance in the people and in the streets; in the stores, in the banks, and in the churches. I could not but observe, too, that there was a much larger predominance of Scotch names over the doors than I had previously seen in any other city of America. Looked upon from any part of itself, Toronto does not greatly impress the imagination; but seen from the deck of one of the ferry steam-boats that ply at regular intervals between the city and the long, low strip of a peninsula that, at a distance of four miles from the shore, protects the harbor, it has all the air of wealth and majesty that belongs to a great city. Its numerous church spires and public buildings; its wharves, factories, and tall chimneys, mark it for what it is—a busy, thriving, and expanding place. In the year 1793, the spot on which it stands was covered with a dense forest, amid which, close to the lake, might be seen the wigwams of the Mississagua Indians. The site was fixed upon by Governor Simcoe, and the future town named York, in honor of the Duke of York, then a favorite with the British army; and the ground cleared in 1794. The Parliament of Upper Canada met here in 1797. But the growth of the place was not rapid; for, in 1821, a quarter of a century after its foundation, it contained but 250 houses and 1336 inhabitants. During the next nine years its progress was more satisfactory; and its ambition was great enough to draw upon it the ill-will of other struggling places upon the lake, by whose inhabitants it was called in derision "Little York," "Dirty Little York," and "Muddy Little York." But "Little York" was well situated; its early inhabitants knew how to turn its advantages to account; and by rapid steps it became the seat of a large trade and of very considerable manufactures, among which those of furniture and machinery are now the most important. The name of Toronto, derived from the original Indian appellation of a collection of wigwams that once stood upon the same site, and signifying "the meeting-place," was adopted in the year 1834, at which time it had become a flourishing place of about 10,000 inhabitants. Since that period its progress has been greater than that of any other city in Canada. In ten years it nearly doubled its population, which in 1844 amounted to 18,420. In 1851 the population had increased to 30,755, and in the spring of 1858 to upward of 50,000. The number of houses in the city is 7476, of which 3212 have been built since 1850. The amount of real property within its limits is assessed at £7,288,150, the yearly value of which is estimated for purposes of local taxation at £437,289. The value of personal property is estimated at £1,296,616. Independently of the real property in the hands of citizens, the corporation of the city holds property in public buildings, lands, and water-lots estimated at upward of £430,000, and yearly increasing in value.

Toronto possesses no less than four daily newspapers, one of which, the *Globe*, circulates every morning about 19,000 copies, and the editor and proprietor of which is a member of the Legislature, and acknowledged leader of the Opposition in the Lower House. The other daily papers, the *Leader*, the

Colonist, and the *Atlas*, are also widely circulated, and conducted with much ability. The weekly and semi-weekly papers are too numerous to specify, and betoken by their success an amount of intellectual activity among the people that is not to be found in any city or town of the same size in the Old Country, or, indeed, any where out of London. It also possesses two small newspapers, of a class of which *Punch* is almost the only representative in England, and which have never yet been successfully established in any city of the United States—the *Poker* and the *Grumbler*—each a *Punch* in its way, without the illustrative wood engravings which make *Punch* so attractive. The Canadians seem to have more of the British and Irish relish for wit than exists among the people of the United States, who, if they enjoy broad humor, are for the most part, unless they have traveled in Europe, or are *littérateurs* by profession, quite unable to appreciate wit.

Toronto possesses a well-endowed University, several colleges and public schools, and may be said to have set an example to all Canada in the cause of public education. It also possesses a park for the health and recreation of the people, as well as for the amenity of the city, objects of which the necessity has not, unfortunately, been so manifest in other cities, both in Canada and the United States, as to induce either the early founders or the existing municipalities of the most populous among them to look so far into the future, or even into the wants of the present, as to purchase land for purposes so desirable.

The Legislature was in full session on my arrival; and having the honor of the acquaintance of one actual and three ex-ministers, and of half a dozen members of the Lower House, I was speedily made free of both chambers, and admitted to all such privileges of the floor as can be accorded to any one not actually a member. The proceedings were almost, if not quite, as devoid of ceremonial and formality as the State Legislatures of the American Union. Indeed, the only difference that I could discover was that at the back of the speaker's chair were the royal arms of Great Britain, and on the table before him, as in the House of Commons at home, a large silver-gilt mace—"that bauble," as Cromwell called it.

The "show-places" of Toronto, after the Houses of Parliament, are the University, the normal and model school, under the superintendence of the Rev. Dr. Egerton Ryerson, to whom education in Canada owes much ; and the furniture manufactory of Messrs. Jacques and Hay. All these establishments are not only interesting in themselves, but suggestive of the present importance and future progress of Canada. At the manufactory of Messrs. Jacques and Hay may be seen the production by machinery of furniture *en gros*, from the commonest stool, chair, table, or bedstead required for the log hut of the humblest settler in the wilderness, to the most costly ottoman and fauteuil demanded by the luxury of the richest merchant. Walnut wood, so expensive in England, is in Canada among the cheapest of the woods of which furniture is made.

Toronto has a great future before it. For the last ten years its progress has been such as to justify the expectation that it will rival, if not surpass Chicago and Milwaukee, still farther west, for it has advantages not possessed by either of these cities, and which will indubitably be turned to proper account when Canada shall be properly known to the emigrants of the British Isles. At present the great tide of emigration sets to the United States. Hereafter it is more than probable that Canada will be the favorite.

In looking at the vast capabilities of the two Canadas—in considering the climate, so much more congenial to the hardy races of the British Isles than that of Ohio, Indiana, Illinois, and Missouri—in considering, above all things, the fact that the immigrant into the Canadas enters into the enjoyment of a much greater degree of political liberty than is possessed in the United States, and that he does not thereby cut himself entirely adrift from the protection and relationship of the old and dear mother country with which he is associated by so many tender ties of memory and sympathy, one can not but feel surprise that the Canadas do not absorb a far larger proportion of the overflow of the teeming population of Great Britain and Ireland.

For one Englishman, Scotchman, or Irishman who fixes his lot in Canada, ten Englishmen, Scotchmen, and Irishmen try their fortunes in the United States; not because there is cheaper, better, and more abundant land to be had—not because there is a greater amount of rational liberty, or a lighter amount of local and imperial taxation, but apparently from a vague fear that a day must come when the Canadians will have to struggle for their freedom, and do over again what was done by the people of the United States in the days of Washington. There seems to be a dread that the battle for independence will have to be fought against England. Emigrants do not choose to run the risk of such a struggle, and to do such violence to their feelings as to take arms against the land of their love and of their childhood; against the land where rest the bones of their fathers; against which they have and can have no natural or even political animosity. If such be the idea or the instinct of the mass of emigrants, nothing can be more erroneous, as far as we can judge from the present politics, interests, and feelings of the Canadians; and as far also as we can judge from the tone and temper, and, let us hope, the increased wisdom of the British government. Should the Canadians ever wish to be independent, they have but to say the word, and the British people, so far from supporting the government in any attempt to thwart their wishes, will say, " Go ! God bless you ! May you increase and prosper ! You are blood of our blood, and bone of our bone ; and all that we desire of you—as we should desire of our dearest son—is that you should flourish, pay your own way, cease to be a burden or an expense to us, and remain forever our dearest friend and best customer." The same feeling would influence the government, whether it were Liberal or Conservative. The mistakes of George III. could no more be repeated in our day than the mistakes of King John or James II. ; and Great Britain, warned by experience, and having learned wisdom in adversity—and having, moreover, a truer appreciation of the value of colonies, and of the duty of the queen bee to the swarms that she sends forth, could not fall into the errors committed in the by-gone and almost antediluvian times of Washington and Lafayette. Public opinion has grown too strong for the commission of such blunders, and would not tolerate their repetition, even if a ministry could be found in our day wrong-headed and foolhardy enough to repeat them. And while the loyalty of the Canadas is an established fact, it is equally established on the other side that the Canadas must make their own way in the world, fight their own battle, and take their own choice. Great Britain, like a fond mother, will rejoice in their prosperity, even though it be acquired by their independence.

These considerations, if properly weighed and understood in the British Isles, will in due time cause a far larger stream of emigration to flow toward those noble provinces, and to the yet undeveloped wildernesses of the Red River and the Saskatchewan, than the superior attractions, though not the superior advantages, of the United States have yet permitted—and farther even than these remote regions—across the whole breadth of the continent, to British Columbia, Vancouver, and the shores of the Pacific.

CHAPTER XLII.

HAMILTON, LONDON, AND OTTAWA.

The flourishing city of Hamilton, in Burlington Bay, may be reached from Toronto, by the Great Western Railway of Canada, in an hour and a half, and by a pleasant drive along the shores of Lake Ontario. Hamilton contains a population of upward of 30,000, and has from small beginnings made as rapid a progress as any city in Canada. It aspires to rival, and looks with considerable jealousy upon Toronto. The principal journal of Hamilton was, at the time of my arrival, in great spirits at the supposed effects of a recent storm in the lake, which had made a breach through the long, narrow peninsula—six miles long, and about twenty yards wide—with its row of trees, which protects the harbor of Toronto. In the estimation of the writer, this catastrophe had ruined Toronto as a port. The people of Toronto, however, were of a different opinion, and looked upon the alleged calamity as a piece of great good fortune, in saving them the expense of cutting a previously projected canal through the very place which the storm had so opportunely broken down.

The inhabitants of Hamilton call it the "ambitious little city;" and if ambition is to be measured by deeds as well as by words, the promise is, in this case, justified by the performance. It is handsomely laid out with broad clean streets, and built upon the level of the lake. Behind it stretches what its people call "the Mountain," but the summit of which is merely the real level of the whole surrounding country—the margin of the great Lake of Ontario at a time, perhaps fifty or a hundred centuries ago, when its waters were on a height with the upper rapids of Niagara; and when between Kingston and the Thousand Isles there stretched toward Quebec and the Gulf of St. Lawrence that other lake, no longer existent, in which Montreal and Bel Œil were islands, and of which the Laurentian range on the one side, and the hills of Vermont on the other, were the boundaries. The position of Hamilton renders it extremely hot and close in the summer months, and such of its inhabitants as can afford the luxury of country villas betake themselves to the upper plateaux of the "mountain" in search of the cool breezes which are denied them in the city. It boasts not only a monster hotel on the American principle, but several fine churches and some commercial buildings which would do honor to St. Paul's Church-yard—among others, that of Mr. M'Innes, whose "dry goods' store" is upon a scale of magnitude that the great wholesale houses of London, whether in St. Paul's Church-yard or elsewhere, have not yet surpassed. Hamilton is of a decidedly Scottish character, Gaelic is often heard in its streets, but not to so great an extent as the Saxon Doric of the Lowlands. The names over the shop doors and stores smack of Sutherlandshire, Invernessshire, and Argyllshire. There are a few Germans and Irish to be found, as there are in every city in America, but the predominating race in Hamilton is the Scotch—both Highland and Lowland—all, or the greater part of them, thriving and well-to-do persons. At Montreal a Highlander introduced himself to me whose cottage or hut had been unroofed by order of the agents of a great Highland proprietor, and he and his wife and destitute family turned out upon the highway to live or die, as they pleased. Resolving not to die, and putting a brave heart to a rough work, he had emigrated to Canada, and, after years of patient industry, had succeeded in establishing himself as a merchant. Fortune had favored him, and he had built a mansion on the base of the hill of Montreal almost as large, substantial, and elegant as Spencer House in the Green Park of London, or the Duke of Sutherland's adjoining. And more than one such instance of prosperity, achieved by indomitable Highlanders cleared out of their small holdings by the supposed necessity that impels great proprietors to make sheep-farms of the valleys, and grouse-shootings or deer-forests of the hill-tops of the Highlands, were reported to me in Hamilton and in other parts of Canada. The desolate glens of Ballahulish, the bleak moorlands of the Black Mount, and the wide-stretching wildernesses of the Reay Forest, or "Mackay country," have contributed many stout hearts, strong arms, and clear heads to till the soil and develop the resources of Upper Canada; and though no thanks be due to such landlords in Scotland as think more of their rents than of the peasantry—more of money than of men—and who derive a larger revenue from bare hill-sides, where the sheep pasture with one solitary shepherd per square mile to guard them, than from the glens and straths which were formerly cultivated by hundreds of honest men who could fight the battles of their country in days of peril, the result has in numberless instances been to the advantage both of the expatriated people and the new land of their adoption. If Scotland have suffered, Canada has gained; and, "there being a soul of goodness in things evil," the pauper of the Old World has, by a little severity—if not too aged and decrepit when the operation was tried upon him—been converted into the flourishing farmer or merchant of the New, by a rough but, perhaps, wholesome process.

Want of time prevented me from extending my journey through the whole length of Western Canada to Sarnia upon the River St. Clair, a place described by a local poet, whose title-page affirms him to be both "satirical and sentimental:"

> "Sarnia is a thriving town,
>   And lately was incorporated,
> Has no rivals to pull her down,
>   Nor none against her can be created."

I also intended to visit the large city of Detroit—once on Canadian soil, but now the principal port of Michigan in the United States—but had only time to proceed as far as London, seventy-six miles beyond Hamilton. This place ought assuredly to have received another name. It is as interesting as any city in Canada for its rapid growth, and more so, perhaps, for the sudden check which its prosperity received in consequence of the recoil caused by the over-eagerness of land and building speculators to force it into premature importance by inadequate means. The name of the place and river was originally "The Forks;" but when its early founder absurdly chose to call it London, the river, on the high bank of which it is built, was with equal absurdity miscalled the Thames. And now, when it is a city of ten or twelve thousand inhabitants, and when its streets are either planned or laid out in anticipation of the day when it shall number fifty thousand or upward, the original idea has been carried out to the full extent in the naming of its principal buildings and thoroughfares. Thus we have in this "Forest City," as it is sometimes called, Blackfriars' and Westminster Bridges, Covent Garden Market and Theatre, Oxford Street, Piccadilly, Pall Mall, Grosvenor Street, and other appellations known in the world's metropolis, and the use of which, coupled with the word "London," very often leads to serious mistakes in the post-office, and sends to Europe letters and orders for goods which are intended for Canada. Every one with whom I came in contact during my visit was loud in denunciation of the folly, and there seemed to be a general wish that the city should receive the name of Huron, as more appropriate and distinctive. When the Anglican bishop for this part of Canada was appointed, it was intended to call him Bishop of London; but the inconvenience of this adoption of an ecclesiastical title already appropriated was felt to be so excessive, that on the representation of the Home Government the new prelate was called the Bishop of Huron, a precedent which will, perhaps, lead to the substitution of Huron for London in the name of a city that deserves, and is important enough to assert its own individuality. Toronto is infinitely better as the name of a city than York; Ottawa is a vast improvement upon Bytown; and, generally, the Indian names, wherever they can be adopted, are far more sonorous, musical, and appropriate than any names derived from the geography of Europe, or from individuals, illustrious or the reverse, who may have chanced to possess the land on which cities are built.

London had scarcely recovered from the effects of its reverse of fortune at the period of my visit. Its "Great American Hotel" was shut up for want of patronage, and a general depression seemed to hang over the place. But there can be little doubt, from its situation on the high road from the Atlantic to the Pacific, or, to speak more moderately, from Quebec, Montreal, and Toronto to Detroit and the Far West, that London will yet become a flourishing place, and justify the sanguine expectations of its early founders. Here, as in Hamilton and Toronto, the Scotch muster in large numbers, and are among the most thriving and respected of the inhabitants.

It was with regret that I left unvisited those rural districts of Upper Canada where the ultra-Highlanders, turned out of their holdings in the north, have founded a new Scotland, and where they unfortunately, in an unwise love of their mother-land, cultivate the Gaelic to the exclusion of the English language, and where, with a more pardonable love of country, they keep up the sports and games, the dress and music of the Gael, and are far more Highland in their habits and prejudices than Highlanders at home. After a short stay in London I turned my steps back toward the east, to accept an invitation to the city of Ottawa, the place selected by her majesty in council as the future capital of the United Provinces. Proceeding by rail beyond Toronto to Prescott, a miserable town at the eastern extremity of Lake Ontario, where it narrows into the St. Lawrence, and threads the mazes of the Thousand Isles, I passed the night in a fourth-rate inn, after the English, and not after the American fashion, and woefully remarked the difference. In the morning I proceeded to the station of the railway, first opened for traffic in December, 1854, and waited for some time the departure of the tardy train, amid a loud and exultant chorus of bull-frogs, amusing myself at times by looking at the frogs, and thinking of the lines of the poet of Sarnia,

"This pond is full of toads and frogs,
And here and there of rotten logs;"

and of his exclamation to the boys who pelted them with stones when they croaked "Strong rum! strong rum!"

"Oh, how can man be so unjust
As thus betray his Maker's trust?
Yes, tyrant man acts thus unholy,
His hopes of heaven's a *hyperboly!*"

But my principal amusement was to watch the antics of an unconscionably numerous family of little ones belonging to an Irish squatter who had taken possession of a piece of land by the road-side, and built himself a very respectable log hut, or wigwam, for it partook more of the nature of a savage than of a civilized edifice. At last we started, and in the course of three hours got over the distance of fifty-one miles, and arrived safely at Ottawa, on the border-line between Upper and Lower Canada—the very place that any intelligent person, unaware of, or making no allowance for established interests or ancient jealousies, would select, after a study of the map, as the most eligible and proper site for the capital of the two Canadas. And if a capital can be artificially created, Ottawa will be the capital of Canada. But as there are more things necessary for a capital than an act of the Legislature and the assembling of a Parliament within its boundaries, and as commerce has laws of its own over which Parliaments—imperial or provincial—are utterly powerless, it is tolerably certain that Ottawa never will become the commercial metropolis or the greatest and most populous city of Canada. As the small city of Albany is to the large city of New York, as Columbus is to Cincinnati, and Baton Rouge to New Orleans, so will the small legislative city of Ottawa be to the great commercial emporium of Montreal. Montreal is the real capital of the Canadas, and will continue to be so, whatever progress may be made either by such rival cities as Toronto on the one side, and Quebec on the other, and by such a neutral city as Ottawa, where the Canadian Parliament may well meet, but where Canadian merchants will most assuredly never congregate to the same extent as in the cities of the St. Lawrence. For the legislative capital Ottawa possesses many advantages of position, especially when considered in reference to the now extinguished jealousies of the Upper and Lower Canadians, and the possibility, though not the probability, of a war with the United States. In the last supposed case, Toronto would be at the mercy of a *coup de main;* and if Canada were independent and the nucleus of another and self-supporting system of allied commonwealths, in case of a purely American war, in which Great Britain had no concern, Montreal, since the abandonment of Rouse's Point and a large portion of Maine by the short-sighted stipulations of the Ashburton Treaty, would scarcely be defensible against an invading force from the United States. Quebec, it is true, with its strong natural position, rendered stronger by art, might bid defiance to any force dispatched against it; but fortresses do not make the most eligible capitals, and for this reason Quebec is objectionable. No such arguments apply against Ottawa; and though the selection made by her majesty, at the request of the Canadians themselves, whose jealousies and predilections in favor of Montreal, Toronto, Quebec, Kingston, and other places, rendered their agreement impossible, was somewhat ungraciously and ungenerously repudiated for a time, the Canadian Parliament has at length acquiesced, and the question may now be considered decided. Ottawa will be the future capital of Canada, town lots will rise in value, and the holders of real property in and around it will grow rich in consequence.

The original name of Ottawa was Bytown, derived from Colonel By, an officer of engineers, who led to its foundation in 1826 by the construction of the famous Rideau Canal, which connects the Ottawa River with Lake Ontario. It was found during the last war with the United States, that the transport of ordnance and other military stores up the St. Lawrence was rendered both difficult and hazardous, in consequence of the attacks made upon the vessels from the American side, and a bill was introduced into the Imperial Parliament for the construction of a canal to obviate this danger and inconvenience. The project was warmly supported for strategical reasons by the Duke of Wellington; and having passed both houses, and received the royal assent, Colonel By, the original projector, was intrusted with the execution of the works, and the canal was opened in 1832. Its cost was upward of £800,000 sterling.

The locks of the canal are of the most substantial masonry, and so many men were employed for some years in completing the works that the little village of Bytown grew in importance, until by degrees it began to arrogate to itself the name of a town, and afterward of a city. In the year 1854 its name was changed to Ottawa, and its present population, including that of its suburb of New Edinburgh, is estimated at about 10,000. The Rideau Canal divides it into the Upper and Lower Town. Its principal commerce is in timber, both sawn and square, the staple of Canada, for the transport of which from the rivers of the interior it possesses unrivaled natural advantages in the Ottawa and the almost equally important streams, the Gatineau and the Rideau. The sites for the new Parliament House and other public buildings have been already selected; and if the edifices themselves are worthy of the imposing situation on which it is proposed to place them, Ottawa will become one of the most picturesque cities in America.

Ottawa is sometimes called the "City of the Woods," but a more appropriate name would be the "City of the Torrents;" for it may truly be said that no city in the world, not even the straggling village, dignified with the name of a city, that has been laid out on the American side of Niagara, contains within it, or near it, such splendid waterfalls as those of which Ottawa can boast. The two falls of the Rideau into the Ottawa at the commencement of the suburb of New Edinburgh would be of themselves objects of great beauty and grandeur were they not eclipsed by the Chaudière, or Falls of the Ottawa, a cataract that possesses many features of sublimity that not even the great Niagara itself can surpass. To stand on the rock below the sawmill, looking down the boiling and foaming flood toward the Suspension Bridge that spans the fearful abyss, is to behold a scene of greater turbulence, if not of greater majesty, than Niagara can show with all its world of waters. The river does not leap precipitously over a sudden impediment as at Niagara, but rushes down a long inclined plane, intersected by ledges of rock, with a fury that turns dizzy the brain of those who gaze too long and earnestly upon the spectacle, and that no power of poet's or painter's genius can describe. No painting can do justice to a waterfall, and words, though capable of more than the pencil and the brush, are but feeble to portray, except in the old, stale set terms that have been well-nigh worn out in the service of enthusiasm, the ineffable magnificence of such mighty forces, obeying forever and ever the simple law of gravitation. If Niagara may claim to be the first and noblest cataract in the world, the Chaudière at Ottawa may claim to rank as second. And if ever the day comes when American travel shall be as fashionable and attractive as travel in Europe, no one will cross the Atlantic without paying a pilgrimage to the multitudinous waterfalls of Canada, or think his journey complete unless he has visited both Niagara and the Ottawa.

CHAPTER XLIII.

SHOOTING THE RAPIDS.

Not having time to visit Kingston, which, although it was once the capital of Upper Canada, has dropped somehow or other out of the line of march, and become a place almost as unprogressive and stagnant as its namesake in England, I was advised to make the town of Prescott my point of departure for a new and more beautiful trip on the St. Lawrence than I had yet undertaken. The scenery of the river between Prescott and Montreal was declared to be grander and more varied than in any other part of its course; for within the distance of 120 miles between the two were to be seen not only a portion of the fairy-like panorama of the Thousand Isles, which commence at Kingston, where the St. Lawrence, issuing from Lake Ontario, first assumes its name, but the long series of rapids, the "shooting" of which is a feat which must be accomplished by every traveler in Canada who desires to sow the seeds of the "pleasures of memory." Upon this advice I shaped my course. Bidding farewell to my kind and hospitable namesakes in the city of Ottawa, I took my seat in the car, and the train soon brought me to the little, dull, insignificant town of Prescott, where, lodged like the great Villiers, Duke of Buckingham, " in the worst inn's worst room," I was compelled to await the arrival of the steamer bound from Toronto to Montreal. Let me qualify the expression. My temporary abode was in reality the "best inn's best room;" but when best and worst are equally intolerable, or not to be distinguished the one from the other by a hair's breadth, it does not greatly signify which epithet be used.

As there had been a storm on the lake during two days previous, the steamer was beyond the advertised time, though hourly expected, and I had to amuse myself as best I could in an inchoate village in which there was nothing whatever to be seen or learned, and not even a newspaper to read. It is true that during the Canadian rebellion Prescott was invaded from the American shore by a too adventurous Pole, named Von Schulze, at the head of a small band of filibusters, and that he was captured by the British commanding officer, and hanged forthwith. But there was nothing in this historical incident to invest Prescott with additional attraction. Right opposite, upon the southern bank of the St. Lawrence, and in hourly communication with Prescott by a steam ferry-boat, stood Ogdensburg, in the State of New York, whence Von Schulze's expedition started. As it was apparently a large and populous city, I very much longed to visit it, if but to pass the time. But it was unsafe to run the risk of an hour's absence, for the Toronto boat might arrive at any moment, and would not delay at the wharf at Prescott above five minutes. As things turned out, I might have safely gone to Ogdensburg, for hour after hour passed away, noon succeeded to morning, evening to noon, and night to evening, lengthening themselves out till they were as attenuated as my weariness, and still there was no tidings of the tardy steamer. At midnight, worn out, sleepy, and, if the truth must be told, somewhat out of patience with the place, I lay down in my clothes upon the bed with strict injunctions to a messenger whom I had kept all day in my pay to arouse me the moment the steamer appeared in sight. At three in the morning, sixteen hours after her time, the lights of the approaching vessel came within view of my scout. I was duly aroused, according to agreement, with two other expectant passengers, the one from Hartford, in Connecticut, and the other from Chicago. Guided through the dark and muddy streets by a man with a lantern, we had the mortification to arrive at the wharf just three minutes too late, the steamer having landed a passenger in hot haste, and started off again without waiting to ascertain whether there were any others to come on board. We saw the lights of her stern-cabins shining brightly through the gloom of the night; and the man of Connecticut, who was very anxious to get on, having vented his wrath and his disgust in a volley of imprecations in the choicest Yankee slang, we retraced our steps, in the worst possible humor, to the inn, and held a council of war around the stove. The Yankee ordered a glass of "whisky-skin," very hot, which restored him to something like equanimity, and the agent of the boat, who was responsible for not having given the captain the proper signal to stop, having, as in duty bound, thrown the entire blame of our disappointment upon the absent skipper, we went quietly to bed, to await the next regular boat, the *Kingston*, due at eight in the morning. Much to our satisfaction, the *Kingston* was punctual to her time. The weather was magnificent, and we started for Montreal, none the worse for our disappointment in body or mind, and but little lighter in pocket; for if the hotel in which we had wasted the day was bad, we had but little to pay, and might have exclaimed with the Englishman who traveled for the first time in a railway car from New York to Philadelphia, "that we never had so large an amount of discomfort for so small an amount of money."

The "Thousand Isles," through which the St. Lawrence winds its way in beautiful intricacy from Lake Ontario to the Rapids of the Long Sault, are said to number in reality considerably upward of a thousand, if not of fifteen hundred; and though, in embarking at Prescott, we may have missed two thirds of them, we saw sufficient to be enabled to judge of their variety and loveliness. Some of them were fringed with trees to the river's bank; others were smooth, flat, and grassy as a bowling-green; some were rocky, bare, and small as a dining-table; while others were of fifty or a hundred acres in extent, and presented hill and dale, wood and coppice, meadow and pasture to our view, as the steamer shot rapidly by, sometimes in a narrow but deep channel, scarcely wider than our deck, and at others through a reach of the river as broad as the Thames at Waterloo Bridge. The man from Connecticut, one of that class of Job's comforters who will never allow a stranger to enjoy the loveliness of any natural scene present and palpable before him without reminding him that he has left unvisited something still finer which he might and ought to have seen, emphatically made me understand that all this beauty was as nothing to the scenery between Kingston and Prescott; that I had been misdirected and misinformed; that I had not seen any portion of the real "Thousand Isles;" and that the little "scraps" of rock and island amid which we were passing, and which to my eyes appeared quite fairy-like in their beauty and multitudinous in their number, were mere "humbugs" and "false pretenders." This personage, hard as he tried, was not able to mar my enjoyment by his companionship; and even he became excited as we approached Dickenson's Landing, shortly below which commences the Great Rapid of the Long Sault, or "Long Leap," pronounced Long *Soo* by the Americans and the English. Having taken in one and disembarked another passenger, we prepared to "shoot" the rapid, and all became bustle and excitement on board. The order was given to let off steam, and at a sudden bend of the river, where the banks seemed as if they had contracted to deepen the channel, the white crests of the waves, foaming like the breakers on a rocky coast, became visible, and the roar of the descending waters was heard, dull, heavy, and monotonous, but grand as a requiem sounded from a cathedral. Most of the ladies, and more than one of the rougher sex, whose nerves were unable to bear the excitement of the scene, retired into their state-rooms or the saloon; and those who had resolved to stay upon deck provided themselves with plaids and wrappers as a protection against any sudden dash of the waters, should our fast-driving keel strike against a billow at an angle too acute. We kept to the northern or Canadian side of the rapid, which, in the days ere steam-vessels plowed these stormy waters, and when the only craft that ventured down were the light canoes of the Indians, was supposed to be more dangerous than the other, and called "La Rapide des Perdus," or the Rapid of the Lost. We were speedily in the midst of great round eddies twenty or thirty feet in diameter, and, ere we had time to admire them, shot down fast as a railway express from London to Brighton, or faster if that be possible, in the bubbling, raging, foaming, thundering, and maddening waters, our prow casting up clouds of spray that drenched the deck, and formed rainbows ere they fell. At intervals there came some tremendous "thud" on the side of the steamer, causing her to stagger and shiver through all her framework, like a living creature mortally wounded, and the spray, mounting as high as the top of the funnel, fell like a torrent upon the deck. Then a moment of comparative calm succeeded, to be followed by another thud and another shower. In the space of five hundred yards, which we shot through in from two to three minutes, but which one lady, very much alarmed and excited, declared had occupied us half an hour, the St. Lawrence falls no less than thirty feet, a declivity more than sufficient to account for this magnificent perturbation and "hell of waters." The whole scene, heightened by the novelty, the excitement, and the danger, impressed itself upon my mind as the third greatest marvel that I had seen in America, and only next to the Rapids and Falls of Niagara and the Chaudière at Ottawa. Now that the feat is accomplished almost every day by large steamers, the Canadians and Americans look upon it as a matter of course, and do not seem to be really aware of the danger of the achievement and the grandeur of the scene. If he were a bold man who ate the first oyster, heroic and of Titanic energy and audacity was the captain or pilot of the first steam-vessel that ever braved the frantic whirlpools of the Long Sault, and came out triumphantly from among them.

We were again in smooth water in much less time than it takes to tell the story, and in about three quarters of an hour stopped for a few minutes at Cornwall, the frontier town of Canada West, and were again in sight of the land of the *Habitans*. Steaming on once more through a succession of small islands—and the St. Lawrence most certainly contains ten times, if not twenty or fifty times, as many islands as any other river known to travelers or geographers—we emerged into the broad, quiet Lake St. Francis, also studded with islands. This lake, or enlargement of the river, is about fifty miles in length, but of a breadth scarcely sufficient to justify its appellation of lake in preference to that of river. At its eastern extremity is the little town of Coteau du Lac, where commences a new series of rapids, all of which we had to "shoot," and the first of which is at a short distance beyond the town. It is one of the rapidest of the rapids; and our steamer shot it like an arrow in two minutes, and launched itself into a deep, and comparatively placid but strong current, where we scarcely required the aid of steam to carry us along at the rate of twelve miles an hour. Becoming *blasés* with rapids, as people will do with almost every thing in this world except sleep, we passed in succession the Cascades and the Cedars, the latter with its little church and tin spire, built upon the shore of the foaming current, suggesting in a new form Byron's beautiful though well-worn simile of "love watching madness." To these succeeded the Rapid of Beauharnais, after shooting which with the accustomed drenching, though with less excitement among the strangers than had been exhibited at the Long Sault, we glided into another expansion of the river, known as the Lake St. Louis, at the extremity of which the dark brown and turbid Ottawa mingles with the blue and clear St. Lawrence. Here we came in sight of the large island of Montreal, which interposes itself between the uniting but not commingling rivers, the one of which rises far in the farthest West, and the other runs through a country scarcely half explored, except by forlorn remnants of the Indians, and the scouts, trappers, and fur-traders of the Hudson's Bay Company. The Ottawa, seen in the distance from Lake St. Louis, looks broad as an estuary widening into a sea, but it speedily narrows and sweeps along the northern shore of Montreal island to effect a second junction with the St. Lawrence, of which the deeper and more vigorous current rushes impetuously to the south, down a steep incline to Lachine, the last of the magnificent series of the rapids. Lachine —so called by an early navigator, who imagined, as Hendrik Hudson did a little farther south, that he had found the western passage to China—is nine miles above the city of Montreal, and the roar of the rapids may be heard in the still midnight in the streets of Montreal, when the wind is from the west, almost as distinctly as if the torrent were in the heart of the town.

The Rapids of Lachine, though they do not run a course so lengthened as the Long Sault, and are not in themselves grander or more picturesque, are far more perilous to navigate. They are jagged, and dotted both with sunken and visible rocks, scattered in most perplexing confusion, lengthways or athwart, at every possible and apparently impossible angle, amid the rushing waters. Any one beholding the turmoil of the flood, and the innumerable Scyllas on the one side, balanced by as many Charybdises on the other, would be quite justified—if no previous adventurer had made the perilous journey—in pronouncing the attempt to " shoot" them, either in large vessel or small skiff, an act beyond foolhardiness—a reckless tempting of Fate, if not a proof of positive insanity. But the feat was continually accomplished by the Indians of

Caughnawaga, opposite to Lachine, at the head of the rapids, in their frail canoes, long before the white man and his steam-vessels had penetrated to the shores of the St. Lawrence; and the danger and the means of surmounting it became alike familiar to them. Whether by treaty, and as a recompense for the surrender of their lands, or whether entirely on account of their superior knowledge of the intricacies of the rapids, or whether for both reasons in combination, was not made clear to my comprehension, either by the individuals, or the books that I consulted on the point; but for some of these reasons, if not for all, the Indians of Caughnawaga—a remnant of the Iroquois—enjoy the legal monopoly of the pilotage. Letting off steam at Caughnawaga, we lay to, opposite the village, for a few minutes, to allow the pilot to come on board. The squaws and other idlers turned out in considerable numbers to the shore to witness our passage, and I saw enough of the village, which is inhabited entirely by the Indians, to excite a desire to visit it, if only to investigate the kind of life they lead in their state of semi-barbarism, and what progress they have made in the arts of civilization. It was evident, even from the shore, that they had not been entirely neglected by the clergy, for a handsome Roman Catholic church, with the glittering tin spire, universal in Lower Canada, proved that their spiritual welfare had been deemed a matter of importance. The zeal of the Roman Catholics for the extension of their faith in Canada, and the wealth they have scraped together for the purpose, should make Protestants blush for their own lukewarmness. The immediate successors of Jacques Cartier, by introducing not only the feudal tenures, but the ecclesiastical zeal of Old France into the New France which they founded, proved that they knew how to colonize upon system. They left nothing to hazard, and, wherever they went, the Pope and the Church went with them; an example which the Church of England seems never to have had the zeal or the wisdom to follow, except lately in a small corner of New Zealand. I was not able to carry into effect my design of visiting the Iroquois in their village, but learned that their advances toward civilization have not extended much beyond

SHOOTING THE RAPIDS. 395

costume and the love of "fire-water;" that the gipsy element is strong in them, and that continuous hard labor is considered fitter for squaws than for men.

Our pilot started from shore in a canoe, and, on reaching the "Kingston," sprang nimbly upon deck—an indubitable Red Man, but without paint and feathers—in the European costume of his vocation. He had a keen black eye and a quick hand, and seemed to be fully aware of the importance of the task he had undertaken, and of the necessity that lay upon him to have every faculty of mind and body on the alert, to carry our vessel in safety down this frantic staircase of seventy feet in a run of about three miles, intersected and encumbered by many rocks, and with a current rushing, in some places, at the rate of fifteen or twenty miles an hour. Our trusty pilot was equal to his work. He was all nerve—and nerves —and at one point more especially of our mad career, when we seemed to be running right upon a point of rock projecting about two feet above the surface of the torrent, to be inevitably dashed to pieces, a sudden turn of his wrist altered our course instantaneously, and sent us down a long reach, amid showers of dashing spray, at reckless speed, like a railway train, full tilt upon another heap of rocks, that seemed absolutely to bar the passage. A delay of one second in altering our course would have been certain perdition; but the mind of the Red Man, quick as electricity, communicated its impulse to his hand, and his hand, with the same rapidity, to the wheel, and away we were again, before we could draw breath, safe in deep waters, dancing along impetuously, but safely, into new dangers, to be as splendidly and triumphantly surmounted. The trees upon either side seemed to pass out of our field of vision as instantaneously as the phantasmagoria seen in a magic lantern; and when we darted at last into the blue water, and saw far behind us the snowy wreaths and feathery crests of the mountainous waves through which our ship had whizzed like an arrow, the propriety of the expression, "shooting the rapids," needed no justification but this scene and its remembrance. It should be stated that, although many canoes and boats have been lost in the rapids, no accident has ever yet happened to a steam-vessel in navigating them.

We speedily arrived at what is called the "Tail of the Rapids," a strong but equable current; after which, having fallen two hundred and seventy feet between the Long Sault and Montreal, the St. Lawrence runs to the sea without farther obstruction, as calmly as our English Thames. Ere sunset the city of Montreal, and the solid piers and masonry of the Tubular Bridge, were in sight, and before dark I was safe again, amid the kindly society and cheerful hospitalities of Rosemount.

CHAPTER XLIV.

EMIGRATION.

Montreal, May, 1858.

THE population of Canada in 1858 is considerably greater than that to which the ancient and illustrious kingdom of Scotland had attained in the first year of the present century, long ere its name and fame in literature, science, art, and arms, had become famous over the civilized world. It is about as great as that of England was when William the Conqueror dispossessed Harold of his throne, and little inferior to that of Norman England when Henry V. gained the victory at Agincourt, and sowed the seeds of that animosity between Englishmen and Frenchmen which have unfortunately germinated since that day into results which philanthropists may deplore, but of which British and French statesmen are bound to take cognizance, if they would govern their countrymen either in war or in peace. It is not because its population is so small, but because its territory is so great, and its resources so little known, that Canada is considered in its infancy, and because it is conterminous with a republic so much older, more developed, and more populous than itself. Stretching westward from the Gulf of St. Lawrence along the northern margin of the great chain of lakes, Canada—even if no additional territories in the fertile regions of the Red River and the Saskatchewan be included hereafter within its boundaries —has room enough for a population as great as that of France or Germany, and only requires men and time to rank among the greatest powers of the earth. Its water communication alone would point it out as a country destined in no very distant Hereafter to play a great part in the drama of civilization. An ordinarily intelligent study of the map is sufficient to show that the line of the southern Canadian frontier, along the shores of Ontario, Erie, Huron, Michigan, and Superior, will become the highway of the trade and travel of Europe to the Pacific Ocean, if what is called the "lay" of the country be more favorable for the development of railway communication than the regions of Central North America to the south of the lakes. And this it appears to be from the reports of all the scientific men who, either in official or non-official capacities, have explored the land. A great railway will inevitably unite the Atlantic and the Pacific Ocean through British territory, although it is possible that a southern line may also be constructed across the centre of the United States. But the Canadian and British line will have the advantage, for the solid and substantial reasons that the engineering difficulties are not nearly so many or so costly; that the country lies on a much lower level, and that there is no high plateau of utterly barren ground, twelve hundred miles in extent, to be traversed in the centre of the line. Between the Canadas, the Red River settlements, and the great districts of the Saskatchewan, and the Fraser River, British Columbia, and Vancouver, there will be but the territory at the head of Lake Superior, which will not ultimately repay, by its own traffic, the expenses of its construction; while the Atlantic and Pacific line, through the centre of the United States, across the Rocky Mountains, will have to traverse a bleak and howling wilderness, never to be settled at any time, because quite incapable of cultivation, and extending for more than twelve hundred miles.

When the outlying British provinces of Nova Scotia, New Brunswick, and Cape Breton are connected by rail with each other and with the Canadas, and when the Grand Trunk

Railway shall be linked with other grand trunk lines as great and useful as itself, British America will become strong enough to rival the United States both in commerce and in politics. There has lately been considerable talk, if not agitation, in Canada in favor of a federation of the North American Colonies, which, in consequence of the want of railway communication, are very little known to each other. But such a federation is not likely to take place while they remain dependencies of the British crown. Their ignorance of each other leads to jealousies sufficiently great to render their union a difficult achievement, if left to themselves to effect; and as the mother country has nothing to gain, but might possibly have something to lose by encouraging the idea, there is no likelihood that it will make much progress or meet with adequate encouragement on either side of the Atlantic. If, from any circumstances in their own or British history, these noble colonies should hereafter declare themselves independent, their federation for mutual protection would either precede that event, or immediately follow it as a matter of course. But, under existing circumstances, the best federation which they can establish is the federation of railways and the union of interests, of which commerce is the best and readiest instrument.

The passion or instinct of loyalty is so strong in Canada, that even the recoil of the great rebellion of 1839 has increased the fervor of the sentiment instead of diminishing it, as it might have done. Both Upper and Lower Canada once possessed a kind of aristocracy composed of what are called the " U. E. Loyalists," or " United Empire Loyalists;" persons who disapproved of the war waged against the mother country by Washington; who, while they deplored the ill-judged proceedings of King George III. and his ministers, held that nothing could justify rebellion, and fled across the St. Lawrence to avoid staining their consciences with an opposition which they stigmatized as treason. Loyalty *à l'outrance* was their motto, as it was that of the Cavaliers of England in the days of Oliver Cromwell. This feeling survives in their descendants. The very rebels pardoned by the British government after the events of 1839 have become as truly loyal and as fervent in the expression of their attachment to the crown of Great Britain as the most zealous living representatives of the U. E. Loyalists of old. The change in the popular feeling is perfectly natural. Throughout the whole of those unhappy disputes, which had well-nigh cost Great Britain her most valuable colony, the government at home, supported by the people, acted with enlightened and far-seeing generosity, forbore to exasperate grievances by superciliousness or neglect on the one side, or by vindictiveness on the other, admitted to the fullest extent the right of the Canadians to self-government, and by a series of truly liberal measures prepared the way for that democratic freedom which the Canadians enjoy, and which could not by any possibility be theirs if their institutions were identified with those of their brethren on the other side of the Lakes, or if they had, like them, to elect a President every four years. Canada enjoys a far greater amount of liberty than any nation on the globe, unless Great Britain be an exception; and if it be, the Canadians have far less to pay for their freedom than their brethren in the Old Country. The national debt of Great Britain touches them not. They are defended by British soldiers and British ships of war without cost. The standard of England, which prevents all nations from insulting them, costs them nothing to uplift. They have but to pay their own way, and to be happy in an allegiance nominal in its burden, but real in the protection which it insures. The Canadians are fully impressed with the value of these advantages, and are not likely to imperil them either by a self-sacrificing annexation to the United States, or by a costly independence of Great Britain, which would entail upon them all the expenses of a nation that had to provide for its own security against the world, and especially against its nearest neighbor.

As already observed, the first want of Upper Canada—for Lower Canada is well peopled—is men; men who will push out into the wilderness, fell and clear the forest, found villages, towns, and cities, and run the race that is run by their kindred in the more popular emigration fields of the "Great

West" of the United States. Men of the right sort are, and will continue to be, the wants of Canada, and of the colonies planted, or to be planted, between the present western limits and the shores of the Pacific Ocean.

But who are the men of the right sort? Let no reader of these pages be deceived. It is but one class of men whose presence will be acceptable to the Canadians or advantageous to themselves. Loiterers about cities—fellows who herd in the back slums, and think the life of the backwoodsman too hard for their dainty fingers, or for their notions of what is right and proper, should remain in Europe, and not presume, with their sickly education, to venture into the free, fresh air and rough work of the wilderness.

Canada requires, and will require, a large stream of immigration; and yet immigrants are hourly arriving who are not wanted, and Montreal, Toronto, Hamilton, and Quebec swarm with young and middle-aged men, who find it quite as difficult to "get on" as they ever could have done in Great Britain. Who, then, are the classes that should emigrate to Canada? This is a question that should be well and thoroughly debated by all who, not having elbow-room at home, imagine that they must, of necessity, have greater scope in America. Those who ought not to emigrate may be designated in a few words as those who expect to live by their brains—by trade, commerce, or professions of any kind. Neither clerks nor shopmen, nor men with ready pens or readier tongues, should try their fortunes in Canada. Such men are always to be had in young communities in greater numbers than young communities require, and are useless in a country where rough work is to be done, and where one good blacksmith, stone-mason, or plowman is worth half a dozen clerks and a score of barristers. The strong men who inherit nothing from their forefathers but their brawny limbs and their good health, and who, by the employment of their physical strength, with more or less of skill and industry, are able to derive their subsistence from the land—these are the people wanted. The classes who, by the exercise either of more than an average amount of talent, or the enjoyment of more than an average amount of social advantages derived from education, desire to live pleasantly, should stay at home. Their existence in this old is far more comfortable than it can be in a new country, which desires them not, and has no adequate field for the exercise of their abilities, except in rare instances, which are speedily taken advantage of by people on the spot.

It is the agriculturist who is the most urgently required; the class that in the British Isles is the most hardly used, whatever Arcadian poets and Belgravian novelists may urge to the contrary. Traditionally and poetically, or telescopically viewed, we are told that in England the cottages of this class peep out from the verdure of the land; that the roses blossom at their doors; that the ivy and the honeysuckle clamber over their walls; that the swallow builds in their thatch; that the lark and the nightingale, the blackbird and the thrush, make music for them; that the honest house-dog watches at their gate; and that their children sport beneath the lofty elms, or make garlands in the fields of the butter-cups and daisies. They are said to be the wealth and the boast of the nation. Out of their ranks, as we are told, is recruited the vigor of the generations. They are a bold and independent race. Honesty is their stay. Health is their portion. A sufficiency is their reward. All this is very fine, but, unluckily, it is not true. Actually or microscopically considered, what are the peasantry of England? Enter one of their cottages and look around, and all the glory and poetry disappear. The peasant is found to be a man of many sorrows. He toils for an insufficiency. He has not wherewithal to cover himself in comfort from the inclemency of the weather. His cottage is ill furnished and dirty, and has no convenient separation of apartments for the decencies of a family. A dung-heap and a cesspool fester at his door. His intellectual life is as degraded as his physical. If he reads at all, which is very doubtful, he has read the Bible, but whether with understanding or without, it is hard to say. He goes to church because his fathers went before him, and because men better dressed than himself have set him the example, and urged upon him the duty of going. He is told when he gets there that he is a miserable wretch; that, by the inscrutable decrees of Providence, the many must ever be the hewers of wood and the drawers of water, and that he is born into that state, and must live in it. He is warned to respect those above him, and to be contented with his lot. If he be a true man, he learns, after his own humble and dejected fashion, that there may be some chance for him in heaven if not on earth. If he be not a true man, if he have no spiritual life in him, if he have no hope for the future, he becomes reckless and brutal, seeking for animal enjoyment wherever he can find it, and seizing eagerly the coarse pleasures and excitements of the passing day, lest death and annihilation should come upon him before he has enjoyed any thing at the expense of any body. His wife is prematurely old with bearing many children and many woes. She labors hard and has no rest. Her children toil before their bones have acquired consistency; and the combined labor of the family, provided they could procure work for the whole year, might maintain them in coarse food indifferently well, and supply them indifferently well with coarse raiment. But they can not procure work all the year round, and the moderate sufficiency of six months so dearly bought is painfully beaten and hammered out into an insufficiency for twelve.

When decrepitude or old age—and the first often precedes the second—comes upon the peasant and his wife, they have no resource but the poor rate. They are a broken-spirited and utterly worn-down couple, and become a burden to the community. If a young, vigorous man of this class wished to possess for himself a small portion of his mother earth, he must expatriate himself. At home, though no serf *de jure*, he is a serf *de facto*. The land is so valuable as to shut utterly against him the slightest chance of his ever obtaining one yard of it to call his own. There are many thousands of such people in England, to whom the Canadas would offer a career of industry, usefulness, and prosperity. Let them depart, and benefit themselves, the country which they quit, and that to which they go. And not only the Englishman of this class, but the Scotchman and the Irishman will be welcome to Canada, if they can fell the forest, plow the land, shoe a horse or

EMIGRATION. 403

a man, or do any kind of hard-hand work, such as is required in the wilderness. As much trash has been spoken of the Scottish as of the English peasant. It is said that, though he live in a cold and moist, it is by no means an unhealthy climate. We are told that the grandeur and the glories of nature surround him; that the everlasting hills rear their magnificent peaks on his horizon; that fresh-water lakes of extreme beauty are imbedded among his hills, and that salt-water lochs wind far into the country from the sea, presenting not only the sublimities and splendor of scenery to his eyes, but wealth for his wants, if he will but labor in search of it. We are told, moreover, that, although the hills are bleak and bare, the glens and straths are green and capable of cultivation. Even if the country be deficient in coal and wood, nature is so bountiful that the peasant need not perish from the inclemency of the climate, inasmuch as great tracts of moorland are spread on every side, affording him an inexhaustible supply of fuel. But how does the so-called fortunate peasant live? What has civilization done for him? What has he done for himself? The answer should be, that he has done nothing for himself; that he is but half civilized; that he is worse off than his forefathers; that he lives in a miserable wigwam built of unshapely stones gathered from the *débris* of the mountains, or lying loose on the uncultivated soil; that the interstices between them are rudely plastered with mud; that he has very often no windows to his hut, and that, if there be a window, a piece of paper commonly serves the purpose of a pane of glass. When there is a chimney—a somewhat rare case—an old tub without top or bottom, stuck amid the rotten heather of the roof, answers for a chimney-pot. The door is low, and he has to stoop before he can enter it. He gathers his fuel from the peat moss, a privilege accorded to him for the labor of a certain number of days upon the farm of which the moorland forms a portion. The smoke from this peat-fire fills his wigwam and exudes from the door. The floor is of earth, and damp; and the cow which he keeps shares the shelter of his own roof. He has a little patch of ground, reclaimed perhaps from the moorland, for which he pays a considerable rent in labor, if not in money, and on this patch of ground he grows potatoes. He has little or no skill in agriculture beyond the skill necessary to plant his potatoes, but does as he is bid in a clumsy way when he works for other people. Oatmeal porridge, on which his forefathers grew strong, is a rare luxury with him. The easily-raised and less nutritious potato is much cheaper, and supplies its place. If his landlord, or his landlord's factor, will permit him, he marries upon his potatoes. If the landlord does not wish that he should marry, for fear of an increase of the population, inconvenient always to landlords who have not the skill, the enterprise, or the capital to employ them, he either dispenses with the ceremonial part of the business, or emigrates to Glasgow or some other great town, and trusts to Providence to live some*how* and some*where*.

If he remains on his potato-patch, and marries by consent, he has a large family; for, by a provision of nature, now beginning to be understood by political economists, each pair of living beings threatened with extinction by habitual insufficiency of nourishment becomes prolific in proportion to the imminency of the danger.[*] He is idle and dirty in his habits, and his children are like him. If he can now and then get a little oatmeal-cake and a herring in addition to his potatoes, a little milk for his children, a pinch of snuff now and then, and much fiery whisky for himself, he envies no man in existence, except, perhaps, the laird and the minister. All around his wigwam are large tracts of country capable of cultivation, if capable people were allowed to undertake the task of clearing, draining, and manuring it, and if the owners of these tracts had the energy and the capital to exercise the duties of proprietorship. Undrained and untilled, these lands, if not valuable for raising corn and men, are admirable for raising sheep and preserving grouse. There is little or no expenditure of capital necessary for this purpose on the part of landlords. The hill-sides afford excellent pasturage; and as sheep and black cattle can be herded in such a country at a small expense of men and money, the land is let out in large farms

[*] See Mr. Doubleday's Theory.

for this purpose, and at very heavy rentals. Additional rentals are procured for the right of grouse-shooting. None of the mutton, none of the beef, none of the grouse or other game, finds its way to the larder of the peasant, unless he steals it—which he sometimes does, taking his chance of the penalty. When peasants grow too numerous for a sheep and cattle feeding country, for the confines of a deer-forest, or for the due cultivation of that more valuable two-legged animal, the grouse, the less valuable two-legged animal, man, is "cleared out." The superabundant and useless people are warned to depart within a certain period. If they neglect the warning, their wigwams are pulled down over their heads, and they are left to the moorland and the hill-side, to enjoy an equality of shelter with the moor-fowl or the sheep. If any of these people have been provident or penurious enough to scrape a few pounds together, or if they have any remote cousins settled in the New World who have lent them a little money for the purpose, they emigrate to the United States, or perhaps to Australia—any where where a man has a likelihood of being considered a man, and of living his life without oppression. These are the men that ought to go to Canada; these are the men that Canada requires; and these are the men who, if they go there, will increase and multiply, and replenish the earth.

The Irish Celtic peasant, when he is at home, leads much the same kind of life, except that he is not quite so closely elbowed as the Highlander is by the grouse and the deer. He is not the patient ass that browses upon the thistle, and takes insults from all comers. Though he, too, lives in a wigwam, and shares it with a pig, the priest comforts him when no one else will take the trouble. When a war breaks out among the nations, this class of men, partly from the misery of their daily fare and the wretchedness of their daily attire, partly from the ignorance which accompanies extreme poverty, and partly from a barbarian love of finery, press or are pressed into the legions of battle, and die in scarlet coats and feathered caps for the supposed good of their country. If war does not require him, and he has neither energy to emigrate nor friends to supply him with the means of paying his passage across the Atlantic, he comes over to England in the harvesting-time, and gains a few pounds to help him through the winter. Some of his good friends, who wish to try experiments at his expense, settle him upon the coast, and lend him a boat and buy him nets, and tell him to fish in the sea, and not allow the Danes and Norwegians to come down hundreds of miles, and take away the wealth that the great deep affords. No doubt the man ought to fish, but he does not. The change is disagreeable to the Celt. He does not like continuous hard work. A potato-diet has weakened his energies. He has no fancy for the sea. He loves the old ways. Could he be allowed to fish in the rivers, he would be willing enough; but fresh-water fish are the property of the landlord, reserved for aristocratic, and not plebeian sport and profit. Salt sea fishing is another matter. There is no landlord right upon the ocean. The great deep is free. There is no possibility of deriving any rents from the billows; but, free as it is, the peasant from the interior can make no use of it. He not only detests sea work, but has no skill in the management of boats or nets. He has, in fact, no liking for or knowledge of the business in any shape or degree. The strange result is that, while on one side of him there is a poor barren soil, with owners who ask a large rent, the Celtic Irishman would rather pay that rent and draw a small subsistence for himself in potatoes out of it than betake himself to the abundant sea on the other side, which has no owners, for which there is no rent to pay, and from which he might draw not subsistence merely, but wealth for himself and for his country. Though we bring the peasant to the sea-shore, we can not make him fish. He prefers to fold his arms in his potato-ground, and trusts in Providence for the better days which never come to those who do not make them. His children swarm half naked about him, and when the potatoes fail, get a miserable subsistence by gathering limpets from the rocks, or plucking seaweed to boil into a jelly.

While such men as these are young, the British possessions in America could absorb any number of them—to dig and delve, to cut down the forest, make canals and railways, and do the work for which they are eminently qualified. In short, it is the peasantry of the British Isles who are wanted in Canada, not clerks, shopmen, and penmen; and, until the peasantry go in larger numbers than they do at present, Canada, like the daughter of the horse-leech, will continue to cry, "Give! give!" and will remain but half or a quarter developed, even in its oldest regions.

CHAPTER XLV.

HOME AGAIN.

It might seem ungracious and ungrateful, after having been received in the United States and in Canada, at every town and city in which I sojourned, with a degree of kindness as great as it was unexpected, to conclude this record of my tour without saying one word in acknowledgment of the popular favor that was showered upon me. Without parading names, detailing private conversations, or indulging in personal gossip, I may be permitted, in a form somewhat less evanescent than a speech after dinner, that perishes with the newspaper of the following morning, even if it find its way to such transient notoriety, to avow my grateful sense of the hospitality of which I was the object, and of the good-will toward the Old Country expressed toward me, as happening to recall its memories to the minds of those with whom I was brought into personal and public intercourse. The following quotation from the *Toronto Globe* will, better than any words of my own, tell all that is necessary to be told of the kindness of which I was the object, and which I should be worse than ungrateful were I ever to forget:

"Charles Mackay in Canada.—The reception given by the Canadians to this distinguished poet has been cordial in the extreme. No English traveler or literary man who has hitherto visited this country has been welcomed with a tithe of the enthusiasm which has greeted the popular songster in every city in Canada in which he has set foot. At Montreal, after his lecture in the Bonsecour Market Hall on "Poetry and Song," which was attended by upward of 1600 persons, he was entertained at a public supper at the Donegana Hotel. The band of the 73d regiment, under the leadership of Mr. Prince, was in attendance during the evening, and honored the poet with a serenade, appropriately playing some of his own melodies. At Toronto, where he has lectured under the auspices of the Mechanics' Institute, he has been honored by the attendance of the largest audiences ever known to have gathered in the city to listen to a lecture. The St. Lawrence Hall was densely crowded on both occasions; many persons were unable to obtain even standing room. At Hamilton, where he lectured twice, the same enthusiasm prevailed, and at the close of the second lecture he was invited to a public entertainment at the Anglo-American Hotel, which was attended by many of the notabilities and leading merchants of the city. At London, where the corporation granted the gratuitous use of the City Hall for the occasion, an audience of 1000 persons was present, and, as in other cities, a public supper was hastily organized, at which the healths went round until the small hours of the morn, and libations were drunk full of loyalty toward the Old Country and of attachment to the new. At Quebec, after the lecture, there was a public supper; and at Ottawa the poet was publicly serenaded in the beautiful grounds of the Hon. Mrs. Mackay, of Rideau Hall. Mr. Mackay will, no doubt, take home the most favorable impressions of Canada. He expresses himself deeply sensible of the kindness shown to him by its warm-hearted people. Mr. Mackay was entertained at supper last night at the Rossin House, and he leaves us this morning *en route* for England."

Leaving Canada with feelings of regret that I had not seen more of it, I took the rail at Montreal for Boston, and engaged my passage home in the steamship *Europa*, Captain Leitch, advertised to sail on the 19th of May. But I was not destined to leave America without receiving a farther proof of kindness and esteem, and this time from people whose names and labors are alike the property and pride of all who speak the English language, and of which the following short record appeared in the Boston newspapers of the 20th of May:

"Mr. Charles Mackay.—This gentleman sailed in the steamer *Europa* yesterday morning from this city. Quite a crowd of his personal friends assembled to take farewells. He carries with him the best wishes of hosts of admirers, who will be glad to see him again on this side the Atlantic. A parting dinner was given to him on Tuesday evening, at which were present some of the most distinguished literati of the country. Among the sentiments drunk with the heartiest enthusiasm was the health of Alfred Tennyson, proposed by Mr. Longfellow—a most graceful and genial recognition of the genius of the author of "In Memoriam" by the author of "Evangeline." The company on the occasion included Professors Longfellow, Holmes, Agassiz, and Lowell; his Excellency N. P. Banks (Governor of Massachusetts); Josiah Quincy, Esq.; Josiah Quincy, Esq., jun.; W. H. Prescott, the historian; Dr. Howe, of the Blind Asylum; Messrs. Ticknor and Fields, the eminent publishers, and many others well known to fame. Mr. J. G. Whittier, Theodore Parker, and Mr. R. W. Emerson were unavoidably absent."

The speeches made on the occasion were not reported. In lieu of a speech, Oliver Wendell Holmes, known to fame in both hemispheres as the "Autocrat of the Breakfast Table," and author of some of the tenderest as well as some of the wittiest poems that American literature has produced, read the following amid much applause:

TO CHARLES MACKAY,

ON HIS DEPARTURE FOR EUROPE.

Brave singer of the coming time,
  Sweet minstrel of the joyous present,
Crowned with the noblest wreath of rhyme,
  The holly-leaf of Ayrshire's peasant,

Good-by! good-by! Our hearts and hands,
  Our lips in honest Saxon phrases,
Cry, God be with him till he stands
  His feet amid his English daisies.

'Tis here we part. For other eyes
  The busy deck, the fluttering streamer,
The dripping arms that plunge and rise,
  The waves in foam, the ship in tremor,
The kerchiefs waving from the pier,
  The cloudy pillar gliding o'er him,
The deep blue desert, lone and drear,
  With heaven above and home before him.

His home! The Western giant smiles,
  And twirls the spotty globe to find it;
"This little speck, the British Isles?
  'Tis but a freckle, never mind it!"
He laughs, and all his prairies roll,
  Each gurgling cataract roars and chuckles,
And ridges, stretched from pole to pole,
  Heave till they shake their iron knuckles.

Then Honor, with his front austere,
  Turned on the sneer a frown defiant,
And Freedom leaning on her spear,
  Laughed louder than the laughing giant:
"Our islet is a world," she said,
  "Where glory with its dust has blended,
And Britain keeps her noble dead
  Till earth, and seas, and skies are rended!"

Beneath each swinging forest bough
  Some arm as stout in death reposes;
From wave-washed foot to heaven-kissed brow,
  Her valor's life-blood runs in roses.
Nay, let our ocean-bosomed West
  Write, smiling, in her florid pages,
"One half her soil has walked the rest
  In poets, heroes, martyrs, sages!"

Hugged in the clinging billows' clasp,
  From seaweed fringe to mountain heather,
The British oak, with rooted grasp,
  Her slender handful holds together.
With cliffs of white and bowers of green,
  And ocean narrowing to caress her,
And hills and threaded streams between—
  Our little Mother Isle, God bless her!

In earth's broad temple, where we stand,
　Fanned by the eastern gales that brought us,
We hold the missal in our hand,
　Bright with the lines our Mother taught us.
Where'er its blazoned page betrays
　The glistening links of gilded fetters,
Behold, the half-turned leaf displays
　Her rubric stained in crimson letters.

Enough. To speed a parting friend,
　'Tis vain alike to speak and listen;
Yet stay—these feeble accents blend
　With rays of light from eyes that glisten.
Good-by! once more. And kindly tell,
　In words of peace, the Young World's story;
And say, besides, we love too well
　Our Mother's soil—our Father's glory.

Among other effusions called forth by the occasion was the following:

You've seen us Yankees, Mr. Mackay,
The white, the red, the brown, the blackey;
The white, they say, who knows no color
But that of the almighty dollar;
The red, who roves as free as nature,
Could give play to the gallant creature;
The black, who laughs, amid his fetters,
More heart-free than his free-born betters;
And the wan hybrid, half his mother
And half his father, yet a brother;
When telling in the little island
Of sights seen here in flood or dry land,
Say, white, red, brown, black, short, or tall,
You found some good among them all.

In conclusion, and for the benefit of Americans, and especially of critics, who are too apt to be oversensitive upon the *Cosas Americanas*, I need but say that time has strengthened every good impression which I formed both of the people and of the country, and weakened every unfavorable one; that, if I have spoken of slavery and one or two other subjects in a manner at which some may take offense, I have spoken conscientiously, and that I could not do my own heart the injustice to witness slavery without raising my voice against it—not to blame the slaveholders, but to condole with them on the burden of their inheritance, and to pray for the day when the evil thing may be either entirely removed, or so diminished by natural, aided by legislative causes, as to lead to the hope that one or two generations at the farthest may witness its extinction. No Englishman can travel in the United States without seeing on every side, and at each step of his progress, the proof of the indomitable energy of the people; and (if he will not judge too rashly from first appearances or from random expressions) of the pride which they feel in their Anglo-Saxon descent, in their relationship to England, and of the noble inheritance of British literature, which is theirs as well as ours. Should the day ever arrive—which may Heaven in its mercy avert—that the "Old Country" should be imperiled by the coalitions of despotism, or by the subjection of Continental Europe to a great and overpowering military barbarism, Great Britain would have but to say the word, and an alliance with the United States, offensive and defensive, would stir the heart of the whole American people, and bring to the green shores of the "Mother Isle"—of which Professor Holmes has sung so sweetly—a greater army of volunteers than England and America have at the present moment ships enough to convey across the ocean.

The voyage home occupied twelve days. The weather was propitious all the way. We saw but one iceberg — a very small one—at a safe distance; and the trip altogether was as pleasant as fair skies, a clever captain (both in the English and in the American sense), and a joyous company could make it. Our run, according to the daily estimate made at noon—an operation always looked forward to with much interest on board ship—was as follows:

	Miles.		Miles.
May 19, 20	232	May 26	290
" 21	195	" 27	280
" 22	180	" 28	305
" 23	240	" 29	312
" 24	250	" 30	295
" 25	268	Total	2847

On the twelfth and last day—within sight of home and the shores of Ireland—the passengers kept no reckoning.

HOME AGAIN.

On arriving once more in England, I may mention the pleasant and novel sensation I experienced at riding over the excellent pavement of the streets of Liverpool, so superior to the bad pavements and worse roads of the United States, and the delight I felt in beholding once more the garden-like beauty and verdure of the landscape. The hawthorn and the wild chestnut, the lilac and the acacia, were in the full flush of their early bloom; and in rolling up to London at the rate of forty miles an hour, I came to the conclusion that not even the magnolia groves of the sunny South, or the exuberant loveliness of the northern landscape in America, were equal to the sylvan beauty and fair blue sky of England. And if, during my absence, I had learned to love America, I had also learned to love my own country better than before; or, if this were not possible, to render to myself better and more cogent reasons for doing so than I had before crossing the Atlantic.

THE END.

COSIMO CLASSICS

COSIMO is an innovative publisher of books and publications that inspire, inform and engage readers worldwide. Our titles are drawn from a range of subjects including health, business, philosophy, history, science and sacred texts. We specialize in using print-on-demand technology (POD), making it possible to publish books for both general and specialized audiences and to keep books in print indefinitely. With POD technology new titles can reach their audiences faster and more efficiently than with traditional publishing.

> **Permanent Availability:** Our books & publications never go out-of-print.

> **Global Availability:** Our books are always available online at popular retailers and can be ordered from your favorite local bookstore.

COSIMO CLASSICS brings to life unique, rare, out-of-print classics representing subjects as diverse as *Alternative Health, Business and Economics, Eastern Philosophy, Personal Growth, Mythology, Philosophy, Sacred Texts, Science, Spirituality* and much more!

COSIMO-on-DEMAND publishes your books, publications and reports. If you are an Author, part of an Organization, or a Benefactor with a publishing project and would like to bring books back into print, publish new books fast and effectively, would like your publications, books, training guides, and conference reports to be made available to your members and wider audiences around the world, we can assist you with your publishing needs.

Visit our website at www.cosimobooks.com to learn more about Cosimo, browse our catalog, take part in surveys or campaigns, and sign-up for our newsletter.

And if you wish please drop us a line at info@cosimobooks.com. We look forward to hearing from you.

LaVergne, TN USA
29 November 2009
165425LV00001B/5/A